CCSP Self-Study

# CCSP Cisco Secure VPN
# Exam Certification Guide

**John F. Roland**
**Mark J. Newcomb**

**Cisco Press**

Cisco Press
201 West 103rd Street
Indianapolis, IN 46290 USA

**CCSP Self-Study**

# CCSP Cisco Secure VPN Exam Certification Guide

John F. Roland and Mark J. Newcomb

Copyright © 2003 Cisco Systems, Inc.

Published by:
Cisco Press
201 West 103rd Street
Indianapolis, IN 46290 USA

Printed in the United States of America   1 2 3 4 5 6 7 8 9 0

First Printing   April 2003

Library of Congress Cataloging-in-Publication Number: 2002108141

ISBN: 1-58720-070-8

## Warning and Disclaimer

This book is designed to provide information about selected topics for the CCSP Cisco Secure VPN exam. Every effort has been made to make this book as complete and as accurate as possible, but no warranty or fitness is implied.

The information is provided on an "as is" basis. The authors, Cisco Press, and Cisco Systems, Inc., shall have neither liability nor responsibility to any person or entity with respect to any loss or damages arising from the information contained in this book or from the use of the discs or programs that may accompany it.

The opinions expressed in this book belong to the authors and are not necessarily those of Cisco Systems, Inc.

## Trademark Acknowledgments

All terms mentioned in this book that are known to be trademarks or service marks have been appropriately capitalized. Cisco Press or Cisco Systems, Inc., cannot attest to the accuracy of this information. Use of a term in this book should not be regarded as affecting the validity of any trademark or service mark.

## Feedback Information

At Cisco Press, our goal is to create in-depth technical books of the highest quality and value. Each book is crafted with care and precision, undergoing rigorous development that involves the unique expertise of members from the professional technical community.

Readers' feedback is a natural continuation of this process. If you have any comments regarding how we could improve the quality of this book, or otherwise alter it to better suit your needs, you can contact us through e-mail at feedback@ciscopress.com. Please make sure to include the book title and ISBN in your message.

We greatly appreciate your assistance.

| | |
|---|---|
| Publisher | John Wait |
| Editor-In-Chief | John Kane |
| Cisco Representative | Anthony Wolfenden |
| Cisco Press Program Manager | Sonia Torres Chavez |
| Manager, Marketing Communications, Cisco Systems | Scott Miller |
| Cisco Marketing Program Manager | Edie Quiroz |
| Executive Editor | Brett Bartow |
| Acquisitions Editor | Michelle Grandin |
| Production Manager | Patrick Kanouse |
| Development Editor | Dayna Isley |
| Senior Editor | Sheri Cain |
| Copy Editor | PIT, John Edwards |
| Technical Editors | Scott Chen, Gert Schauwers, Thomas Scire |
| Team Coordinator | Tammi Ross |
| Book Designer | Gina Rexrode |
| Cover Designer | Louisa Adair |
| Composition | Octal Publishing, Inc. |
| Indexer | Tim Wright |
| Media Developer | Jay Payne |

CISCO SYSTEMS

**Corporate Headquarters**
Cisco Systems, Inc.
170 West Tasman Drive
San Jose, CA 95134-1706
USA
http://www.cisco.com
Tel: 408 526-4000
   800 553-NETS (6387)
Fax: 408 526-4100

**European Headquarters**
Cisco Systems Europe
11 Rue Camille Desmoulins
92782 Issy-les-Moulineaux
Cedex 9
France
http://www-europe.cisco.com
Tel: 33 1 58 04 60 00
Fax: 33 1 58 04 61 00

**Americas Headquarters**
Cisco Systems, Inc.
170 West Tasman Drive
San Jose, CA 95134-1706
USA
http://www.cisco.com
Tel: 408 526-7660
Fax: 408 527-0883

**Asia Pacific Headquarters**
Cisco Systems Australia,
Pty., Ltd
Level 17, 99 Walker Street
North Sydney
NSW 2059 Australia
http://www.cisco.com
Tel: +61 2 8448 7100
Fax: +61 2 9957 4350

Cisco Systems has more than 200 offices in the following countries. Addresses, phone numbers, and fax numbers are listed on the Cisco Web site at www.cisco.com/go/offices

Argentina • Australia • Austria • Belgium • Brazil • Bulgaria • Canada • Chile • China • Colombia • Costa Rica • Croatia • Czech Republic • Denmark • Dubai, UAE • Finland • France • Germany • Greece • Hong Kong Hungary • India • Indonesia • Ireland • Israel • Italy • Japan • Korea • Luxembourg • Malaysia • Mexico The Netherlands • New Zealand • Norway • Peru • Philippines • Poland • Portugal • Puerto Rico • Romania Russia • Saudi Arabia • Scotland • Singapore • Slovakia • Slovenia • South Africa • Spain • Sweden Switzerland • Taiwan • Thailand • Turkey • Ukraine • United Kingdom • United States • Venezuela • Vietnam Zimbabwe

# About the Authors

**John F. Roland,** CCNA, CCDA, CCNP, CCDP, CSS-1, MCSE, is a security specialist who works for Ajilon Consulting. John has worked in the IT field for more than 22 years, from COBOL programming on IBM mainframes to LAN/WAN design and implementation on United States military networks and, more recently, to the development of Cisco and Microsoft certification training materials. John's current assignment has him designing and implementing enterprise network certification testing at one of the largest banks in America.

John holds a bachelor's degree in accounting from Tiffin University, Tiffin, Ohio, with minors in math and electrical engineering from General Motors Institute, Flint, Michigan.

**Mark J. Newcomb** is the owner and lead security engineer for Secure Networks in Spokane, Washington. Mark has over 20 years of experience in the networking industry, focusing on the financial and medical industries. The last six years have been devoted to designing security solutions for a wide variety of clients throughout the Pacific Northwest. Mark was one of the first people to obtain the CCNA certification from Cisco and has since obtained CCDA, CCNP, and CCDP certifications. He is the co-author of *Cisco Secure Internet Security Solutions*, published by Cisco Press, and two other networking books. He has been a technical reviewer on over 20 texts regarding networking for a variety of publishers. He can be reached by e-mail at mnewcomb@wanlansecurity.com.

## About the Technical Reviewers

**Scott Chen** has worked in the IT field for the past seven years holding various positions, including senior NT engineer, senior network engineer, and lead network engineer/network manager. Scott is currently a lead network engineer/network manager at Triad Financial Corporation, which is a wholly owned subsidiary of Ford Motor. He has implemented VPN solutions for remote access and LAN-to-LAN for several enterprises. Scott has extensive experience designing, implementing, and supporting enterprise networks and working with various technologies that Cisco offers, including routing, switching, security, content switching, wireless, BGP, EIGRP, and NAT. Scott graduated from the University of California, Irvine, with a bachelor's degree. He also holds several certifications, including MCSE, CCNA, CCNP, and CCIE Written/Qualification. Scott can be reached through e-mail at scottchen@cox.net.

**Gert Schauwers** is a triple Cisco Certified Internet Expert (CCIE No. 6942)—Routing and Switching, Security, and Communication and Services. He has more than four years experience in internetworking and holds an Engineering degree in Electronics/Communication. Gert is currently working in the Brussels CCIE lab where he's a proctor and content engineer for the Routing and Switching, Security, and Communication and Services exams.

**Thomas Scire** has been working in the network infrastructure industry since 1996. Thomas specializes in LAN, WAN, security, and multiservice infrastructure from Cisco Systems, Checkpoint, and Nokia. Thomas works for Accudata Systems, Inc., an independent IT professional services and solutions firm that specializes in enterprise network and security infrastructure. Some of his more notable projects include enterprise VPN and IP telephony deployments and an international Voice over Frame Relay network deployment. Thomas holds a bachelor's degree in Computer Engineering from Polytechnic University and holds several certifications, including Cisco CCNA/CCDA, Cisco IP Telephony Design Specialist, Checkpoint Certified Security Engineer, Checkpoint Certified Security Instructor, and Nokia Security Administrator.

# Dedications

**From John Roland:**

This book is dedicated to my wife of 28 years, Mariko, and to our son, Michael, for their understanding and support. Their steady love and encouragement has kept me on target through some trying times during the development of this book. You're the greatest! I further dedicate this book to my late parents, Hazel and Forrest Roland, for nurturing me, teaching me right from wrong, setting a shining example of a loving partnership, and showing me the benefits of a good day's work. I like to believe that they will be kicking up their heels together throughout eternity.

**From Mark Newcomb:**

This book is dedicated to my wife, Jacqueline, and my daughter, Isabella Rumiana. Jacqueline's patience and understanding while I am in the process of writing never fails to amaze me.

# Acknowledgments

**From John Roland:**

Writing this book has provided me with an opportunity to work with some very fine individuals. I want to thank Brett Bartow from Cisco Press for believing in the project and for getting the ball rolling. I would also like to thank him for turning this project over to Michelle Grandin, Cisco Press, for editorial support. Michelle helped me in many ways during this project and was always there to lend an encouraging word or a guiding hand. Dayna Isley, Cisco Press, provided developmental guidance and feedback and was way too easy on my less-than-perfect submissions, and I want to thank her for turning the work into a professional document. It has been a real pleasure to work with you three over these several months.

Next, I would like to thank my co-author, Mark Newcomb, for stepping in to author half of this book when personal problems brought me to a standstill. Thank you, Mark, for your professionalism and expertise and for helping to bring this project to fruition.

I would also like to thank the technical reviewers, Gert Schauwers, Scott Chen, and Thomas Scire for their comments, suggestions, and careful attention to detail. Without their help, this book would not be the valuable resource that it has become. Thank you all.

**From Mark Newcomb:**

I heartily acknowledge John Roland's contribution to this effort and thank him for inviting me to assist in this endeavor.

No text of any size is ever truly a work of just the authors. After nearly five years of writing, technical editing, and working with a variety of publishers, I commend every employee of Cisco Press. Michelle Grandin, Dayna Isley, John Kane, and Brett Bartow are people at Cisco Press I have come to know and respect for their professional efforts. I also want to give special thanks to Tammi Ross. Within any organization, there is one individual that seems to be able to solve any unsolvable problem. Tammi has proven herself to be that person at Cisco Press.

The technical reviewers working with Cisco Press are world class. Technical reviewers are the most valuable assets a good publisher can have. They do not receive the recognition or compensation that they so richly deserve. I thank Gert Schauwers, Scott Chen, and Thomas Scire for their efforts to make this work what it is today.

# Contents at a Glance

# Table of Contents

# Introduction

The Cisco Systems series of certifications provide you with a means of validating your expertise in certain core areas of study to current or prospective employers and to your peers. More network professionals are pursuing the Cisco Certified Security Professional (CCSP) certification because network security has become a critical element in the overall security plan of 21st-century businesses. This book is designed to help you attain this prestigious certification.

## Goals and Methods

The primary goal of this book is to help you prepare to pass either the 9E0-121 or 642-511 Cisco Secure VPN (CSVPN) exams as you strive to attain the CCSP certification or a focused VPN certification. Adhering to the premise that, as individuals, we each retain information better through different media, this book provides a variety of formats to help you succeed in passing this exam. Questions make up a significant portion of this book, because they are what you are confronted with on the exam and because they are a useful way to gauge your understanding of the material. The accompanying CD-ROM provides additional questions to help you with your exam preparation.

Along with the extensive and comprehensive questions within this book and on the CD, this book also covers all the published topics for the exam in detail, using charts, diagrams, and screenshots as appropriate to help you understand the concepts. The book assumes that you have a moderate understanding of networking (Cisco's prerequisite for CCSP certification is that you possess the CCNA certification and pass five additional exams), and does not attempt to bore you with material that you should already know. Some published topics are stated with the assumption that you possess certain knowledge that the CCNA certification did not bestow upon you. In those cases, this book attempts to fill in the missing material to catch you up to the material covered by the exam topic. Because this is an exam certification guide, the goal is to provide you with enough information to understand the published topics and to pass the exam, in effect right-sizing the material to the topics of the exam.

This book can help you pass the Cisco Secure VPN exam using the following methods:

- Self-assessment questions at the beginning of each chapter help you discover what you need to study.

- Detailed topic material is provided to clarify points that you might not already understand.

- End-of-chapter exercises and scenarios help you determine what you learned from the chapter's material.

- Additional questions on the CD give you a chance to look at the material from different perspectives.

## Who Should Read This Book?

This book was designed as an aid to help you pass the CCSP Cisco Secure VPN exam. Because that is the primary goal of this book, it stands to reason that the CCSP candidate will derive the most benefit from this book. Everyone who attempts to obtain the CCSP certification must take the Cisco Secure VPN exam, making every CCSP candidate a potential beneficiary of the material in this book.

That doesn't mean that this is just another one of those cramming aids that you use to pass the test and then place on your shelf to collect dust. The material covered in this book provides practical solutions to 80–90% of the VPN configuration challenges that you can encounter in your day-to-day networking experiences. This book can become a valuable reference tool for the security-conscious network manager. Designers can also find the foundation material and foundation summaries valuable aids for network design projects.

## The Organization of This Book

Although this book could be read cover to cover, it is designed to be flexible and allows you to easily move between chapters and sections of chapters to cover just the material that you need more work with. Chapter 1 provides an overview of the CCSP certification and offers some strategies for how to prepare for the exams. Chapters 2 through 11 are the core chapters and can be covered in any order. If you intend to read all the chapters, their order in this book is an excellent sequence to use.

The core chapters—Chapters 2 through 11—cover the following topics:

- **Chapter 2, "Overview of VPN and IPSec Technologies"**—This chapter discusses VPN protocols and concepts, concentrating on the IPSec protocol. Exam objectives covered in this chapter include the following:
  - 1  Cisco products enable a secure VPN
  - 2  IPSec overview
  - 3  IPSec protocol framework
  - 4  How IPSec works

- **Chapter 3, "Cisco VPN 3000 Concentrator Series Hardware Overview"**—This chapter looks at the Cisco VPN 3000 Concentrator Series and describes the capabilities of each VPN concentrator model. Exam objectives covered in this chapter include the following:
  - 5  Overview of the Cisco VPN 3000 Concentrator Series
  - 6  Cisco VPN 3000 Concentrator Series models
  - 7  Benefits and features of the Cisco VPN 3000 Concentrator Series
  - 8  Cisco VPN 3000 Concentrator Series Client support

- **Chapter 4, "Configuring Cisco VPN 3000 for Remote Access Using Preshared Keys"**—This chapter describes the process of configuring VPN concentrators for remote access with preshared keys. Initial CLI and browser configuration of the concentrator are covered. Advanced configuration issues are discussed. Installation and configuration of the Cisco VPN Client for Windows is also discussed in this chapter. Exam objectives covered in this chapter include the following:
  - 9  Overview of remote access using preshared keys
  - 10 Initial configuration of the Cisco VPN 3000 Concentrator Series for remote access
  - 11 Browser configuration of the Cisco VPN 3000 Concentrator Series
  - 12 Configuring users and groups
  - 13 Advanced configuration of the Cisco VPN 3000 Series Concentrator
  - 14 Configuring the IPSec Windows Client

- **Chapter 5, "Configuring Cisco VPN 3000 for Remote Access Using Digital Certificates"**—This chapter discusses digital certificates and Certificate Authority (CA) support. Enrolling and installing certificates, generating public/private key pairs, and validating certificates are also discussed. The VPN concentrator and VPN Client are configured to use digital certificates in this chapter. Exam objectives covered in this chapter include the following:
  - — **15** CA support overview
  - — **16** Certificate generation
  - — **17** Validating certificates
  - — **18** Configuring the Cisco VPN 3000 Concentrator Series for CA support

- **Chapter 6, "Configuring the Cisco VPN Client Firewall Feature"**—This chapter discusses the VPN Client's firewall feature set, including the Are You There feature, central policy protection, and monitoring firewall statistics. Exam objectives covered in this chapter include the following:
  - — **19** Overview of software client's firewall feature
  - — **20** Software client's Are You There feature
  - — **21** Software client's Stateful Firewall feature
  - — **22** Software client's Central Policy Protection feature
  - — **23** Client firewall statistics
  - — **24** Customizing firewall policy

- **Chapter 7, "Monitoring and Administering the Cisco VPN 3000 Series Concentrator"**—Earlier chapters in this book work with the Configuration menus of the VPN Manager. This chapter works with the remaining sections of the VPN Manager, the Monitoring and Administration sections. Exam objectives covered in this chapter include the following:
  - — **25** Monitoring the Cisco VPN 3000 Series Concentrator
  - — **26** Administering the Cisco VPN 3000 Series Concentrator

- **Chapter 8, "Configuring Cisco 3002 Hardware Client for Remote Access"**—The Cisco VPN 3002 Hardware Client is thoroughly discussed in this chapter. Interactive and integrated hardware and client authentication are discussed. Client statistics monitoring is also covered in this chapter. Exam objectives covered in this chapter include the following:
  - — **27** Cisco VPN 3002 Hardware Client remote access with preshared keys
  - — **28** Overview of VPN 3002 interactive unit and user authentication feature
  - — **29** Configuring VPN 3002 integrated unit authentication feature
  - — **30** Configuring VPN 3002 user authentication
  - — **31** Monitoring VPN 3002 user statistics

- **Chapter 9, "Configuring Scalability Features of the VPN 3002 Hardware Client"**—The Cisco VPN 3002 Hardware Client is well suited to large organizations. This chapter discusses the scalability features of load balancing, PAT, auto-update, and backup server. Exam objectives covered in this chapter include the following:

  - **32** Overview of the VPN 3002 Reverse Route Injection feature
  - **33** Configuring the VPN 3002 backup server feature
  - **34** Configuring the VPN 3002 load-balancing feature
  - **35** Overview of the VPN 3002 Auto-Update feature
  - **36** Configuring the VPN 3002 Auto-Update feature
  - **37** Monitoring VPN 3002 Auto-Update events
  - **38** Overview of Port Address Translation
  - **39** Configuring IPSec over UDP
  - **40** Configuring IPSec over TCP

- **Chapter 10, "Cisco VPN 3000 LAN-to-LAN with Preshared Keys"**—While ideal for remote access implementations, the Cisco VPN 3000 Concentrator Series is also an excellent platform for LAN-to-LAN VPN connections. This chapter discusses the LAN-to-LAN concept and shows you how to configure the VPN concentrator for that role. Exam objectives covered in this chapter include the following:

  - **41** Cisco VPN 3000 IPSec LAN-to-LAN
  - **42** LAN-to-LAN configuration
  - **43** SCEP support overview
  - **44** Root certificate installation
  - **45** Identity certificate installation

- **Chapter 11, "Scenarios"**—This chapter presents scenarios that test your ability to analyze various VPN situations and to apply your knowledge to solving problems and implementing solutions.

# Icons and Symbols Used in This Book

Cisco uses the following standard icons to represent different networking devices.
You will encounter several of these icons within this book.

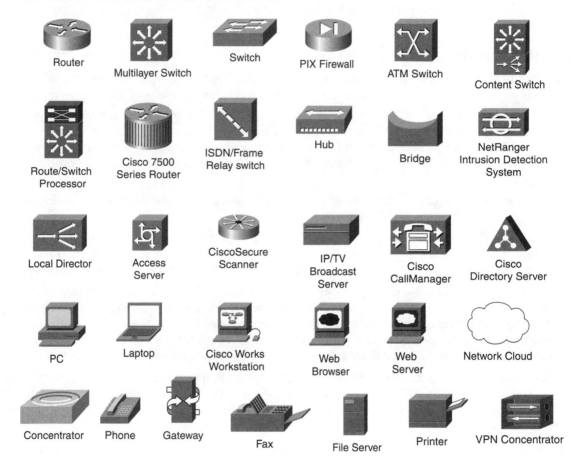

# Command Syntax Conventions

The conventions used to present command syntax in this book are the same conventions used in the IOS Command Reference. The Command Reference describes these conventions as follows:

- Vertical bars (|) separate alternative, mutually exclusive elements.
- Square brackets [ ] indicate optional elements.
- Braces { } indicate a required choice.
- Braces within brackets [( )] indicate a required choice within an optional element.

- **Boldface** indicates commands and keywords that are entered literally as shown. In actual configuration examples and output (not general command syntax), boldface indicates commands that are manually input by the user (such as a **show** command).
- *Italics* indicate arguments for which you supply actual values.

# Features of Each Chapter

Example test questions allow simulated exams for final practice. Each of these chapters uses several features to help you make the best use of your time in that chapter. The features are as follows:

- **"Do I Know This Already?" Quiz and Quizlets**—Each chapter begins with a quiz that helps you determine the amount of time you need to spend studying that chapter. The quiz is broken into subdivisions, called "quizlets," that correspond to a section of the chapter. Following the directions at the beginning of each chapter, the "Do I Know This Already?" quiz directs you to study all or parts of the chapter.
- **Foundation Topics**—This is the core section of each chapter that explains the protocols, concepts, and configuration for the topics in the chapter.
- **Foundation Summary**—Near the end of each chapter, a summary collects the most important tables and figures from the chapter. This section helps you review the key concepts in the chapter if you score well on the "Do I Know This Already?" quiz, and these concepts are excellent tools for last-minute review.
- **Q&A**—These end-of-the-chapter questions focus on recall, covering subjects in the "Foundation Topics" section by using several types of questions. Because the "Do I Know This Already?" quiz questions can help increase your recall as well, these questions are restated in the Q&A section. Restating these questions, along with presenting new questions, provides a larger set of practice questions for testing your knowledge when you finish a chapter and for final review when your exam date is approaching.
- **Scenarios**—Located at the end of most chapters, the scenarios allow a more in-depth examination of a network implementation. Rather than posing a simple question asking for a single fact, the scenarios let you design and build networks (at least on paper) without the inherent clues of a multiple-choice quiz format.

# About the CD-ROM

The companion CD-ROM contains more than 200 questions that are not included in this book. You can answer these questions by using the simulated exam feature or by using the topical review feature. This is the best tool to help you prepare for the test-taking process.

# CHAPTER 1

# All About the Cisco Certified Security Professional

Network security is a hot topic, and network security specialists are hot commodities in today's job market. It's no surprise, then, that the Cisco Certified Security Professional (CCSP) distinguishes itself as one of the most sought-after networking certifications available today.

The CCSP was promoted in late 2002 from a Cisco Qualified Specialist program to a full-fledged track, paralleling Cisco Certified Network Professional (CCNP), Cisco Certified Design Professional (CCDP), and Cisco Certified Internetworking Professional (CCIP). Like the other three primary certification tracks, the CCSP has the CCNA exam as a prerequisite.

Accomplishing the CCSP certification requires you to pass five challenging exams, which cover a wide range of Cisco hardware and application software. You work with routers and firewalls at your network perimeter or in your demilitarized zone (DMZ). You establish Virtual Private Network (VPN) concentrators for your remote access users. Intrusion detection systems can covertly keep tabs on your network, and you learn how to configure and administer those systems. You work with Cisco Works components, such as Cisco Secure Policy Manager (CSPM) and Cisco Secure Access Control Server (CSACS). You use web browser applications to configure the hardware devices that protect your network. You ensure secure connectivity in small and medium networks, based on the SAFE blueprint.

Some of the information contained in this book overlaps material from the other four topics covered by the CCSP series of exams. VPN technology is an important element in network security, and it is no accident that more than one CCSP course includes additional information on Internet Protocol Security (IPSec) VPNs.

The exam is a computer-based exam that has multiple-choice, fill-in-the-blank, and drag-and-drop matching and ordering questions. The CCSP series of exams are some of the most interesting exams to take because of the variety of presentation methods used during the questioning. When you are required to enter a command, you must be precise in your syntax, and you must not use abbreviations.

You can take the exam at any Thompson Prometric or VUE testing center. Both of these testing organizations have websites that allow you to find a testing center and register for tests online. You can also call them to accomplish the same thing. Cisco's website has information about registering for the exams, including links and telephone numbers for Prometric and VUE. Go to Cisco's website and search for "registering for exams." The first search result should contain the most recent information regarding exam registration.

Both organizations have an official registration process that you need to complete the first time you work with them. When you arrive at the testing facility to take your exam, be absolutely sure that you have a photo ID on hand. You will not be allowed to take an exam without positive identification. Also, be aware that you will not be permitted to take materials into the testing booth—instead, the test proctor provides you with a pencil and supply of scratch paper.

As you take the exam, remember to read each question carefully before selecting your answer. Understand what the question is asking before attempting to answer it. Some electronic certification tests allow you to review and modify your answers if you finish before time expires. Cisco exams are not of that variety. You have one opportunity to answer each question. Take your time, and be sure to supply an answer for each question. If you don't understand the question, try restating it to see if you can figure out what is being asked. If a question stumps you, try to eliminate obviously false answers and make an educated guess from the remaining choices. Be sure to jot down "stumper" topics on your scratch paper.

You will most likely be given little more than an hour to complete the exam. Passing scores vary—typically, somewhere in the range of 790 or 800 on a scale of 300 to 1000 points is considered passing. If you turn that into a percentage, you need to answer slightly more than 70 percent of the questions correctly to pass the exam.

---

**NOTE**    Certification candidates should check the Cisco Systems certification website frequently (www.cisco.com/go/training) as exam criteria such as time allotted, number of questions, and passing scores are subject to change without notice.

---

You might not pass the exam the first time. If that is the case, use the experience as a learning tool. Now you know what the test looks like, and you don't need to worry about the mechanics of the test. Make notes to yourself of the questions that were asked, especially the ones that stumped you. You can make notes on your scratch paper during the exam.

At the end of the exam, you don't have to leave the testing booth immediately, and you can review your notes several times to remember them. (Remember that the proctor collects your scratch paper before you leave.) After you leave the test facility, try to write down as many questions and topics as you can remember from the exam. Be prepared by bringing a notebook to jot down your answers. Use these brain dumps as your study guide in preparation for the next time you take the exam. Although you will not get exactly the same questions each time you take the exam, the questions are pulled from a pool, and you will most likely see some of the same questions each time you take the test. You will certainly see similar questions.

Stick with it if you don't succeed the first time. You can do it, and you will find the CCSP material interesting and on target for the needs of most businesses. Also, the exams are a refreshing change from those you might have taken in the past.

# How This Book Can Help You Pass the CCSP Cisco Secure VPN Exam

The primary focus of this book is to crystallize knowledge that you might have gained from instructor-led or on-the-job training into the facts and procedures you need to know to pass the CCSP Cisco Secure VPN exam. Material is not covered to the depth that you might see in an instructor-led class. This book concentrates on the core material and does not delve too deeply into the more esoteric aspects of this topic.

The audience for this book includes candidates who have successfully completed the Cisco Secure Virtual Private Networks (CSVPN) class or those who gained some experience in VPNs through other means. If you have taken the CSVPN class, you will find that much of the material is familiar, and you can benefit most from the prechapter and postchapter questions and from the scenarios that you find throughout this book. If you have not taken the CSVPN class, you are going to find those questions and scenarios especially beneficial as you prepare for the exam.

The most recent version of the CSVPN exam has been greatly modified from the original. You no longer need to be able to configure VPNs on routers and firewalls; this exam concentrates on remote access VPNs through VPN Concentrators, including the Cisco VPN 3002 Hardware Client, which was not covered on the original exam.

# Overview of CCSP Certification and Required Exams

The CCSP certification is a main certification track, beginning at the CCNA and ending at the CCIE level, as do the CCNP and CCIP certifications.

The CCSP certification requires you to pass five exams. The prerequisite for being awarded your CCSP certification upon completion of these exams is that you hold a current CCNA certification. Table 1-1 contains a list of the exams in the CCSP certification series. Because all exam information is managed by Cisco Systems and is therefore subject to change, candidates should continually monitor the Cisco Systems website for course and exam updates at www.cisco.com/go/training.

The CCSP certification is valid for 3 years, after which you must perform the requirements for recertification. Currently, the requirement is that you retake the current version of the appropriate exams. You can find out more about the Cisco Certified Security Professional track at the Cisco website, www.cisco.com, where you can search for "Career Certifications."

**Table 1-1**   *CCSP Certification Exams*

| Exam Number | Exam Name | Comments on Upcoming Exam Changes |
|---|---|---|
| 640-100 | MCNS 3.0, Managing Cisco Network Security | In Summer 2003, a new exam, SECUR 642-501, will become available. This exam will eventually replace the 640-100 exam. If recertification candidates pass this exam, they will be considered recertified at the CCNA or CCDA level. |
| 9E0-111 | CSPFA 3.0, Cisco Secure PIX Firewall Advanced Exam | By Summer 2003, a new exam will be available to certification candidates taking the PIX exam: 642-521. Note that the renumbering signifies that those that pass this exam will be considered recertified at the CCNA or CCDA level. There are no significant changes between the 9E0-111 exam and the 642-521 exam. |
| 9E0-100 | CSIDS 3.0, Cisco Secure Intrusion Detection Systems | There are no anticipated changes to this exam as of the time that this book was printed. Be sure to refer to the Cisco Systems website for current information regarding exam numbers and content. |
| 9E0-121 | CSVPN 3.0, Cisco Secure Virtual Private Networks | By Summer 2003, a new exam will be available to certification candidates taking the VPN exam: 642-511. Note that the renumbering signifies that those that pass this exam will be considered recertified at the CCNA or CCDA level. There are no significant changes between the 9E0-121 exam and the 642-511 exam. |
| 9E0-131 | CSI 1.0, Cisco SAFE Implementation | There are no anticipated changes to this exam as of the time that this book was printed. Be sure to refer to the Cisco Systems website for current information regarding exam numbers and content. |

# The Cisco Secure VPN Exam

The Cisco Secure VPN exam was designed to test your knowledge of configuring, monitoring, and administering Cisco's purpose-built VPN 3000 Series Concentrators. Because IPSec is the VPN tunneling protocol of choice for these products, the exam deals mostly with the IPSec protocol on these devices. The CSVPN exam covers the concentrators, software clients, and the Cisco VPN 3002 Hardware Client.

You will most likely be given little more than an hour to complete the exam. Passing scores vary— typically, somewhere in the range of 790 or 800 on a scale of 300 to 1000 points is considered passing. The exam is a mixture of multiple-choice questions with a single answer, multiple-choice questions with multiple answers, drag-and-drop questions, simulation questions, and fill-in-the-blank questions. All CCSP exams now contain a simulation lab item. For this exam, this means that you may have to actually configure a VPN 3000 Concentrator for remote access. This exam item is worth multiple points and you may qualify for partial credit. There are no true-or-false questions. (Remember that exam criteria such as time allotted, number of questions, and passing scores, are subject to change without notice. Test takers should frequently refer to the Cisco Systems certification site for the latest information at www.cisco.com/go/training.)

Once you are in the testing booth in front of the workstation, you are asked to log in. Next, you are asked to complete a short survey about how you prepared for the exam and what you consider your expertise level to be. The time you take for the survey is not deducted from the time allotted for the exam. After you complete the survey, you are asked to accept the terms of Cisco's non-disclosure agreement (which is the reason that the authors cannot tell you about actual test questions). If you decline to accept the agreement, you are not permitted to take the exam. Upon accepting the nondisclosure agreement, the exam begins.

You are presented with one question at a time. A timer and a counter are running to show you how many minutes you have remaining for the exam and how many questions you have attempted. The questions in Cisco exams tend to be straightforward, for example, "How do you configure the. . .," "What do you call the. . .," "What is the command to. . .," and so on. The questions are comprehensive, however, so you need to know your material. A multiple-choice question might encompass two or three topics. Some of the trickier questions tend to be the drag-and-drop questions. However, you can undo your answers to those questions and reposition your choices if you find you've made a mistake before committing your answer.

Always take a couple of seconds to review your answer before moving on to the next question. You are not permitted to review your answers or to change them once you go to the next question. If you get to the end before time runs out, click the Finish button to end the exam. If time expires, the testing software does that for you.

At the end of the exam, you are allowed to make comments to Cisco about any of the questions in the exam. If you find questions that don't work properly, are poorly worded, seem unfair, or are wrong, this is your opportunity to tell Cisco about them. Be sure to keep notes as you take the exam if you want to make comments at the end.

Once you finish the comments section, the software presents a "thank you for taking the exam" screen. When you clear that, the system displays your score and declares whether you have passed the exam. When you have spent many hours preparing for an exam, you can't believe the relief you feel when the word PASS is shown on the screen!

At the same time you see the results of your exam, a copy of the results is printed at the proctor's desk. When you leave the testing booth, the proctor presses a seal onto the exam results and stamps them DO NOT LOSE THIS REPORT. You also receive a printed copy of the non-disclosure agreement that you consented to prior to taking the exam.

A few weeks after you have completed all the requirements for a given certification, you receive your certification through the mail. You also receive a laminated card that you can carry with you attesting to the fact that you are, indeed, a Cisco Certified Security Professional.

# Topics on the Cisco Secure VPN Exam

Although you might not know what questions you are going to see on the exam, you do have access to the exam topics. If you study these topic areas, you should do well on this exam. The design of this book is based on the exam topics. Each chapter in this book corresponds to a major topic area and contains the information that you need to study to thoroughly cover the exam topic material. Table 1-2 shows the topics for the Cisco Secure VPN exam.

**Table 1-2**   *CSVPN Exam Topics*

| Chapter and Chapter Title | Exam Topics |
|---|---|
| **Chapter 2**<br>Overview of VPN and IPSec Technologies | **1** Cisco products enable a secure VPN |
| | **2** IPSec overview |
| | **3** IPSec protocol framework |
| | **4** How IPSec works |
| **Chapter 3**<br>Cisco VPN 3000 Concentrator Series Hardware Overview | **5** Overview of the Cisco VPN 3000 Concentrator Series |
| | **6** Cisco VPN 3000 Concentrator Series models |
| | **7** Benefits and features of the Cisco VPN 3000 Concentrator Series |
| | **8** Cisco VPN 3000 Concentrator Series Client support |
| **Chapter 4**<br>Configuring Cisco VPN 3000 for Remote Access Using Preshared Keys | **9** Overview of remote access using preshared keys |
| | **10** Initial configuration of the Cisco VPN 3000 Concentrator Series for remote access |
| | **11** Browser configuration of the Cisco VPN 3000 Concentrator Series |
| | **12** Configure users and groups |
| | **13** Advanced configuration of the Cisco VPN 3000 Series Concentrator |
| | **14** Configure the IPSec Windows Client |
| **Chapter 5**<br>Configuring Cisco VPN 3000 for Remote Access Using Digital Certificates | **15** CA support overview |
| | **16** Certificate generation |
| | **17** Validating certificates |
| | **18** Configuring the Cisco VPN 3000 Concentrator Series for CA support |

**Table 1-2**    *CSVPN Exam Topics (Continued)*

| Chapter and Chapter Title | Exam Topics |
|---|---|
| **Chapter 6**<br><br>Configuring the Cisco VPN Client Firewall Feature | **19** Overview of software client's firewall feature |
| | **20** Software client's Are You There feature |
| | **21** Software client's Stateful Firewall feature |
| | **22** Software client's Central Policy Protection feature |
| | **23** Client firewall statistics |
| | **24** Customizing firewall policy |
| **Chapter 7**<br><br>Monitoring and Administering the Cisco VPN 3000 Series Concentrator | **25** Monitoring the Cisco VPN 3000 Series Concentrator |
| | **26** Administering the Cisco VPN 3000 Series Concentrator |
| **Chapter 8**<br><br>Configuring Cisco 3002 Hardware Client for Remote Access | **27** Cisco VPN 3002 Hardware Client remote access with preshared keys |
| | **28** Overview of VPN 3002 interactive unit and user authentication feature |
| | **29** Configuring VPN 3002 integrated unit authentication feature |
| | **30** Configuring VPN 3002 user authentication |
| | **31** Monitoring VPN 3002 user statistics |
| **Chapter 9**<br><br>Configuring Scalability Features of the VPN 3002 Hardware Client | **32** Overview of the VPN 3002 Reverse Route Injection feature |
| | **33** Configuring the VPN 3002 backup server feature |
| | **34** Configuring the VPN 3002 load balancing feature |
| | **35** Overview of the VPN 3002 Auto-Update feature |
| | **36** Configuring the VPN 3002 Auto-Update feature |
| | **37** Monitoring VPN 3002 Auto-Update events |
| | **38** Overview of Port Address Translation |
| | **39** Configuring IPSec over UDP |
| | **40** Configuring IPSec over TCP |

*continues*

**Table 1-2**      *CSVPN Exam Topics (Continued)*

| Chapter and Chapter Title | Exam Topics |
|---|---|
| **Chapter 10**<br>Cisco VPN 3000 LAN-to-LAN with Preshared Keys | **41** Cisco VPN 3000 IPSec LAN-to-LAN |
| | **42** LAN-to-LAN configuration |
| | **43** SCEP support overview |
| | **44** Root certificate installation |
| | **45** Identity certificate installation |

# Recommended Training Path for the CCSP Certification

The Cisco recommended training path for the CCSP certification is to attend the instructor-led training courses offered by Cisco Learning Partner. The following courses are designed around lots of lab work so that you can get practical experience configuring or managing the devices that you are studying:

- **Securing Cisco IOS Networks (SECUR)**—This five-day course is an update to Version 3.0 of the Managing Cisco Network Security (MCNS) course. This task-oriented course teaches the knowledge and skills needed to secure Cisco IOS router networks.

- **Cisco Secure PIX Firewall Advanced (CSPFA)**—This four-day course teaches you how to describe, configure, verify, and manage all aspects of the PIX Firewall product.

- **Cisco Secure Intrusion Detection System (CSIDS)**—This three-day course teaches you how to use the Cisco Intrusion Detection System to detect and respond to network attacks. Additionally, you learn how to manage, administer, and monitor your intrusion detection systems.

- **Cisco Secure VPN (CSVPN)**—This four-day course teaches you how to describe, configure, verify, and manage the Cisco VPN 3000 Concentrator, the Cisco VPN 3.1 Software Client, and the Cisco VPN 3002 Hardware Client.

- **Cisco SAFE Implementation (CSI)**—This four-day course teaches you how to understand and apply the axioms described in the SAFE blueprint as applied to small, medium, and remote user networks.

Many students find the labs an invaluable learning aid. That fact, coupled with knowledgeable instructors, helps to make these courses popular and effective. You can couple these training classes with the associated Cisco Press Exam Certification Guide or Self-Study Guide to obtain broad knowledge and experience with the subject material in the class and then target that knowledge and experience toward the specific topics of the exam.

# Using This Book to Pass the Exam

Each of the following chapters in this book contains four components, and many contain a fifth optional component. The four main components within each chapter and the optional component are as follows:

- A short preassessment quiz titled "Do I Know This Already?".
- A "Foundation Topics" section that contains the major topics of the chapter.
- A "Foundation Summary" section that summarizes the key points of the chapter.
- A longer postassessment quiz entitled "Q&A".
- The optional section includes scenarios and scenario-related questions and exercises. Scenarios are included in chapters where the content lends itself to hands-on, critical-thinking exercises. The scenarios section is not included in chapters that are conceptual in nature; these chapters do not lend themselves to scenario-based questions and exercises.

You should begin each chapter by honestly taking the "Do I Know This Already?" quiz at the beginning. The questions are all fill-in-the-blank types that ask for objective—rather than subjective—answers. You can find the answers to the questions in Appendix A. If you miss only one or two of the questions, you already have a good understanding of the chapter's material, and you can opt to skip the chapter and move on to the next.

If you only miss a few questions on the prechapter test, you should plan on studying the Foundation Summary and completing the Q&A and the Scenarios sections at the end of the chapter. These three areas should provide the extra information that would allow you to master the chapter's material. If you miss any more than four or five questions in the "Do I Know This Already?" quiz, plan on devoting time to study the entire chapter.

Do not skip the chapter quizzes! You are preparing for an exam that consists of questions about the subject of VPNs and VPN concentrators. The more questions you attempt that cover the same topics, the better the odds that you will have seen most of the questions that are on the exam. Just as a baseball hitter gains confidence by taking batting practice before stepping up to the plate to face a pitcher, you too can gain confidence by attempting the chapter quizzes before taking the exam.

# Final Exam Preparation Tips

This book contains most of the material that you need to pass the Cisco Secure VPN exam. Remember, you do not need to know all the answers to pass the exam. Few individuals become certified having received 100 percent on any of the required exams. For the record, the tests are only graded Pass or Fail. Passing by one point is just as good as passing with 100 percent as far as the certification process is concerned.

Although you do not need to answer 100 percent of the questions correctly, you should study all the material in this book because you do not know what areas will be covered by the test you are given. The questions that you get for your exam are drawn from a large pool. The tests attempt to cover most of the published objectives, but a given test might skip questions for some objectives.

Take the chapter quizzes. If you do poorly on these quizzes, review the material and take the quizzes again. Once you can answer 85–90 percent of the questions correctly, move on to the next chapter. The questions in the chapters are representative of the questions that you encounter on the exam, but they probably do not cover everything that you will see on the exam. If you can accept the notion that it's okay not to ace the CSVPN exam, you will most likely do well.

Try to spend no more than a few days on each chapter, and keep a consistent study schedule. Information is volatile, and the shorter you can keep your preparation period, the fresher the information is when you take the exam. If you get off schedule, review the summaries from each chapter you have completed thus far, retake the end-of-chapter Q&A quizzes for those chapters, and then move on. When you are within two weeks of completing your study, schedule your exam so that you have a fixed date to keep you motivated and on target. Before you take the exam, spend a day reviewing the Foundation Summary material from each chapter and retaking the "Do I Know This Already?" tests at the beginning of each chapter.

If you can do consistently well on the chapter quizzes, you will pass the CSVPN exam. The authors wish you good luck in achieving your career certification goals.

# Exam Topics Discussed in This Chapter

This chapter covers the following topics, which you need to master in your pursuit of certification as a Cisco Certified Security Professional:

1 Cisco products enable a secure VPN

2 IPSec overview

3 IPSec protocol framework

4 How IPSec works

# CHAPTER 2

# Overview of VPN and IPSec Technologies

The Internet is an integral part of business communications today. Corporations use it as an inexpensive extension of their local- or wide-area networks. A local connection to an Internet service provider (ISP) enables far-reaching communications for e-commerce, mobile users, sales personnel, and global business partners. The Internet is cheap, easily enabled, stable, resilient, and omnipresent. But it is not secure, at least not in its native state.

As a corporate user, you want to shield your communications from misdirection, misappropriation, and misuse, especially if you are discussing trade secrets, personnel issues, or financial information. Ideally, you want to be able to establish a pipeline through the Internet cloud that goes from point A to point B and shields your data from prying eyes along the way. TCP/IP is the foundation of the Internet and provides little in the way of security.

That is where Virtual Private Networks (VPNs) come to the rescue. This clever concept can provide the security that you need with a variety of features. VPNs can provide security through point-to-point encryption of data, data integrity by ensuring that the data packets have not been altered en route, and authentication to ensure that the packets are coming from the right source. VPNs enable an efficient and cost-effective method for secure communications across the Internet's public infrastructure. Internet Protocol Security (IPSec) is the Cisco protocol of choice for establishing VPNs. This chapter provides an overview of VPNs and IPSec and discusses the technologies that Cisco products bring to this useful technology.

## How to Best Use This Chapter

By taking the following steps, you can make better use of your time:

- Keep your notes and answers for all your work with this book in one place for easy reference.

- Take the "Do I Know This Already?" quiz, and write down your answers. Studies show that retention is significantly increased through writing facts and concepts down, even if you never look at the information again.

- Use the diagram in Figure 2-1 to guide you to the next step.

**Figure 2-1** *How to Use This Chapter*

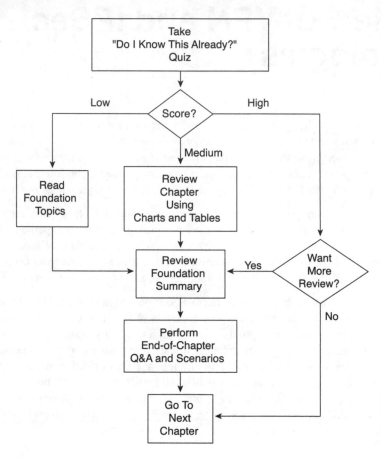

## "Do I Know This Already?" Quiz

The purpose of the "Do I Know This Already?" quiz is to help you decide what parts of the chapter to use. If you already intend to read the entire chapter, you do not need to answer these questions now.

This 16-question quiz helps you determine how to spend your limited study time. The quiz is sectioned into four smaller "quizlets," which correspond to the four major topic headings in the chapter. Figure 2-1 outlines suggestions on how to spend your time in this chapter based on your quiz score. Use Table 2-1 to record your scores.

**Table 2-1**    *Score Sheet for Quiz and Quizlets*

| Quizlet Number | Foundations Topics Section Covering These Questions | Questions | Score |
|---|---|---|---|
| 1 | Cisco products enable a secure VPN | 1–4 | |
| 2 | IPSec overview | 5–8 | |
| 3 | IPSec protocol framework | 9–12 | |
| 4 | How IPSec works | 13–16 | |
| All questions | | 1–16 | |

1  Which Cisco hardware product families support IPSec VPN technology?

_____

_____

_____

2  What are the two IPSec protocols?

_____

_____

_____

3  Which type of VPNs use a combination of the same infrastructures that are used by the other two types of VPNs?

_____

_____

_____

4  Which of the Cisco VPN 3000 Series Concentrators is a fixed-configuration device?

_____

_____

_____

5  What key element is contained in the AH or ESP packet header?

_____

_____

_____

**6** What are the two modes of operation for AH and ESP?

_____

_____

_____

**7** How many Security Associations (SAs) does it take to establish bidirectional IPSec communications between two peers?

_____

_____

_____

**8** What is a message digest?

_____

_____

_____

**9** Which current RFCs define the IPSec protocols?

_____

_____

_____

**10** What message integrity protocols does IPSec use?

_____

_____

_____

**11** What is the triplet of information that uniquely identifies a security association?

_____

_____

_____

**12** You can select to use both authentication and encryption when using the ESP protocol. Which is performed first when you do this?

_____

_____

_____

**13** What five parameters are required by IKE Phase 1?

_____

_____

_____

**14** What is the difference between the **deny** keyword in a crypto Access Control List (ACL) and the **deny** keyword in an access ACL?

_____

_____

_____

**15** What transform set would allow SHA-1 authentication of both AH and ESP packets and would also provide Triple Data Encryption Standard (3DES) encryption for ESP?

_____

_____

_____

**16** What are the five steps of the IPSec process?

_____

_____

_____

The answers to this quiz are listed in Appendix A, "Answers to the "Do I Know This Already?" Quizzes and Q&A Sections." The suggestions for your next steps, based on quiz results, are as follows:

- **2 or less score on any quizlet**—Review the appropriate portions of the "Foundation Topics" section of this chapter, based on Table 2-1. Proceed to the "Foundation Summary" section and the "Q&A" section.

- **8 or less overall score**—Read the entire chapter, including the "Foundation Topics," "Foundation Summary" sections, and the "Q&A" section.

- **9 to 12 overall score**—Read the "Foundation Summary" section and the "Q&A" section. If you are having difficulty with a particular subject area, read the appropriate portion of the "Foundation Topics" section.

- **13 or more overall score**—If you feel that you need more review on these topics, go to the "Foundation Summary" section, then to the "Q&A" section. Otherwise, skip this chapter and go to the next chapter.

# Foundation Topics

## Cisco VPN Product Line

> **1**   Cisco products enable a secure VPN

VPNs are typically deployed to provide improved access to corporate resources while providing tighter control over security at a reduced cost for WAN infrastructure services. Telecommuters, mobile users, remote offices, business partners, clients, and customers all benefit because corporations see VPNs as a secure and affordable method of opening access to corporate information.

Surveys have shown that most corporations implementing VPNs do so to provide access for telecommuters to access the corporate network from home. They cite security and reduced cost as the primary reasons for choosing VPN technology and single out monthly service charges as the cost justification for the decision.

VPN technology was developed to provide private communication wherever and whenever needed, securely, while behaving as much like a traditional private WAN connection as possible. Cisco offers a variety of platforms and applications that are designed to implement VPNs. The next section looks at these various products and Cisco's recommended usage in the deployment of VPNs.

# Enabling VPN Applications Through Cisco Products

Through product development and acquisitions, Cisco has a variety of hardware and software components available that enable businesses of all sizes to quickly and easily implement secure VPNs using IPSec or other protocols. The types of hardware and software components you choose to deploy depend on the infrastructure you already have in place and on the types of applications that you are planning to use across the VPN.

This section covers the following topics:

- Typical VPN applications
- Using Cisco VPN products

## Typical VPN Applications

The business applications that you choose to run on your VPNs go hand in hand with the type of VPN that you need to deploy. Remote access and extranet users can use interactive applications such as e-mail, web browsers, or client/server programs. Intranet VPN deployments are designed to support data streams between business locations.

The benefits most often cited for deploying VPNs include the following:

- **Cost savings**—Elimination of expensive dedicated WAN circuits or banks of dedicated modems can provide significant cost savings. Third-party Internet service providers (ISPs) provide Internet connectivity from anywhere at any time. Coupling ISP connectivity with the use of broadband technologies, such as digital subscriber line (DSL) and cable, not only cuts the cost of connectivity but can also deliver high-speed circuits.

- **Security**—The cost savings from the use of public infrastructures could not be recognized if not for the security provided by VPNs. Encryption and authentication protocols keep corporate information private on public networks.

- **Scalability**—With VPN technologies, new users can be easily added to the network. Corporate network availability can be scaled quickly with minimal cost. A single VPN implementation can provide secure communications for a variety of applications on diverse operating systems.

VPNs fall into three basic categories:

- Remote access
- Intranet
- Extranet

The following sections cover these three areas in more detail.

## Remote Access VPNs

Telecommuters, mobile workers, and remote offices with minimal WAN bandwidth can all benefit from remote access VPNs. Remote access VPNs extend the corporate network to these users over publicly shared infrastructures, while maintaining corporate network policies all the way to the user. Remote access VPNs are the primary type of VPN in use today. They provide secure access to corporate applications for telecommuters, mobile users, branch offices, and business partners. These VPNs are implemented over common public infrastructures using ISDN, dial, analog, mobile IP, DSL, and cable technology. These VPNs are considered ubiquitous because they can be established any time from practically anywhere over the Internet. E-mail is the primary application used by these connections, with database and office automation applications following close behind.

Some of the advantages that might be gained by converting from privately managed networks to remote access VPNs are as follows:

- Modems and terminal servers, and their associated capital costs, can be eliminated.

- Long-distance and 1-800 number expenses can be dramatically reduced as VPN users dial in to local ISP numbers, or connect directly through their always-on broadband connections.

- Deployments of new users are simplified, and the increased scalability of VPNs allows new users to be added without increased infrastructure expenses.

- Turning over the management and maintenance of the dial-up network to third parties allows a corporation to focus on its business objectives rather than on circuit maintenance.

Although there are many advantages, be aware of the following disadvantages when implementing a VPN solution:

- IPSec has a slight overhead because it has to encrypt data as they leave the machine and decrypt data as they enter the machine via the tunnel. Though the overhead is low, it can impact some applications.

- For users with analog modem connections to the Internet at 40 kbps or less, VPNs can cause a slight reduction to throughput speed because the overhead of IPSec takes time to process the data.

- IPSec is sensitive to delays. Because the public Internet infrastructure is used, there is no guarantee of the amount of delay that might be encountered on each connection leg as the tunneled data traverse the Internet. This should not cause major problems, but it is something to keep in mind. Users might need to periodically reestablish connections if delay thresholds are exceeded.

Remote access VPNs can initiate tunneling and encryption either on the dial-up client or on the network access server (NAS). Table 2-2 outlines some of the differences between the two approaches.

**Table 2-2**    *Remote Access Models*

| Model Type | Characteristics |
|---|---|
| Client-initiated model | Uses IPSec, Layer 2 Tunnel Protocol (L2TP), or Point-to-Point Tunneling Protocol (PPTP) for establishing the encrypted tunnel at the client. |
| | Ubiquitous. ISP network is used only as a transport vehicle for the encrypted data, permitting the use of multiple ISPs. |
| | Data is secured end to end from the point of origin (client) to the destination, permitting the establishment of VPNs over any infrastructure without fear of compromise. |
| | Third-party security software packages, such as Cisco's VPN Client, can be used to provide more enhanced security than system-embedded security software like PPTP. |
| | A drawback is that you must install a VPN Client onto every remote user's system. The initial configuration and subsequent maintenance require additional resources from an organization. |
| NAS-initiated model | VPNs are initiated at the service provider's point of presence (POP) using L2TP or Layer 2 Forwarding (L2F). |
| | Eliminates the need for client-based VPN software, simplifying installation and reducing administrative cost. |
| | A drawback is that the data circuits from the POP to the client remain unprotected. |
| | Another drawback is that you must use the same service provider end to end, eliminating the Internet as a transport vehicle. |

Figure 2-2 depicts the two types of remote access VPNs that can be accommodated by Cisco equipment and software.

**Figure 2-2**   *Remote Access VPNs*

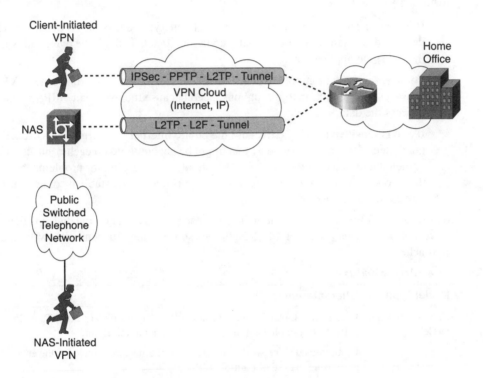

## Site-to-Site Intranet VPNs

You can use site-to-site intranet VPNs to connect remote offices and branch offices to the headquarters internal network over a shared infrastructure. These connections typically use dedicated circuits to provide access to employees only. These VPNs still provide the WAN characteristics of scalability, reliability, and support for a variety of protocols at a reduced cost in a flexible manner.

Intranet VPNs are typically built across service provider-shared network infrastructures like Frame Relay, Asynchronous Transfer Mode (ATM), or point-to-point circuits. Some of the benefits of using intranet VPNs include the following:

- Reduction of WAN costs, especially when used across the Internet.

- Partially or fully meshed networks can be established, providing network redundancy across one or more service providers.

- Ease of connecting new sites to the existing infrastructure.

Figure 2-3 shows a diagram of a typical intranet VPN network. The corporation manages the edge routers, providing flexible management and maintenance opportunities over intranet VPNs.

**Figure 2-3**   *Intranet VPNs*

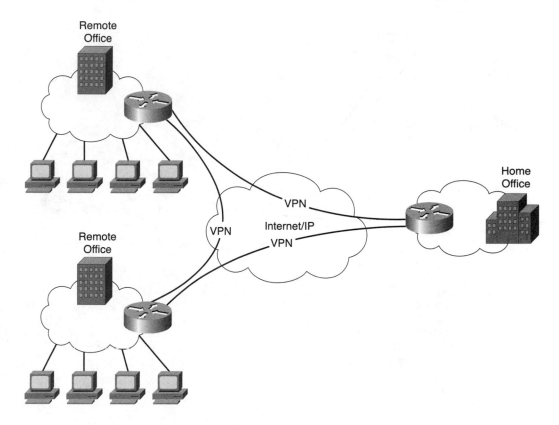

## Business-to-Business Extranet VPNs

Business-to-business extranet VPNs are the VPNs that give corporate network access to customers, suppliers, business partners, or other interested communities who are not employees of the corporation. Extranet VPNs use a combination of the same infrastructures that are used by remote access and intranet VPNs. The difference is found in the privileges that are extended to the extranet users. Security policies can limit access by protocol, ports, user identity, time of day, source or destination address, or other controllable factors.

Fixed, business-to-business connections and ubiquitous dial-up or broadband Internet connections are depicted in Figure 2-4.

**Figure 2-4** *Extranet VPNs*

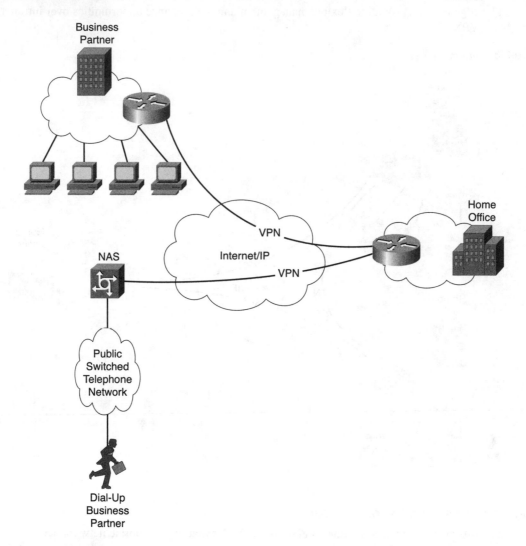

## Using Cisco VPN Products

Cisco can supply hardware and software to cover almost every possible VPN requirement. From routers and firewalls for intranet applications to VPN concentrators and clients for remote access applications, this section introduces you to some of the key features of Cisco VPN products.

## Cisco VPN Routers

Cisco VPN routers are the best choice for constructing intranet or extranet site-to-site VPNs. These routers use Cisco IOS Software and can be used to deliver multicast, routing, and multi-protocol across the VPN. You can enable quality of service (QoS) on these devices, and the firewall feature option can turn these routers into robust firewalls. Some routers also have integrated DSL and cable modems to provide VPN access to small offices/home offices (SOHOs).

Some VPN routers can be equipped with special modules to handle encryption processing for VPN tunnels. These modules free memory and CPU cycles that can then be used for switching packets, which is the routers' primary function.

These VPN routers offer the full range of VPN protocols and services. Table 2-3 shows some of the Cisco routers that are available for VPN service and identifies the application where they would most likely be applied.

**Table 2-3**    *Cisco VPN Routers*

| Site | Model | VPN Performance | Features |
|------|-------|-----------------|----------|
| SOHO<br>Remote access VPN<br>Extranet VPN | Cisco 827H ADSL Router | 384 kbps<br>Up to 50 tunnels | Fixed configuration<br>Integrated DSL modem<br>4-port 10BaseT hub<br>Support for EzVPN Remote |
| SOHO<br>Remote access VPN<br>Extranet VPN | Cisco uBR905 Cable Router | 6 Mbps<br>Up to 50 tunnels | Fixed configuration<br>Integrated cable modem<br>4-port 10BaseT hub<br>Support for EzVPN Remote and Server |
| SOHO<br>Remote access VPN<br>Extranet VPN | Cisco 806 Broadband Router | 384 kbps<br>Up to 50 tunnels | Fixed configuration<br>Installed behind broadband modem<br>10BaseT Ethernet WAN interface<br>4-port 10BaseT LAN hub<br>Support for EzVPN Remote |
| SOHO<br>Remote access VPN<br>Extranet VPN | Cisco 1710 Router | 3 Mbps<br>Up to 100 tunnels | Fixed configuration<br>10/100 Fast Ethernet port<br>10BaseT Ethernet port<br>Support for EzVPN Remote and Server |

*continues*

**Table 2-3** *Cisco VPN Routers (Continued)*

| Site | Model | VPN Performance | Features |
|------|-------|-----------------|----------|
| Small remote office<br>Remote access VPN<br>Intranet VPN<br>Extranet VPN | Cisco 1700 Router Series | 4 Mbps<br>Up to 100 tunnels with VPN Module | Modular configuration<br>Support for VPN Module<br>Support for EzVPN Remote and Server |
| Branch office<br>Intranet VPN<br>Extranet VPN | Cisco 2600 Router Series | 14 Mbps<br>Up to 800 tunnels with VPN Module | Modular configuration<br>Support for VPN Module<br>Support for EzVPN Server |
| Large branch office<br>Intranet VPN<br>Extranet VPN | Cisco 3600 Router Series | 40 Mbps<br>Up to 1800 tunnels with VPN Module | Modular configuration<br>Support for VPN Module<br>Support for EzVPN Server |
| Central hub site<br>Intranet VPN<br>Extranet VPN | Cisco 7100 Router Series | 145 Mbps<br>Up to 5000 tunnels with VPN Acceleration Module (VAM) | Modular configuration<br>Supports VAM<br>Support for EzVPN Server |
| Central hub site<br>Intranet VPN<br>Extranet VPN | Cisco 7200 Router Series | 145 Mbps<br>Up to 5000 tunnels with VAM | Modular configuration<br>Supports VAM<br>Support for EzVPN Server |

## Cisco PIX Firewalls

The next set of major hardware components that support VPNs are the series of Cisco PIX Firewalls. The PIX Firewalls feature a hardened, purpose-built operating system and provide a wide range of security and networking services. Along with IPSec VPN support, the PIX Firewalls also support PPTP and L2TP VPNs from Microsoft Windows clients. Network Address Translation (NAT), Port Address Translation (PAT), content and URL filtering, Remote Authentication Dial-In User Service (RADIUS) and Terminal Access Controller Access Control System Plus (TACACS+) AAA support, Dynamic Host Configuration Protocol (DHCP), and X.509 Public Key Infrastructure (PKI) are some of the features that are supported on these devices.

Some of the PIX Firewalls can accept special VPN modules to handle the CPU- and memory-intensive IPSec encryption process. Cisco PIX Firewalls support a range of operating systems as VPN Clients as well as Cisco's hardware VPN 3002 Client. Table 2-4 depicts the current series of PIX Firewalls, identifies their VPN capabilities, and shows some of the features of the devices.

**Table 2-4**    *Cisco PIX Firewalls*

| Site | Model | VPN Performance | Features |
|------|-------|-----------------|----------|
| SOHO<br><br>Remote access VPN<br>Intranet VPN<br>Extranet VPN | Cisco PIX 501 Firewall | 3 Mbps<br><br>Up to 5 simultaneous VPN peers | Fixed configuration<br><br>Up to 10 Mbps of firewall throughput<br><br>Ideal for securing always-on broadband connections<br><br>10BaseT outside interface<br><br>Integrated 4-port 10/100 switch<br><br>Support for EzVPN Client |
| Remote office/branch office (ROBO)<br><br>Remote access VPN<br>Intranet VPN<br>Extranet VPN | Cisco PIX 506E Firewall | 16 Mbps<br><br>Up to 25 simultaneous VPN peers | Fixed configuration<br><br>Up to 20 Mbps of firewall throughput<br><br>10BaseT outside and inside interfaces |
| Small- to medium-size business<br><br>Intranet VPN<br>Extranet VPN | Cisco PIX 515E Firewall | 63 Mbps<br><br>Up to 2000 tunnels with VPN Accelerator Card (VAC) | Modular configuration<br><br>Support for up to 125,000 concurrent connections<br><br>Capacity for up to 6 10/100 Fast Ethernet (FE) interfaces<br><br>Support for 2 single-port FE modules or one 4-port FE module<br><br>Failover port for high availability<br><br>Support for VAC |

*continues*

**Table 2-4**   *Cisco PIX Firewalls (Continued)*

| Site | Model | VPN Performance | Features |
|------|-------|-----------------|----------|
| Enterprise and service provider<br><br>Intranet VPN<br><br>Extranet VPN | Cisco PIX 525 Firewall | 70 Mbps<br><br>Up to 2000 tunnels with VAC | Modular configuration<br><br>Support for up to 280,000 concurrent connections<br><br>Support for single-port or four-port 10/100 Fast Ethernet interfaces<br><br>Support for Gigabit Ethernet interfaces<br><br>Failover port for high availability<br><br>Support for VAC |
| Enterprise and service provider<br><br>Intranet VPN<br><br>Extranet VPN | Cisco PIX 535 Firewall | 95 Mbps<br><br>Up to 2000 tunnels with VAC | Modular configuration<br><br>Support for up to 500,000 concurrent connections<br><br>Support for single-port or four-port 10/100 Fast Ethernet interfaces<br><br>Support for 66-MHz Gigabit Ethernet interface<br><br>Failover port for high availability<br><br>Support for VAC |

## Cisco VPN 3000 Concentrators

Cisco identified the need for a purpose-built, remote access VPN device and developed the Cisco VPN 3000 Series Concentrator family of products. While much of the rest of this book deals with these devices, this section introduces them along with the other VPN products.

The Cisco VPN 3000 Series Concentrator was designed to be a high-performance, scalable solution offering high availability and state-of-the-art encryption and authentication techniques. Scalable Encryption Processor (SEP) modules can be easily used to add capacity and throughput.

The Cisco VPN 3000 Series Concentrator comes in a variety of models that can support small offices of 100 or fewer VPN connections to large enterprises of 10,000 or more simultaneous VPN connections. Redundant and nonredundant configurations are available to help ensure the high reliability of these devices. Cisco VPN 3000 Concentrators also support wireless clients such as Personal Digital Assistants (PDAs) and Smart Phones. Mobile professionals using

Cisco Mobile Office can quickly and securely connect to the Cisco VPN 3000 Series Concentrator from airports, hotels, client offices, or other remote locations.

Table 2-5 describes the current Cisco VPN 3000 Series Concentrator line.

**Table 2-5**    *Cisco VPN 3000 Series Concentrators*

| Concentrator | Features |
|---|---|
| Cisco VPN 3005 Concentrator | Fixed configuration |
| | Supports up to 100 simultaneous sessions |
| Cisco VPN 3015 Concentrator | Upgradeable to 3030 Concentrator |
| | Supports up to 100 simultaneous sessions |
| Cisco VPN 3030 Concentrator | Accepts SEP modules |
| | Upgradeable to 3060 Concentrator |
| | Supports up to 1500 simultaneous sessions |
| | Redundant and nonredundant configurations available |
| Cisco VPN 3060 Concentrator | Accepts SEP modules |
| | Upgradeable to 3080 Concentrator |
| | Supports up to 5000 simultaneous sessions |
| | Redundant and nonredundant configurations available |
| Cisco VPN 3080 Concentrator | Accepts SEP modules |
| | Supports up to 10,000 simultaneous sessions |
| | Fully redundant configuration only |

## VPN Clients

Cisco has several VPN Clients available that can simplify the administration and maintenance of VPN connections. This section covers the software and hardware VPN Clients offered by Cisco.

### Cisco VPN Client

Sometimes called the Unity Client, the Cisco VPN Client is the current iteration of the Cisco VPN 3000 Client. This software comes bundled as a no-cost extra with Cisco VPN 3000 Series Concentrators and allows end stations to establish IPSec VPNs to any Cisco remote access VPN product at a central site. Although relatively easy to configure, the client can be preconfigured for mass deployments, making the initial configuration even easier. This method of installation is performed by pushing the client to the user's system upon initial login to the network, making the application of the Cisco VPN Client scalable. The Cisco VPN Client supports an assortment of operating systems, including versions of Linux, Solaris, MAC OS, and Windows 95, 98, Me,

NT 4.0, 2000, and XP. This client is covered more extensively in Chapter 3, "Cisco VPN 3000 Concentrator Series Hardware Overview," and Chapter 4, "Configuring Cisco VPN 3000 for Remote Access Using Preshared Keys."

### Cisco VPN 3002 Hardware Client

An alternative solution to deploying software clients on every connecting workstation is to use the Cisco VPN 3002 Hardware Client. These devices are deployed at remote office facilities and can provide a VPN tunnel for the entire facility and any operating system that communicates in IP, including Windows, Solaris, MAC, and Linux.

The Cisco VPN 3002 Hardware Client supports Easy VPN (EzVPN) Remote, allowing the device to establish IPSec VPN connections with any EzVPN Server system. These hardware clients can be configured to operate like a software client or to establish a permanent, secure VPN connection with the central site. The Cisco VPN 3002 Hardware Client can be configured with or without an integrated 8-port 10/100 Ethernet switch.

### Cisco Easy VPN

In the past, configuring VPNs between devices was a chore. Both ends of the VPN connection had to be configured identically, or the VPN tunnel could not be established. With the introduction of Easy VPN (EzVPN), Cisco has changed that. EzVPN has two components: Cisco Easy VPN Remote and Cisco Easy VPN Server. Once you have configured EzVPN Server on a device, you can configure an EzVPN Remote device to establish IPSec with it by simply supplying the correct password. Table 2-6 identifies the devices that support each of the EzVPN components.

**Table 2-6** *Cisco Easy VPN*

| Component | Cisco Model |
|---|---|
| Cisco Easy VPN Remote | Cisco 800 Series Routers |
| | Cisco 1700 Series Routers |
| | Cisco uBR900 Series Routers |
| | Cisco PIX 501 Firewalls |
| | Cisco VPN 3002 Hardware Clients |
| Cisco Easy VPN Server | Cisco IOS Software version 12.2(8)T Routers, including 1700 Series, 7100 Series, 7200 Series, as well as other Cisco IOS Routers. |
| | Cisco PIX Firewalls |
| | Cisco VPN 3000 Series Concentrators |

Because the EzVPN Remote and Server are built upon the Cisco Unified Client Framework, a Cisco Easy VPN Server can terminate Cisco VPN Client connections that originate with mobile users or telecommuters. EzVPN is an ideal solution for businesses with many remote facilities and little or no IT support at those facilities. EzVPNs are a highly scalable and secure method of deploying VPNs across widely dispersed organizations.

### Wireless Client Support

Also bundled with Cisco VPN 3000 Series Concentrators is a trial copy of Certicom Corporation's Movian VPN Client. This client is an Elliptic Curve Cryptosystem (ECC)–compliant VPN client for use with IP-enabled wireless devices such as PDAs and Smart Phones. All Cisco VPN 3000 Series Concentrators support ECC, which is a new Diffie-Hellman group that allows faster processing of keying information. Ideal for devices with limited processing power, these ECC-compliant VPN clients open the world of secure VPN connectivity to a new class of users.

### Cisco Internet Mobile Office

The Cisco Internet Mobile Office is a program that aims to bring secure, flexible, manageable, and scalable VPN support to users on the road, at home, and at work. In fact, the three phases of Cisco Mobile Office are called On The Road, At Home, and At Work.

Cisco Mobile Office On The Road is a global collaborative effort designed to provide secure, high-speed Internet and intranet access from public facilities such as airports and hotels. Using wireless LANs and many of the routers, firewalls, and concentrators that have been discussed in this chapter, accompanied by similar Cisco Mobile Office At Work networks and remote access devices for at-home connectivity, the Cisco Mobile Office provides a seamless networking environment for mobile professionals.

## Management Software

Cisco provides a robust selection of management tools to help manage and maintain Cisco devices and supported protocols, including VPNs. There is some overlap in the capabilities of these tools, and you might want to choose one product over another. Many of these tools are web based, using standard web browsers and simplifying their administration and maintenance. The following sections discuss several of those tools.

### Cisco VPN Device Manager

The Cisco VPN Device Manager (VDM) is an embedded device manager that is installed directly into a supporting router's flash memory. VDM then allows management of that router from a web browser using wizards to simplify the management process. VDM is currently supported on Cisco 7100, 7200, and 7400 Series Routers, allowing the simplified configuration of VPNs. A monitoring and graphing capability allows an administrator to view and graph statistics on VPN tunnel throughput, traffic volume, system utilization, tunnel counts, and errors. VDM is a no-cost option for these routers and can either be ordered with the router or downloaded from Cisco.com.

### CiscoWorks 2000

CiscoWorks 2000 is a family of network management tools that enable you to manage the protocols and Cisco products in your network. This comprehensive set of tools is modular, with overlapping components in some areas. The following list identifies some of the components found in the CiscoWorks family:

- Cisco Catalyst 6500 Network Analysis Module (NAM)
- Cisco Hosting Solution Engine
- Cisco Secure Access Control Server (ACS)
- Cisco User Registration Tool (URT)
- CiscoWorks for Windows
- CiscoWorks LAN Management Solution (LMS)
- CiscoWorks QoS Policy Manager (QPM)
- CiscoWorks Routed WAN (RWAN) Management Solution
- CiscoWorks Small Network Management Solution (SNMS)
- CiscoWorks Voice Manager (CVM)
- CiscoWorks VoIP Health Monitor (VoIP-HM)
- CiscoWorks VPN/Security Management Solution (VMS)
- CiscoWorks Wireless LAN Solution Engine (WLSE)

These products provide extensive monitoring and management capabilities for your Cisco network. Two of these product families have more direct ties to VPN control than the others: Cisco Secure Access Control Server (ACS) and CiscoWorks VMS.

Part of the CiscoWorks product line, the Cisco Secure ACS is Cisco's Authentication, Authorization, and Accounting (AAA) server. This device supports both TACACS+ and RADIUS. Sporting a web-based, graphical interface, this product is easy to install and administer.

AAA is supported on a many products and services, including routers, firewalls, concentrators, VPNs, switches, DSL and cable solutions, voice over IP (VoIP), and wireless solutions. You can team up Cisco Secure ACS servers to provide failover support with automatic database synchronization between servers. Cisco Secure ACS allows you to establish groups for easy application of restrictions, such as time of day and day of week.

Cisco Secure ACS comes in the following configurations:

- **Cisco Secure for NT**—Cisco Secure ACS for NT version 3.0 requires either a Microsoft Windows NT 4.0 Server or a Microsoft Windows 2000 Server. Cisco Secure ACS for NT version 3.1 operates only on the Windows 2000 platform.

- **Cisco Secure for UNIX**—Cisco Secure ACS for UNIX runs on the Sun Solaris operating system, versions 2.51, 2.6, 7, and 8.

CiscoWorks VPN/Security Management Solution (VMS) is a highly scalable solution for configuring, monitoring, and troubleshooting remote access, intranet, and extranet VPNs for small- and large-scale VPN deployments. VMS can also be used to configure network perimeter security. This CiscoWorks bundled solution consists of CiscoWorks VPN Monitor, Cisco IDS Host Sensor, CiscoWorks Auto Update Server Software, CiscoWorks CiscoView, CiscoWorks CD One, CiscoWorks Common Services Software, CiscoWorks Management Center for IDS Sensors, CiscoWorks Management Center for PIX Firewalls, CiscoWorks Management Center for VPN Routers, CiscoWorks Monitoring Center for Security, and CiscoWorks Resource Manager Essentials. Some of these products are discussed in more depth in the following list:

- **CiscoWorks VPN Monitor**—This is a web-based management tool that supports Cisco VPN 3000 Series Concentrators as well as the 1700, 2600, 3600, 7100, and 7200 VPN Routers. VPN Monitor collects, stores, and presents information on IPSec VPN connections used in remote access or site-to-site configurations. Graphical monitoring lets administrators view IPSec VPN status at a glance and helps troubleshoot problems through drill-down and graphing capabilities.

- **Cisco IDS Host Sensor**—This is a system of agent and console components that turn critical Windows or Sun servers into intrusion detection sensors. Cisco IDS Host Sensor detects and prevents attacks before unauthorized transactions can occur.

  IDS Host Sensor agents are available for Microsoft Windows NT or 2000 Server, and for Sun Solaris Ultrasparc systems running Solaris versions 2.6, 7, and 8. IDS Host Sensor consoles are available for Microsoft Windows NT or 2000 Server.

  The agent software running on a critical server obtains configuration and attack signatures from the console systems. If an attack occurs, the agent takes appropriate action to thwart the attack and reports the attempt to the console for immediate alerts or subsequent reporting.

- **CiscoView**—This is a web-based management tool that displays a physical representation of each managed device. Modules, ports, and indicators are depicted with color coding to indicate the current, dynamically updated status of the element. Performance and other statistics can be viewed through comprehensive monitoring capabilities. Administrators with the appropriate security privileges can also modify configurations on monitored devices.

- **CiscoWorks Resource Management Essentials (RME)**—Cisco switches, access servers, and routers can be managed through this product. RME is a suite of applications designed to provide central management of these devices. RME includes Inventory Manager, Change Audit, Device Configuration Manager, Software Image Manager, Availability Manager, Syslog Analyzer, and Cisco Management Connection.

# An Overview of IPSec Protocols

| 2 | IPSec overview |
|---|---|
| 3 | IPSec protocol framework |

IP Security Protocol (IPSec) is a collection of open standards that work together to establish data confidentiality, data integrity, and data authentication between peer devices. These peers can be pairs of hosts or pairs of security gateways (routers, firewalls, VPN concentrators, and so on), or they can be between a host and a security gateway, as in the case of remote access VPNs. IPSec can protect multiple data flows between peers, and a single gateway can support many simultaneous, secure IPSec tunnels between different pair partners.

IPSec works at the IP layer and can use the Internet Key Exchange (IKE) protocol to negotiate protocols between peers and generate encryption and authentication keys to be used by IPSec. IPSec was first described in a series of Requests for Comment (RFCs) from RFC 1825 through RFC 1829. RFCs 1825, 1826, and 1827 have since been updated by subsequent RFCs. Table 2-7 presents a list of the IPSec-related RFCs.

**Table 2-7** *IPSec RFCs*

| RFC | Title | Topic | Author | Date |
|---|---|---|---|---|
| 1825 (obsolete) | Security Architecture for the Internet Protocol | IPSec | R. Atkinson | Aug. 1995 |
| 1826 (obsolete) | IP Authentication Header | AH | R. Atkinson | Aug. 1995 |
| 1827 (obsolete) | IP Encapsulating Security Payload (ESP) | ESP | R. Atkinson | Aug. 1995 |
| 1828 | IP Authentication Using Keyed MD5 | MD5 | P. Metzger W. Simpson | Aug. 1995 |
| 1829 | The ESP DES-CBC Transform | DES | P. Karn P. Metzger W. Simpson | Aug. 1995 |

**Table 2-7**    *IPSec RFCs (Continued)*

| RFC | Title | Topic | Author | Date |
|-----|-------|-------|--------|------|
| 2104 | HMAC: Keyed-Hashing for Message Authentication | HMAC | K. Krawczyk<br>M. Bellare<br>R. Canetti | Feb. 1997 |
| 2202 | Test Cases for HMAC-MD5 and HMAC-SHA-1 | HMAC-MD5<br>HMAC-SHA-1 | P. Cheng<br>R. Glenn | Sep. 1997 |
| 2401 | Security Architecture for the Internet Protocol | IPSec | S. Kent<br>R. Atkinson | Nov. 1998 |
| 2402 | IP Authentication Header | AH | S. Kent<br>R. Atkinson | Nov. 1998 |
| 2403 | The Use of HMAC-MD5-96 within ESP and AH | HMAC-MD5 | C. Madson<br>R. Glenn | Nov. 1998 |
| 2404 | The Use of HMAC-SHA-1-96 within ESP and AH | HMAC-SHA-1 | C. Madson<br>R. Glenn | Nov. 1998 |
| 2405 | The ESP DES-CBC Cipher Algorithm With Explicit IV | DES | C. Madson<br>N. Doraswamy | Nov. 1998 |
| 2406 | IP Encapsulating Security Payload (ESP) | ESP | S. Kent<br>R. Atkinson | Nov. 1998 |
| 2407 | The Internet IP Security Domain of Interpretation for ISAKMP | ISAKMP | D. Piper | Nov. 1998 |
| 2408 | Internet Security Association and Key Management Protocol | ISAKMP | D. Maughan<br>M. Schertler<br>M. Schneider<br>J. Turner | Nov. 1998 |
| 2409 | The Internet Key Exchange (IKE) | IKE | D. Harkins<br>D. Carrel | Nov. 1998 |
| 2410 | The NULL Encryption Algorithm and Its Use With IPSec | NULL | R. Glenn<br>S. Kent | Nov. 1998 |
| 2451 | The ESP CBC-Mode Cipher Algorithms | CBC | R. Periera<br>R. Adams | Nov. 1998 |

This is not an exhaustive list of IPSec-related RFCs, but you can find these RFCs and others at the Internet Engineering Task Force (IETF) website:

www.ietf.org/rfc.html

Specific RFCs that relate to IPSec can be found at the following website:

www.ietf.org/html.charters/ipsec-charter.html

Notice that just three years after IPSec was introduced, a veritable army of IPSec tools was developed and quickly accepted by the networking industry.

Some things to remember when you are planning an IPSec deployment are as follows:

- IPSec supports High-Level Data-Link Control (HDLC), ATM, Point-to-Point Protocol (PPP), and Frame Relay serial encapsulation.
- IPSec also works with Generic Routing Encapsulation (GRE) and IP-in-IP (IPinIP) Encapsulation Layer 3 tunneling protocols. IPSec does not support the data-link switching (DLSw) standard, source-route bridging (SRB), or other Layer 3 tunneling protocols.
- IPSec does not support multipoint tunnels.
- IPSec works strictly with unicast IP datagrams only. It does not work with multicast or broadcast IP datagrams.
- IPSec is slower than Cisco Encryption Technology (CET) because IPSec provides per-packet data authentication.
- IPSec provides packet expansion that can cause fragmentation and reassembly of IPSec packets, creating another reason that IPSec is slower than CET.
- When using NAT, be sure that NAT occurs before IPSec encapsulation so that IPSec has global addresses to work with.

Table 2-7 shows the major protocols that you can encounter when working with IPSec. The following is a quick review of these standard protocols:

- IP Security Protocol (IPSec)
  - Authentication Header (AH)
  - Encapsulating Security Payload (ESP)
- Message Encryption
  - Data Encryption Standard (DES)
  - Triple DES (3DES)
- Message Integrity (Hash) Functions
  - Hash-based Message Authentication Code (HMAC)
  - Message Digest 5 (MD5)
  - Secure Hash Algorithm-1 (SHA-1)

- Peer Authentication
  - Rivest, Shamir, and Adelman (RSA) Digital Signatures
  - RSA Encrypted Nonces
- Key Management
  - Diffie-Hellman (D-H)
  - Certificate Authority (CA)
- Security Association
  - Internet Key Exchange (IKE)
  - Internet Security Association and Key Management Protocol (ISAKMP)

**NOTE**     IKE and ISAKMP are interchangeable in Cisco implementations.

These protocols are examined in more detail in the following sections.

## The IPSec Protocols

The protocols that IPSec uses to provide traffic security are Authentication Header (AH) and Encapsulating Security Payload (ESP). These two protocols are considered purely IPSec protocols and were developed strictly for IPSec. Each protocol is described in its own RFC, which was identified in Table 2-7. You can use AH and ESP independently on an IPSec connection, or you can combine their use.

IKE and IPSec negotiate encryption and authentication services between pairs. This negotiation process culminates in establishing Security Associations (SAs) between security pairs. IKE SAs are bidirectional, but IPSec SAs are unidirectional and must be established by each member of the VPN pair to establish bidirectional traffic. There must be an identical SA on each pair to establish secure communications between pairs. The information associated with each SA is stored in a Security Association Database, and each SA is assigned a Security Parameters Index (SPI) number that, when combined with the destination IP address and the security protocol (AH or ESP), uniquely identifies the SA.

The key to IPSec is the establishment of these SAs. SAs are negotiated once at the beginning of an IPSec session and periodically throughout a session when certain conditions are met. To avoid having to negotiate security for each packet, there had to be a way to communicate the use of an already agreed upon SA between security pairs.

That is where the AH and ESP protocols come into use. These two protocols are simply a means of identifying which prenegotiated security features to use for a packet going from one peer to another. Both of these protocols add an extra header to the IP datagram between the Layer 3

(IP) and Layer 4 (usually TCP or UDP) protocol headers. A key element contained in each protocol's header is the SPI, giving the destination peer the information it needs to authenticate and decrypt the packet.

## Authentication Header

The Authentication Header (AH) protocol is defined in RFCs 1826 and 2402 and provides for data integrity, data origin authentication, and an optional antireplay service. AH does not provide encryption, which means that the packets are sent as clear text. AH is slightly quicker than ESP, so you might choose to use AH when you need to be certain of the source and integrity of the packet but confidentiality is not a concern.

Devices configured to use AH insert an extra header into the IP datagrams of "interesting traffic," between the IP header and the Layer 4 header. Because a processing cost is associated with IPSec, VPNs can be configured to choose which traffic to secure, and IPSec and non-IPSec traffic can coexist between security pairs. You might choose to secure e-mail traffic but not web traffic, for example. The process of inserting the AH header is shown in Figure 2-5.

**Figure 2-5**   *AH Header in IPSec Datagram*

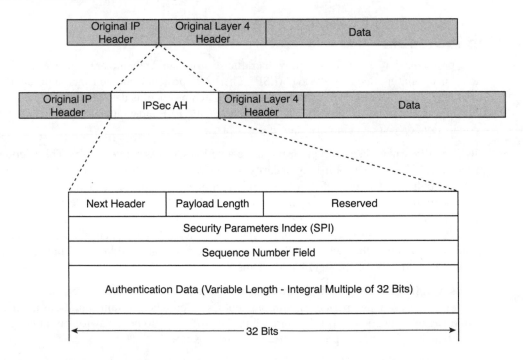

The fields included in the AH are as follows:

- **Next Header (8 bits)**—This field contains the protocol number of the Layer 4 header that follows the IPSec header. If the Layer 4 protocol were TCP, this field would contain the number 6. For UDP, it would contain the number 17.

---

**NOTE**    The Next Header or Protocol value within the IP header preceding the IPSec header contains the value of 51 when AH is used as the IPSec protocol.

---

- **Payload Length (8 bits)**—This field contains the length of the IPSec header in 32-bit words, minus 2. The fixed portion of the header is 96 bits long, or 3 words. The Authentication Data portion is of variable length but has a standard length of 96 bits, also 3 words. That makes a total of six 32-bit words. Deduct 2 and the value entered in the Payload Length field would be 4.

- **Reserved (16 bits)**—Currently unused, this portion of the header must be filled with 0s.

- **Security Parameters Index (SPI) (32 bits)**—The destination IP address, the IPSec protocol, and this number uniquely identify the SA for this packet.

- **Sequence Number Field (32 bits)**—This is an unsigned, monotonically increasing counter that enables antireplay services for a specific SA. This information does not have to be used by the receiving peer, but it must be included by the sender. This number is initialized to 0 when an SA is established. If antireplay is used, this number can never be allowed to repeat. Because the sender does not know if the receiver is using the antireplay function, the fact that this number cannot be repeated requires that the SA be terminated and a new one established prior to transmitting the $2^{32}$ packet.

- **Authentication Data (Variable)**—This field contains the Integrity Check Value (ICV) for the packet. The field must be an integral multiple of 32 bits and can contain padding to fill it out to the next 32-bit increment.

  The ICV is computed using authentication algorithms, including keyed Message Authentication Codes (MACs). MACs are based on symmetric encryption algorithms, such as DES and 3DES, or on one-way functions, such as MD5 or SHA-1. When computing the ICV, the computation is done using the entire new packet. To keep the elements aligned properly, any mutable fields that cannot be predicted and the Authentication Data field of the IPSec header are set to 0. Predictable, mutable fields are set to their predictable value. Upper-layer data are assumed to be immutable. A shared secret key is used in the MAC calculation, making it difficult to spoof.

  Each peer at the end of the VPN calculates this ICV independently. If these ICVs do not match, the packet is discarded, thereby assuring that the packet has not been tampered with during transit.

## Encapsulating Security Payload

The other IPSec protocol is the Encapsulating Security Payload (ESP) protocol. This protocol provides confidentiality by enabling encryption of the original packet. Additionally, ESP provides data origin authentication, integrity, antireplay service, and some limited traffic flow confidentiality. This is the protocol to use when you require confidentiality in your IPSec communications.

ESP acts differently than does AH. As its name implies, ESP encapsulates all or portions of the original IP datagram by surrounding it with both a header and a trailer. Figure 2-6 shows this encapsulation process.

**Figure 2-6**  *ESP Encapsulation Process*

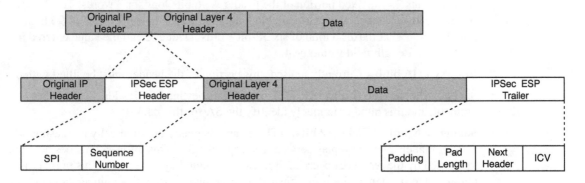

Figure 2-7 shows more detail about the lengths and placement of the various ESP components.

**Figure 2-7**  *Encapsulating Security Payload*

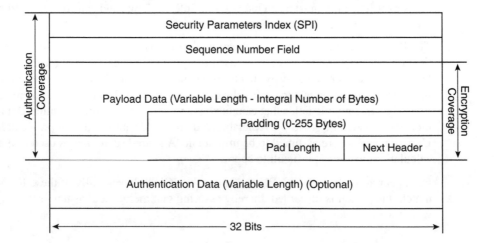

The fields included in the ESP are as follows:

- **Security Parameters Index (SPI) (32 bits)**—The destination IP address, the IPSec protocol, and this number uniquely identify the SA for this packet.

- **Sequence Number Field (32 bits)**—This is an unsigned, monotonically increasing counter that enables antireplay services for a specific SA. This information does not have to be used by the receiving peer, but it must be included by the sender. This number is initialized to 0 when an SA is established. If antireplay is used, this number can never be allowed to repeat. Because the sender does not know if the receiver is using the antireplay function, the fact that this number cannot be repeated requires that the SA be terminated and a new one established prior to transmitting the $2^{32}$ packet.

- **Payload (Variable)**—This is the original IP datagram or portions of that datagram. Whether this is the entire datagram depends on the mode used. When using tunnel mode, this Payload includes the entire original IP datagram. In transport mode, it includes only the upper-layer portions of the original IP datagram. IPSec modes are discussed in an upcoming section. The length of the Payload is always an integral number of bytes.

- **Padding (0–255 bytes)**—The Pad Length and Next Header fields must be right aligned within a 4-byte (32-bit) boundary, as shown in Figure 2-7. If the Payload does not accomplish this, padding must be added to ensure this alignment. Additionally, padding can be added to support the multiple block size requirements of encryption algorithms. Padding can also be added to conceal the true length of the Payload.

- **Pad Length (8 bits)**—This field contains the number of bytes of padding that were included in the previous field.

- **Next Header (8 bits)**—This field contains the protocol number of the Layer 4 header that follows the IPSec header. If the Layer 4 protocol were TCP, this field would contain the number 6. For UDP, it would contain the number 17.

---

**NOTE**      The Next Header or Protocol value within the IP header preceding the IPSec header contains the value of 50 when ESP is used as the IPSec protocol.

---

- **Authentication Data (Variable)**—This field contains the ICV for the packet. The field must be an integral multiple of 32 bits and can contain padding to fill it out to the next 32-bit increment. This field is optional when authentication has been specified in the SA.

Figure 2-7 shows the data areas that are covered by encryption and authentication. If encryption is specified in the SA, the fields from Payload through Next Header are encrypted. If authentication is specified, that occurs on the immutable fields from the SPI field through the Next Header field.

## AH and ESP Modes of Operation

The previous discussion talked about the AH and ESP protocols using several examples that showed sliding the IP header of an IP datagram to the left, inserting either an AH or ESP header, and then appending the upper-layer portion of the datagram to that. This is a classic description of one of the modes of operation for IPSec, namely the Transport mode. The other mode of operation for IPSec is the Tunnel mode.

These two modes provide a further level of authentication or encryption support to IPSec. The next sections discuss these two IPSec modes.

### Transport Mode

Transport mode is primarily used for end-to-end connections between hosts or devices acting as hosts. Tunnel mode is used for everything else. An IPSec gateway (that is, a Cisco IOS Software router, Cisco PIX Firewall, or Cisco VPN 3000 Series Concentrator) might act as a host when being accessed by an administrator for configuration or other management operations.

Figure 2-8 shows how the Transport mode affects AH IPSec connections. The Layer 3 and Layer 4 headers are pried apart, and the AH is added between them. Authentication protects all but mutable fields in the original IP header.

**Figure 2-8**  *AH Transport Mode*

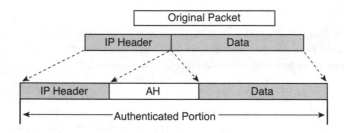

Figure 2-9 shows ESP Transport mode. Again, the IP header is shifted to the left, and the ESP header is inserted. The ESP trailer and ICV are then appended to the end of the datagram. If encryption is desired (not available with AH), only the original data and the new ESP trailer are encrypted. Authentication extends from the ESP header through the ESP trailer.

Even though the original header has been essentially left intact in both situations, the AH Transport mode does not support NAT because changing the source IP address in the IP header causes authentication to fail. If you need to use NAT with AH Transport mode, you must ensure that NAT happens before IPSec.

Notice that this problem does not exist with ESP Transport mode. The IP header remains outside of the authentication and encryption areas for ESP Transport mode datagrams.

**Figure 2-9**  *ESP Transport Mode*

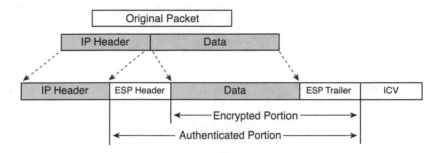

## Tunnel Mode

IPSec tunnel mode is used between gateways such as Cisco IOS Software routers, Cisco PIX Firewalls, and Cisco VPN 3000 Series Concentrators. It is also typically used when a host connects to one of these gateways to gain access to networks controlled by that gateway, as would be the case with most remote access users dialing in to a router or concentrator.

In Tunnel mode, instead of shifting the original IP header to the left and then inserting the IPSec header, the original IP header is copied and shifted to the left to form the new IP header. The IPSec header is then placed between the original and the copy of the IP header. The original datagram is left intact and is wholly secured by authentication or encryption algorithms.

Figure 2-10 shows the AH Tunnel mode. Once again, notice that the new IP header is under the auspices of the authentication algorithm and that it does not support NAT.

**Figure 2-10**  *AH Tunnel Mode*

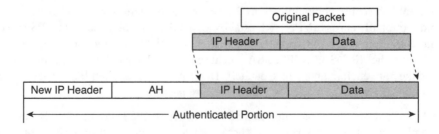

In Figure 2-11, you see a depiction of the ESP Tunnel mode. The entire original datagram can be encrypted and/or authenticated with this method. If you select to use both ESP authentication and encryption, encryption is performed first. This allows authentication to be done with assurance that the sender does not alter the datagram before transmission, and the receiver can authenticate the datagram before decrypting the package.

**Figure 2-11**  *ESP Tunnel Mode*

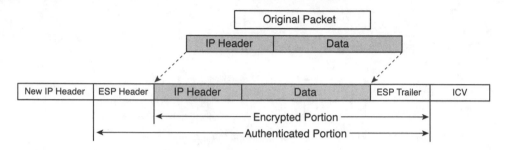

ESP supports NAT in either Tunnel or Transport mode, and only ESP supports encryption. If you need encryption, you must use ESP. If you also want authentication with ESP, you must select ESP HMAC service. HMAC uses the MD5 and SHA-1 keyed hashing algorithms.

## Security Associations

Depending on the IPSec protocol you choose to use, you can ensure data integrity and source authenticity, provide encryption, or do both. Once you decide the service you need, the peers then begin a negotiation process to select a matching set of algorithms for authentication, encryption, and/or hashing as well as a matching SA lifetime. This negotiation process is done by comparing requested services from the source peer with a table of acceptable services maintained on the destination peer.

Once the negotiation process has been completed, it would be convenient not to have to do it again for a while. The IETF named this security service relationship between two or more entities to establish secure communications the Security Association (SA). When traffic needs to flow bidirectionally across a VPN, IKE establishes a bidirectional SA and then IPSec establishes two more unidirectional SAs, each having their own lifetime. Get into the habit of identifying these SAs as either IKE SAs or IPSec SAs because they each have their own configuration attributes and they are each maintained separately. IKE SAs are used when IPSec tries to establish a connection. IPSec SAs are used with every secure packet.

SAs are only good for one direction of data across an IPSec connection. Because SAs are simplex, establishing conversations between peers requires two IPSec SAs, one going and one coming, for each peer and two underlying IKE SAs. IPSec SAs are also protocol specific. If you are going to be using both AH and ESP between security pairs, you need separate SAs for each.

Each SA is assigned a unique random number called a Security Parameters Index (SPI). This number, the destination IP address of a packet, and the IPSec protocol used create a unique triplet that identifies a security association. When a system wants to send IPSec traffic to a peer, it checks to see if an SA already exists for that peer using the desired security services. If it finds an existing SA, it places the SPI of the SA into the IPSec header and sends the packet. The destination peer takes the SPI, combines it with the IPSec protocol and the destination IP address (itself), and locates the existing SA in the Security Association Database it maintains for incoming traffic on that interface. Once it finds the SA, the destination peer knows how to unwrap the data for use.

# Existing Protocols Used in the IPSec Process

IPSec makes use of numerous existing encryption, authentication, and key exchange standards. This approach maintains IPSec as a standards-based application, making it more universally acceptable in the IP community. Many of these standard protocols are described in the following sections.

## Message Encryption

Available when using the ESP IPSec protocol, message encryption enables you to send highly sensitive information across the public networks without fear of having those data easily compromised. Two encryption standards are available with Cisco VPN equipment, the Data Encryption Standard (DES) and its more robust cousin, the Triple Data Encryption Standard (3DES or Triple DES).

### Data Encryption Standard

The standard encryption method used by many VPN deployments is the Data Encryption Standard (DES) method of encryption. DES applies a 56-bit key to every 64 bits of data. DES provides over 72,000,000,000,000,000 (72 quadrillion) possible encryption keys. Developed by IBM in 1977 and adopted by the U.S. Department of Defense, DES was once considered such a strong encryption technique that it was barred from export from the continental United States. It was considered unbreakable at the time of its adoption, but faster computers have rendered DES breakable within a relatively short period of time (less than a day), so DES is no longer in favor in high-security applications.

Cisco products support 56-bit DES-CBC with Explicit IV. Cipher Block Chaining (CBC) is one of several methods of implementing DES. CBC requires an initialization vector (IV) to start encryption. IPSec ensures that both VPN peers have the same IV or shared secret key. The shared secret key is input into the DES encryption algorithm, and clear text is then supplied in 64-bit blocks. The clear text is converted to ciphertext and is passed to ESP for transmission to the waiting peer, where the process is reversed using the same shared secret key to reproduce the clear text message.

### Triple DES

One version of the Data Encryption Standard is Triple DES (3DES) so named because it performs three encryption operations on the data. It performs an encryption process, a decryption process, and then another encryption process, each with a different 56-bit key. This triple process produces an aggregate 168-bit key, providing strong encryption. Cisco VPN products and software all support the 168-bit 3DES encryption algorithm as well as the 56-bit DES algorithm.

## Message Integrity

Message integrity is accomplished by using a hashing algorithm to compute a condensed representation of a message or data file. These condensed representations are called message digests (MDs) and are of a fixed length that depends on the hashing algorithm used. All or part of this message digest is transmitted with the data to the destination host, which executes the same hashing algorithm to create its own message digest. The source and destination message digests are then compared. Any deviation means that the message has been altered since the original message digest was created. A match means that you can be fairly certain that the data have not been altered during transit.

When using the IPSec AH protocol, the message digest is created using the immutable fields from the entire IP datagram, replacing mutable fields with 0s or predictable values to maintain proper alignment. The computed MD is then placed into the Authentication Data (or ICV) field of the AH. The destination device then copies the MD from the AH and zeroes out the Authentication Data field to recalculate its own MD. Refer to Figures 2-8 and 2-10 to refresh your memory about the structure of the AH datagram.

With the IPSec ESP protocol, the process is similar. The message digest is created using the immutable data in the portion of the IP datagram from the beginning of the ESP header to the end of the ESP trailer. The computed MD is then placed into the ICV field at the end of the datagram. With ESP, the destination host does not need to zero out the ICV field because it sits outside of the scope of the hashing routine. Refer to Figures 2-9 and 2-11 for the structure of the ESP datagram.

Cisco VPN products support Message Digest 5 (MD5) and Secure Hash Algorithm-1 (SHA-1) algorithms, which use a keyed hashing mechanism called Hashed Method Authentication Code (HMAC). These three message integrity tools are described in the following sections.

### Hash-Keyed Message Authentication Code

RFC 2104 describes the HMAC algorithm, because it was developed to work with existing hashing algorithms like MD5 and SHA-1. Many security processes involved in sharing data involve the use of secret keys and a mechanism called Message Authentication Codes (MACs). One party creates the MAC using the secret key and transmits the MAC to its peer partner. The peer partner creates its own MAC using the same secret key and compares the two MACs.

MD5 and SHA-1 share a similar concept, except that they do not use secret keys. That is where HMAC comes in. HMAC was developed to add a secret key into the calculation of the message digests produced by standard hashing algorithms. The secret key added to the formula is the same length as the resulting message digest for the hashing algorithm used.

### Message Digest 5—HMAC Variant

Message Digest 5 (MD5) was developed by Ronald Rivest of the Massachusetts Institute of Technology and RSA Data Security Incorporated. MD5 takes any message or data file and creates a 128-bit condensed representation (message digest) of the data.

The HMAC variant used by Cisco is designated HMAC-MD5-96. This version uses a 128-bit secret key to produce a 128-bit MD. AH and ESP-HMAC only use the left-most 96 bits, placing them into the authentication field. The destination peer then calculates a complete 128-bit message digest but then only uses the left-most 96 bits to compare with the value stored in the authentication field.

MD5 creates a shorter message digest than does SHA-1 and is considered less secure but offers better performance. MD5 without HMAC has some known weaknesses that make it a poor choice for high-security applications. HMAC-MD5 has not yet been successfully attacked.

### Secure Hash Algorithm-1

The Secure Hash Algorithm was developed by the National Institute of Standards and Technology (NIST) and was first documented in the Federal Information Processing Standards (FIPS) Publication 180. The current version is SHA-1, as described in FIPS 180-1 and RFC 2404.

SHA-1 produces a 160-bit message digest, and the HMAC-SHA-1 variant uses a 160-bit secret key. Cisco's implementation of HMAC-SHA1-96 truncates the 160-bit MD to the left-most 96 bits and sends those in the authentication field. The receiving peer re-creates the entire 160-bit message digest using the same 160-bit secret key but then only compares the leading 96 bits against the MD fragment in the authentication field.

The 160-bit SHA-1 message digest is more secure than the 128-bit MD5 message digest. There is a price to pay in performance for the extra security, but if you need to use the most secure form of message integrity, you should select the HMAC-SHA-1 algorithm.

## Peer Authentication

One of the processes that IKE performs is the authentication of peers. This is done during IKE Phase 1 using a keyed hashing algorithm with one of three possible key types:

- Preshared
- RSA digital signatures
- RSA encrypted nonces

These three key types and their associated authentication processes are outlined in the next sections.

## Preshared Keys

The process of sharing preshared keys is manual. Administrators at each end of the IPSec VPN agree on the key to use and then manually enter the key into the end device, either host or gateway. This method is fairly secure, but it does not scale well to large applications.

## RSA Digital Signatures

Ronald Rivest, Adi Shamir, and Leonard Adelman developed the RSA public-key cryptosystem in 1977. Ronald Rivest also developed the MD5 hashing algorithm. A Certificate Authority (CA) provides RSA digital certificates upon registration with that CA. These digital certificates allow stronger security than do preshared keys. Once the initial configuration has been completed, peers using RSA digital certificates can authenticate with one another without operator intervention.

When an RSA digital certificate is requested, a public and a private key are generated. The host uses the private key to create a digital signature. The host sends this digital signature along with its digital certificate to its IPSec peer partner. The peer uses the public key from the digital certificate to validate the digital signature received from the peer.

## RSA Encrypted Nonces

A twist in the way digital signatures are used is the process of using RSA encrypted nonces for peer authentication. A *nonce* is a pseudorandom number. This process requires registration with a CA to obtain RSA digital certificates. Peers do not share public keys in this form of authentication. They do not exchange digital certificates. The process of sharing keys is manual and must be done during the initial setup.

RSA encrypted nonces permit repudiation of the communication, where either peer can plausibly deny that it took part in the communication. Cisco is the only vendor that offers this form of peer authentication.

# Key Management

Key management can be a huge problem when working with IPSec VPNs. It seems like there are keys lurking everywhere. In reality, only five permanent keys are used for every IPSec peer relationship. These keys are described as follows:

- Two are private keys that are owned by each peer and are never shared. These keys are used to sign messages.

- Two are public keys that are owned by each peer and are made available to anyone. These keys are used to verify signatures.

- The fifth key is the shared secret key. Both peer members use this key for encryption and hashing functions. This is the key created by the Diffie-Hellman protocol, which is discussed in the next section.

That does not seem like many keys. In fact, the private and public keys are used for multiple IPSec connections on a given peer. In a small organization, these keys could all probably be managed manually. The problem arises when trying to scale the processes to support hundreds or thousands of VPN sessions. The next sections discuss the Diffie-Hellman protocol and Certificate Authorities, which are two excellent ways of automatically managing this potential nightmare.

## Diffie-Hellman Protocol

In 1976, Whitfield Diffie and Martin Hellman developed the first public key cryptographic technique. The Diffie-Hellman (D-H) key agreement protocol allows two peers to exchange a secret key without having any prior secrets. This protocol is an example of an asymmetrical key exchange process in which peers exchange different public keys to generate identical private keys. This protocol is over 20 years old and has withstood the test of time.

The Diffie-Hellman protocol is used in IPSec VPNs, but you have to look hard to find it. It is used in the process of establishing the secure channel between peers that IPSec rides on. The trail is as follows:

1  IPSec uses the Internet Security Association and Key Management Protocol (ISAKMP) to provide a framework for authentication and key exchange.

2  ISAKMP uses the IKE Protocol to securely negotiate and provide authenticated keying material for security associations.

3  IKE uses a protocol called OAKLEY, which describes a series of key exchanges and details the service provided by each.

4  OAKLEY uses Diffie-Hellman to establish a shared secret key between peers.

Symmetric key encryption processes then use the shared secret key for encryption or authentication of the connection. Peers that use symmetric key encryption protocols must share the same secret key. Diffie-Hellman provides an elegant solution for providing each peer with a shared secret key without having to keep track of the keys used.

Diffie-Hellman is such a clean process that you might wonder why we need symmetric key encryption processes. The answer is that asymmetric key encryption processes are much too slow for the bulk encryption required in high-speed VPN circuits. That is why the Diffie-Hellman protocol has been relegated to creating the shared secret key used by symmetric key encryption protocols.

IPSec peers use the Diffie-Hellman Protocol to generate the shared secret key that is used by AH or ESP to create authentication data or to encrypt an IP datagram. The receiving peer uses the D-H shared secret key to authenticate the datagram and decrypt the payload.

No discussion of Diffie-Hellman would be complete without showing the mechanisms involved in creating the shared secret key. Table 2-8 shows the Diffie-Hellman process of creating the key between two IPSec peers called Able and Baker. Notice that the shared secret key never travels over the network between the peers.

**NOTE**    Recall from your high school math that the modulus operation returns the remainder that results from dividing one number by another. For example, 7 mod 4 returns the number 3.

**Table 2-8**    *Diffie-Hellman Process*

| ABLE | NETWORK | BAKER |
|------|---------|-------|
| Agrees with BAKER to use a large prime number:<br><br>**P** | $\rightarrow \leftarrow$ | Agrees with ABLE to use a large prime number:<br><br>**P** |
| Further agrees on an integer to use as a generator:<br><br>**G** | $\rightarrow \leftarrow$ | Further agrees on an integer to use as a generator:<br><br>**G** |
| Picks a secret number:<br><br>**A** | | Picks a secret number:<br><br>**B** |
| Computes a public number:<br><br>$X = G^A \bmod P$ | | Computes a public number:<br><br>$Y = G^B \bmod P$ |
| Sends **X** to BAKER | $X \rightarrow \leftarrow Y$ | Sends **Y** to ABLE |
| Now knows:<br><br>**P, G, A, X, Y** | | Now knows:<br><br>**P, G, B, X, Y** |
| Computes:<br><br>$K_A = Y^A \bmod P$ | | Computes:<br><br>$K_B = X^B \bmod P$ |
| Now knows shared secret key:<br><br>$K_A = K_B = K$ | | Now knows shared secret key:<br><br>$K_B = K_A = K$ |
| | | |
| Proof:<br><br>$K_A = (G^B \bmod P)^A \bmod P$<br>$K_A = (G^B)^A \bmod P$<br>$K_A = G^{BA} \bmod P$<br>$K_A$ | $=$ | Proof:<br><br>$K_B = (G^A \bmod P)^B \bmod P$<br>$K_B = (G^A)^B \bmod P$<br>$K_B = G^{AB} \bmod P$<br>$K_B$ |

## Certificate Authorities

Another method of handling keys that does not take a lot of administrative support is to use Certificate Authorities (CAs) as a trusted entity for issuing and revoking digital certificates and for providing a means to verify the authenticity of those certificates. CAs are usually third-party agents such as VeriSign or Entrust, but for cost savings, you could also set up your own CA using Windows 2000 Certificate Services.

The following list describes how CAs work:

1  A client that wants to use digital certificates creates a pair of keys, one public and one private. Next, the client prepares an unsigned certificate (X.509) that contains, among other things, the client's ID and the public key that was just created. This unsigned certificate is then sent to a CA using some secure method.

2  The CA computes a hash code of the unsigned certificate. The CA then takes that hash and encrypts it using the CA's private key. This encrypted hash is the digital signature, and the CA attaches it to the certificate and returns the signed certificate to the client. This certificate is called an Identity Certificate and is stored on the client device until it expires or is deleted. The CA also sends the client its own digital certificate, which becomes the root certificate for the client.

3  The client now has a signed digital certificate that it can send to any other peer partner. If the peer partner wants to authenticate the certificate, it decrypts the signature using the CA's public key.

It is important to note that a CA only sends a client's certificate to that client itself. If the client wants to establish IPSec VPNs with another client, it trades digital certificates with that client, thereby sharing public keys.

When a client wants to encrypt data to send to a peer, it uses the peer's public key from the digital certificate. The peer then decrypts the package with its private key.

When a client wants to digitally sign a package, it uses its own private key to create a "signed" hash of the package. The receiving peer then uses the client's public key to create a comparison hash of the package. When the two hash values match, the signature has been verified.

Another function of a CA is to periodically generate a list of certificates that have expired or have been explicitly voided. The CA makes these Certificate Revocation Lists (CRLs) available to its customers. When a client receives a digital certificate, it checks the CRL to find out if the certificate is still valid.

You learn more about CAs and digital certificates in Chapter 5, "Configuring Cisco VPN 3000 for Remote Access Using Digital Certificates."

## Authenticating IPSec Peers and Forming Security Associations

The protocol that brings all the previously mentioned protocols together is the Internet Key Exchange (IKE) Protocol. IKE operates in two separate phases when establishing IPSec VPNs. In IKE Phase 1, it is IKE's responsibility to authenticate the IPSec peers, negotiate an IKE security association between peers, and initiate a secure tunnel for IPSec using the Internet Security Association and Key Management Protocol (ISAKMP).

In IKE Phase 2, the peers use the authenticated, secure tunnel from Phase 1 to negotiate the set of security parameters for the IPSec tunnel. Once the peers have agreed on a set of security parameters, the IPSec tunnel is created and stays in existence until the Security Associations (SAs) (either IKE or IPSec) are terminated or until the SA lifetimes expire.

## Combining Protocols into Transform Sets

Configuring IPSec in Cisco devices is fairly simple. You need to identify the five parameters that IKE uses in Phase 1 to authenticate peers and establish the secure tunnel. Those five parameters and their default settings for the VPN 3000 Concentrator Series are as follows:

- **Encryption algorithm**—56-bit DES (default) or the stronger 168-bit 3DES.
- **Hash algorithm**—MD5 (default) or the stronger SHA-1.
- **Authentication method**—Preshared keys, RSA encrypted nonces, or the most secure, RSA digital signatures (also the default).
- **Key exchange method**—768-bit Diffie-Hellman Group 1 (default) or the stronger 1024-bit Diffie-Hellman Group 2.
- **IKE SA lifetime**—The default is 86,400 seconds or 1 day. Shorter durations are more secure but come at a processing expense.

Whatever parameters you choose for IKE Phase 1 must be identical on the prospective peer, or the connection is not established. Once you have these configured, the only other values you need to supply to establish the IPSec tunnel in IKE Phase 2 are as follows:

- **IPSec protocol**—AH or ESP
- **Hash algorithm**—MD5 or SHA-1 (These are always HMAC assisted for IKE Phase 2.)
- **Encryption algorithm if using ESP**—DES or 3DES

---

**NOTE**     The AH Protocol is seldom used in production environments today. SHA-HMAC and MD5-HMAC are now available to provide additional packet integrity for ESP. A second argument for not using AH is that AH does not support NAT or PAT, essential components of secure networks and useful tools for extending IPv4 addresses into private networks.

---

In a VPN network environment, you can have different security requirements for each VPN. If you are going router to router within a physically secured building, you might not want the added processing expense of ESP on that VPN. VPN connections to one of the routers from the Internet, however, might need ESP's encryption.

To facilitate the configuration process for devices that need to support a variety of IPSec VPNs, the IPSec parameters are grouped into predefined configurations called *transforms*. The transforms identify the IPSec protocol, hash algorithm, and when needed, the encryption algorithm. Only a handful of valid transforms are available; they are identified in Table 2-9.

**Table 2-9**    *IPSec Transforms*

| Type | Transform | Description |
|---|---|---|
| AH authentication transforms | ah-md5-hmac | IPSec AH Protocol using HMAC-MD5 for message integrity. |
| | ah-sha-hmac | IPSec AH Protocol using HMAC-SHA-1 for message integrity. |
| | ah-rfc1828 | IPSec AH Protocol using MD5 for message integrity. This transform is used to support older RFC 1828 IPSec implementations. |
| ESP encryption transforms | esp-des | IPSec ESP Protocol using DES encryption. |
| | esp-3des | IPSec ESP Protocol using 3DES encryption. |
| | esp-null | IPSec ESP Protocol with no encryption. This can be used in test environments in combination with either of the ESP authentication transforms to provide ESP authentication with no encryption. esp-null should not be used in production environments. |
| | esp-rfc1829 | IPSec ESP Protocol using DES-CBC encryption. This transform is used to support older RFC 1829 IPSec implementations. |
| ESP authentication transforms | esp-md5-hmac | IPSec ESP Protocol using HMAC-MD5 for message integrity. |
| | esp-sha-hmac | IPSec ESP Protocol using HMAC-SHA-1 for message integrity. |

Transforms are used to identify the types of IPSec tunnels that a host supports. A specific IPSec tunnel can support up to three transforms in a strictly regulated structure called a *transform set*. You can configure multiple transform sets within a device's crypto policy to identify acceptable combinations that can be used for establishing IPSec tunnels. A transform set can be any of the following valid combinations.

- One AH authentication transform:
  - ah-md5-hmac
  - ah-sha-hmac
  - ah-rfc1828
- One ESP encryption transform:
  - esp-des
  - esp-3des
  - esp-null
  - esp-rfc1829
- One ESP encryption transform <AND> one ESP authentication transform:
  - esp-des esp-md5-hmac
  - esp-des esp-sha-hmac
  - esp-3des esp-md5-hmac
  - esp-3des esp-sha-hmac
  - esp-null esp-md5-hmac
  - esp-null esp-sha-hmac
- One AH authentication transform <AND> one ESP encryption transform in the following combination only:
  - ah-rfc1828 esp-rfc1829
- One AH authentication transform <AND> one ESP encryption transform <AND> one ESP authentication transform:
  - ah-md5-hmac esp-des esp-md5-hmac
  - ah-md5-hmac esp-des esp-sha-hmac
  - ah-md5-hmac esp-3des esp-md5-hmac
  - ah-md5-hmac esp-3des esp-sha-hmac
  - ah-md5-hmac esp-null esp-md5-hmac
  - ah-md5-hmac esp-null esp-sha-hmac
  - ah-sha-hmac esp-des esp-md5-hmac
  - ah-sha-hmac esp-des esp-sha-hmac
  - ah-sha-hmac esp-3des esp-md5-hmac
  - ah-sha-hmac esp-3des esp-sha-hmac
  - ah-sha-hmac esp-null esp-md5-hmac
  - ah-sha-hmac esp-null esp-sha-hmac

**NOTE**    One additional transform can be used with Cisco VPN devices, and that is the *comp-lzs* transform. This transform activates the Stacker LZS compression algorithm on the VPN. LZS was designed to be used on slow-speed WAN connections to enable conservation of bandwidth resources. This transform is not well documented in Cisco reference materials, and this book does not mention it again, other than to say that you might see it as an option when configuring transform sets on Cisco devices.

# Establishing VPNs with IPSec

### 4   How IPSec works

As you can see from the previous discussion, IPSec was designed to use a robust set of protocols and processes. You could establish VPNs without knowing much about these protocols, but the results would be haphazard at best. Good practice dictates a sequence of preparation steps that you should take before you can effectively configure a device for IPSec. Those preconfiguration steps are as follows:

**Step 1**    **Establish an IKE policy**—This policy must be identical on both ends of a VPN. The following elements go into the IKE policy:

— **Key distribution method**—Manual or certificate authority.

— **Authentication method**—Mostly determined by the key distribution method you select. Manual distribution uses preshared keys. Certificate authority distribution uses RSA encrypted nonces or RSA digital signatures.

— **IP address and host names of peers**—IP needs to know where to locate potential peers, and access control lists on intermediate devices need to permit the peers to communicate. IPSec configuration requires the fully qualified domain name (FQDN) of the device as well as the IP address.

— **IKE policy parameters**—Used by ISAKMP to establish the secure tunnel of IKE Phase 1. IKE policies consist of the following five parameters:

Encryption algorithm (DES/3DES)

Hash algorithm (MD5/SHA-1)

Authentication method (Preshared, RSA encryption, RSA signatures)

Key exchange (D-H Group 1/D-H Group 2)

IKE SA lifetime (86,400 seconds by default)

**Step 2** **Establish an IPSec policy**—The IPSec security and authentication capabilities are applied to certain traffic that passes between peers. You can choose to send all traffic between peers through the IPSec tunnel, but there is a significant performance penalty when using IPSec, so you should be selective in its application. However you choose to implement the IPSec tunnel, both ends of the tunnel must implement identical IPSec policies. Careful planning and documentation can simplify this process. You need the following information for your IPSec policy:

— **IPSec protocol**—AH or ESP

— **Authentication**—MD5 or SHA-1

— **Encryption**—DES or 3DES

— **Transform or transform set**—ah-sha-hmac esp-3des esp-md5-hmac or one of the other allowable combinations

— **Identify traffic to be protected**—Protocol, source, destination, and port

— **SA establishment**—Manual or IKE

**Step 3** **Examine the current configuration**—Avoid issues with conflicting configuration parameters by checking existing IPSec settings on your device.

**Step 4** **Test the network before IPSec**—Can you **ping** the peers that are going to participate in IPSec with your device? If not, you must fix that before you go any further.

**Step 5** **Permit IPSec ports and protocols**—If you have enabled ACLs on any devices along the path of the proposed IPSec VPN, be sure that those devices permit IPSec traffic. You must ensure that the following are permitted through the network:

— **UDP port 500**—ISAKMP, identified by the keyword **isakmp**

— **Protocol 50**—ESP, identified by the keyword **esp**

— **Protocol 51**—AH, identified by the keyword **ahp**

---

**NOTE**     Protocols 50 and 51 are actual protocols within the TCP/IP stack. They are not ports used within a protocol, such as port 500 for ISAKMP within UDP.

---

After you have ensured network connectivity, cleaned up your existing configuration, enabled IPSec traffic, and established your IKE and IPSec policies, you can begin the configuration process. Configuration processes for the Cisco VPN 3000 Series Concentrators are covered in detail throughout the remainder of this book.

You can think of the IPSec process as the following five-step process:

**Step 1**    Interesting traffic initiates the setup of an IPSec tunnel.

**Step 2**    IKE Phase 1 authenticates peers and establishes a secure tunnel for IPSec negotiation.

**Step 3**    IKE Phase 2 completes the IPSec negotiations and establishes the IPSec tunnel.

**Step 4**    Once the tunnel has been established, secured VPN communications occur.

**Step 5**    When there is no more traffic to use IPSec, the tunnel is torn down, either explicitly or through timeout of the SA lifetimes.

The following sections examine these five processes in more detail.

## Step 1: Interesting Traffic Triggers IPSec Process

As previously stated, you have absolute control over the traffic that gets processed by IPSec. You might want certain traffic between peers authenticated only, for example, for mail or intranet traffic. You might want to encrypt client/server traffic that interacts with your financial server. Maybe you want to encrypt everything going from peer A to peer B.

Whatever your security policy dictates is mirrored in access lists. Peers must contain the same access lists, and you can have multiple access lists for different purposes between peers. These ACLs are called crypto ACLs because of their application. They are simply extended IP access lists, but they work slightly differently because the **permit** and **deny** keywords have a different purpose for crypto ACLs. Figure 2-12 shows the effect of **permit** and **deny** statements on source and destination peers.

The **permit** and **deny** keywords have different functions on the source and destination devices. The following list describes those functions:

- **permit at the source peer**—Passes the traffic to IPSec for authentication, encryption, or both. IPSec modifies the packet by inserting an AH or ESP header and possibly encrypting some of or all of the original packet and then places it on the wire to the destination.

- **deny at the source peer**—Bypasses IPSec and puts the clear-text packet on the wire to the destination.

- **permit at the destination peer**—Passes the traffic to IPSec for authentication, decryption, or both. The ACL uses the information in the header to make its decision. In ACL logic, if the header contains the correct source, destination, and protocol, the packet must have been processed by IPSec at the sender and must now be processed by IPSec at the receiver.

- **deny at the destination peer**—Bypasses IPSec and assumes that the traffic has been sent in the clear.

**Figure 2-12** *Crypto ACLs*

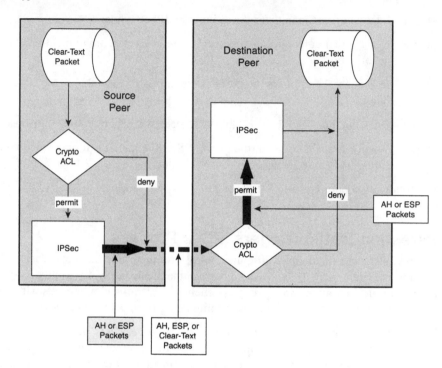

When these **permit** and **deny** keywords are used in the proper combinations, data are successfully protected and transferred. When they are not used in the proper combinations, data are discarded. Table 2-10 shows the various **permit** and **deny** keyword combinations and the actions that result from the combinations.

**Table 2-10** *Crypto ACL Actions*

| Source | Destination | Action |
|--------|-------------|--------|
| **permit** | **permit** | Packet processed correctly |
| **permit** | **deny** | Packet misunderstood and dropped |
| **deny** | **permit** | Packet misunderstood and dropped |
| **deny** | **deny** | Packet processed correctly |

You can readily see why it is so important for crypto ACLs to match on both ends of the IPSec VPN. Remember that Cisco ACLs always have an implicit **deny all** as the last entry. If your permit statements do not match on both ends, the destination is not able to process the packet information and the packet is discarded.

| | |
|---|---|
| **NOTE** | Remember that IPSec is an IP-only function. All your crypto ACLs must be extended IP ACLs, permitting you to identify source, destination, and protocol. |

## Step 2: Authenticate Peers and Establish IKE SAs

IKE Phase 1 uses two different mode types to authenticate IPSec peers and establish an IKE SA policy between peers. These two modes are the Main mode and the Aggressive mode.

Main mode protects the identity of both peers during key exchange. This is the mode that is used by default on Cisco VPN products. When using Main mode, IKE performs three bidirectional exchanges between peers. Those three exchanges are as follows:

- Algorithms and hashes are agreed upon.
- Diffie-Hellman exchange is made, producing matching shared secret keys.
- Verification of the other peer's identity is made.

Only three messages are exchanged during Aggressive mode. More information is packed into the first message, providing key information to eavesdroppers that might be watching the traffic before the connection has been secured. Cisco products answer in Aggressive mode to products that initiate IKE Phase 1 in Aggressive mode, but their preference is for Main mode operation. Whether using Main mode or Aggressive mode, the end result of IKE Phase 1 is a secure tunnel between peers that protects the ISAKMP exchanges of IKE Phase 2 as the IPSec SA is negotiated.

## Step 3: Establish IPSec SAs

IKE Phase 2 has one mode of operation, Quick mode, which begins immediately after the secured tunnel is established in IKE Phase 1. The following tasks are accomplished during IKE Phase 2:

1 IPSec SA parameters are negotiated and agreed on by both peers within the protection of the IKE SA established in Phase 1.

2 IPSec SAs are established.

3 IPSec SAs are renegotiated periodically as needed.

4 IPSec SAs an optionally perform an additional Diffie-Hellman key exchange.

## Step 4: Allow Secured Communications

Once the IPSec SAs have been established in Step 3, secured traffic can be exchanged over the connection. IP packets across this IPSec tunnel are authenticated and/or encrypted, depending on the transform set selected. Figure 2-13 shows the use of a secure IPSec tunnel between peers.

**Figure 2-13** *IPSec Secure Tunnel*

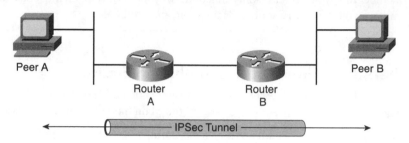

## Step 5: Terminate VPN

In normal operation, IPSec VPN tunnels can be terminated when one of the peers goes away, as might be the case in remote access VPNs when the mobile user packs up his system for the day. More frequently, however, they out based on the negotiated SA lifetimes in the IPSec SA and the IKE SA. When the SA terminates, keys are discarded.

When an IPSec SA times out and IPSec traffic still exists, the peers immediately go into IKE Phase 2 negotiations and reestablish the IKE SA using new keys. If the IKE SA times out, the peers must start with IKE Phase 1 negotiations to establish new IKE SAs and then renegotiate IPSec SAs.

# Foundation Summary

The Foundation Summary is a collection of tables, figures, and best practices that provide a convenient review of many key concepts in this chapter. For those who are already comfortable with the topics in this chapter, this summary could help you recall a few details. For those who just read this chapter, this review should help solidify some key facts. For anyone doing final preparation before the exam, these tables and figures are a convenient way to review the day before the exam.

## Table of Protocols Used with IPSec

IPSec was designed to be able to use existing protocols and multipurpose protocols. The only two that are considered strictly IPSec protocols are Authentication Header and Encapsulating Security Payload. Table 2-11 outlines the protocols discussed in this chapter.

**Table 2-11**   *Protocols Used with IPSec*

| Process | Protocol | Description |
| --- | --- | --- |
| IP Security (IPSec) Protocol | Authentication Header (AH) | A security protocol that provides data authentication and optional antireplay services. AH is embedded in the data to be protected (a full IP datagram). |
| | Encapsulating Security Payload (ESP) | Security protocol that provides data privacy services, optional data authentication, and antireplay services. ESP encapsulates the data to be protected. |
| Message encryption | Data Encryption Standard (DES) | Standard cryptographic algorithm developed by the U.S. National Bureau of Standards using 56-bit key. |
| | Triple DES (3DES) | Standard cryptographic algorithm based on DES, using 168-bit key. |
| Message integrity (hash) functions | Hash-based Message Authentication Code (HMAC) | A mechanism for message authentication using cryptographic hash functions. HMAC can be used with any iterative cryptographic hash function, for example, MD5 or SHA-1, in combination with a secret shared key. The cryptographic strength of HMAC depends on the properties of the underlying hash function. |

*continues*

**Table 2-11**   *Protocols Used with IPSec (Continued)*

| Process | Protocol | Description |
|---|---|---|
| Message integrity (hash) functions (*continued*) | Message Digest 5 (MD5) | A one-way hashing algorithm that produces a 128-bit hash. Both MD5 and Secure Hash Algorithm (SHA) are variations on MD4 and are designed to strengthen the security of the MD4 hashing algorithm. Cisco uses hashes for authentication within the IPSec framework. |
| | Secure Hash Algorithm-1 (SHA-1) | Algorithm that takes a message of less than 264 bits in length and produces a 160-bit message digest. The large message digest provides security against brute-force collision and inversion attacks. SHA-1 [NIS94c] is a revision to SHA that was published in 1994. |
| Peer authentication | Preshared keys | A shared secret key that must be communicated between peers through some manual process. |
| | RSA digital signatures | Public-key cryptographic system that can be used for encryption and authentication. The digital signature is a value computed with the RSA algorithm and appended to a data object in such a way that any recipient of the data can use the signature to verify the data's origin and integrity. |
| | RSA encrypted nonces | Nonces are random numbers used in security protocols to prove recentness of messages, but they can also be used as symmetric session keys. |
| Key management | Diffie-Hellman (D-H) | A public-key cryptography protocol that allows two parties to establish a shared secret over insecure communications channels. Diffie-Hellman is used within Internet Key Exchange (IKE) to establish session keys. Diffie-Hellman is a component of OAKLEY key exchange. Cisco IOS Software supports 768-bit and 1024-bit Diffie-Hellman groups. |
| | Certificate Authority (CA) | Entity that issues digital certificates (especially X.509 certificates) and vouches for the binding between the data items in a certificate. |

**Table 2-11**  *Protocols Used with IPSec (Continued)*

| Process | Protocol | Description |
|---------|----------|-------------|
| Security Association (SA) | Internet Key Exchange (IKE) | IKE establishes a shared security policy and authenticates keys for services (such as IPSec) that require keys. Before any IPSec traffic can be passed, each router/firewall/host must verify the identity of its peer. This can be done by manually entering preshared keys into both hosts or by a CA service. |
| | Internet Security Association and Key Management Protocol (ISAKMP) | Internet IPSec protocol [RFC 2408] that negotiates, establishes, modifies, and deletes security associations. It also exchanges key generation and authentication data (independent of the details of any specific key generation technique), key establishment protocol, encryption algorithm, or authentication mechanism. |

# IPSec Preconfiguration Processes

Most projects go much easier if you spend some careful planning time before you begin. The same is true for implementing IPSec security. Take the following steps before you begin the task of configuring IPSec on your Cisco devices:

**Step 1**   Establish an IKE policy.

**Step 2**   Establish an IPSec policy.

**Step 3**   Examine the current configuration.

**Step 4**   Test the network before IPSec.

**Step 5**   Permit IPSec ports and protocols.

# Creating VPNs with IPSec

After you configure your Cisco devices for IPSec, the setup and termination of IPSec happens automatically. The following steps are involved in that process:

**Step 1**   Interesting traffic triggers IPSec process.

**Step 2**   Authenticate peers and establish IKE SAs (IKE Phase 1).

**Step 3**   Establish IPSec SAs (IKE Phase 2).

**Step 4**   Allow secured communications.

**Step 5**   Terminate VPN.

## Chapter Glossary

The following terms were introduced in this chapter or have special significance to the topics within this chapter.

**antireplay**   A security service where the receiver can reject old or duplicate packets to protect itself against replay attacks. IPSec provides this optional service by use of a sequence number combined with the use of data authentication.

**Cisco Unified Client Framework**   A consistent connection, policy, and key management method across Cisco routers, security appliances, and VPN Clients.

**data authentication**   Process of verifying that data have not been altered during transit (data integrity), or that the data came from the claimed originator (data origin authentication).

**data confidentiality**   A security service where the protected data cannot be observed.

**data flow**   A grouping of traffic, identified by a combination of source address/mask, destination address/mask, IP next protocol field, and source and destination ports, where the protocol and port fields can have the values of any. In effect, all traffic matching a specific combination of these values is logically grouped together into a data flow. A data flow can represent a single TCP connection between two hosts, or it can represent all the traffic between two subnets. IPSec protection is applied to data flows.

**Elliptic Curve Cryptography (ECC)**   A public-key encryption technique based on elliptic curve theory that can be used to create faster, smaller, and more efficient cryptographic keys. ECC generates keys through the properties of the elliptic curve equation instead of using the traditional method of generation as the product of large prime numbers. The technology can be used in conjunction with most public-key encryption methods, such as RSA and Diffie-Hellman.

**peer**   In the context of this document, a router, firewall, VPN concentrator, or other device that participates in IPSec.

**Perfect Forward Secrecy (PFS)**   A cryptographic characteristic associated with a derived shared secret value. With PFS, if one key is compromised, previous and subsequent keys are not compromised, because subsequent keys are not derived from previous keys.

**Scalable Encryption Processing (SEP)**   Cisco VPN 3000 Series Concentrator modules that enable users to easily add capacity and throughput.

**Security Association (SA)**   An IPSec security association (SA) is a description of how two or more entities use security services in the context of a particular security protocol (AH or ESP) to communicate securely on behalf of a particular data flow. It includes things such as the transform and the shared secret keys to be used for protecting the traffic.

**Security Parameters Index (SPI)**   This is a number that, together with an IP address and security protocol, uniquely identifies a particular security association. When using IKE to establish the security associations, the SPI for each security association is a pseudo-randomly derived number. Without IKE, the SPI is manually specified for each security association.

**transform**   A transform lists a security protocol (AH or ESP) with its corresponding algorithms. For example, one transform is the AH protocol with the HMAC-MD5 authentication algorithm; another transform is the ESP protocol with the 56-bit DES encryption algorithm and the HMAC-SHA authentication algorithm.

**tunnel**   In the context of this document, a secure communication path between two peers, such as two routers. It does not refer to using IPSec in Tunnel mode.

# Q&A

As mentioned in Chapter 1, these questions are more difficult than what you should experience on the CCSP exam. The questions do not attempt to cover more breadth or depth than the exam; however, the questions are designed to make sure you know the answer. Rather than allowing you to derive the answer from clues hidden inside the question itself, your understanding and recall of the subject are challenged. Questions from the "Do I Know This Already?" quiz from the beginning of the chapter are repeated here to ensure that you have mastered the chapter's topic areas. Hopefully, these questions will help limit the number of exam questions on which you narrow your choices to two options and guess!

1 What are the Cisco hardware product families that support IPSec VPN technology?

_____

_____

_____

2 What are the two IPSec protocols?

_____

_____

_____

3 What are the three major VPN categories?

_____

_____

_____

4 What is an SEP module used for?

_____

_____

_____

5 What are the primary reasons cited for choosing VPN technology?

_____

_____

_____

**6**  Why are remote access VPNs considered ubiquitous?

_____

_____

_____

**7**  What types of VPNs are typically built across service provider shared network infrastructures?

_____

_____

_____

**8**  Which type of VPNs use a combination of the same infrastructures that are used by the other two types of VPNs?

_____

_____

_____

**9**  What hardware would you use to build intranet and extranet VPNs?

_____

_____

_____

**10**  Which Cisco routers provide support for Cisco EzVPN Remote?

_____

_____

_____

**11**  Which Cisco router series supports VAMs?

_____

_____

_____

**12**  Which Cisco router series supports ISMs?

_____

_____

_____

**13** Which of the Cisco PIX Firewall models are fixed-configuration devices?

_____

_____

_____

**14** Which Cisco PIX Firewall models offer a failover port for high availability and support VACs?

_____

_____

_____

**15** Which series of Cisco hardware devices are purpose-built remote access VPN devices?

_____

_____

_____

**16** Which of the Cisco VPN 3000 Series Concentrators is a fixed-configuration device?

_____

_____

_____

**17** Which of the Cisco VPN 3000 Series Concentrators can accept SEP modules?

_____

_____

_____

**18** What feature of the Cisco Unity Client makes it scalable?

_____

_____

_____

**19** Which of Cisco's VPN clients can be used with any operating system that communicates in IP?

_____

_____

_____

**20**  What protocol enables IP-enabled wireless devices such as PDAs and Smart Phones to participate in VPN communications?

_____

_____

_____

**21**  What are the three phases of Cisco Mobile Office?

_____

_____

_____

**22**  What is the distinctive characteristic of Cisco VPN Device Manager?

_____

_____

_____

**23**  What is Cisco's AAA server, and what AAA systems does it support?

_____

_____

_____

**24**  Which web-based management tool can display a physical representation of each managed device?

_____

_____

_____

**25**  What are the current RFCs that define the IPSec protocols?

_____

_____

_____

**26** What are three shortcomings of IPSec?

_____

_____

_____

**27** What message encryption protocols does IPSec use?

_____

_____

_____

**28** What message integrity protocols does IPSec use?

_____

_____

_____

**29** What methods does IPSec use to provide peer authentication?

_____

_____

_____

**30** What methods does IPSec use for key management?

_____

_____

_____

**31** What is the key element contained in the AH or ESP packet header?

_____

_____

_____

**32** Which IPSec protocol does not provide encryption services?

_____

_____

_____

**33** What is the triplet of information that uniquely identifies a Security Association?

_____

_____

_____

**34** What is an ICV?

_____

_____

_____

**35** What IPSec protocol must you use when confidentiality is required in your IPSec communications?

_____

_____

_____

**36** What is the primary difference between the mechanisms used by AH and ESP to modify an IP packet for IPSec use?

_____

_____

_____

**37** What are the two modes of operation for AH and ESP?

_____

_____

_____

**38** Which IPSec protocol should you use if your system is using NAT?

_____

_____

_____

**39** You can select to use both authentication and encryption when using the ESP protocol. Which is performed first when you do this?

_____

_____

_____

**40** How many SAs does it take to establish bidirectional IPSec communications between two peers?

_____

_____

_____

**41** Which encryption protocol was considered unbreakable at the time of its adoption?

_____

_____

_____

**42** What process does 3DES use to obtain an aggregate 168-bit key?

_____

_____

_____

**43** What is a message digest?

_____

_____

_____

**44** What does HMAC-MD5-96 mean?

_____

_____

_____

**45**  What does HMAC-SHA1-96 mean?

_____

_____

_____

**46**  How are preshared keys exchanged?

_____

_____

_____

**47**  What does the Diffie-Hellman key agreement protocol permit?

_____

_____

_____

**48**  Why is D-H not used for symmetric key encryption processes?

_____

_____

_____

**49**  What is a CRL?

_____

_____

_____

**50**  What are the five parameters required by IKE Phase 1?

_____

_____

_____

**51**  What are the valid AH authentication transforms?

_____

_____

_____

52 What transform set would allow for SHA-1 authentication of both AH and ESP packets and would also provide 3DES encryption for ESP?

_____

_____

_____

53 What steps should you take before you begin the task of configuring IPSec on a Cisco device?

_____

_____

_____

54 What are the five steps of the IPSec process?

_____

_____

_____

55 What is the difference between the **deny** keyword in a crypto ACL and the **deny** keyword in an access ACL?

_____

_____

_____

# Exam Topics Discussed in This Chapter

This chapter covers the following topics, which you need to master in your pursuit of certification as a Cisco Certified Security Professional:

**5** Overview of the Cisco VPN 3000 Concentrator Series

**6** Cisco VPN 3000 Concentrator Series models

**7** Benefits and features of the Cisco VPN 3000 Concentrator Series

**8** Cisco VPN 3000 Concentrator Series Client support

# CHAPTER 3

# Cisco VPN 3000 Concentrator Series Hardware Overview

Ever striving to meet the needs of its customers, Cisco has put together a complete lineup of VPN products. As you learned in Chapter 2, "Overview of VPN and IPSec Technologies," the Cisco IOS Software feature set used on Cisco routers offers robust IP Security (IPSec) capability for site-to-site VPN requirements. The Cisco Secure PIX Firewall also provides VPN capability, moving the CPU-intensive encryption operations away from the busy border routers.

With the introduction of the Cisco VPN 3000 Concentrator Series, Cisco has implemented solutions that are built for the unique purpose of remote access VPNs. These versatile, reliable systems are designed to only process VPNs, and to process them quickly and efficiently.

Five models are available in the Cisco VPN 3000 Concentrator line: 3005, 3015, 3030, 3060, and 3080. The 3005 is a fixed configuration, while the others share the same chassis and are configurable, providing an unrestricted upgrade path from the 3015 model all the way to the 3080 model. These configurable models also allow for the use of multiple Scalable Encryption Processor (SEP) modules that offload processor-intensive encryption activities from the central processor of the concentrator.

This chapter present the products in this concentrator series and analyzes their benefits and features. Additionally, the chapter introduces the clients that support these products.

## How to Best Use This Chapter

By taking the following steps, you can make better use of your time:

- Keep your notes and answers for all your work with this book in one place for easy reference.

- Take the "Do I Know This Already?" quiz, and write down your answers. Studies show retention is significantly increased through writing facts and concepts down, even if you never look at the information again.

- Use Figure 3-1 to guide you to the next step.

**Figure 3-1**   *How to Use This Chapter*

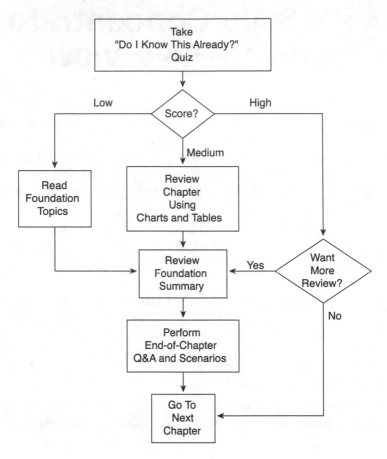

## "Do I Know This Already?" Quiz

The purpose of the "Do I Know This Already?" quiz is to help you decide what parts of the chapter to use. If you already intend to read the entire chapter, you do not need to answer these questions now.

This 18-question quiz helps you determine how to spend your limited study time. The quiz is sectioned into three smaller "quizlets," which correspond to the three major topic headings in the chapter. Figure 3-1 outlines suggestions on how to spend your time in this chapter based on your quiz score. Use Table 3-1 to record your scores.

**Table 3-1**    *Score Sheet for Quiz and Quizlets*

| Quizlet Number | Foundations Topics Section Covering These Questions | Questions | Score |
|---|---|---|---|
| 1 | Overview of the Cisco VPN 3000 Concentrator Series<br><br>Cisco VPN 3000 Concentrator Series models | 1–6 | |
| 2 | Benefits and features of the Cisco VPN 3000 Concentrator Series | 7–12 | |
| 3 | Cisco VPN 3000 Concentrator Series Client support | 13–18 | |
| All questions | | 1–18 | |

**1** What models are available in the Cisco VPN 3000 Concentrator Series?

_____

_____

_____

**2** What is the maximum number of simultaneous sessions that can be supported on the Cisco VPN 3015 Concentrator?

_____

_____

_____

**3** What is the maximum number of simultaneous sessions that can be supported on the Cisco VPN 3080 Concentrator?

_____

_____

_____

**4** On a Cisco VPN 3005 Concentrator, what does a blinking green system LED indicate?

_____

_____

_____

**5** What is the maximum encryption throughput rate for the VPN 3000 series?

_____

_____

_____

**6** What tunneling protocols do Cisco VPN 3000 Concentrators support?

_____

_____

_____

**7** How do VPN concentrators reduce communications expenses?

_____

_____

_____

**8** What other authentication capability exists if standard authentication servers are not available?

_____

_____

_____

**9** What routing protocols do the Cisco VPN 3000 Concentrators support?

_____

_____

_____

**10** What protocol permits multichassis redundancy and failover?

_____

_____

_____

11  List some of the methods that can be used to interface with the embedded Cisco VPN Manager software on VPN concentrators?

_____

_____

_____

12  What four options are available under the Configuration menu of the VPN Manager?

_____

_____

_____

13  What mechanism is used by Cisco VPN Clients to monitor firewall activity between the client and the concentrator?

_____

_____

_____

14  What optional feature on the Cisco VPN 3002 Hardware Client allows you to connect Ethernet devices to the client?

_____

_____

_____

15  During large-scale implementations, how can VPN 3000 Concentrators be configured to simplify client configuration?

_____

_____

_____

16  Which of Cisco's client offerings has no limitations with regard to the types of client operating systems it can support?

_____

_____

_____

**17** What two operating modes can a Cisco VPN 3002 Hardware Client be configured to support?

_____

_____

_____

**18** What operating systems does the Cisco VPN Client support?

_____

_____

_____

The answers to this quiz are listed in Appendix A, "Answers to the "Do I Know This Already?" Quizzes and Q&A Sections." The suggestions for your next steps, based on quiz results, are as follows:

- **10 or less overall score**—You should read the entire chapter, including the "Foundation Topics" and "Foundation Summary" sections, as well as the "Q&A" section.

- **11 to 14 overall score**—Read the "Foundation Summary" section and the "Q&A" section. If you are having difficulty with a particular subject area, read the appropriate section in the "Foundation Topics" section.

- **15 or more overall score**—If you feel you need more review on these topics, go to the "Foundation Summary" section, then the "Q&A" section. Otherwise, skip this chapter and go to the next chapter.

# Foundation Topics

In January 2000, Cisco purchased Altiga Networks of Franklin, Massachusetts. With that purchase, Cisco acquired Altiga's nifty line of VPN concentrators, client software, and web-based management software. These products became the Cisco VPN 3000 Series Concentrators and supporting software. Since that time, Cisco has enhanced the product line by adding a top-end concentrator and a hardware client, and has made improvements to the software client. This chapter explores the advantages, features, and specifications of the Cisco VPN 3000 Concentrator Series.

# Major Advantages of Cisco VPN 3000 Series Concentrators

> 5    Overview of the Cisco VPN 3000 Concentrator Series
>
> 7    Benefits and features of the Cisco VPN 3000 Concentrator Series

The Cisco VPN 3000 Series Concentrators are extremely versatile, delivering high performance, security, and fault tolerance. The centralized management tool is standards-based and enables real-time statistics gathering and reporting. These devices allow corporations to reduce communications expenses by permitting clients to connect to corporate assets through local ISP connections to the Internet rather than through long-distance or 800 number connections to access servers. VPNs provide the productivity-enhancing ability to access corporate network assets while reducing expenses.

Dial-up connections using modems are prevalent throughout many corporate communities, especially on laptop systems. For some types of users, however, broadband VPN services provide speed and always-on connectivity that permit corporations to extend their office LANs into small office/home office (SOHO) environments. The popularity of cable modems and DSL modems has made broadband services commonplace for the home office user. Connecting these high-speed networks to the corporate network via IPSec tunnels gives SOHO users secure, full access to network assets at speeds up to 25 times faster than 56-kbps modems. Figure 3-2 shows typical modem and broadband connectivity to a VPN concentrator.

**Figure 3-2** *Remote Access Types*

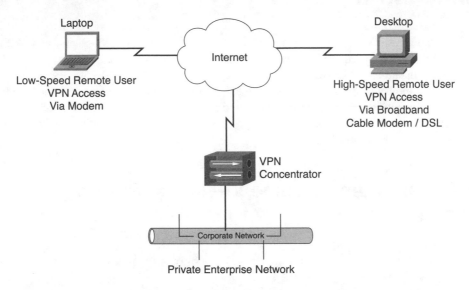

Not shown in Figure 3-2, wireless VPN clients provide an additional layer of encryption security to wireless communications. IPSec encryption end-to-end between client and concentrator can be combined with the encryption provided by the wireless Wired Equivalent Privacy (WEP) standard to enable a high level of security for wireless communications. IPSec with 3DES encryption for wireless communications is one of the recommendations of Cisco's SAFE security guidelines.

**NOTE**      SAFE is the Cisco secure blueprint for enterprise networks that provides information to interested parties on the best practices to use for designing and implementing secure networks.

The Cisco VPN 3000 Series Concentrators are versatile, full-featured systems. Some of the characteristics that make them so popular are as follows:

- Ease with which you can deploy them
- Performance and scalability
- Security
- Fault tolerance
- Management interface
- Ease with which you can upgrade them

The following sections cover these areas in more detail.

## Ease of Deployment and Use

The Cisco VPN 3000 Series Concentrators were designed to be inserted into the current network without forcing infrastructure changes. These concentrators work with existing Remote Authentication Dial-In User Service (RADIUS), Terminal Access Controller Access Control System Plus (TACACS+), NT Domain, or Security Dynamics servers. This capability presents the same authentication interface to the users as they attempt to connect to the network. When these authentication servers are not available, the VPN concentrators have the ability to authenticate users from an internal database.

One of the interesting capabilities of the Cisco VPN 3000 Concentrator is its flexibility in placement. These systems can be installed in front of, behind, or in parallel with a firewall. The Cisco VPN Concentrator has firewall features that make it possible to customize the access permitted to individual connections coming through the concentrator. To avoid static route configurations on neighboring devices when inserting these concentrators into routed networks, the Cisco VPN 3000 Series Concentrators are routers, supporting RIP versions 1 and 2 and OSPF.

The VPN concentrators are equipped with numerous LED indicator lights that make it easy to verify system status. These indicators can even be "viewed" remotely through the web-based VPN 3000 Concentrator Series Manager software so that you can perform a quick system health check from your desk.

The Cisco VPN 3000 Series Concentrators are standards-based systems that can easily mesh with existing tunneling protocols such as Point-to-Point Tunneling Protocol (PPTP) in the Microsoft environment, or IPSec when more security is desired. The Cisco VPN concentrators can push the client policies to the user when they first connect through the concentrator. The Cisco VPN Client is shipped with the VPN concentrators and includes an unlimited distribution license, which means you do not have to worry about whether you have enough client licenses.

## Performance and Scalability

The 3DES-encrypted throughput on the Cisco VPN Concentrators is rated at up to 100 Mbps without performance degradation. This is accomplished by using Scalable Encryption Processors (SEPs) on the modular devices. These SEPs are powered by programmable digital signal processors (DSPs) in the encryption engine. Each SEP provides 25 Mbps of 3DES encryption, making the VPN concentrators scalable.

The software-based DSPs give Cisco the ability to respond to changing standards without the need for customers to replace cards or chipsets in the VPN devices. DSPs also enable Cisco developers to tune the software to maximize performance for various applications. For the Cisco VPN 3000 Series Concentrators, that means maximizing the remote access performance characteristics. Hardware-assisted encryption makes these VPN concentrators extremely fast in comparison to software-based encryption devices.

The Cisco VPN Concentrators were designed specifically as VPN communication devices. They are not performing the function as an afterthought. Cisco VPN Concentrators have been optimized for connectivity, throughput, management, and standards support.

The Cisco VPN Concentrators support the following tunneling protocols:

- Internet Protocol Security (IPSec)
- Point-to-Point Tunneling Protocol (PPTP)
- Layer 2 Tunneling Protocol (L2TP)
- L2TP/IPSec
- Network Address Translation (NAT) Transparent IPSec

The Cisco VPN 3000 Series Concentrators are true routers and offer the following routing options:

- RIP
- RIP2
- OSPF
- Static
- Automatic endpoint discovery
- Network Address Translation (NAT)
- Classless interdomain routing (CIDR)
- Reverse Route Injection (RRI)

Table 3-2 lists additional important features of these concentrators.

**Table 3-2**    *Cisco VPN 3000 Concentrator Series Capabilities*

| Description | | Specification |
|---|---|---|
| Compatibility | Client Software Compatibility | Cisco VPN Client (IPSec) for Windows 95, 98, Me, NT 4.0, and 2000, including centralized split-tunneling control and data compression. |
| | | Cisco VPN 3002 Hardware Client. |
| | | Microsoft Point-to-Point Tunneling Protocol (PPTP)/Microsoft Point-to-Point Encryption (MPPE)/Microsoft Point-to-Point Compression (MPPC). |
| | | Microsoft L2TP/IPsec for Windows 2000. |
| | | MovianVPN (Certicom) Handheld VPN Client with ECC. |

**Table 3-2**    *Cisco VPN 3000 Concentrator Series Capabilities (Continued)*

| Description | | Specification |
| --- | --- | --- |
| Compatibility *(Continued)* | Encryption/Authentication | IPSec Encapsulating Security Payload (ESP) using DES/3DES (56/168-bit) with Message Digest 5 (MD5) or Secure Hash Algorithm (SHA); MPPE using the 40/128-bit RC4 encryption algorithm from RSA. |
| | Key Management | Internet Key Exchange (IKE). Perfect Forward Secrecy (PFS). |
| | Third-Party Compatibility | Certicom, iPass Ready, Funk Steel Belted RADIUS certified, NTS TunnelBuilder VPN Client (Mac and Windows), Microsoft Internet Explorer, Netscape Communicator, Entrust, GTE Cybertrust, Baltimore, RSA Keon, VeriSign. |
| | High Availability | VRRP protocol for multichassis redundancy and failover. Destination pooling for client-based failover and connection reestablishment. Redundant SEP modules (optional), power supplies, and fans (3015–3060). Redundant SEP modules, power supplies, and fans (3080). |
| Management | Configuration | Embedded management interface is accessible via console port, Telnet, Secure Shell (SSH), and Secure HTTP. Administrator access is configurable for five levels of authorization. Authentication can be performed externally via TACACS+. Role-based management policy separates functions for service provider and end-user management. |
| | Monitoring | Event logging and notification via e-mail (SMTP). Automatic FTP backup of event logs. SNMP MIB-II support. Configurable SNMP traps. Syslog output. System status. Session data. General statistics. |

*continues*

**Table 3-2** *Cisco VPN 3000 Concentrator Series Capabilities (Continued)*

| Description | | Specification |
|---|---|---|
| Security | Authentication and Accounting Servers | Support for redundant external authentication servers: <br> • RADIUS <br> • Microsoft NT Domain authentication <br> • RSA Security Dynamics (SecurID Ready) <br> Internal Authentication server for up to 100 users. <br> TACACS+ Administrative user authentication. <br> X.509v3 Digital Certificates. <br> RADIUS accounting. |
| | Internet-Based Packet Filtering | Source and destination IP address. <br> Port and protocol type. <br> Fragment protection. <br> FTP session filtering. |
| | Policy Management | By individual user or group: <br> • Filter profiles <br> • Idle and maximum session timeouts <br> • Time and day access control <br> • Tunneling protocol and security authorization profiles <br> • IP Pool <br> • Authentication servers |

# Security

Because the Cisco VPN Concentrators have such a high throughput level for encrypted communications, you can set up all your users for the highest security levels without a loss of functionality or performance. Currently, the highest security option would be IPSec with 3DES encryption. Robust authentication options permit you to set up authentication using either an internal database or external authentication servers. Digital certificates and tokens can also be used to add an extra measure of security.

With the integral firewall capabilities, you have options in where you can locate the concentrators. You can augment the protection of your existing firewall by placing the VPN concentrator in front of or behind the existing firewall. Additionally, you can allow the concentrator to provide its own firewall protection by placing the VPN concentrator in parallel with your existing firewall.

Many firewalls also provide an isolated network called a demilitarized zone (DMZ), which is often used to house public access facilities such as Internet web servers. When the firewall does provide a DMZ, the VPN concentrator can be placed there, providing a fourth method of installing the Cisco VPN 3000 Concentrator in conjunction with a firewall. The following figures illustrate the four methods of implementing a VPN concentrator with a firewall.

Figure 3-3 shows the VPN concentrator placed in front of the firewall.

**Figure 3-3**    *VPN Concentrator in Front of Firewall*

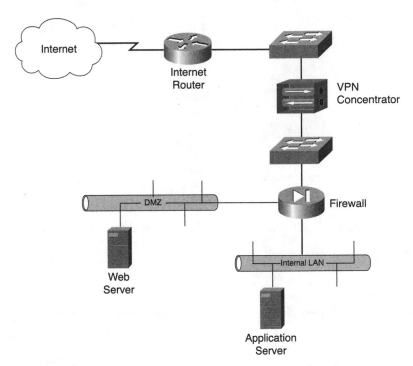

Figure 3-4 shows the VPN concentrator placed behind the firewall.

**Figure 3-4** *VPN Concentrator Behind Firewall*

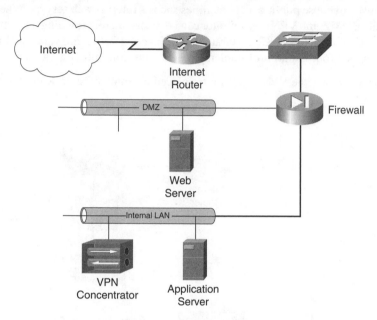

Figure 3-5 shows the VPN concentrator placed parallel with the firewall.

**Figure 3-5** *VPN Concentrator Parallel with Firewall*

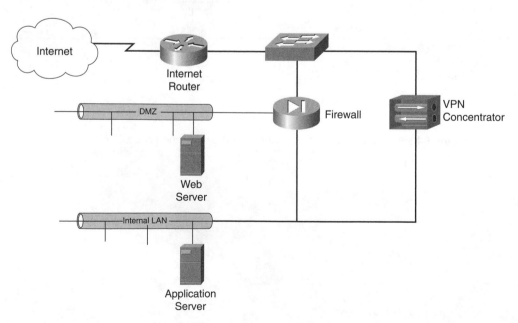

Figure 3-6 shows the VPN concentrator placed in the firewall's DMZ.

**Figure 3-6**    *VPN Concentrator in DMZ*

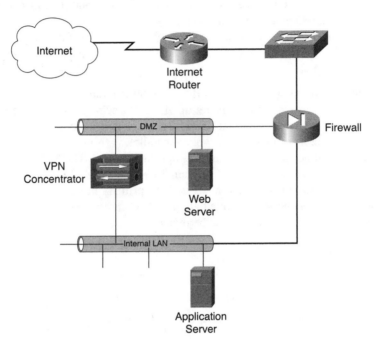

You can establish filters to permit or deny almost any kind of traffic, and you can handshake with client-based firewalls. The Cisco VPN 3000 Series Concentrators can push firewall settings to the VPN Client, which then monitors firewall activity through an enforcement mechanism called *Are You There (AYT)*. The AYT policy causes the client to poll the firewall every 30 seconds. If the firewall doesn't respond, the VPN client drops the connection.

Centralized management of concentrators and clients is another powerful security feature. The VPN manager is a web-based management tool that can be secured using HTTPS or through an encrypted tunnel.

The Cisco VPN 3000 Concentrators and the Cisco VPN Client also provide additional security by providing 3DES encryption over IPSec for wireless transmissions. While the wireless WEP protocol provides some encryption for a portion of the connection, IPSec with 3DES enables end-to-end encryption security from the client to the concentrator.

# Fault Tolerance

As more of your network users connect through the VPN concentrator, you might begin to wonder what happens if the device fails. Cisco thought about that too, and built in redundant system images, redundant fans, optional load-sharing redundant power supplies, and support for optional multiple hardware encryption modules. The mean time between failure (MTBF) rating of the Cisco VPN 3000 Series Concentrators is 200,000 hours, or slightly over 22 years, making them reliable products.

However, even with that kind of reliability, systems can fail. If your installation requires 99.9% uptime, simply trusting the lifetime rating of the device might not suffice for you. Cisco has an answer for that, too: the Virtual Router Redundancy Protocol (VRRP). With VRRP, two concentrators are placed into the network in parallel, as shown in Figure 3-7. One of the devices becomes the online unit and the other the hot standby unit. The VPN concentrators constantly monitor the health of each other. If the standby unit detects a failure of the primary unit, it assumes the IP address and MAC address of the primary unit and takes over as the connecting device. This process happens without administrator intervention. When failover occurs, alerts are sent so that the failed device can be repaired.

**Figure 3-7**   *VPN Concentrators and VRRP*

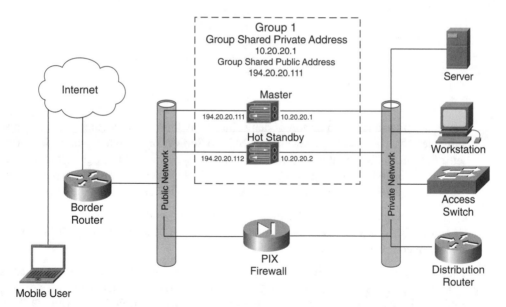

# Management Interface

Versatile management options make the VPN 3000 Concentrators easy to administer. They can be managed using the command-line interface (CLI), and in fact, some CLI administration is necessary during the initial configuration stages. The login screen and main menu of the CLI are shown in Example 3-1. But the web interface is the tool that you want to use. Intuitive menu systems, onscreen help, drop-down-box selection windows, error checking, and security make this one of the slickest management interfaces in Cisco's product line.

**Example 3-1**   *VPN Concentrator Command Line Interface*

```
Login: admin
Password:


            Welcome to
          Cisco Systems
    VPN 3000 Concentrator Series
        Command Line Interface
Copyright (C) 1998-2002 Cisco Systems, Inc.


1) Configuration
2) Administration
3) Monitoring
4) Save changes to Config file
5) Help Information
6) Exit

Main ->
```

The VPN Concentrator Manager breaks the concentrator management process into three management areas: Configuration, Administration, and Monitoring. Figure 3-8 shows the main menu screen of the manager.

**Figure 3-8**   *VPN Concentrator Manager Main Page*

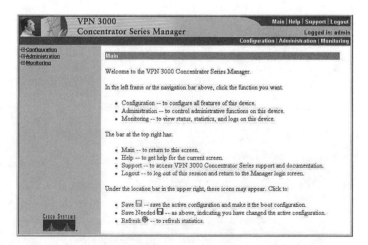

Configuration changes are stored within the memory of the VPN concentrator and take effect immediately. This feature allows the administrator to make configuration modifications on the fly without having to reboot the system or disrupt users. The next sections take a little closer look at the three major management areas of the VPN Concentrator Manager.

## Configuration

Figure 3-9 shows the Configuration menu that appears when you click that option from the main menu. This menu identifies the four subheadings under the Configuration portion of the manager: Interfaces, System, User Management, and Policy Management.

**Figure 3-9** *VPN Concentrator Manager—Configuration*

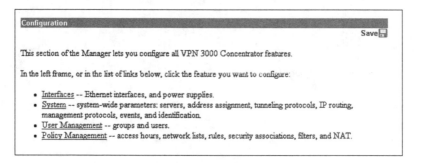

Clicking the Interfaces option brings up the window shown in Figure 3-10. This window shows an image of the concentrator and allows you to select the interface that you need to configure. This screen gives a quick synopsis of the status of the interfaces and shows their IP configuration properties.

**Figure 3-10** *VPN Concentrator Manager—Configuration | Interfaces*

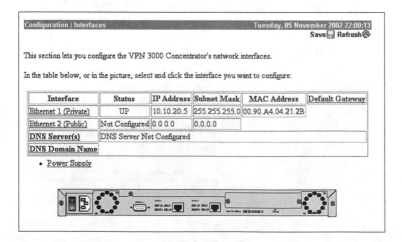

The other three options on the Configuration menu cover the following areas:

- **System**—Server access, address assignment, tunneling protocols, IP routing, built-in management servers, system events, and system identification

- **User Management**—Attributes for groups and users that determine their access to and use of the VPN

- **Policy Management**—Policies that control data traffic through the VPN via filters, rules, and IPSec Security Associations; network lists; access times; and NAT

A hierarchy in the User Management section determines the inherited properties that groups and users assume. The root of all inherited properties is the group called the Base Group. The properties within this group are the default properties for all users, unless the users are members of specific groups. When specific groups are defined, for example, Accounting, Topeka Sales, or Network, those groups inherit their default settings from the Base Group. Those settings can be overridden within the specific groups. Users inherit the properties of the group when they are added to specific groups. If a user is not a member of a specific group, he or she defaults to the settings of the Base Group. It is a simple yet effective method of assigning properties to groups and users.

The following two sections present an overview of the Administration and Monitoring sections of the VPN Manager. Chapter 7, "Monitoring and Administering the Cisco VPN 3000 Series Concentrator," provides more detail on these topics.

## Administration

The Administration screen is shown in Figure 3-11.

**Figure 3-11** *VPN Concentrator Manager—Administration*

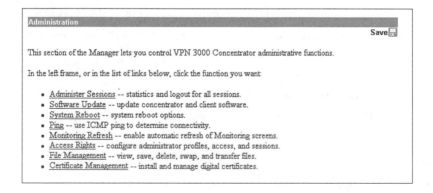

The administration functions available from this menu are as follows:

- **Administer Sessions**—View statistics for logout and ping sessions.
- **Software Update**—Update concentrator and client software images to the most current versions using the appropriate choice from these two selections:
  - **Concentrator**—Upload and update the VPN concentrator software image.
  - **Clients**—Upload and update the VPN client software image.
- **System Reboot**—Set options for VPN concentrator shutdown and reboot.
- **Ping**—Use Internet Control Message Protocol (ICMP) ping to determine connectivity.
- **Monitoring Refresh**—Enable automatic refresh of status and statistics in the Monitoring section of the Manager.
- **Access Rights**—Configure administrator profiles, access, and sessions. The Access Rights option provides these four selections:
  - **Administrators**—Configure administrator usernames, passwords, and rights.
  - **Access Control List**—Configure IP addresses for workstations with access rights.
  - **Access Settings**—Set administrative session idle timeout and limits.
  - **AAA Servers**—Set administrative authentication using TACACS+.
- **File Management**—Manage system files in flash memory. The File Management option provides these four selections:
  - **Files**—Copy, view, and delete system files.
  - **Swap Configuration Files**—Swap backup and boot configuration files.
  - **TFTP Transfer**—Use TFTP to transfer files to and from the VPN concentrator.
  - **File Upload**—Use HTTP to transfer files to the VPN concentrator.
- **Certificate Management**—Install and manage digital certificates. The Certificate Management option provides these three selections:
  - **Enrollment**—Create a certificate request to send to a Certificate Authority.
  - **Installation**—Install digital certificates.
  - **Certificates**—View, modify, and delete digital certificates.

## Monitoring

The Monitoring screen is shown in Figure 3-12.

**Figure 3-12**  *VPN Concentrator Manager—Monitoring*

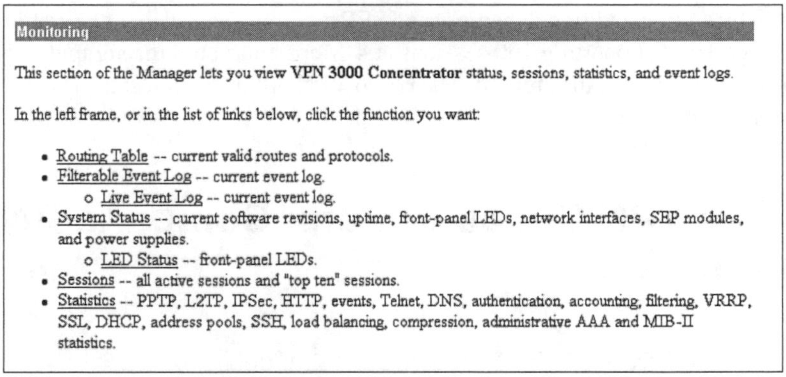

The monitoring functions available from this menu are as follows:

- **Routing Table**—Current valid routes, protocols, and metrics.

- **Filterable Event Log**—Current event login memory, filterable by event class, severity, IP address, and so on. Within this monitoring section, you also find access to current log entries from the following selection:

  — **Live Event Log**—Current event log, continuously updated.

- **System Status**—Current software revisions, uptime, SEP modules, system power supplies, Ethernet interfaces, front-panel LEDs, and hardware sensors. To monitor the LED status indicator panel, select the following System Status option:

  — **LED Status**—Current status of the VPN Concentrator front-panel LED indicators.

- **Sessions**—Currently active sessions sorted by protocol, SEP, and encryption. "Top ten" sessions sorted in descending order by data (total bytes transmitted and received), duration (total time connected), and throughput (average bytes per second).

- **Statistics**—Current statistics for PPTP, L2TP, IPSec, HTTP, events, Telnet, DNS, authentication, accounting, filtering, VRRP, SSL, DHCP, address pools, SSH, load balancing, and data compression. MIB-II statistics for interfaces, TCP/UDP, IP, RIP, OSPF, ICMP, the ARP table, Ethernet traffic, and SNMP.

# Ease of Upgrades

There are only two basic chassis for the Cisco VPN 3000 Series Concentrators: the 1U-high fixed-configuration box, used for the 3005 Concentrator, and the 2U-high modular box, used for all others. The 3005 is not upgradeable, but it is still a powerful performer capable of supporting up to 100 simultaneous sessions.

The 2U-high modular system used for the other four concentrator models is clever. If you begin with the 3015 Concentrator, it is progressively upgradeable to the 3030 and then to the 3060 simply by adding additional memory and SEP modules. This elegant migration approach allows you to go from supporting 100 sessions at 4-Mbps encrypted throughput to 5000 sessions at 100-Mbps encrypted throughput. The Cisco VPN 3080 Concentrator is the top of the line and cannot be upgraded.

# Cisco Secure VPN Concentrators: Comparison and Features

| 6 | Cisco VPN 3000 Concentrator Series models |
|---|---|

Now that you've learned about some of the features of the Cisco VPN 3000 Series Concentrators, this section takes a closer look at the individual products in the series. Each of the concentrators in this series is shipped with the Cisco VPN Client, with unlimited distribution licensing. Additionally, each of these concentrators contains the powerful Cisco VPN Manager software in memory. These systems come as a complete package, ready to drop into your network. Figure 3-13 shows one of the 3015–3080 systems.

**Figure 3-13**  *Cisco VPN Concentrator*

This section covers the following topics:

- Cisco VPN 3005 Concentrator
- Cisco VPN 3015 Concentrator
- Cisco VPN 3030 Concentrator
- Cisco VPN 3060 Concentrator
- Cisco VPN 3080 Concentrator
- Cisco VPN 3000 Concentrator Series LED indicators

# Cisco VPN 3005 Concentrator

Designed for small- to medium-sized organizations, the Cisco VPN 3005 Concentrator can deliver up to full-duplex T1/E1, 4 Mbps of encryption throughput, and support for up to 100 simultaneous sessions. Figure 3-14 shows front and rear views of the 3005 chassis.

**Figure 3-14** *Cisco VPN 3005 Concentrator*

Table 3-3 shows the major features of the Cisco VPN 3005 Concentrator. Notice that encryption is performed in software on this system and that the system is not upgradeable.

**Table 3-3** *Cisco VPN 3005 Concentrator*

| Feature | Cisco 3005 |
| --- | --- |
| Typical application | Small to medium |
| Simultaneous sessions | 100 |
| Encryption throughput | 4 Mbps |
| Encryption method | Software |
| Encryption (SEP) module | 0 |
| Redundant SEP | N/A |
| Available expansion slots | 0 |
| Upgrade capability | No |
| System memory | 32 MB (fixed) |
| Hardware | 1U, fixed |
| Power supply | Single |
| Client license | Unlimited |
| Processor | Motorola PowerPC |
| Console port | Async DB9 |
| Flash | 32 MB SRAM |
| Memory | Fixed |

# Cisco VPN 3015 Concentrator

Also designed for small- to medium-sized organizations, the Cisco VPN 3015 Concentrator can deliver up to full-duplex T1/E1, 4 Mbps of encryption throughput, and support for up to 100 simultaneous sessions. The biggest difference between the 3005 and 3015 concentrators is the fact that the 3015 is upgradeable, whereas the 3005 is not. Figure 3-15 shows front and rear views of the 3015, 3030, 3060, and 3080 chassis. These models all share the same case.

**Figure 3-15**   *Cisco VPN 3015 Concentrator*

Table 3-4 shows the major features of the Cisco VPN 3015 Concentrator. Notice that, like the VPN 3005 Concentrator, encryption is performed in software on this system; however, this system is upgradeable.

**Table 3-4**   *Cisco VPN 3015 Concentrator*

| Feature | Cisco 3015 |
|---|---|
| Typical application | Small to medium |
| Simultaneous sessions | 100 |
| Encryption throughput | 4 Mbps |
| Encryption method | Software |
| Encryption (SEP) module | 0 |
| Redundant SEP | N/A |
| Available expansion slots | 4 |
| Upgrade capability | Yes |
| System memory | 128 MB |
| Hardware | 2U, scalable |
| Power supply | Single or dual |

**Table 3-4**    *Cisco VPN 3015 Concentrator (Continued)*

| Feature | Cisco 3015 |
|---------|-----------|
| Client license | Unlimited |
| Processor | Motorola PowerPC |
| Console port | Async DB9 |
| Flash | Redundant |
| Memory | Variable |

# Cisco VPN 3030 Concentrator

Designed for medium- to large-sized organizations, the Cisco VPN 3030 Concentrator can deliver from full-duplex T1/E1 through T3/E3, 50 Mbps of encryption throughput, and support for up to 1500 simultaneous sessions.

Table 3-5 shows the major features of the Cisco VPN 3030 Concentrator. The 3030 VPN Concentrator uses SEPs to perform hardware encryption and can be purchased in either redundant or nonredundant configurations. This system is field-upgradeable to the Cisco 3060 Concentrator.

**Table 3-5**    *Cisco VPN 3030 Concentrator*

| Feature | Cisco 3030 |
|---------|-----------|
| Typical application | Medium to large |
| Simultaneous users | 1500 |
| Encryption throughput | 50 Mbps |
| Encryption method | Hardware |
| Encryption (SEP) module | 1 |
| Redundant SEP | Option |
| Available expansion slots | 3 |
| Upgrade capability | Yes |
| System memory | 128 MB |
| Hardware | 2U, scalable |
| Power supply | Single or dual |
| Client license | Unlimited |
| Processor | Motorola PowerPC |
| Console port | Async DB9 |
| Flash | Redundant |
| Memory | Variable |

# Cisco VPN 3060 Concentrator

Designed for large organizations requiring high performance and reliability, the Cisco VPN 3060 Concentrator can deliver from fractional T3 through T3/E3 or greater, 100 Mbps of encryption throughput, and support for up to 5000 simultaneous sessions.

Table 3-6 shows the major features of the Cisco VPN 3060 Concentrator. The 3060 VPN Concentrator uses SEPs to perform hardware encryption and can be purchased in either redundant or nonredundant configurations. This system is field-upgradeable to the Cisco 3080 Concentrator.

**Table 3-6** *Cisco VPN 3060 Concentrator*

| Feature | Cisco 3060 |
|---|---|
| Typical application | Large |
| Simultaneous users | 5000 |
| Encryption throughput | 100 Mbps |
| Encryption method | Hardware |
| Encryption (SEP) module | 2 |
| Redundant SEP | Option |
| Available expansion slots | 2 |
| Upgrade capability | N/A |
| System memory | 256 MB |
| Hardware | 2U, scalable |
| Power supply | Single or dual |
| Client license | Unlimited |
| Processor | Motorola PowerPC |
| Console port | Async DB9 |
| Flash | Redundant |
| Memory | Variable |

# Cisco VPN 3080 Concentrator

Designed for large organizations demanding the highest level of performance and reliability, the Cisco VPN 3080 Concentrator delivers 100 Mbps of encryption throughput and support for up to 10,000 simultaneous sessions.

Table 3-7 shows the major features of the Cisco VPN 3080 Concentrator. The 3080 VPN Concentrator uses SEPs to perform hardware encryption and is available only in a fully redundant configuration. The 3080 is the top of the line and is not upgradeable.

**Table 3-7**     *Cisco VPN 3080 Concentrator*

| Feature | Cisco 3080 |
|---|---|
| Typical application | Large |
| Simultaneous users | 10,000 |
| Encryption throughput | 100 Mbps |
| Encryption method | Hardware |
| Encryption (SEP) module | 4 |
| Redundant SEP | Yes |
| Available expansion slots | N/A |
| Upgrade capability | N/A |
| System memory | 256 MB |
| Hardware | 2U |
| Power supply | Dual |
| Client license | Unlimited |
| Processor | Motorola PowerPC |
| Console port | Async DB9 |
| Flash | Redundant |
| Memory | Variable |

## Cisco VPN 3000 Concentrator Series LED Indicators

While the LED indicator panel for the 3005 Concentrator only provides information for system status, the front panel on the 3015 through 3080 Concentrators, shown in Figure 3-16, has numerous LEDs that you can use to quickly check the health of the unit.

**Figure 3-16**     *Cisco VPN Concentrator 3015–3080 Front LED Display Panel*

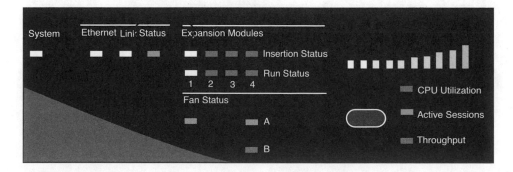

A description of the LEDs on the front panel of the Cisco 3000 Series Concentrators is given in Table 3-8.

**Table 3-8**   *Cisco VPN Concentrator Front Panel LEDs*

| LED Indicator | Green | Amber | Off |
|---|---|---|---|
| **The following details pertain to Model 3005.** | | | |
| System | Power on. Normal. Blinking green— System is in a shutdown (halted) state, ready to power off. | System has crashed and halted. *Error.* | Power off. (All other LEDs are also off.) |
| **The following details pertain to Models 3015–3080.** | | | |
| Ethernet Link Status 1 2 3 | Connected to network and enabled. Blinking green— Connected to network and configured, but disabled. | N/A | Not connected to network or not enabled. |
| Expansion Modules Insertion Status 1 2 3 4 | SEP module installed in system. | N/A | Module not installed in system. |
| Expansion Modules Run Status 1 2 3 4 | SEP module operational. | Module failed during operation. *Error.* | If installed, module failed diagnostics, or encryption code is not running. *Error.* |
| Fan Status | Operating normally. | Not running or RPM below normal range. *Error.* | N/A |
| Power Supplies A B | Installed and operating normally. | Voltage(s) outside of normal ranges. *Error.* | Not installed. |
| CPU Utilization | This statistic selected for usage gauge display. | N/A | Not selected. |
| Active Sessions | This statistic selected for usage gauge display. | N/A | Not selected. |
| Throughput | This statistic selected for usage gauge display. | N/A | Not selected. |

The rear panel on the 3015 through 3080 Concentrators also has numerous indicator LEDs that you can use to quickly check the health of the unit. Figure 3-17 shows the typical LED indicator configuration that is associated with each Ethernet port on a concentrator.

**Figure 3-17**  *Cisco VPN Concentrator Ethernet Port LEDs*

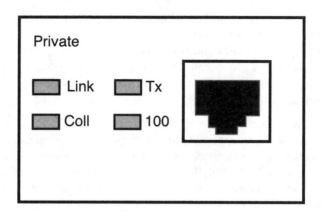

A description of the LEDs on this display is given in Table 3-9.

**Table 3-9**    *Cisco VPN Concentrator Rear Panel LEDs*

| LED Indicator | Green | Amber | Off |
|---|---|---|---|
| Link | Carrier detected. Normal. | N/A | No carrier detected. *Error.* |
| Tx | Transmitting data. Normal. Intermittent on. | N/A | Not transmitting data. Idle. Intermittent off. |
| Coll | N/A | Data collisions detected. | No collisions. Normal. |
| 100 | Speed set at 100 Mbps. | N/A | Speed set at 10 Mbps. |

SEP modules that are included on VPN Concentrator Models 3015 through 3080 have additional LEDs. Table 3-10 describes those LEDs.

**Table 3-10**    *Cisco VPN Concentrator SEP LEDs*

| SEP Module LED | Green | Amber | Off |
|---|---|---|---|
| Power | Power on. Normal. | N/A | Power is not reaching the module. It might not be seated correctly. *Error.* |
| Status | Encryption code is running. Normal. | Module failed during operation. *Error.* | Module failed diagnostics, or encryption code is not running. *Error.* |

# Cisco Secure VPN Client Features

> **8**    Cisco VPN 3000 Concentrator Series Client support

Cisco now offers two types of clients that can be used to negotiate and maintain IPSec VPN tunnels with Cisco VPN 3000 Series Concentrators, as well as equipment from other hardware vendors that support the full standards-based implementation of IPSec. The Cisco VPN Client is shipped with every VPN concentrator that Cisco sells. The Cisco VPN Client is supplied at no extra charge, is licensed for an unlimited number of installations, and can be used on most popular operating systems.

A new entry into the field, the Cisco VPN 3002 Hardware Client has no limitations as far as the operating systems it can support. As long as the attaching client can support TCP/IP, the VPN 3002 Hardware Client can provide secure IPSec communications. The next sections provide a brief overview of the VPN 3002 Hardware Client and the Cisco VPN Client. More information on the VPN Client is given in Chapter 4, "Configuring Cisco VPN 3000 for Remote Access Using Preshared Keys," and Chapter 6, "Configuring the Cisco VPN Client Firewall Feature." The VPN 3002 Hardware Client is discussed in Chapter 8, "Configuring Cisco 3002 Hardware Client for Remote Access," and Chapter 9, "Configuring Scalability Features of the Cisco VPN 3002 Hardware Client."

This section covers the following topics:

- Cisco VPN 3002 Hardware Client
- Cisco VPN Client

## Cisco VPN 3002 Hardware Client

The Cisco VPN 3002 Hardware Client was designed for remote office environments that normally have little direct IT support. These facilities need an easy-to-install, scalable, reliable, stable platform that can support any attached TCP/IP device, regardless of the operating system. The VPN 3002 is just such a device. Figure 3-18 shows the Cisco VPN 3002 Hardware Client equipped with the optional 8-port Ethernet switch.

**Figure 3-18**  *Cisco VPN 3002 Hardware Client*

The Cisco VPN 3002 Hardware Client is a full-featured VPN client. It supports IPSec and other VPN protocols. With IPSec, it supports both DES and 3DES encryption, providing either 56-bit or 168-bit encryption. The client can be configured in either a client mode or a network mode. The VPN 3002 uses Easy VPN and uses a push policy that enables it to scale to large numbers. The optional 8-port 10/100BaseTX switch allows immediate connection to local network devices.

## Cisco VPN Client

The client that is included with every VPN concentrator, the Cisco VPN Client, is easy to deploy and operate. The client can connect with any Easy VPN server and can be preconfigured to simplify mass deployments, requiring little user intervention. For these deployments, the VPN access policies and configurations are pulled from the central gateway and pushed to the client upon initial connection. This highly scalable client supports the full range of Microsoft Windows operating systems, including Windows 95, 98, Me, NT 4.0, 2000, and XP. The Cisco VPN Client also supports Linux (Intel), Solaris (UltraSparc-32bit), and MAC OS X 10.1. Figure 3-19 shows the initial screen of the Windows version of the Cisco VPN Client.

The VPN client is easy to deploy throughout a large corporation. The client installation is customizable, where the configuration can be preconfigured and installation can be automated. In addition, installation via CD-ROM can be automatically started using the autorun feature. By using this autorun feature, it requires no intervention from the user. Whenever possible, the client should connect to the VPN concentrator using the Cisco VPN Client because it provides the highest available security mechanism using IPSec and 3DES encryption.

**Figure 3-19**  *Cisco VPN Client*

## Other Client Software

Non-Cisco client software can also be used to establish a VPN connection to the Cisco VPN 3000 Concentrator. Microsoft provides a client called Microsoft L2TP/IPScc client that can be used to connect to the concentrator. However, using this client limits the client to an L2TP connection with IPSec. Microsoft also has the capability to establish a connection with the concentrator using Point-to-Point Tunneling Protocol (PPTP).

# Foundation Summary

The Foundation Summary is a collection of tables and figures that provides a convenient review of many key concepts in this chapter. For those of you who are already comfortable with the topics in this chapter, this summary can help you recall a few details. For those of you who just read this chapter, this review should help solidify some key facts. For anyone doing his or her final preparation before the exam, these tables and figures are a convenient way to review the material the day before the exam.

## Table of Cisco VPN 3000 Concentrators

The features of the Cisco VPN 3000 Concentrators are shown in Table 3-11.

**Table 3-11**    *Cisco VPN 3000 Series Concentrators*

| Feature | Cisco 3005 | Cisco 3015 | Cisco 3030 | Cisco 3060 | Cisco 3080 |
|---|---|---|---|---|---|
| Typical application | Small to medium | Small to medium | Medium to large | Large | Large |
| Simultaneous users | 100 | 100 | 1500 | 5000 | 10,000 |
| Encryption throughput | 4 Mbps | 4 Mbps | 50 Mbps | 100 Mbps | 100 Mbps |
| Encryption method | Software | Software | Hardware | Hardware | Hardware |
| Encryption (SEP) module | 0 | 0 | 1 | 2 | 4 |
| Redundant SEP | N/A | N/A | Option | Option | Yes |
| Available expansion slots | 0 | 4 | 3 | 2 | N/A |
| Upgrade capability | No | Yes | Yes | N/A | N/A |
| System memory | 32 MB (fixed) | 128 MB | 128 MB | 256 MB | 256 MB |
| Hardware | 1U, fixed | 2U, scalable | 2U, scalable | 2U, scalable | 2U |
| Power supply | Single | Single or dual | Single or dual | Single or dual | Dual |
| Client license | Unlimited | Unlimited | Unlimited | Unlimited | Unlimited |
| Processor | Motorola PowerPC | Motorola PowerPC | Motorola PowerPC | Motorola PowerPC | Motorola PowerPC |
| Console port | Async DB9 | Async DB9 | Async DB9 | Async DB9 | Async DB9 |
| Flash | 32 MB SRAM | Redundant | Redundant | Redundant | Redundant |
| Memory | Fixed | Variable | Variable | Variable | Variable |

# Table of Cisco VPN 3000 Concentrator Capabilities

Table 3-12 shows the various protocols that are supported by the Cisco VPN 3000 Series Concentrators.

**Table 3-12**    *Cisco VPN 3000 Concentrator Series Capabilities*

| Description | | Specification |
| --- | --- | --- |
| Compatibility | Client Software Compatibility | Cisco VPN Client (IPSec) for Windows 95, 98, Me, NT 4.0, 2000, and XP, including centralized split-tunneling control and data compression. |
| | | Cisco VPN 3002 Hardware Client. |
| | | Microsoft PPTP/MPPE/MPPC. |
| | | Microsoft L2TP/IPsec for Windows 2000. |
| | | MovianVPN (Certicom) Handheld VPN Client with ECC. |
| | Tunneling Protocols | IPSec, PPTP, L2TP, L2TP/IPsec, NAT Transparent IPSec. |
| | Encryption/Authentication | IPSec Encapsulating Security Payload (ESP) using DES/3DES (56/168-bit) with MD5 or SHA; MPPE using 40/128-bit RC4. |
| | Key Management | Internet Key Exchange (IKE). |
| | | Perfect Forward Secrecy (PFS). |
| | Routing Protocols | RIP, RIP2, OSPF, Static, automatic endpoint discovery, Network Address Translation (NAT), classless interdomain routing (CIDR). |
| | Third-Party Compatibility | Certicom, iPass Ready, Funk Steel Belted RADIUS certified, NTS TunnelBuilder VPN Client (Mac and Windows), Microsoft Internet Explorer, Netscape Communicator, Entrust, GTE Cybertrust, Baltimore, RSA Keon, VeriSign. |
| | High Availability | VRRP protocol for multichassis redundancy and failover. |
| | | Destination pooling for client-based failover and connection reestablishment. |
| | | Redundant SEP modules (optional), power supplies, and fans (3015–3060). |
| | | Redundant SEP modules, power supplies, and fans (3080). |

**Table 3-12**    *Cisco VPN 3000 Concentrator Series Capabilities (Continued)*

| Description | | Specification |
|---|---|---|
| Management | Configuration | Embedded management interface is accessible via console port, Telnet, SSH, and Secure HTTP.<br><br>Administrator access is configurable for five levels of authorization. Authentication can be performed externally via TACACS+.<br><br>Role-based management policy separates functions for service provider and end-user management. |
| | Monitoring | Event logging and notification via e-mail (SMTP).<br>Automatic FTP backup of event logs.<br>SNMP MIB-II support.<br>Configurable SNMP traps.<br>Syslog output.<br>System status.<br>Session data.<br>General statistics. |
| Security | Authentication and Accounting Servers | Support for redundant external authentication servers:<br>• RADIUS<br>• Microsoft NT Domain authentication<br>• RSA Security Dynamics (SecurID Ready)<br>Internal Authentication server for up to 100 users.<br>TACACS+ Administrative user authentication.<br>X.509v3 Digital Certificates.<br>RADIUS accounting. |
| | Internet-Based Packet Filtering | Source and destination IP address.<br>Port and protocol type.<br>Fragment protection.<br>FTP session filtering. |
| | Policy Management | By individual user or group<br>• Filter profiles<br>• Idle and maximum session timeouts<br>• Time and day access control<br>• Tunneling protocol and security authorization profiles<br>• IP pool<br>• Authentication servers |

# Chapter Glossary

The following terms were introduced in this chapter or have special significance to the topics within this chapter:

**Are You There (AYT)**   A process where the VPN Client enforces firewall policy defined on the local firewall by monitoring that firewall to make sure it is running. The client sends periodic "Are you there?" messages to the firewall. If no response is received, the VPN Client terminates the connection to the VPN concentrator.

**classless interdomain routing (CIDR)**   Technique supported by BGP4 and based on route aggregation. CIDR allows routers to group routes together to reduce the quantity of routing information carried by the core routers. With CIDR, several IP networks appear to networks outside the group as a single, larger entity. With CIDR, IP addresses and their subnet masks are written as four octets, separated by periods, followed by a forward slash and a two-digit number that represents the subnet mask.

**demilitarized zone (DMZ)**   Network that is isolated from a corporation's production environment. The DMZ is often used as a location for public-access servers, where the effects of successful intrusion attempts can be minimized and controlled.

**digital signal processor (DSP)**   Segments the voice signal into frames and stores them in voice packets.

**Elliptic Curve Cryptosystem (ECC)**   A public-key cryptosystem for mobile/wireless environments. ECC uses smaller key sizes to provide security equivalent to cryptosystems like RSA, resulting in faster computations, lower power consumption, and reduced memory and bandwidth use. ECC is particularly well suited for mobile devices that have limited CPU and memory capabilities.

**Internet Engineering Task Force (IETF)**   Task force consisting of over 80 working groups responsible for developing Internet standards. The IETF operates under the auspices of the ISOC.

**Layer 2 Forwarding Protocol (L2FP)**   Protocol that supports the creation of secure virtual private dial-up networks over the Internet.

**Layer 2 Tunneling Protocol (L2TP)**   An Internet Engineering Task Force (IETF) standards track protocol defined in RFC 2661 that provides tunneling of PPP. Based on the best features of L2F and PPTP, L2TP provides an industry-wide interoperable method of implementing VPDN.

**Microsoft Point-to-Point Compression (MPPC)**   A compression protocol used to compress Point-to-Point Protocol (PPP) packets between Cisco and Microsoft client devices. This protocol optimizes bandwidth usage to support multiple simultaneous connections.

**Microsoft Point-to-Point Encryption (MPPE)**   An encryption technology that was developed to encrypt point-to-point links over dial-up lines or VPN tunnels. MPPE works as a subfeature of MPPC.

**Network Address Translation (NAT)**   Mechanism for reducing the need for globally unique IP addresses. NAT allows an organization with addresses that are not globally unique to connect to the Internet by translating those addresses into globally routable address space. Also known as Network Address Translator.

**Open Shortest Path First (OSPF)**   Link-state, hierarchical IGP routing algorithm proposed as a successor to RIP in the Internet community. OSPF features include least-cost routing, multipath routing, and load balancing. OSPF was derived from an early version of the Intermediate System–to–Intermediate System (IS-IS) Protocol.

**Perfect Forward Secrecy (PFS)**   Cryptographic characteristic associated with a derived shared secret value. With PFS, if one key is compromised, previous and subsequent keys are not compromised because subsequent keys are not derived from previous keys.

**Point-to-Point Tunneling Protocol (PPTP)**   A protocol that enables secure data transfer between remote clients and enterprise servers by creating on-demand, multiprotocol VPNs across TCP/IP-based public data networks, such as the Internet.

**Remote Authentication Dial-In User Service (RADIUS)**   A standards-based protocol for authentication, authorization, and accounting (AAA).

**Reverse Route Injection (RRI)**   Used to populate the routing table of an internal router running OSPF or RIP for remote VPN clients or LAN-to-LAN sessions.

**Scalable Encryption Processing (SEP)**   VPN concentrator modules that perform hardware-based cryptographic functions, including random number generation, hash transforms (MD5 and SHA-1) for authentication, and encryption and decryption (DES and Triple-DES).

**Secure Shell (SSH)**   Sometimes called Secure Socket Shell, a UNIX-based command interface and protocol for gaining access to a remote computer securely.

**Secure Sockets Layer (SSL)**   Encryption technology for the web used to provide secure transactions, such as the transmission of credit card numbers for e-commerce.

**Terminal Access Controller Access Control System Plus (TACACS+)**   A Cisco proprietary protocol for authentication, authorization, and accounting (AAA).

**Virtual Router Redundancy Protocol (VRRP)**   In installations of two or more VPN concentrators in a parallel, redundant configuration, VRRP provides automatic switchover to a backup system in case the primary system is out of service, thus ensuring user access to the VPN.

**Wired Equivalent Privacy (WEP)**   An encryption protocol used on data signals transmitted between wireless LAN (WLAN) devices.

# Q&A

As mentioned in Chapter 1, these questions are more difficult than what you should experience on the CCSP exam. The questions do not attempt to cover more breadth or depth than the exam; however, the questions are designed to make sure you know the answer. Rather than allowing you to derive the answer from clues hidden inside the question itself, your understanding and recall of the subject are challenged. Questions from the "Do I Know This Already?" quiz from the beginning of the chapter are repeated here to ensure that you have mastered the chapter's topic areas. Hopefully, these questions will help limit the number of exam questions on which you narrow your choices to two options and guess!

The answers to this quiz are listed in Appendix A, "Answers to the "Do I Know This Already?" Quizzes and Q&A Sections."

**1**  How do VPN concentrators reduce communications expenses?

_____

_____

_____

**2**  What are two of the standard authentication servers that Cisco VPN 3000 Concentrators can use for authentication?

_____

_____

_____

**3**  What other authentication capability exists if standard authentication servers are not available?

_____

_____

_____

**4**  With respect to firewalls, where can you install Cisco VPN 3000 Concentrators?

_____

_____

_____

**5**  What routing protocols do the Cisco VPN 3000 Concentrators support?

_____

_____

_____

**6**  During large-scale implementations, how can Cisco VPN 3000 Concentrators be configured to simplify client configuration?

_____

_____

_____

**7**  What is the maximum encryption throughput rate for the VPN 3000 Concentrator Series?

_____

_____

_____

**8**  What hardware device is required to achieve maximum encryption throughput on the Cisco VPN 3000 Concentrators?

_____

_____

_____

**9**  What element on SEPs permits them to be so fast and flexible?

_____

_____

_____

**10**  Why are Cisco VPN Concentrators so good at supporting VPN communications?

_____

_____

_____

**11**  What tunneling protocols do Cisco VPN 3000 Concentrators support?

_____

_____

_____

**12** In addition to RIP and OSPF, what other routing capabilities do Cisco VPN Concentrators have?

_____

_____

_____

**13** What encryption and authentication protocols do Cisco VPN 3000 Concentrators support?

_____

_____

_____

**14** What protocol permits multichassis redundancy and failover?

_____

_____

_____

**15** What hardware items can be made redundant on Cisco VPN 3000 Concentrators?

_____

_____

_____

**16** What are some of the methods that can be used to interface with the embedded Cisco VPN Manager software on VPN concentrators?

_____

_____

_____

**17** What are the most secure forms of authentication that can be used with Cisco VPN 3000 Series Concentrators?

_____

_____

_____

**18** What mechanism is used by Cisco VPN Clients to monitor firewall activity between the client and the concentrator?

_____

_____

_____

**19** What is the rated mean time between failure (MTBF) for Cisco VPN 3000 Concentrators?

_____

_____

_____

**20** You have installed two Cisco VPN 3000 Concentrators in parallel on your network. Both devices have redundant power supplies, fans, and SEPs. You need to ensure 99.9% uptime. How can you achieve this rate of fault tolerance?

_____

_____

_____

**21** During the initial configuration of the VPN concentrators, what management interface must you use?

_____

_____

_____

**22** What do you need to do to activate configuration changes to Cisco VPN Concentrators that are made through the Cisco VPN Manager?

_____

_____

_____

**23** What four options are available under the Configuration menu of the VPN Manager?

_____

_____

_____

**24** What is the hierarchical order of property inheritance on Cisco VPN Concentrators?

_____

_____

_____

**25** What options are available on the Administration menu of the Cisco VPN Manager?

_____

_____

_____

**26** What options are available on the Monitoring menu of the Cisco VPN Manager?

_____

_____

_____

**27** Where in the Cisco VPN Manager could you go to view the current IP address for the private interface on a Cisco VPN 3000 Concentrator?

_____

_____

_____

**28** What models are available in the Cisco VPN 3000 Concentrator Series?

_____

_____

_____

**29** Which of the Cisco VPN 3000 Series Concentrators is a fixed configuration that is not upgradeable?

_____

_____

_____

**30**  How can purchasers of a Cisco VPN 3000 Series Concentrator obtain a license for the Cisco VPN Client?

_____

_____

_____

**31**  What is the maximum number of simultaneous sessions that can be supported on the Cisco VPN 3005 Concentrator?

_____

_____

_____

**32**  What is the maximum number of simultaneous sessions that can be supported on the Cisco VPN 3015 Concentrator?

_____

_____

_____

**33**  What is the maximum number of simultaneous sessions that can be supported on the Cisco VPN 3030 Concentrator?

_____

_____

_____

**34**  What is the maximum number of simultaneous sessions that can be supported on the Cisco VPN 3060 Concentrator?

_____

_____

_____

**35**  What is the maximum number of simultaneous sessions that can be supported on the Cisco VPN 3080 Concentrator?

_____

_____

_____

**36** Which of the Cisco VPN 3000 Series Concentrators is only available in a fully redundant configuration?

_____

_____

_____

**37** On a Cisco VPN 3005 Concentrator, what does a blinking green system LED indicate?

_____

_____

_____

**38** On a Cisco VPN 3000 Concentrator, what does a blinking amber system LED indicate?

_____

_____

_____

**39** What does a blinking green Ethernet link status LED indicate on a Cisco VPN Concentrator?

_____

_____

_____

**40** What does an amber SEP status LED indicate?

_____

_____

_____

**41** Which of Cisco's client offerings has no limitations with regard to the types of client operating systems it can support?

_____

_____

_____

**42** What optional feature on the Cisco VPN 3002 Hardware Client allows you to connect Ethernet devices to the client?

_____

_____

_____

**43** What two operating modes can a Cisco VPN 3002 Hardware Client be configured to support?

_____

_____

_____

**44** What operating systems does the Cisco VPN Client support?

_____

_____

_____

# Exam Topics Discussed in This Chapter

This chapter covers the following topics, which you need to master in your pursuit of certification as a Cisco Certified Security Professional:

9    Overview of remote access using preshared keys

10   Initial configuration of the Cisco VPN 3000 Concentrator Series for remote access

11   Browser configuration of the Cisco VPN 3000 Concentrator Series

12   Configuring users and groups

13   Advanced configuration of the Cisco VPN 3000 Concentrator Series

14   Configuring the IPSec Windows Client

# Configuring Cisco VPN 3000 for Remote Access Using Preshared Keys

From a procedural perspective, it is easier to configure the Cisco VPN 3000 Concentrator Series for remote access using preshared keys. While the alternative method is to use the services of a Certificate Authority (CA), that method entails additional steps. Using preshared keys, the client only needs to know the address of the VPN concentrator and the shared secret key.

While VPN configuration is relatively easy with preshared keys, this manual process does not scale well for large implementations. The VPN administrator must provide the password and implementation instructions to prospective users. This could be accomplished by preconfiguring client software on a floppy disk or CD-ROM, but even that process can be labor intensive in large implementations.

Once all of your users have successfully configured their remote systems with the current shared key, the process of changing passwords periodically, as every good security plan requires, would require notifying all users of the new password and providing modification instructions. You can imagine how it would be easy to forget about this important security consideration.

While scaling VPN implementations can be better handled by using CA support and digital certificates, preshared keys are easy to implement and can be used in many applications. This chapter discusses the process of implementing Internet Protocol Security (IPSec) using preshared keys on the Cisco VPN 3000 Series Concentrators. The clever graphical user interface (GUI) makes the implementation process easy.

## How to Best Use This Chapter

By taking the following steps, you can make better use of your time:

- Keep your notes and answers for all your work with this book in one place for easy reference.
- Take the "Do I Know This Already?" quiz, and write down your answers. Studies show retention is significantly increased through writing facts and concepts down, even if you never look at the information again.
- Use the diagram in Figure 4-1 to guide you to the next step.

**Figure 4-1**   *How to Use This Chapter*

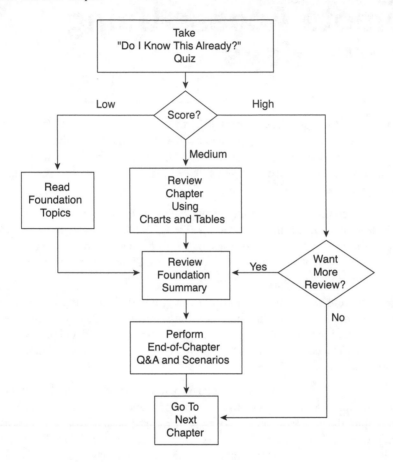

# "Do I Know This Already?" Quiz

The purpose of the "Do I Know This Already?" quiz is to help you decide what parts of the chapter to use. If you already intend to read the entire chapter, you do not need to answer these questions now.

This 24-question quiz helps you determine how to spend your limited study time. The quiz is sectioned into six smaller "quizlets," which correspond to the six major topic headings in the chapter. Figure 4-1 outlines suggestions on how to spend your time in this chapter based on your quiz score. Use Table 4-1 to record your scores.

**Table 4-1**   *Score Sheet for Quiz and Quizlets*

| Quizlet Number | Foundations Topics Section Covering These Questions | Questions | Score |
|---|---|---|---|
| 1 | Overview of remote access using preshared keys | 1–4 | |
| 2 | Initial configuration of the Cisco VPN 3000 Concentrator Series for remote access | 5–8 | |
| 3 | Browser configuration of the Cisco VPN 3000 Concentrator Series | 9–12 | |
| 4 | Configuring users and groups | 13–16 | |
| 5 | Advanced configuration of the Cisco VPN 3000 Concentrator Series | 17–20 | |
| 6 | Configuring the IPSec Windows Client | 21–24 | |
| All questions | | 1–24 | |

1   What methods can you use for user authentication on the Cisco VPN 3000 Series Concentrators?

_____

_____

_____

2   What methods can you use for device authentication between VPN peers?

_____

_____

_____

3   What are the three types of preshared keys?

_____

_____

_____

4   What is a unique preshared key?

_____

_____

_____

**5** When you boot up a Cisco VPN 3000 Concentrator with the default factory configuration, what happens?

_____

_____

_____

**6** What information do you need to supply in the command-line interface (CLI) portion of Quick Configuration?

_____

_____

_____

**7** Which interface do you need to configure using the browser-based VPN Manager?

_____

_____

_____

**8** What is the default administrator name and password for VPN concentrators?

_____

_____

_____

**9** How do you get your web browser to connect to the VPN concentrator's Manager application?

_____

_____

_____

**10** What is the default administrator name and password for the GUI VPN Manager?

_____

_____

_____

**11** What are the three major sections of the VPN Manager system?

_____

_____

_____

**12** What hot keys are available in the standard toolbar of the VPN Manager?

_____

_____

_____

**13** From where do users inherit attributes on the VPN concentrator?

_____

_____

_____

**14** How many groups can a user belong to in the VPN concentrator's internal database?

_____

_____

_____

**15** What is an external group in the VPN Manager system?

_____

_____

_____

**16** When reviewing the list of attributes for a group, what does it mean when an attribute's Inherit? box is checked?

_____

_____

_____

**17** What are the nine subcategories under the Configuration | System option in the VPN Manager's table of contents?

_____

_____

_____

**18**   Where would you configure information for Network Time Protocol (NTP) and Dynamic Host Configuration Protocol (DHCP) servers within the VPN Manager?

_____

_____

_____

**19**   What tunneling protocol can you configure on the VPN concentrator to support the Microsoft Windows 2000 VPN Client?

_____

_____

_____

**20**   What dynamic routing protocols are available on the VPN 3000 Concentrators?

_____

_____

_____

**21**   What Microsoft Windows operating systems can support the Cisco VPN Client?

_____

_____

_____

**22**   How do you start the Cisco VPN Client on a Windows system?

_____

_____

_____

**23**   How do you start the Cisco VPN Client installation process?

_____

_____

_____

**24**   What variables can you supply during the installation process of the Cisco VPN Client?

_____

_____

_____

The answers to this quiz are listed in Appendix A, "Answers to the "Do I Know This Already?" Quizzes and Q&A Sections." The suggestions for your next steps, based on quiz results, are as follows:

- **2 or less score on any quizlet**—Review the appropriate parts of the "Foundation Topics" section of this chapter, based on Table 4-1. Then proceed to the section, "Foundation Summary," the section, "Q&A," and the scenarios at the end of the chapter.

- **12 or less overall score**—Read the entire chapter, including the "Foundation Topics" and "Foundation Summary" sections, the "Q&A" section, and the scenarios at the end of the chapter.

- **13 to 18 overall score**—Begin with the section, "Foundation Summary," continue with the section, "Q&A," and read the scenarios. If you are having difficulty with a particular subject area, read the appropriate section in the "Foundation Topics" section.

- **19 or more overall score**—If you feel you need more review on these topics, go to the "Foundation Summary" section, then to the "Q&A" section, then to the scenarios. Otherwise, skip this chapter and go to the next chapter.

# Foundation Topics

# Using VPNs for Remote Access with Preshared Keys

> **9** Overview of remote access using preshared keys

For site-to-site VPN connections, peer devices must authenticate one another before IPSec communications can occur. In addition to requiring device authentication, remote access VPN connections require user authentication to make certain that the user is permitted to use the applications that are protected by the IPSec connection.

User authentication can be handled in a variety of ways. You can configure Remote Authentication Dial-In User Service (RADIUS), NT Domain, and Security Dynamics International (SDI) authentication on most Cisco devices, and the VPN 3000 Concentrators have the additional ability to authenticate users through an internal database.

If you want to use internal authentication, create a username and password for each user and assign the users to the group that is to be used for IPSec device authentication. Once the devices have established the IPSec tunnel, the user is prompted to enter a username and password to continue. Failure to authenticate causes the tunnel to drop. A similar login prompt is displayed if you are using RADIUS, NT Domain, or SDI authentication.

You can establish device authentication by using either preshared keys or digital certificates. (For more information, see Chapter 5, "Configuring Cisco VPN 3000 for Remote Access Using Digital Certificates.") With preshared keys, the system administrator chooses the key and then shares that key with users or other system administrators. Combining a preshared key with some other metric establishes three different uses for preshared keys, as follows:

- Unique
- Group
- Wildcard

The following sections describe each type of preshared key in more detail.

## Unique Preshared Keys

When a preshared key is tied to a specific IP address, the combination makes the preshared key unique. Only the peer with the correct IP address can establish an IPSec session using this key. Ideal for site-to-site VPNs where the identity of the peer devices is always known, unique preshared keys are not recommended for remote access VPNs. Unique preshared keys scale particularly poorly because each new user requires a new key and the administrative burden that entails.

While this type of preshared key is the most secure of the three types, it is not practical for remote access applications, where users are typically connecting through a commercial Internet service provider (ISP). Most users are not willing to pay for the luxury of a permanently assigned IP address from their ISP and are assigned an IP address from an available pool of addresses when they connect to the service. If you had a large installed base of VPN users, keeping up with these dynamically assigned IP addresses to provide this level of security would be a maintenance nightmare.

## Group Preshared Keys

If you begin using unique preshared keys, at some point you can decide to just use the same password for discrete groups of users. If you decide to do that, and shed the association with the IP address, you have begun to use the next type of preshared key, the group preshared key. A group preshared key is simply a shared key that is associated with a specific group. In a VPN 3000 Concentrator configuration, the group can be the Base Group or any other group that you define.

A group preshared key is well suited for remote access VPNs and is the method used by Cisco VPN 3000 Concentrators. It is good practice to use groups to establish Internet Key Exchange (IKE) and IPSec settings and to provide other capabilities that are unique to a specific set of users. If you choose to use the Cisco VPN 3000 Concentrator's internal database for user authentication, you can assign your users to specific groups, making the process of managing preshared keys much easier.

## Wildcard Preshared Keys

The final type of preshared key classification is the wildcard preshared key. This type of key does not have an IP address or group assigned to it and can be used by any device holding the key to establish an IPSec connection with your VPN concentrator. When you set up your concentrator to use wildcard preshared keys, every device connecting to the concentrator must also use preshared keys. If any device is compromised, you must change the key for all the devices in your network. This type of key is also open to man-in-the-middle attacks and should not be used for site-to-site applications.

---

**NOTE**    Man-in-the-middle attacks happen when an intruder has access to data packets that are in transit between connection endpoints. The intruder can then modify information within the packets in an attempt to gain access to the endpoints or for some other nefarious purpose. The intruder might just extract information from the packets. Obtaining a wildcard preshared key this way would permit an attacker to establish a VPN connection to the host from any other system.

---

# VPN Concentrator Configuration

10 Initial configuration of the Cisco VPN 3000 Concentrator Series for remote access

11 Browser configuration of the Cisco VPN 3000 Concentrator Series

12 Configuring users and groups

13 Advanced configuration of the Cisco VPN 3000 Series Concentrator

Three major categories of activities that should be performed on network devices are configuration, administration, and monitoring. The browser-based VPN 3000 Concentrator Series Manager was designed with those functions in mind. The remainder of this chapter focuses on the configuration capabilities of the VPN concentrator.

Remote access VPNs can be established with minimal equipment. Most of your users connect through the Internet, so their infrastructure costs are minimal. While you should place the concentrator behind or in parallel with a firewall, you could establish a robust VPN network with just a border router and your concentrator.

Administration requirements for the Cisco VPN 3000 Concentrator Series are fairly standard. You could configure the concentrators completely from the CLI using either a directly connected console monitor or by Telnetting to the concentrator. However, the best option for configuring this series of concentrators is through the GUI that you access through a web browser.

Microsoft Internet Explorer version 4.0 or higher is the recommended browser to use, but you can also use Netscape Navigator/Communicator version 4.0 or higher. You must enable the use of JavaScript and cookies in the browser application in order for the Cisco VPN 3000 Concentrator Manager to work properly. Nothing needs to be installed on your workstation other than the browser software.

This section covers the following topics:

- Cisco VPN 3000 Concentrator configuration requirements
- Cisco VPN 3000 Concentrator initial configuration
- Configuring IPSec with preshared keys through the VPN 3000 Concentrator Series Manager
- Advanced configuration of the VPN concentrator

## Cisco VPN 3000 Concentrator Configuration Requirements

Figure 4-2 shows a typical VPN concentrator configuration using a Cisco VPN 3005 Concentrator. The Public interface connects to the Internet through a security device such as a firewall or border router (not shown in this diagram). The Private interface connects to the local network, in this case supporting Domain Name System (DNS), Windows Internet Naming Service (WINS), and DHCP servers. On those models that have a third interface, you can establish a demilitarized zone (DMZ), which could contain some of these elements and, most likely, your Internet server. Connection to the Public and Private 10/100-Mbps Ethernet interfaces is done using UTP/STP CAT-5 cabling with RJ-45 connectors.

**Figure 4-2**    *VPN 3005 Concentrator Configuration*

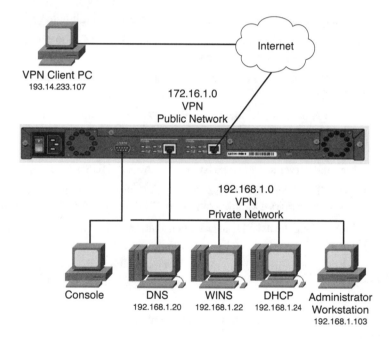

You need to attach a console for the initial configuration. The console port takes a standard straight-through RS-232 serial cable with a female DB-9 connector, which Cisco supplies with the system. Once the Private interface has been configured, you can access the concentrator from your administrator workstation using a web browser such as Internet Explorer or Netscape Navigator.

In addition to the physical connections, you also need to plan your IKE phase 1 and phase 2 settings. If you are going to be using preshared keys, you must select that key as well. The following is a list of the data values you need to obtain to completely configure your Cisco VPN 3000 Series Concentrator:

- Private interface IP address, subnet mask, speed, and duplex mode.
- Public interface IP address, subnet mask, speed, and duplex mode.
- VPN concentrator's device or system name.
- System date and time of day.
- VPN tunnel protocol that you will use, either IPSec, PPTP, or L2TP.
- Your local DNS server's IP address.
- Your registered domain name.
- The IP address or host name for the concentrator's default gateway.
- (Optional) Additional interfaces (for example, for a DMZ, on models 3015–3080 only), IP addresses, subnet masks, speed, and duplex mode.
- (Optional) IP address or host name of your DHCP server, if your concentrator will be using DHCP to assign addresses to remote users.
- (Optional) A pool of IP addresses if the VPN concentrator will be assigning addresses to remote users.
- (Optional) For external RADIUS user authentication, the IP address or host name, port number, and server secret or password for the RADIUS server.
- (Optional) For external Windows NT Domain user authentication, the IP address, port number, and Primary Domain Controller (PDC) host name for your domain.
- (Optional) For external SDI user authentication, the IP address and port number for the SDI server.
- (Optional) For internal VPN concentrator user authentication, the username and password for each user. If you specify per-user address assignment, you also need the IP address and subnet mask for each user.
- (Optional) For the IPSec tunneling protocol, a name and password for the IPSec tunnel group.

## Cisco VPN 3000 Concentrator Initial Configuration

When the Cisco VPN 3000 Concentrator is powered on for the first time, it boots up the factory default configuration, which offers a Quick Configuration option. The data requested by the Quick Configuration mode are enough to make the concentrator operational. Once you have the basic configuration entered through this mode, you can fine-tune the configuration through normal menu options.

The Quick Configuration can be accomplished from the CLI, but the HTML version of the concentrator manager provides a more intuitive tool for performing the essential configuration of the concentrator. The Quick Configuration steps are as follows:

**Step 1**  CLI: Set the system time, date, and time zone.

**Step 2**  CLI: Enable network access for your web browser by setting the Private interface's IP address, subnet mask, speed, and duplex mode.

**Step 3**  Browser: Configure the Public interface and any other Ethernet or WAN interfaces of the concentrator. To do that, you need to set the IP address, subnet mask, speed, and duplex mode for each of these interfaces.

**Step 4**  Browser: Identify the system by supplying system name, date, time, DNS, domain name, and default gateway.

**Step 5**  Browser: Select the tunneling protocol to use and the encryption options.

**Step 6**  Browser: Identify the method the concentrator is to use for assigning IP addresses to clients as a tunnel is established.

**Step 7**  Browser: Select the type of user authentication to use, and provide the identity of the authentication server. You can choose to authenticate from the internal server, RADIUS, NT Domain, or SDI.

**Step 8**  (Optional) Browser: When using the internal authentication server, populate the internal user database with group and user identities.

**Step 9**  (Optional) Browser: When using IPSec as the tunneling protocol, assign a name and password to the IPSec tunnel group.

**Step 10**  (Optional, but recommended) Browser: Change the admin password for security.

**Step 11**  Browser: Save the configuration settings.

## Quick Configuration Using the CLI

The VPN 3000 Concentrator enters into Quick Configuration mode the first time it is powered up. Quick Configuration is a configuration wizard that guides you through the initial configuration settings. To begin performing the 11 steps outlined above from the CLI, connect your console to the concentrator and power on the concentrator. As the system boots, various information is displayed on the console screen. After the system has performed the boot functions, you should see the login prompt. When prompted, supply the default administrator login name of **admin** and the default password, which is also **admin**. Note that the password is not displayed on the console screen as you type it, as shown in the following CLI output.

```
Login: admin
Password:
```

Once you have entered the correct login name and password, the concentrator displays a welcome screen, as shown in Example 4-1.

**Example 4-1**   *Quick Configuration Welcome Screen*

```
                      Welcome to
                    Cisco Systems
           VPN 3000 Concentrator Series
               Command Line Interface
   Copyright (C) 1998-2001 Cisco Systems, Inc.



    -- : Set the time on your device. The correct time is very important,
    -- : so that logging and accounting entries are accurate.

    -- : Enter the system time in the following format:
    -- :        HH:MM:SS.  Example 21:30:00  for 9:30 PM

   > Time

   Quick -> [ 08:57:13 ]
```

## Setting the System Time, Date, and Time Zone

At this point, the concentrator is waiting for you to verify the current time by pressing Enter or to type in a new time, as shown in Example 4-2. Notice that the system prompt changes to Quick -> to indicate that the system is waiting for you to confirm or enter data. The following example also shows the entries that are required (in boldface type) to complete the configuration of the date, time zone, and daylight-savings time support information.

**Example 4-2**   *Setting the System Time and Date*

```
   Quick -> [ 08:57:13 ] 08:15:22

    -- : Enter the date in the following format.
    -- : MM/DD/YYYY  Example 06/12/1999  for June 12th 1999.

   > Date

   Quick -> [ 03/29/2002 ] 09/01/2002

    -- : Set the time zone on your device. The correct time zone is very
    -- : important so that logging and accounting entries are accurate.

    -- : Enter the time zone using the hour offset from GMT:
    -- : -12 : Kwajalein  -11 : Samoa     -10 : Hawaii       -9 : Alaska
    -- :  -8 : PST         -7 : MST        -6 : CST          -5 : EST
    -- :  -4 : Atlantic    -3 : Brasilia  -2 : Mid-Atlantic  -1 : Azores
```

**Example 4-2**  *Setting the System Time and Date (Continued)*

```
-- :    0 : GMT        +1 : Paris    +2 : Cairo     +3 : Kuwait
-- :   +4 : Abu Dhabi  +5 : Karachi  +6 : Almaty    +7 : Bangkok
-- :   +8 : Singapore  +9 : Tokyo   +10 : Sydney   +11 : Solomon Is.
-- : +12 : Marshall Is.

> Time Zone

Quick -> [  0 ] -6

1) Enable Daylight Savings Time Support
2) Disable Daylight Savings Time Support

Quick -> [ 1 ] 2
```

## Configuring the Private LAN Interface

The next phase of the CLI Quick Configuration steps is to configure the Private LAN interface. This is simply a matter of setting the IP address and subnet mask information and then specifying the speed and duplex mode to use for the interface. Those steps are shown in the output in Example 4-3, which is displayed as soon as you enter your preference for daylight-savings support.

**Example 4-3**  *Configuring the Private Interface*

```
This table shows current IP addresses.

   Intf         Status        IP Address/Subnet Mask          MAC Address
------------------------------------------------------------------------------
Ether1-Pri¦Not Configured¦      0.0.0.0/0.0.0.0         ¦
Ether2-Pub¦Not Configured¦      0.0.0.0/0.0.0.0         ¦
------------------------------------------------------------------------------
DNS Server(s): DNS Server Not Configured
DNS Domain Name:
Default Gateway: Default Gateway Not Configured

** An address is required for the private interface. **

> Enter IP Address

Quick Ethernet 1 -> [ 0.0.0.0 ] 192.168.1.3

Waiting for Network Initialization...

> Enter Subnet Mask

Quick Ethernet 1 -> [ 255.255.255.0 ]

1) Ethernet Speed 10 Mbps
```

*continues*

**Example 4-3** *Configuring the Private Interface (Continued)*

```
2) Ethernet Speed 100 Mbps
3) Ethernet Speed 10/100 Mbps Auto Detect

Quick Ethernet 1 -> [ 3 ] 2

1) Enter Duplex - Half/Full/Auto
2) Enter Duplex - Full Duplex
3) Enter Duplex - Half Duplex

Quick Ethernet 1 -> [ 1 ] 2

1) Modify Ethernet 1 IP Address (Private)
2) Modify Ethernet 2 IP Address (Public)
3) Save changes to Config file
4) Continue
5) Exit
```

In Example 4-3, the administrator wanted to use a 24-bit subnet mask. When he entered a Class C IP address for the interface, the system automatically brought up the 24-bit Class C default subnet mask. The administrator simply pressed Enter to accept this subnet mask setting. Also notice that the administrator explicitly set the speed of the interface to 100 Mbps and to Full Duplex rather than accepting the default automatic detection settings.

From the menu displayed at the end of the previous output display, you can see that you have the option of also configuring the Public interface. If the hardware configuration had additional interfaces, you would see menu options for configuring those interfaces, too.

The browser-based manager is the configuration tool of choice for the VPN 3000 Concentrator. The CLI is used only to enable network connectivity so that you can communicate with the concentrator through the network from your administration workstation. Configuration of additional interfaces and all remaining concentrator settings is accomplished through the browser-based manager.

To finish the CLI initial configuration of the VPN concentrator, simply save your changes to the Config file and then exit the Quick Configuration mode. Those steps are shown in the output in Example 4-4.

**Example 4-4** *Saving Configuration Settings and Exiting the CLI*

```
1) Modify Ethernet 1 IP Address (Private)
2) Modify Ethernet 2 IP Address (Public)
3) Save changes to Config file
4) Continue
5) Exit

Quick -> 3

1) Modify Ethernet 1 IP Address (Private)
```

**Example 4-4**  *Saving Configuration Settings and Exiting the CLI (Continued)*

```
2) Modify Ethernet 2 IP Address (Public)
3) Save changes to Config file
4) Continue
5) Exit

Quick -> 5
```

The concentrator only presents the Quick Configuration process upon initial bootup using the default configuration. After you have configured the concentrator, the normal CLI menus look as follows:

Model 3005 menu:

```
1) Modify Ethernet 1 IP Address (Private)
2) Modify Ethernet 2 IP Address (Public)
3) Configure Expansion Cards
4) Save changes to Config file
5) Continue
6) Exit

Quick -> _
```

Model 3015–3080 menu:

```
1) Modify Ethernet 1 IP Address (Private)
2) Modify Ethernet 2 IP Address (Public)
3) Modify Ethernet 3 IP Address (External)
4) Configure Expansion Cards
5) Save changes to Config file
6) Continue
7) Exit

Quick -> _
```

If you need to go through the Quick Configuration again for any reason, simply select the **Reboot with Factory/Default Configuration** option from the **Administration | System Reboot** menu in the VPN 3000 Concentrator Manager.

This finishes the CLI configuration steps. The remainder of the configuration steps are completed using the Cisco VPN 3000 Concentrator Manager application that is resident on each VPN concentrator and is accessible using the web browser on your administrator PC.

## Quick Configuration Using the Browser-Based Manager

Now that you have configured the Private interface on the VPN concentrator, make sure that your workstation has an IP address on the same subnet as the concentrator and verify that you can reach the concentrator by pinging to it from the workstation. Once you have verified connectivity, open your web browser application and connect to the concentrator by entering the IP address of the concentrator in the Address field of the browser, as shown in Figure 4-3.

**Figure 4-3** *HTTP Addressing for VPN 3000 Concentrator Series Manager*

The browser connects to the VPN concentrator and presents the initial login screen, as shown in Figure 4-4.

**Figure 4-4** *VPN 3000 Concentrator Series Manager Login Screen*

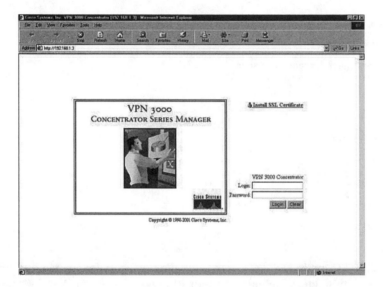

Notice the hotlink option on the screen labeled Install SSL Certificate. You can use Secure Sockets Layer (SSL) encryption to establish a secure session between your management workstation and the concentrator. Using this secure session capability encrypts all VPN Manager communications with the concentrator at the IP socket level. SSL uses the HTTPS protocol and uses https:// addressing on the browser. You might want to use SSL if your VPN Manager workstation connects to the concentrator across a public network. There can be a slight performance penalty when using SSL, depending on the capability of the administration workstation, but it should not be a serious consideration for management functions.

When the VPN concentrator boots for the first time, it generates a self-signed SSL server certificate. To use SSL with your browser, install this server certificate into the browser. If you have multiple concentrators, you must install the certificate from each of the concentrators into your browser, but you only need to do that once for each concentrator. Once the SSL server certificate is installed, you can begin using HTTPS for communications with the concentrator.

Clicking the Install SSL Certificate hotlink takes you to the browser's certificate installation wizard. Netscape and Microsoft browsers have slightly different installation routines, but in either case, accept the default settings presented, supply a nickname for the certificate if requested, and continue through the installation process by clicking Next or Finish. You can then immediately connect to the concentrator using HTTPS once the installation wizard has finished.

To continue with the Quick Configuration that you started from the CLI, log in with the administrator login name and password. Using the login screen shown in Figure 4-4, follow these steps:

**Step 1**    Position your cursor in the Login field.

**Step 2**    Type **admin** and the press Tab.

**Step 3**    With the cursor in the Password field, type **admin** again. The window displays **\*\*\*\*\***.

**Step 4**    Click the **Login** button to initiate the login process.

If you make a mistake, click on the **Clear** button to refresh the screen so that you can start over.

After the VPN concentrator has accepted your administrator login, the screen shown in Figure 4-5 is displayed in your browser window.

**Figure 4-5**    *First-Time Quick Start Option Menu*

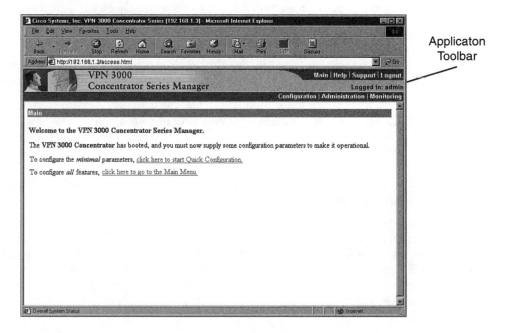

The top portion of the screen is the application toolbar, and it is displayed on every other manager screen. Because this is a consistent header, it is not shown in subsequent screen displays.

On the right-hand portion of the header, you see the standard toolbar, which contains the following elements:

- Hotlinks to the following items:
  - Main menu
  - Manager's Help system
  - A support page that provides web addresses and phone numbers to Cisco support sites
  - Logout, so that you can exit the system or log in as a different user
- Information on the login name of the current user
- Hotlinks to the Main Menu screen for the three major sections of the VPN 3000 Concentrator Manager system:
  - Configuration
  - Administration
  - Monitoring

The first time that you enter the VPN Manager after booting from the default configuration, you are presented with a screen that allows you to enter the Quick Configuration mode to continue the process that you started at the CLI. Figure 4-5 shows this screen.

If you click here to start Quick Configuration, the VPN Manager leads you through a series of screens to complete the 11 initial configuration steps. This is a continuation of the Quick Configuration wizard that was started at the CLI. You only have this opportunity once.

If you click here to go to the Main Menu, you can configure the same settings, but you must select the configuration windows from the table of contents. After you have completed the Quick Configuration, this screen is not displayed again, and the system boots into the standard VPN Manager window.

## Configuring Remaining Interface Settings

When you click to start Quick Configuration, the VPN Manager displays the IP Interfaces screen. If your system is a 3005 series with only two fixed interfaces, the screen looks like that shown in Figure 4-6. Notice that the screen's title bar shows the complete path to this screen (Configuration | Quick | IP Interfaces), as it would be shown if you had worked down to this screen through the table of contents. This 3005 display shows that the Private interface is configured and operational and that the Public interface is not yet configured.

**Figure 4-6**  *3005 Concentrator—Configuration | Quick | IP Interfaces*

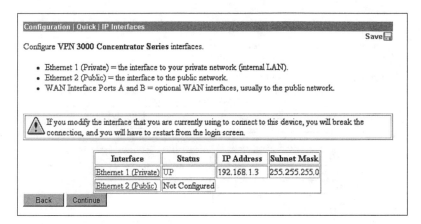

Figure 4-7 shows the IP Interfaces screen for the Model 3015–3080 VPN Concentrator. This system has two unconfigured Ethernet interfaces and two unconfigured WAN interfaces. The listings in the Interface column are hotlinks to the configuration screen for each of the interfaces.

**Figure 4-7**  *3015–3080 Concentrator—Configuration | Quick | IP Interfaces*

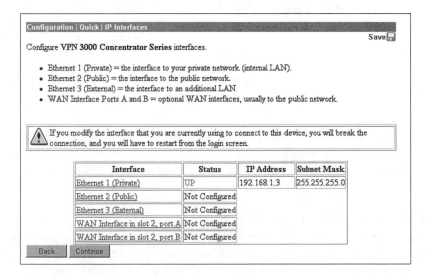

If you click the hotlink to Ethernet 1 (Private), the configuration screen for Ethernet 1 appears, as shown in Figure 4-8. You can select to disable the interface, to obtain addressing from a DHCP server, or to assign static IP addressing.

**Figure 4-8** *Configuration | Quick | IP Interfaces | Ethernet 1*

Configuration | Quick | IP Interfaces | Ethernet 1

> ⚠ You are modifying the interface you are using to connect to this device. If you make any changes, you will break the connection and you will have to restart from the login screen.

**Configuring Ethernet Interface 1 (Private).**

| | | General Parameters | |
|---|---|---|---|
| Sel | Attribute | Value | Description |
| ○ | Disabled | | Select to disable this interface. |
| ○ | DHCP Client | | Select to obtain the IP Address, Subnet Mask and Default Gateway via DHCP (System Name may be required for DHCP). |
| | System Name | | |
| ⊙ | Static IP Addressing | | Select to configure the IP Address and Subnet Mask. Enter the IP Address and Subnet Mask for this interface. |
| | IP Address | 192.168.1.3 | |
| | Subnet Mask | 255.255.255.0 | |
| | Public Interface | ☐ | Check to make this interface a "public" interface. |
| | MAC Address | 00.90.A4.00.00.13 | The MAC address for this interface. |
| | Filter | —None— ▼ | Select the filter for this interface. |
| | Speed | 100 Mbps ▼ | Select the speed for this interface. |
| | Duplex | Full-Duplex ▼ | Select the duplex mode for this interface. |

Apply   Cancel

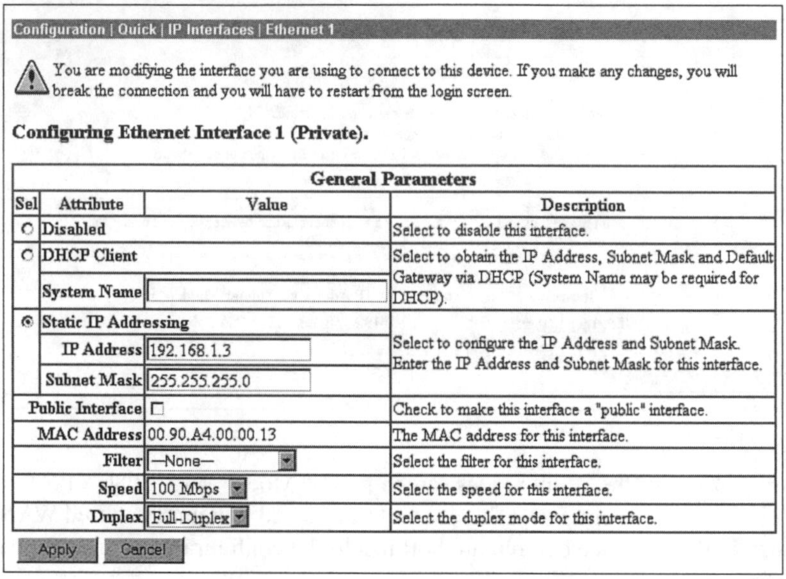

**NOTE** If you disable the Private interface, you lose your browser connection to the concentrator.

The Speed and Duplex settings were configured from the CLI in this example. The default settings for these two fields are 10/100 Auto and Auto, respectively, allowing the systems to negotiate speed and duplex mode.

When you have completed entering the configuration settings for an interface, click the Apply button to save the settings and return to the IP Interfaces screen. Once you have configured all the interfaces, click the Continue button to proceed to the next Quick Configuration screen.

### Configuring System Information

The System Info screen is the next screen displayed. Figure 4-9 shows this screen. The date and time settings were entered during the CLI configuration steps. You can enter a system name here along with DNS server, domain name, and default gateway information.

**Figure 4-9**  *Configuration | Quick | System Info*

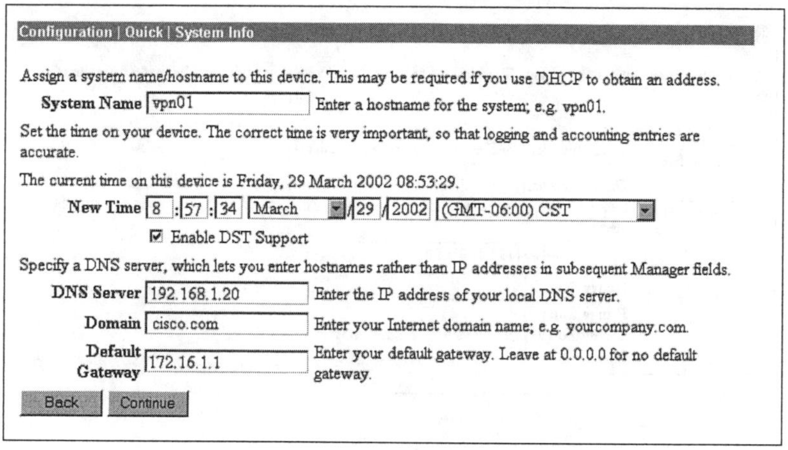

## Configuring the Tunneling Protocol

Clicking the Continue button takes you to the Protocols screen, as shown in Figure 4-10. You can select all protocols, if you like. The configuration described in this chapter works with IPSec only, so that is the only protocol selected on this screen.

**Figure 4-10**  *Configuration | Quick | Protocols*

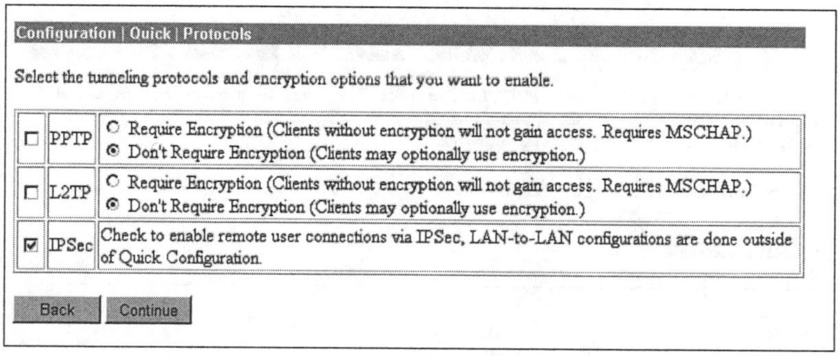

## Configuring Address Assignment Method

After you have selected the protocol to use, you must select the method the VPN concentrator is to use to assign an address to clients as they establish tunnels with the concentrator. The method of address assignment selected in Figure 4-11 is to use a DHCP server. You could select multiple methods; the concentrator tries each method in order until it is successful in assigning an address to the client.

**Figure 4-11** *Configuration | Quick | Address Assignment*

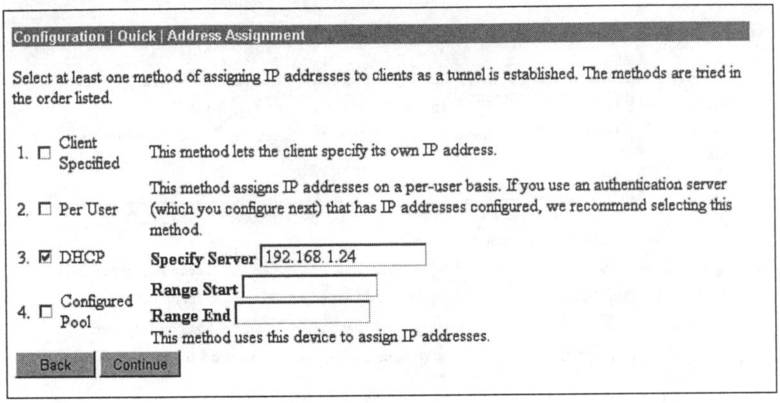

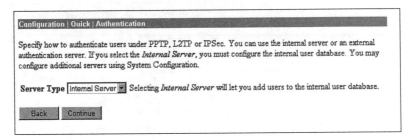

## Configuring User Authentication Method

Next, you determine how users connecting over the VPN tunnel are to be authenticated. Figure 4-12 shows the selection screen. Users can be authenticated from RADIUS servers, NT Domain controllers, external SDI servers, and the concentrator's internal server. The option you select brings up the appropriate next screen so that you can continue configuring user authentication.

**Figure 4-12** *Configuration | Quick | Authentication*

```
Configuration | Quick | Authentication

Specify how to authenticate users under PPTP, L2TP or IPSec. You can use the internal server or an external
authentication server. If you select the Internal Server, you must configure the internal user database. You may
configure additional servers using System Configuration.

Server Type  [Internal Server ▼]  Selecting Internal Server will let you add users to the internal user database.

   [Back]  [Continue]
```

## Configuring Users for Internal Authentication

The example shown in Figure 4-12 has selected the Internal Server option and brings up the User Database screen, shown in Figure 4-13, so that you can enter the usernames and passwords. This screen also requests an IP address and subnet mask because, in this case, the concentrator's administrator selected Per User address assignment on the screen displayed in Figure 4-11.

**Figure 4-13**  *Configuration | Quick | User Database*

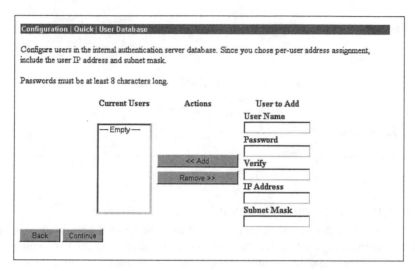

There is a maximum combined number of groups and users that you can configure on a VPN 3000 Concentrator. The number varies by concentrator model, as shown in Table 4-2.

**Table 4-2**    *Maximum Number of Combined Groups and Users per VPN Model*

| Model | Maximum Combined Number of Groups and Users |
|-------|---------------------------------------------|
| 3005  | 100                                         |
| 3015  | 100                                         |
| 3030  | 500                                         |
| 3060  | 1000                                        |
| 3080  | 1000                                        |

## Configuring the IPSec Tunnel Group

When you select IPSec as the tunneling protocol from the screen shown in Figure 4-10, the concentrator prompts you to define a group during the Quick Configuration phase. This group is used by every user unless you change the association later from the standard configuration section of the VPN Manager. Figure 4-14 shows the configuration information for the IPSec group. The password for this group becomes the preshared key for remote access users.

**Figure 4-14**  *Configuration | Quick | IPSec Group*

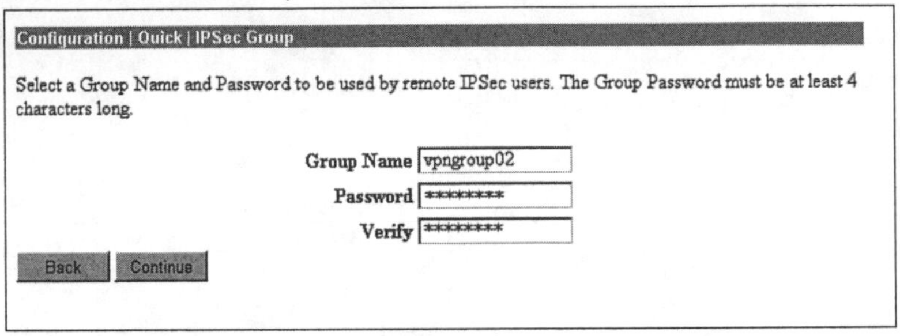

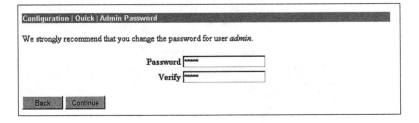

### Configuring the Admin Password

The final setting that you should configure during the Quick Configuration is the password for the admin user. Figure 4-15 shows the Quick Configuration screen for completing this task and displays the message that strongly recommends changing the admin password. For maximum password security, select a password containing at least eight characters that are a mixture of uppercase and lowercase letters, numbers, and special characters.

**Figure 4-15**  *Configuration | Quick | Admin Password*

### Saving Configuration Settings

When you click the Continue button after changing the admin password, the VPN Manager presents you with the Quick Configuration Done screen, as shown in Figure 4-16. At this point, you have configured the system information, LAN and WAN interfaces, users, and IPSec group, completing the basic configuration of the VPN concentrator.

**Figure 4-16**  *Configuration | Quick | Done*

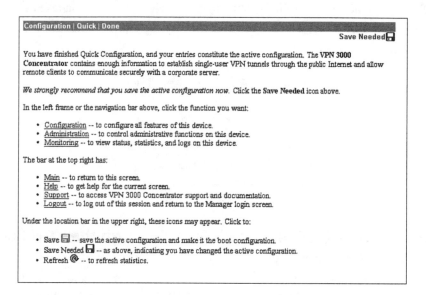

Notice the Save Needed icon in the upper-right corner of the main screen. Click that icon to save the active configuration changes you have made to the boot configuration. As you continue with additional configuration steps, this icon appears from time to time. As you can see from Figure 4-16, the icon can display Save, Save Needed, or Refresh depending on the type of screen you are on and whether you have made modifications to the active configuration.

As with most Cisco products, configuration changes are done to the active configuration and take effect immediately. To ensure that your changes are still in effect after a system reboot, you must copy the active configuration to the boot configuration. The VPN Manager's Save Needed reminder is a nice touch, providing a gentle reminder and an easy method of execution.

Clicking the Save Needed icon executes the requested save and provides you with a status screen. Figure 4-17 shows the screen that is returned upon the completion of a successful save. After you clear this screen by clicking the OK button, VPN Manager displays the Main Menu.

In addition to the Save, Save Needed, and Refresh options, the Configuration | Quick | Done screen shows Configuration, Administration, and Monitoring in the upper-left corner (refer to Figure 4-16). These three keys are the primary navigation tools for the daily VPN Manager functions. Similar to a directory display from a product such as Microsoft Windows Explorer, the plus sign indicates that the indicated function has subfunctions. Clicking the plus sign displays an indented list of the subfunctions, and clicking the option takes you to the window for that function.

**Figure 4-17** *Save Successful Message*

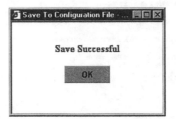

## Configuring IPSec with Preshared Keys Through the VPN 3000 Concentrator Series Manager

The Quick Configuration allows you to configure the basic operational settings of the concentrator, but the IPSec settings have not been established yet. Those settings are made using features in the Configuration portion of the Cisco VPN 3000 Concentrator Manager.

Figure 4-18 shows the Main screen that appears after you log in to the concentrator through VPN Manager. Normally the root Configuration, Administration, and Monitoring levels are the only options displayed in the table of contents. In this case, each of those major sections has been opened to the first layer of subfunctions. You can see the following major subfunctions under the Configuration option:

- **Interfaces**—Ethernet interfaces and power supplies
- **System**—System-wide parameters: servers, address assignment, tunneling protocols, IP routing, management protocols, events, and identification
- **User Management**—Groups and users
- **Policy Management**—Access hours, network lists, rules, security associations, filters, and NAT

**Figure 4-18**  *IPSec Configuration*

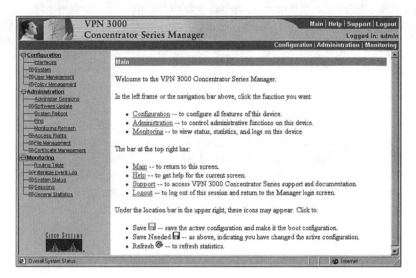

The interfaces have already been configured using the Quick Configuration option. If you chose to use internal authentication, the Quick Configuration wizard then asked you to enter usernames and passwords and then requested a group name to use for IPSec traffic.

Recall from previous chapters that there is a hierarchy to the way groups are used on the Cisco VPN 3000 Concentrator. The following basic rules govern group usage:

- Groups and users have attributes that can be modified to control how they can use the services of the concentrator.

- Users are always members of groups, and groups are always members of the Base Group. The Base Group is a default group that cannot be deleted but which can be modified.

- Inheritance rules state that, by default, users inherit rights from groups, and groups inherit rights from the Base Group.

- A user can only be a member of one concentrator group and, if not explicitly assigned to a different group, is a member of the Base Group by default.

- Users and groups have names and passwords.

- If you change the attributes of a group, it affects all group members.

- If you delete a group, user membership reverts to the Base Group.

Because the Base Group had not been modified before Quick Configuration set up the new group for IPSec use, that new group has default settings that it inherited from the Base Group. Additionally, all the users that you created were placed in this single group. That might be adequate for your organization. The final step you need to perform to set up the concentrator for remote access using preshared keys is to validate the entries that were placed in the IPSec group.

---

**NOTE**     The discussions in this chapter assume that you would be performing the configuration on a new concentrator. You could be setting up remote access services on a concentrator that has been used for other purposes, such as LAN-to-LAN VPNs. In that case, you would start at this point in the configuration process. While this discussion looks at modifying the group that was established through Quick Configuration, you would simply need to add a new group from the Configuration I User Management I Groups screen.

---

To modify the settings for the IPSec group previously created, work down to the Configuration I User Management I Groups screen (see Figure 4-19). In this screen, you find the vpngroup02 group listed in the Current Groups window. There are internal and external groups. External groups are those that would be used with external authentication servers such as RADIUS or NT Domain. The vpngroup02 group is an internal group and is to be used with internal database users.

**Figure 4-19**  *Configuration I User Management I Groups*

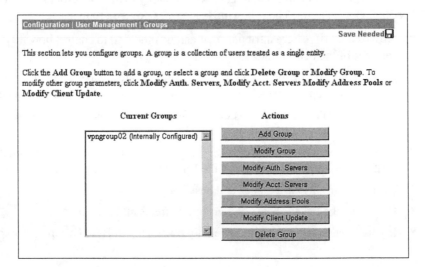

## Modify Groups—Identity Tab

To modify the group, click the group to highlight it, and then click the **Modify Group** button. The screen shown in Figure 4-20 shows the Modify screen for an internal group. Internal groups have multiple tabs. External groups only have the Identity tab. The information in this screen should match the data you entered during Quick Configuration. If not, you can correct it here. When everything looks correct, click the **General** tab.

**Figure 4-20**  *Configuration | User Management | Groups | Modify > Identity*

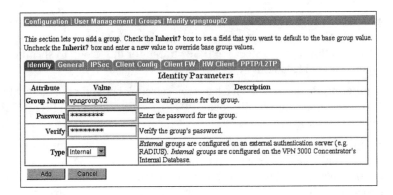

## Modify Groups—General Tab

Figure 4-21 depicts the General tab for the group's Modify function. Notice that each attribute listed has a Value, Inherit?, and Description column. If the Inherit? box is checked, that attribute's value is inherited from the Base Group, regardless of what you enter into the Value field. To change the value for an attribute, uncheck the Inherit? box.

The following information is shown on the General tab:

- **Access Hours**—Selected from the drop-down menu, this attribute determines when the concentrator is open for business for this group. Currently set to No Restrictions, you could also select Never, Business Hours (9 a.m. to 5 p.m., Monday through Friday), or named access hours that you created elsewhere in the VPN Manager.

- **Simultaneous Logins**—Default is 3. Minimum is 0. There is no upper limit, but you should limit this value to 1 for security purposes.

- **Minimum Password Length**—The allowable range is 1 to 32 characters. A value of 8 provides a good level of security for most applications.

- **Allow Alphabetic-Only Passwords**—Notice that the Inherit? box has been unchecked. The default is to allow alphabetic-only passwords, which is not a good idea. This value has been modified.

- **Idle Timeout**—A value of 30 minutes is good here. The minimum allowable value is 1 and the maximum is a value that equates to over 4000 years! 0 disables idle timeout.

- **Maximum Connect Time**—0 disables maximum connect time. The range here is again 1 minute to over 4000 years.

- **Filter**—Filters determine whether IPSec traffic is permitted or denied for this group. There are three default filters: Public, Private, and External. You can select from those or from any that you can define in the drop-down box. The default None option permits IPSec to handle all traffic.

- **Primary/Secondary DNS/WINS**—These have been modified from the Base Group's default settings.

- **SEP Card Assignment**—Some models of the VPN concentrator can contain up to four Scalable Encryption Processing (SEP) modules that handle encryption functions. This attribute allows you to steer the IPSec traffic for this group to specific SEPs to perform your own load balancing.

- **Tunneling Protocols**—IPSec has been selected, but you could allow the group to use Point-to-Point Tunneling Protocol (PPTP), Layer 2 Tunneling Protocol (L2TP), and L2TP over IPSec as well.

- **Strip Realm**—The default operation of the VPN concentrator verifies users against the internal database using a combination of the username and realm qualifier, as in *username@group*. The *@group* portion is called the realm. You can have the VPN concentrator use name only by checking the value for this attribute.

**Figure 4-21** *Configuration | User Management | Groups | Modify > General*

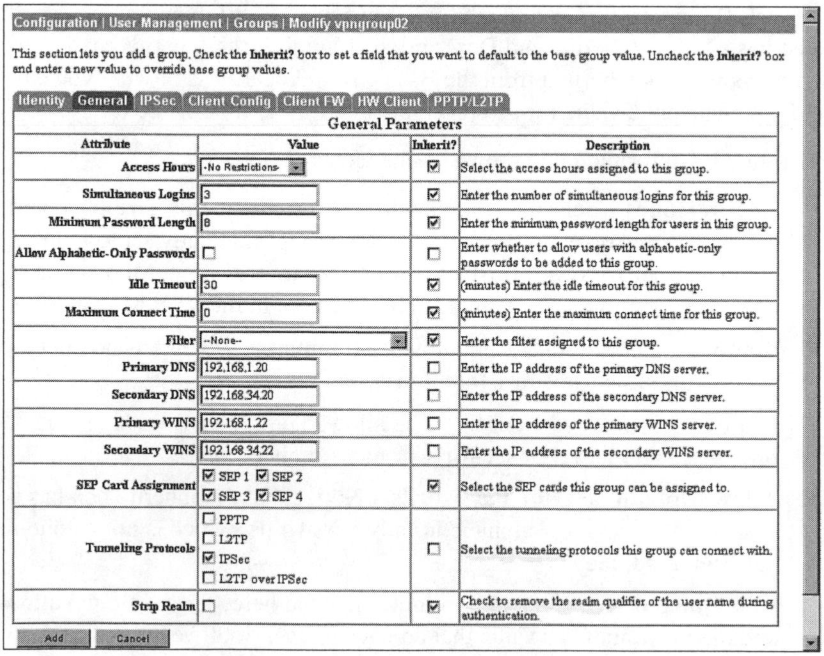

## Modify Groups—IPSec Tab

Clicking the IPSec tab brings up the screen shown in Figure 4-22. The attributes on this screen are as follows:

- **IPSec SA**—For remote access clients, you must select an IPSec Security Association (SA) from this list of available combinations. If you have created additional SA types, those are also displayed here as selection options. The client and server negotiate an SA that governs authentication, encryption, encapsulation, key management, and so on based on your selection here.

  The following are the default selections supplied by the VPN concentrator:

  — **None**—No SA is assigned.

  — **ESP-DES-MD5**—This SA uses DES 56-bit data encryption for both the IKE tunnel and IPSec traffic, ESP/MD5/HMAC-128 authentication for IPSec traffic, and MD5/HMAC-128 authentication for the IKE tunnel.

  — **ESP-3DES-MD5**—This SA uses Triple-DES 168-bit data encryption and ESP/MD5/HMAC-128 authentication for IPSec traffic, and DES-56 encryption and MD5/HMAC-128 authentication for the IKE tunnel.

  — **ESP/IKE-3DES-MD5**—This SA uses Triple-DES 168-bit data encryption for both the IKE tunnel and IPSec traffic, ESP/MD5/HMAC-128 authentication for IPSec traffic, and MD5/HMAC-128 authentication for the IKE tunnel.

  — **ESP-3DES-NONE**—This SA uses Triple-DES 168-bit data encryption and no authentication for IPSec traffic, and DES-56 encryption and MD5/HMAC-128 authentication for the IKE tunnel.

  — **ESP-L2TP-TRANSPORT**—This SA uses DES 56-bit data encryption and ESP/MD5/HMAC-128 authentication for IPSec traffic (with ESP applied only to the transport layer segment), and it uses Triple-DES 168-bit data encryption and MD5/HMAC-128 for the IKE tunnel. Use this SA with the L2TP over IPSec tunneling protocol.

  — **ESP-3DES-MD5-DH7**—This SA uses Triple-DES 168-bit data encryption and ESP/MD5/HMAC-128 authentication for both IPSec traffic and the IKE tunnel. It uses Diffie-Hellman Group 7 (ECC) to negotiate Perfect Forward Secrecy. This option is intended for use with the movianVPN client, but you can use it with other clients that support D-H Group 7 (ECC).

- **IKE Peer Identity Validation**—This option applies only to VPN tunnel negotiation based on certificates. This field enables you to hold clients to tighter security requirements.

- **IKE Keepalives**—Monitors the continued presence of a remote peer and notifies the remote peer that the concentrator is still active. If a peer no longer responds to the keepalives, the concentrator drops the connection, preventing hung connections that could clutter the concentrator.

- **Tunnel Type**—You can select either LAN-to-LAN or Remote Access as the tunnel type. If you select LAN-to-LAN, you do not need to complete the remainder of this screen.

- **Group Lock**—Checking this field forces the user to be a member of this group when authenticating to the concentrator.

- **Authentication**—This field selects the method of user authentication to use. The available options are as follows:

  - **None**—No user authentication occurs. Use this with L2TP over IPSec.

  - **RADIUS**—Uses an external RADIUS server for authentication. The server address is configured elsewhere.

  - **RADIUS with Expiry**—Uses an external RADIUS server for authentication. If the user's password has expired, this method gives the user the opportunity to create a new password.

  - **NT Domain**—Uses an external Windows NT Domain system for user authentication.

  - **SDI**—Uses an external RSA Security, Inc., SecurID system for user authentication.

  - **Internal**—Uses the internal VPN concentrator authentication server for user authentication.

- **IPComp**—This option permits the use of the Lempel Zif Stac (LZS) compression algorithm for IP traffic developed by Stac Electronics. This can speed connections for users connecting through low-speed dial-up circuits.

- **Reauthentication on Rekey**—During IKE phase 1, the VPN concentrator prompts the user to enter an ID and password. When you enable reauthentication, the concentrator prompts for user authentication whenever a rekey occurs, such as when the IKE SA lifetime expires. If the SA lifetime is set too short, this could be an annoyance to your users, but it provides an additional layer of security.

- **Mode Configuration**—During SA negotiations, this option permits the exchange of configuration parameters with the client. To pass configuration information to the client, such as DNS or WINS addresses, you must enable this option. If you check this box, you need to continue to the Mode Config tab to complete the selection of attributes there.

**Figure 4-22**  *Configuration | User Management | Groups | Modify > IPSec*

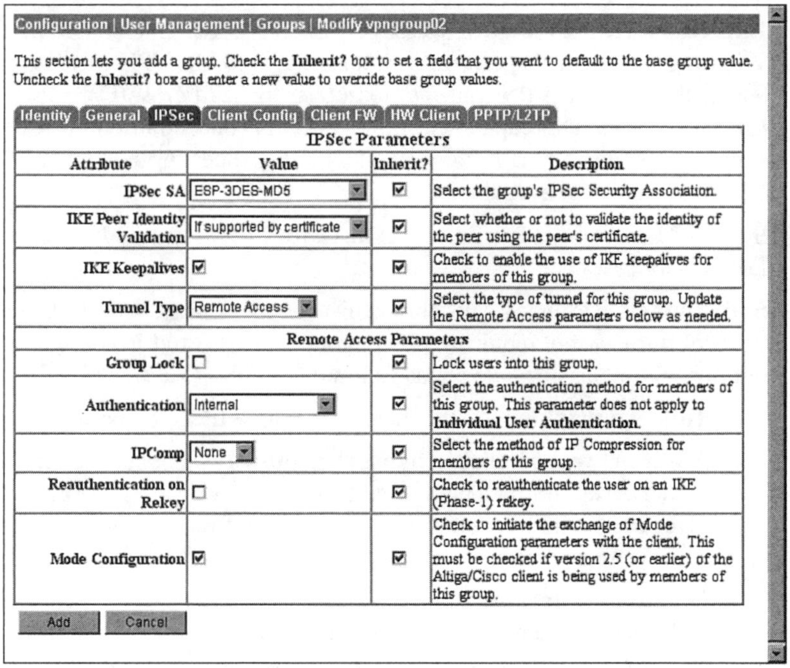

## Modify Groups—Client Config Tab

The Client Config tab screen is shown in Figure 4-23. Configuration of the attributes on this screen is only necessary if you selected Mode Configuration from the IPSec tab screen. The attributes on this page have the following meanings:

- **Banner**—You can enter up to a 510-character greeting banner that is displayed to IPSec software clients each time they log in to the system.

- **Allow Password Storage on Client**—This option allows the client PC to store the user's password. For security reasons, this is not a good policy. The default is to have this capability disabled.

- **IPSec over UDP**—This option permits clients to connect to the VPN concentrator via UDP through a firewall or router using NAT.

- **IPSec over UDP Port**—This attribute lets you set the port to use through the firewall. The default is 10,000.

- **IPSec Backup Servers**—This attribute is used on Cisco VPN 3002 Hardware Clients and is not required for remote access users.

- **Intercept DHCP Configure Message**—Enable DHCP intercept to permit Microsoft Windows XP clients to perform split tunneling with the VPN concentrator. When you enable this field, the VPN concentrator replies to the Microsoft Windows XP client DHCP Inform message. This capability allows the VPN concentrator to provide the client with a subnet mask, domain name, and classless static routes for the tunnel IP address when a DHCP server is not available.

- **Subnet Mask**—Enter a valid subnet mask for Microsoft Windows clients requesting DHCP services.

- **Split Tunneling Policy**—This option, disabled by default, permits clients to specify some types of traffic as not requiring IPSec protection. This traffic is sent in clear text. The options within this attribute are as follows:

  - **Tunnel everything**—All data use the secure IPSec tunnel.

  - **Allow networks in list to bypass the tunnel**—All data use the secure IPSec tunnel except for data being sent to addresses on the network list. This option gives users who have elected to tunnel all traffic the ability to access devices such as printers on their local networks without having that traffic encrypted.

  - **Only tunnel networks in list**—Uses the secure IPSec tunnel for data sent to addresses on the network list. All other traffic is sent as clear text. This option allows remote users to access public networks without requiring IPSec tunneling through the corporate network.

- **Split Tunneling Network List**—If you select the Allow networks in list to bypass the tunnel option, then this list is an exclusion list, allowing traffic to pass over the network without going through IPSec. If you select the Only tunnel networks in list option, then this list is an inclusion list that determines which traffic is handled via IPSec. You can establish these lists elsewhere in the concentrator, or you can use the VPN Client Local LAN option.

- **Default Domain Name**—If you supply a domain name here, the concentrator passes this name to the client. Fully qualified domain names sent over the IPSec tunnel have this domain name appended to the end.

- **Split DNS Names**—Enter a list of domain names that you want the VPN concentrator's internal DNS server to resolve for traffic going over the tunnel. This option is useful in split-tunneling connections, permitting the internal DNS server to resolve domain names for traffic through the tunnel. The ISP-assigned DNS servers resolve DNS requests that travel in the clear to the Internet.

**Figure 4-23**  *Configuration | User Management | Groups | Modify > Client Config*

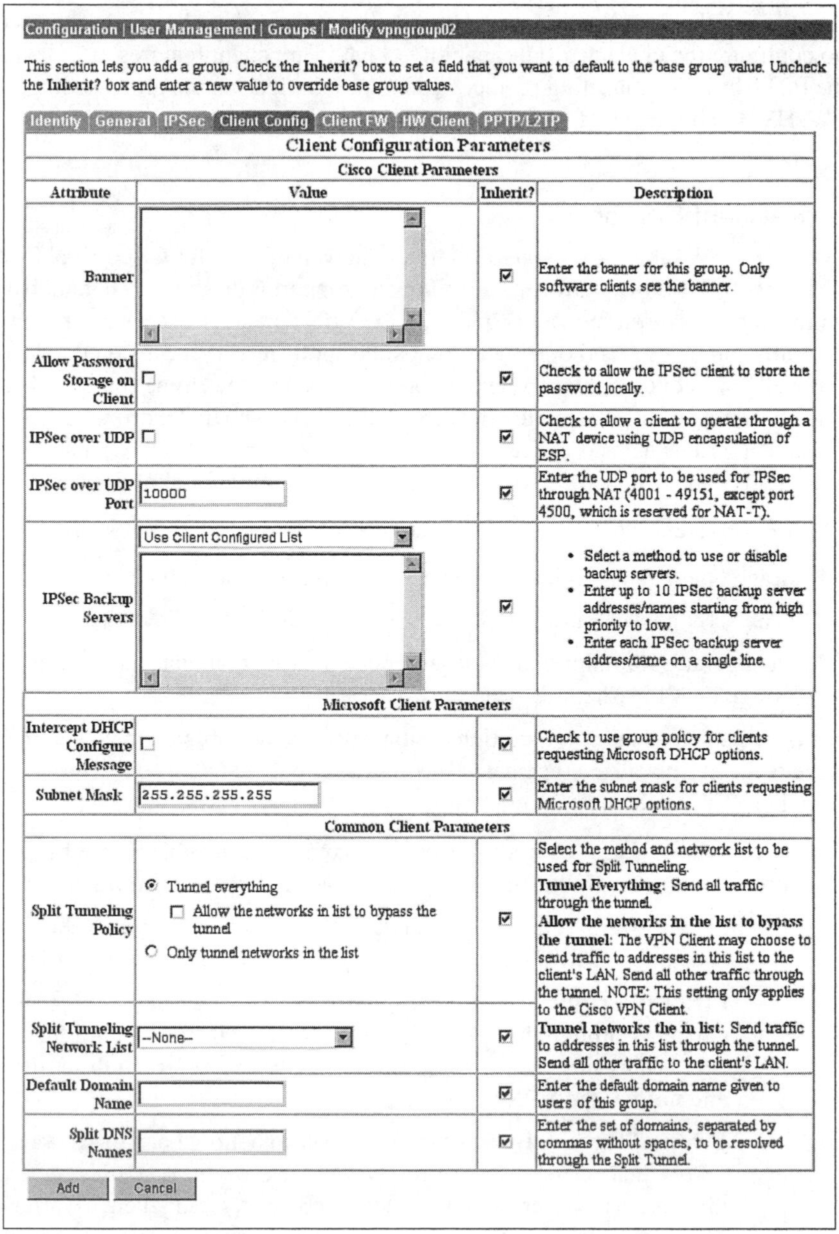

Configuration | User Management | Groups | Modify vpngroup02

This section lets you add a group. Check the **Inherit?** box to set a field that you want to default to the base group value. Uncheck the **Inherit?** box and enter a new value to override base group values.

Identity | General | IPSec | Client Config | Client FW | HW Client | PPTP/L2TP

### Client Configuration Parameters

#### Cisco Client Parameters

| Attribute | Value | Inherit? | Description |
|---|---|---|---|
| Banner | | ☑ | Enter the banner for this group. Only software clients see the banner. |
| Allow Password Storage on Client | ☐ | ☑ | Check to allow the IPSec client to store the password locally. |
| IPSec over UDP | ☐ | ☑ | Check to allow a client to operate through a NAT device using UDP encapsulation of ESP. |
| IPSec over UDP Port | 10000 | ☑ | Enter the UDP port to be used for IPSec through NAT (4001 - 49151, except port 4500, which is reserved for NAT-T). |
| IPSec Backup Servers | Use Client Configured List | ☑ | • Select a method to use or disable backup servers.<br>• Enter up to 10 IPSec backup server addresses/names starting from high priority to low.<br>• Enter each IPSec backup server address/name on a single line. |

#### Microsoft Client Parameters

| | | | |
|---|---|---|---|
| Intercept DHCP Configure Message | ☐ | ☑ | Check to use group policy for clients requesting Microsoft DHCP options. |
| Subnet Mask | 255.255.255.255 | ☑ | Enter the subnet mask for clients requesting Microsoft DHCP options. |

#### Common Client Parameters

| | | | |
|---|---|---|---|
| Split Tunneling Policy | ⦿ Tunnel everything<br>☐ Allow the networks in list to bypass the tunnel<br>◯ Only tunnel networks in the list | ☑ | Select the method and network list to be used for Split Tunneling.<br>**Tunnel Everything:** Send all traffic through the tunnel.<br>**Allow the networks in the list to bypass the tunnel:** The VPN Client may choose to send traffic to addresses in this list to the client's LAN. Send all other traffic through the tunnel. NOTE: This setting only applies to the Cisco VPN Client.<br>**Tunnel networks the in list:** Send traffic to addresses in this list through the tunnel. Send all other traffic to the client's LAN. |
| Split Tunneling Network List | --None-- | ☑ | |
| Default Domain Name | | ☑ | Enter the default domain name given to users of this group. |
| Split DNS Names | | ☑ | Enter the set of domains, separated by commas without spaces, to be resolved through the Split Tunnel. |

Add     Cancel

That is all that you need to configure on the VPN concentrator. Click the Modify button to save your work to the active configuration and return to the Groups screen shown in Figure 4-19. Be sure to click the Save Needed icon to save your configuration changes to the boot configuration. To configure the client firewall capability or hardware client features, or if you are using either the PPTP or L2TP tunneling protocols, continue configuring the group settings using the Client FW, HW Client, and PPTP/L2TP tabs discussed in the following sections.

## Modify Groups—Client FW Tab

The Client FW tab permits you to configure firewall options for Cisco VPN Clients running on a Microsoft Windows platform. Client firewall support is disabled by default but can be enabled on this tab. A stateful firewall is built into the VPN Client, but other commercially available firewalls can be used and operate as a separate application that runs on the Windows platform. Firewalls inspect each inbound and outbound packet to determine if the packet should be forwarded toward its destination or whether the packet should be dropped. These decisions are made using rules defined in firewall policies. Firewalls provide an extra measure of protection to systems and corporate networks, especially when split tunneling is used.

The VPN concentrator can support client firewalls in three different ways:

- Each client can individually manage its own personal firewall policy.
- The VPN concentrator can push a centralized firewall policy to each client.
- A separate, standalone firewall server can be used to manage and enforce firewall policy usage on VPN Client devices.

Figure 4-24 shows the configuration options that are available on the Client FW tab for these three types of firewall management. The following bulleted items discuss the options shown on the Client FW tab screen:

- **Firewall Setting**—This attribute is used to enable or disable firewall support for the users connecting through this group. The available settings are as follows:
  - **No Firewall**—This is the default setting for a new group. When this option is checked, the VPN concentrator ignores VPN Client firewall settings.
  - **Firewall Required**—When this option is checked, every VPN Client peer that connects through this group must use the firewall specified for this group. If the peer is not using the correct firewall, the VPN concentrator drops the connection and notifies the VPN Client of the mismatch.
  - **Firewall Optional**—Setting the firewall to optional can be used when all your VPN Client users are not currently running firewalls on their systems. Choosing this option lets users without firewalls connect, giving them a warning message. Those users with firewalls installed must be using the correct firewall; the VPN concentrator and VPN Client then manage the firewall policy according to the settings contained on this Client FW tab.

- **Firewall**—Select the firewall that members of the group are to use. The available options are as follows:

    - **Cisco Integrated Client Firewall**—The stateful firewall built into the VPN Client.

    - **Network ICE BlackICE Defender**—The Network ICE BlackICE Agent or Defender personal firewall.

    - **Zone Labs ZoneAlarm**—The Zone Labs ZoneAlarm personal firewall.

    - **Zone Labs ZoneAlarm Pro**—The Zone Labs ZoneAlarm Pro personal firewall.

    - **Zone Labs ZoneAlarm or ZoneAlarm Pro**—Either the Zone Labs Zone-Alarm personal firewall or the Zone Labs ZoneAlarm Pro personal firewall.

    - **Zone Labs Integrity**—The Zone Labs Integrity Client.

    - **Custom Firewall**—This option is primarily for future use. Choose this option when you cannot use any of the previous options or when you want to combine two or more of these options. When you choose this option, you must detail your firewall selection(s) in the Custom Firewall attribute settings.

- **Custom Firewall**—All the supported options are currently selectable from the list available in the Firewall attribute setting. In the future, additional options might be available. At that time, you could use this section to identify those new firewalls.

    - **Vendor ID**—You can only enter one vendor ID code in this field. Currently, the available vendor codes are Cisco Systems (Vendor ID 1), Zone Labs (Vendor ID 2), and Network ICE (Vendor ID 3).

    - **Product ID**—For the vendor selected, you can enter multiple product ID codes in this field. When entering multiple code numbers, separate them with a comma or use a hyphen to designate a range, such as 1-3 for Zone Labs. To use all available products for a given vendor, enter 255 as the Product ID. Table 4-3 shows the current product codes.

**Table 4-3**    *Custom Firewall Product Codes*

| Vendor | Product | Product Code |
|---|---|---|
| Cisco | Cisco Integrated Client (CIC) | 1 |
| Zone Labs | Zone Alarm | 1 |
|  | Zone Alarm Pro | 2 |
|  | Zone Labs Integrity | 3 |
| Network ICE | BlackIce Defender/Agent | 1 |

    - **Description**—You can enter an optional description for your custom firewall in this field.

- **Firewall Policy**—You can select from three different methods for administering the firewall policy for your VPN Client systems. Those methods are as follows:

  - **Policy Defined by Remote Firewall (AYT)**—The user of the VPN Client system has established firewall policy settings for a personalized firewall that runs on the user's system. That firewall can be a third-party firewall that works with the Cisco VPN Client and VPN concentrator. The VPN Client uses the Are You There (AYT) enforcement mechanism to periodically poll the firewall. If the firewall doesn't respond to the periodic "Are you there?" messages, the VPN Client drops the connection to the VPN concentrator. A system administrator can initially configure and install the firewall for these users, but each user is allowed to configure his or her own policies beyond the initial settings. This option is available for use with the Network ICE BlackIce Defender, Zone Labs ZoneAlarm, and Zone Labs ZoneAlarm Pro firewall products.

  - **Policy Pushed (CPP)**—When a corporation's security policy mandates that all VPN Clients use the same firewall policy, the system administrator can configure the VPN concentrator to push a centralized, standardized firewall policy to each VPN Client, which then passes the policy on to the local firewall for enforcement. The administrator creates a set of traffic management rules on the VPN concentrator, associates the rules with a filter, and designates the filter as the firewall policy from the drop-down window for this attribute. This type of firewall policy management is called *push policy* or *Central Protection Policy (CPP)*. This option is available for use with the Cisco Integrated Client Firewall, Zone Labs ZoneAlarm, and Zone Labs ZoneAlarm Pro firewall products.

  - **Policy from Server**—You can use the Zone Labs Integrity Server (IS), a standalone firewall server, to manage firewall policy management and enforcement through the VPN Client. A centralized firewall policy is maintained on the IS. The IS then pushes this policy to each monitored VPN Client host and then monitors the use of the policy on those hosts. The Zone Labs IS also communicates with the VPN concentrator to manage connections and share session, user, and status information. This option is only available for the Zone Labs Integrity Server firewall product.

## Modify Groups—HW Client Tab

Cisco VPN 3002 Hardware Clients provide additional authentication capabilities for peer and user authentication. The VPN 3002 Hardware Client communicates with the VPN concentrator to establish the tunnel and the user systems connect to the hardware client via Ethernet connections. The user systems do not require the VPN Client.

**Figure 4-24**  *Configuration | User Management | Groups | Modify > Client FW*

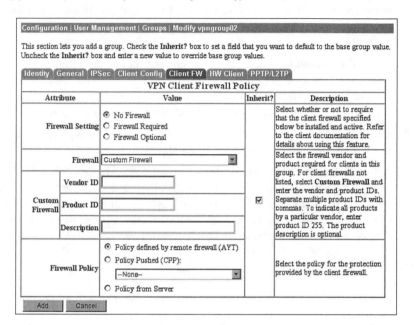

When you configure the VPN 3002 Hardware Client for the IPSec tunneling protocol, you enter the IPSec group name and password that you configured on the VPN concentrator onto the Configuration | System | Tunneling Protocols | IPSec screen of the VPN 3002 Hardware Client. You must also enter a single username and password on that same screen, which are used to establish user authentication for all users connected to the VPN 3002 Hardware Client. Both the group name and username must be valid to establish the IPSec tunnel. Once the VPN 3002 Hardware Client and the VPN concentrator have established the VPN tunnel, any users connected to the hardware client can use the secure tunnel.

To provide additional security, you can enable interactive authentication for the establishment of the IPSec tunnel and for interactive user authentication. The HW Client tab, shown in Figure 4-25, permits you to enable the following authentication features:

- **Require Interactive Hardware Client Authentication**—When this field is checked, the username and password that were configured on the VPN 3002 Hardware Client are ignored. The first user connected to the VPN 3002 Hardware Client that wants to begin using secure IPSec communications is prompted to enter a valid username and password. The method of authentication was selected earlier on the group's IPSec tab. Once the initial user establishes the IPSec tunnel, no other users are prompted for the tunnel authentication username and password.

- **Require Individual User Authentication**—You can also require all other users connected to the VPN 3002 Hardware Client to authenticate before using the IPSec tunnel by checking this attribute box. Each user is prompted for a username and password and is authenticated using whatever method the IPSec group requires.

- **User Idle Timeout**—The default idle timeout for a user's connection is 30 minutes. The smallest idle timeout period you can use is 1 minute. You can enter 0 to tell the concentrator to never drop an idle connection. When a user's connection has been idle for the period of time specified by the idle timeout period, the concentrator drops the connection.

- **Cisco IP Phone Bypass**—Checking this field tells the VPN concentrator not to negotiate individual user authentication for IP phones.

- **Allow Network Extension Mode**—You can configure the VPN 3000 Concentrator to support Network Extension mode with VPN 3002 Hardware Clients in site-to-site networks by checking this field. The VPN 3002 Hardware Client must also be configured to support network extension mode, or the two devices can never connect to one another. The default connection mode is Port Address Translation (PAT).

**Figure 4-25** *Configuration | User Management | Groups | Modify > HW Client*

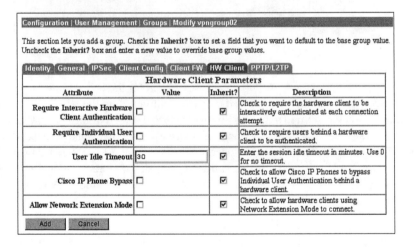

## Modify Groups—PPTP/L2TP Tab

If you selected PPTP, L2TP, or L2TP over IPSec as an allowable tunneling protocol to be used for VPN connections, you might need to make adjustments to the attributes displayed on the PPTP/L2TP Tab, shown in Figure 4-26. Client and VPN concentrator settings must match during VPN tunnel negotiations, or the tunnel is not established. The following attributes are shown on this screen:

- **Use Client Address**—You can allow clients to supply their own address for the client end of the VPN tunnel. This is not a good idea from a security perspective, so be careful about enabling this capability. The default mode for this attribute is disabled, forcing the VPN concentrator to supply the address through one of the various means available to the concentrator.

- **PPTP Authentication Protocols**—During tunnel negotiation, prospective peers generally authenticate one another through some mechanism. By checking none of the available options, you can permit the tunnel to be negotiated with no authentication, but you should only use that for test purposes. The available authentication protocols are as follows:
  - **PAP**—The Password Authentication Protocol (PAP) passes the username and password in clear text and is therefore not secure. Although this is the default setting, it is not a recommended choice for a secure environment. PAP does not provide data encryption.
  - **CHAP**—The Challenge-Handshake Authentication Protocol (CHAP) is also permitted by default, but is also not particularly secure. In response to a challenge from the server, the client encrypts the challenge plus password and returns that to the server along with the clear text username. CHAP does not provide data encryption.
  - **MSCHAPv1**—The Microsoft Challenge-Handshake Authentication Protocol version 1 (MSCHAPv1) is more secure than CHAP because the server only stores and compares encrypted passwords. MSCHAPv1 can encrypt data using the Microsoft Point-to-Point Encryption (MPPE) Protocol.
  - **MSCHAPv2**—The Microsoft Challenge-Handshake Authentication Protocol version 2 (MSCHAPv2) is a step up from MSCHAPv1 because it requires mutual client-server authentication. MPPE can also be used here for data encryption using keys that are unique for each session. MSCHAPv2 also uses different keys for the send and receive functions.
  - **EAP Proxy**—The Extensible Authentication Protocol (EAP) Proxy lets the VPN concentrator offload the authentication process to an external RADIUS server, providing additional authentication services such as EAP/MD5, Smartcards and certificates (EAP/TLS), and RSA SecurID (EAP/SDI). EAP Proxy does not support encryption.
- **PPTP Encryption**—Select the type of PPTP encryption that you want to use from these options:
  - **Required**—If you select this option, clients must use MPPE encryption. This means that you can only select MSCHAPv1 and MSCHAPv2 as the allowable authentication protocols when using this option. You must also select either 40-bit and/or 128-bit encryption in this category.
  - **Require Stateless**—Under this encryption scheme, the encryption key is changed with each packet transferred.

- **40-bit**—Clients can use the RSA RC4 encryption algorithm using a 40-bit key when this option is checked.

- **128-bit**—Clients can use the RSA RC4 encryption algorithm using a 128-bit key when this option is checked.

- **PPTP Compression**—If many of your clients connect via dial-up connections, you might want to enable PPTP compression to decrease the amount of data being transferred. If you enable compression, the Microsoft Point-to-Point Compression (MPPC) algorithm is used.

- **L2TP Authentication Protocols**—L2TP authentication protocol options are the same as the PPTP options previously discussed.

- **L2TP Encryption**—L2TP encryption options are the same as the PPTP options previously discussed.

- **L2TP Compression**—L2TP compression options are the same as the PPTP options previously discussed.

**Figure 4-26** *Configuration | User Management | Groups | Modify > PPTP/L2TP*

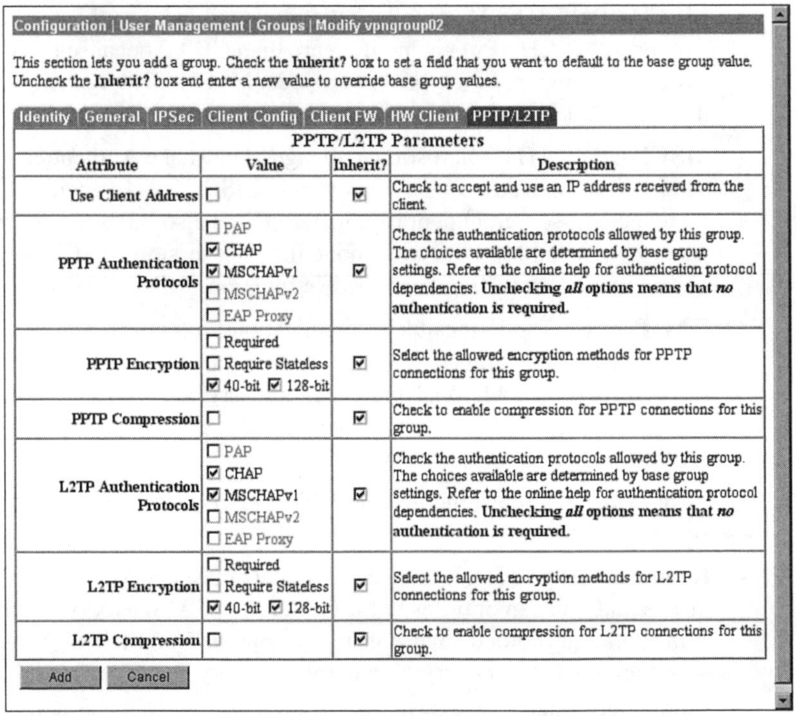

# Advanced Configuration of the VPN Concentrator

The previous sections of this chapter looked at a small part of the Configuration portion of the VPN Manager. There is much more to the Manager than installing groups, users, or system identification. This section looks at the other aspects of the Configuration portion of the VPN Manager.

## Configuration | System

The functions that fall under the Configuration | System section have to do with configuring parameters for system-wide functions in the VPN concentrator. The following subcategories under System let you control the VPN concentrator:

- Configuration | System | Servers
- Configuration | System | Address Management
- Configuration | System | Tunneling Protocols
- Configuration | System | IP Routing
- Configuration | System | Management Protocols
- Configuration | System | Events
- Configuration | System | General
- Configuration | System | Client Update
- Configuration | System | Load Balancing Cisco VPN Clients
- Configuration | User Management
- Configuration | Policy Management

The following sections describe each subcategory in more detail.

### Configuration | System | Servers

The Configuration | System | Servers section of the VPN Manager allows you to configure the various types of servers that communicate with the concentrator. Those servers include the following:

- **Authentication Servers**—Used for user authentication
- **Accounting Servers**—Used for RADIUS user accounting
- **DNS Servers**—Domain Name System address lookup functions
- **DHCP Servers**—Dynamic Host Configuration Protocol to assign IP addresses for client connections
- **Firewall Servers**—Firewall enforcement by means of the Zone Labs Integrity Server

- **NTP Servers**—Network Time Protocol to ensure that all systems use the same time for ease of synchronizing log entries
- **Internal Authentication**—Used for user authentication

## Configuration | System | Address Management

When an IPSec tunnel is established between a VPN concentrator and client, a new set of IP addresses is required to identify the endpoints of the tunnel. This section of the VPN Manager allows you to define how these addresses are managed.

The Assignment portion of Address Management allows you to select the methods that can be used to assign addresses. Quick Configuration used this portion as part of its setup steps.

The Pools portion of Address Management allows you to define a pool of internal addresses that the concentrator draws from when assigning addresses to clients.

## Configuration | System | Tunneling Protocols

Cisco VPN 3000 Concentrators are capable of establishing tunnels using the three most popular VPN tunneling protocols:

- PPTP
- L2TP
- IPSec

To provide support for the Microsoft Windows 2000 VPN client, the VPN concentrators also support L2TP over IPSec.

This section of the VPN Manager allows you to configure the parameters that are associated with each of these protocols.

## Configuration | System | IP Routing

Cisco VPN 3000 Concentrators have the ability to act as routers for IP traffic. This allows the concentrator to communicate with other routers in the network to determine the best path for traffic to take. This section of the VPN Manager allows you to configure the following:

- **Static Routes**—Manually configured routing tables
- **Default Gateways**—Routes for traffic for which routes cannot be determined
- **OSPF**—Open Shortest Path First routing protocol
- **OSPF Areas**—Subnet areas within the OSPF domain
- **DHCP**—Dynamic Host Configuration Protocol global parameters

- **Redundancy**—Virtual Router Redundancy Protocol parameters
- **Reverse Route Injection**—Reverse Route Injection global parameters

Routing Information Protocol (RIP) and interface-specific OSPF parameters are configured on the network interfaces. You access the interfaces to make those configurations through the Configuration I Interfaces screen.

## Configuration I System I Management Protocols

The Configuration I System I Management Protocols portion of the VPN Manager allows you to control various management protocols and servers. These utilities can be an asset to you in managing your total network. Those management protocols are as follows:

- **FTP**—File Transfer Protocol
- **HTTP/HTTPS**—Hypertext Transfer Protocol and HTTP over SSL (Secure Sockets Layer) protocol
- **TFTP**—Trivial File Transfer Protocol
- **Telnet**—Terminal emulation protocol and Telnet over SSL
- **SNMP**—Simple Network Management Protocol
- **SNMP Community Strings**—Identifiers for valid SNMP clients
- **SSL**—Secure Sockets Layer Protocol
- **SSH**—Secure Shell
- **XML**—Extensible Markup Language

## Configuration I System I Events

Significant occurrences within or that could affect a VPN 3000 Concentrator are classified as events. Typical events include alarms, traps, error conditions, network problems, task completions, breaches of threshold levels, and status changes. Events are stored in an event log in nonvolatile memory. Events can also be sent to a backup server via FTP or to Syslog servers. Events can be identified to trigger console messages, send e-mail messages, or send SNMP system traps.

Event attributes include class and severity level, as follows:

- **Event Class**—Specifies the source of the event and refers to a specific hardware or software subsystem within the VPN concentrator.
- **Event Severity Level**—Indicates how serious or significant the event is. Level 1 is the most significant.

## Configuration | System | General

The General section of the VPN Manager enables you to configure these general VPN concentrator parameters:

- **Identification**—System name, contact person, system location
- **Time and Date**—System time and date
- **Sessions**—The maximum number of sessions
- **Authentication**—General authentication parameters

## Configuration | System | Client Update

You can configure the Cisco VPN 3000 Concentrators to manage client updates for VPN Client and VPN 3002 Hardware Clients. In the case of the software clients, the concentrator notifies the clients of the acceptable client versions and provides the location where the appropriate versions can be obtained. For VPN 3002 Hardware Clients, the concentrator pushes the correct version to the client via TFTP.

This section of the VPN 3000 Concentrator Manager lets you configure the client update feature, as follows:

- **Enable**—Enables or disables client update
- **Entries**—Configures updates by client type, acceptable firmware and software versions, and their locations

## Configuration | System | Load Balancing Cisco VPN Clients

When you have two or more VPN 3000 Concentrators on the same subnet handling remote access VPN services, you can group those devices together to perform load balancing across the devices. The private and public subnets are grouped into a virtual cluster. One of the concentrators acts as the cluster master and directs incoming calls to the device that has the smallest load, including itself. If, for any reason, the master fails, one of the other concentrators in the cluster takes over the role.

Clients first connect to the virtual IP address of the cluster. The cluster master intercepts the call and sends the client the public IP address of the least-loaded available concentrator. The client then uses that IP address to initiate the VPN tunnel with the concentrator. If a concentrator in the cluster fails, the terminated clients immediately try to reconnect with the virtual IP, and the cluster master reassigns them to available devices.

After you have made certain that the public and private interfaces have been fully configured and are operational, you use this section of the VPN 3000 Concentrator Manager to define the load-sharing cluster.

## Configuration | User Management

Configuration | User Management is the section that you used in the "Configuring IPSec with Preshared Keys Through the VPN 3000 Concentrator Series Manager" section of this chapter to configure the group for remote access with preshared keys. In addition to working with specific groups, this section is used to configure the Base Group and to manage user accounts for the internal authentication database.

With the default settings, new groups inherit the attributes of the Base Group. Those attributes can be individually overridden for each group so that you can have a variety of groups with different properties. You could have a group using L2TP, one using IPSec with preshared keys, another using IPSec with digital certificates, another using RADIUS for user authentication, and still another using the concentrator's internal database for user authentication.

If you are using the concentrator for internal authentication and have defined your groups, this section of the VPN Manager also allows you to create and manage user accounts. User accounts inherit the attributes of their group, and user accounts can only belong to one group. If you do not explicitly assign a user account to a group, it inherits the attributes of the Base Group.

## Configuration | Policy Management

Policies control the actions of users as they connect to the VPN concentrator. User management determines which users are allowed to use the device. Policy management determines when users can connect, from where they can connect, and what kind of data are permitted in the tunnels. The section of the VPN Manager established filters that determine whether to forward or drop packets and whether to pass the traffic through a tunnel or to send it in the clear. Filters are applied to interfaces, groups, and users.

The Policy Management section contains the following sections:

- **Access Hours**—Establishes when remote users can access the VPN concentrator.
- **Traffic Management**—Controls what data traffic can flow through the VPN concentrator. Traffic Management is further divided into the following configuration sections:
  - **Network Lists**—Allows you to group lists of networks together as single objects.
  - **Rules**—Provides detailed parameters that let you specify the handling of data packets.
  - **SAs**—Lets you choose the options to be used in establishing IPSec Security Associations. This is where you set the authentication, encryption, encapsulation, and SA lifetime. You can modify predefined SAs or create your own.
  - **Filters**—Lets you combine the network lists, rules, and SAs into single packages that you can then apply to interfaces, groups, and users.
  - **NAT**—The Cisco VPN 3000 Concentrators can perform Network Address Translation, which you would configure in this section.

# Installing and Configuring the VPN Client

| 14 | Configuring the IPSec Windows Client |

The Cisco VPN Client is packaged with every VPN concentrator sold by Cisco. The VPN Client can be installed on several different operating systems, including Linux, Sun Solaris, Apple MAC OS X, and Microsoft Windows. This section looks at the Microsoft Windows version of the VPN Client.

The following topics are covered in this section:

- Overview of the VPN Client
- VPN Client features
- VPN Client installation
- VPN Client configuration

## Overview of the VPN Client

The Microsoft Windows version of the VPN Client runs on Windows 95, 98, 98 SE, Me, NT, 2000, and XP platforms. The client is designed to work as a remote access client connecting through a secure data tunnel to an enterprise network over the Internet. This permits remote users to access the services of a private network as though the users were attached directly to the network, with the security of encrypted communications between the client and the host.

To use the VPN Client after it has been installed, the user first connects to the Internet and then starts the VPN Client to negotiate a tunnel with the VPN host. For remote access services, that host is most commonly a VPN concentrator, but it could be a router or firewall, or some other network device.

To start the VPN Client from a Windows-based PC, select **Start**, **Programs**, **Cisco Systems VPN Client**, and then select one of the following programs:

- **Certificate Manager**—Manage digital certificates for the client to be used when authenticating with VPN devices.
- **Help**—View the complete online manual with full instructions on using the VPN Client application.
- **Log Viewer**—View events from the log file.
- **Set MTU**—Control the maximum transmission unit (MTU) size that the VPN Client is to use to communicate with the host.

- **Uninstall VPN Client**—Uninstall the application. You can choose to retain connection and certificate information.

- **VPN Dialer**—Manage connection information and start a connection with a VPN host device. This poorly named function is the main functional area of the VPN Client.

You can use the VPN Client with dial-up, ISDN, cable, or DSL modems as well as with direct LAN connections. How you get to the Internet does not matter to the VPN Client. The only requirement is that the client device can "see" the host device using TCP/IP.

# VPN Client Features

The VPN Client is a feature-packed application. Most of the functions of the client are handled automatically and require little configuration. This section describes the important features of the Cisco VPN Client.

Program features include the following:

- Browser-based, context-sensitive HTML help

- VPN 3000 Series Concentrator support

- Command-line interface to the VPN Dialer application

- Access to local LAN resources while connected through a secure VPN

- Automatic VPN Client configuration option

- Log Viewer application to collect, view, and analyze events

- Ability to set the MTU size

- Application launcher

- Automatic connection via Microsoft Dial-Up Networking and other third-party dialers

- Software update notifications from the connecting VPN device

- Launch software update site from update notification

NT features include the following:

- Password expiration information from RADIUS authentication servers

- Start Before Logon, providing the ability to establish a VPN connection before logging on to a Windows NT platform

- Automatic disconnect disable when logging off to allow for roaming profile synchronization

IPSec features include the following:

- IPSec tunneling protocol

- Transparent tunneling

- IKE key management protocol

- IKE keepalives
- Split tunneling
- LZS data compression

Authentication features include the following:

- User authentication via the following:
  - VPN concentrator internal database
  - RADIUS
  - NT Domain (Windows NT)
  - RSA (formerly SDI) SecurID or SoftID
- Certificate Manager to manage client identity certificates
- Ability to use Entrust Entelligence certificates
- Ability to authenticate using smart cards with certificates

Firewall features include the following:

- Support for Cisco Secure PIX Firewall platforms
- Support for the following personal firewalls:
  - Cisco Integrated Firewall (CIF)
  - ZoneAlarmPro 2.6.3.57
  - ZoneAlarm 2.6.3.57
  - BlackIce Agent and BlackIce Defender 2.5
- Centralized Protection Policy provides support for firewall policies pushed to the VPN Client from the VPN 3000 Concentrator.

VPN Client IPSec attributes include the following:

- Main and aggressive modes for negotiating phase 1 of establishing ISAKMP Security Associations
- Authentication algorithms:
  - HMAC (Hashed Message Authentication Coding) with MD5 (Message Digest 5) hash function
  - HMAC with SHA-1 (Secure Hash Algorithm) hash function
- Authentication modes:
  - Preshared keys
  - X.509 Digital Certificates
- Diffie-Hellman Groups 1, 2, and 5

- Encryption algorithms:
  - 56-bit DES
  - 168-bit Triple-DES
- Extended Authentication (XAUTH)
- Mode Configuration (also known as ISAKMP Configuration Method)
- Tunnel Encapsulation Mode
- IP compression (IPCOMP) using LZS

## VPN Client Installation

Installing the VPN Client is a simple task. System requirements call for 10 MB of hard drive space and up to 64 MB of RAM for Windows 2000 systems. Once you have confirmed those requirements, simply insert the Cisco VPN Client CD-ROM into the system and allow the Autorun program to start, as shown in Figure 4-27.

**Figure 4-27**  *Cisco VPN Client Autorun*

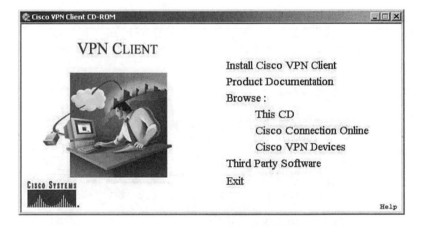

Click the option to **Install Cisco VPN Client**. The system might respond with a message like the one shown in Figure 4-28, stating that the installer needs to disable the IPSec Policy Agent. Simply click the **Yes** button to continue the installation process.

**Figure 4-28**  *Initial Warning Message*

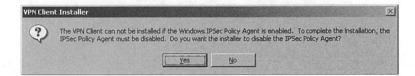

The Welcome screen appears, as shown in Figure 4-29. Click **Next** to continue.

**Figure 4-29** *VPN Client Install Setup Welcome*

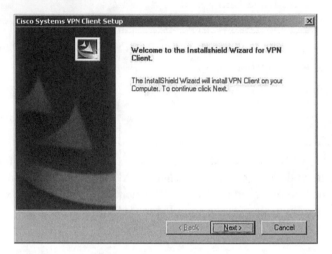

Figure 4-30 shows the next screen to be displayed, the license agreement screen. Scroll down through the agreement, and then click **Yes** to continue if you agree to the terms of the license agreement.

**Figure 4-30** *VPN Client License Agreement*

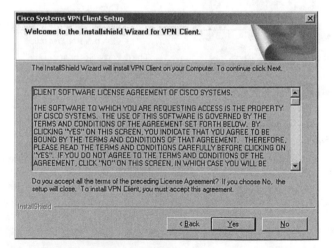

The file location screen is displayed, as shown in Figure 4-31. To accept the default location, click **Next**. If not, click **Browse** to select the folder where the installation wizard is to install the client application.

**Figure 4-31**  *VPN Client Install File Location*

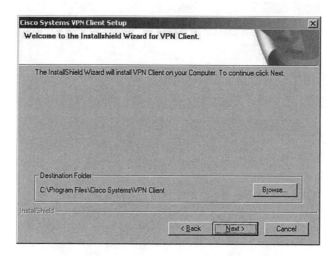

The next screen to be displayed, shown in Figure 4-32, asks you to select the Windows folder for the application. Click **Next** to accept the default, or select another location for the application.

**Figure 4-32**  *VPN Client Install Windows Folder Selection*

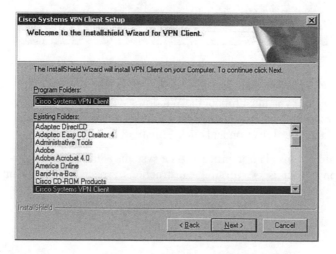

The installation wizard then copies the files from the CD to your system, as shown in Figure 4-33. This portion of the installation takes less than a minute.

**Figure 4-33**  *Cisco VPN Client Installation*

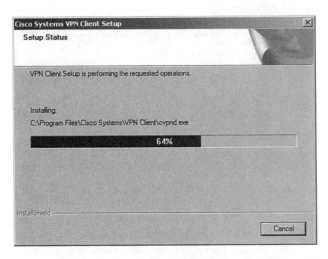

The installation wizard then updates the Windows Registry settings. While it does this, the wizard presents the message shown in Figure 4-34. While the message indicates that it can take several minutes, the wizard is, in fact, fast in accomplishing this task.

**Figure 4-34**  *VPN Client Install Network Settings*

The final screen of the installation process is shown in Figure 4-35. After the installation has been completed, you must reboot the Windows system. The completion screen gives you the option of rebooting when you click the Finish button or waiting until a later time to restart the system. Make your selection and click **Finish**.

This is a simple installation process. As a systems administrator, you could provide the application to your users with simple instructions, especially if you want them to use the default settings.

**Figure 4-35**  *VPN Client Installation Complete*

## VPN Client Configuration

The configuration process is almost as easy as the installation process. The user must enter several pieces of information. Your installation instructions should provide all the entries that your users must make.

To start the configuration process, start the VPN Client application. From the Windows Desktop, choose **Start**, **Programs**, **Cisco Systems VPN Client** to display the Option menu shown in Figure 4-36. The next step is not self-evident. To start the client, click the **VPN Dialer** menu option.

**Figure 4-36**  *Starting the Cisco VPN Client*

Figure 4-37 shows the main interface screen for the VPN Client. Notice that the Connection Entry window is blank, indicating that you have not yet configured the connection information. The Connect button is also grayed out and stays that way until you have a valid connection defined. Create the first connection entry; click **New** to begin that process.

**Figure 4-37**  *Connection Entry Screen*

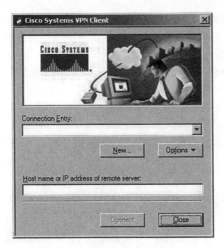

The first screen of the creation process is shown in Figure 4-38. On this screen, you identify the connection by supplying a name and a brief description. The screen is initially blank. The name **CorpConnect** and the description **Connection to the Corporate Network via VPN** were added to describe the connection. Try to make the name fairly descriptive because it is used to make the connection. After you have entered a name and description, click **Next**.

**Figure 4-38**  *Create New Connection*

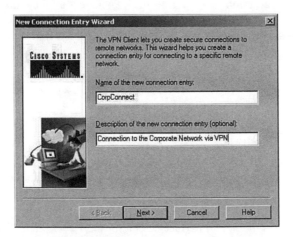

Figure 4-39 shows the next screen to be displayed. This screen asks you to identify the VPN server to which you will be connecting. In this case, you are connecting to the VPN 3000 Concentrator that you configured in the "Configuring IPSec with Preshared Keys Through the

VPN 3000 Concentrator Series Manager" section of this chapter. Enter either the IP address of the device or the fully qualified domain name (FQDN), if you know it. The public IP address of the VPN concentrator is required, so enter 172.16.1.3 to reach the concentrator you configured earlier. Click **Next** after you have identified the host server.

**Figure 4-39**  *New Connection Address*

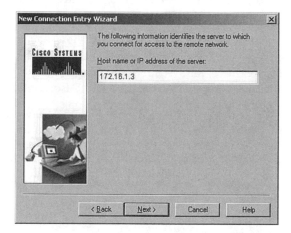

Because you have not yet installed any digital certificates onto your PC, the next screen presents only one option to use for authenticating the IPSec connection. In Figure 4-40 you can see that the Certificate option is grayed out. To configure the client to use a preshared key for the IPSec connection, simply enter the IPSec group name and password in the appropriate fields of the Group Access Information section.

**Figure 4-40**  *Entering the Preshared Key*

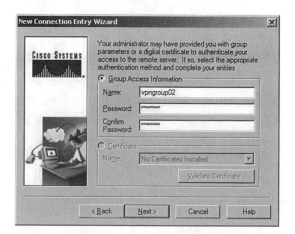

The group name that you established earlier was **vpngroup02**. Enter that in the Name field and the associated password into the Password and Confirm Password fields. The password for the IPSec group is the preshared key for the IPSec connection authentication. Click **Next** to continue.

That's all there is to it. Figure 4-41 shows that the new VPN connection, CorpConnect, has been successfully created. Notice that you did not enter any IKE or IPSec configuration information. Those values are pushed from the VPN concentrator during the initial connection.

Because anyone with the VPN Client and the correct group name and password can now create a secure connection to your VPN 3000 Concentrator, you can see how important the group password is to the security of the system. Be sure to use a strong password for this purpose, and exercise strict control over issuing the password. Also, consider changing the password frequently, even though your user community might object.

Click **Finish** to complete the creation process.

**Figure 4-41** *New Connection Complete*

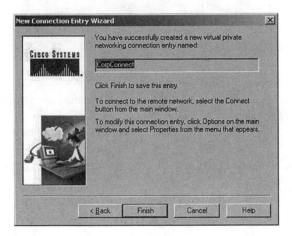

Clicking Finish returns you to the main VPN Client window, shown in Figure 4-42. Notice that CorpConnect now shows in the Connection Entry window and the IP address of the remote server shows in the lower window. Also notice that the Connect button is now active.

If you had additional connections defined to different servers or for different purposes (for example, stricter security), you could access those other connections by clicking the arrow to open the drop-down menu.

**Figure 4-42**  *Using the New VPN Connection*

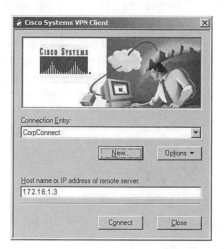

To connect to the VPN 3000 Concentrator, simply click the Connect button. The client attempts to negotiate IKE and IPSec SAs with the concentrator. If that is successful, the IPSec tunnel is created and the client prompts you for your username and password. Once that has been authenticated, you can begin using the VPN Client for secure remote access to the VPN concentrator.

# Foundation Summary

The Foundation Summary is a collection of tables and figures that provides a convenient review of many key concepts in this chapter. For those of you already comfortable with the topics in this chapter, this summary could help you recall a few details. For those of you who just read this chapter, this review should help solidify some key facts. For anyone doing his or her final preparation before the exam, these tables and figures are hopefully a convenient way to review the material the day before the exam.

## Types of Preshared Keys

The types of preshared keys are as follows:

- **Unique**—Tied to a specific IP address
- **Group**—Tied to a group
- **Wildcard**—Not tied to anything

## VPN 3000 Concentrator CLI Quick Configuration Steps

The steps to VPN 3000 Concentrator CLI Quick Configuration are as follows:

**Step 1**  Boot the VPN concentrator with default configuration.

**Step 2**  Login as admin/admin.

**Step 3**  Set the system time.

**Step 4**  Set the system date.

**Step 5**  Set the time zone.

**Step 6**  Set the daylight-savings time support.

**Step 7**  Enter an IP address for the Private interface.

**Step 8**  Enter a subnet mask for the Private interface.

**Step 9**  Select the speed of the interface.

**Step 10**  Select the duplex mode of the interface.

**Step 11**  Save and exit the CLI.

# VPN 3000 Concentrator Browser-Based Manager Quick Configuration Steps

The steps to the VPN 3000 Concentrator browser-based Manager Quick Configuration are as follows:

**Step 1**  Ping the VPN concentrator from the administrator PC to verify connectivity.

**Step 2**  Start the web browser.

**Step 3**  Enter the address of the VPN concentrator (be sure to use https:// if you need to enable the VPN concentrator's SSL Certificate on your browser).

**Step 4**  Log in as admin/admin.

**Step 5**  Select **Click here to start Quick Configuration**.

**Step 6**  Select hotlink to Ethernet 2 (Public) interface.

**Step 7**  Enter the IP address, subnet mask, speed, and duplex mode.

**Step 8**  Verify the system name, date, time, time zone, and DST support.

**Step 9**  Enter the DNS server address.

**Step 10**  Enter the domain name.

**Step 11**  Enter the default gateway address.

**Step 12**  Select the tunneling protocols to use—IPSec.

**Step 13**  Select the methods of assigning IP address for the IPSec tunnel endpoints.

**Step 14**  Choose the method for user authentication (Internal Server).

**Step 15**  Add usernames and passwords.

**Step 16**  Supply the IPSec group name and password.

**Step 17**  Change the admin password.

**Step 18**  Click the **Save Needed** icon to save the configuration changes.

# VPN Client Installation Steps

The steps for installing the VPN Client are as follows:

**Step 1**  Insert the Cisco VPN Client CD into your CD-ROM drive.

**Step 2**  View the CD's menu after Autorun starts the CD.

**Step 3**  Select **Install Cisco VPN Client**.

**Step 4**    Click **Yes** to permit disabling IPSec Policy Agent (if asked).

**Step 5**    Click **Next** on the Welcome screen.

**Step 6**    Read and accept the license agreement.

**Step 7**    Click **Next** to accept the default file location.

**Step 8**    Click **Next** to accept the default application location.

**Step 9**    Select the reboot option (now or later) and click **Finish**.

# VPN Client Configuration Steps

The steps for configuring the VPN Client are as follows:

**Step 1**    Choose **Start**, **Programs**, **Cisco Systems VPN Client**, **VPN Dialer** to start the application.

**Step 2**    Click **New** to create a new connection.

**Step 3**    Enter the connection name and description.

**Step 4**    Enter the IP address or host name of the VPN concentrator.

**Step 5**    Enter the IPSec group name and password that you created on the VPN concentrator.

**Step 6**    Click **Finish** to complete the connection creation.

---

**NOTE**    You can customize the installation process to suit different client configurations. See the Cisco website, www.cisco.com, for more information.

---

# VPN Client Program Options

VPN Client program options include the following:

- Certificate Manager
- Help
- Log Viewer
- Set MTU
- Uninstall VPN Client
- VPN Dialer

# Limits for Number of Groups and Users

Table 4-4 shows the maximum number of groups and users.

**Table 4-4**    *Maximum Combined Groups and Users per VPN Model*

| Model | Maximum Combined Number of Groups and Users |
|-------|---------------------------------------------|
| 3005  | 100 |
| 3015  | 100 |
| 3030  | 500 |
| 3060  | 1000 |
| 3080  | 1000 |

# Complete Configuration Table of Contents

Table 4-5 shows the complete configuration table of contents (TOC).

**Table 4-5**    *Complete Expansion of the Configuration TOC*

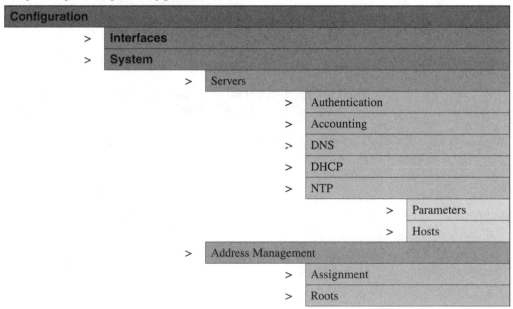

*continues*

**Table 4-5**   *Complete Expansion of the Configuration TOC (Continued)*

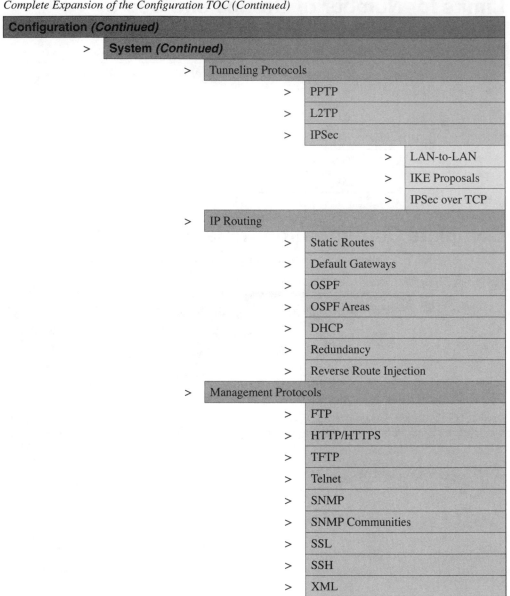

**Table 4-5**  *Complete Expansion of the Configuration TOC (Continued)*

| Configuration *(Continued)* | | | |
|---|---|---|---|
| > | System *(Continued)* | | |
| | > | Events | |
| | | > | General |
| | | > | FTP Backup |
| | | > | Classes |
| | | > | Trap Destinations |
| | | > | Syslog Servers |
| | | > | SMTP Servers |
| | | > | E-mail Recipients |
| | > | General | |
| | | > | Identification |
| | | > | Time and Date |
| | | > | Sessions |
| | | > | Authentication |
| | > | Client Update | |
| | | > | Enable |
| | | > | Entries |
| | > | Load Balancing | |
| > | User Management | | |
| | > | Base Group | |
| | > | Groups | |
| | > | Users | |
| > | Policy Management | | |
| | > | Access Hours | |
| | > | Traffic Management | |
| | | > | Network Lists |
| | | > | Rules |
| | | > | SAs |

*continues*

**Table 4-5** *Complete Expansion of the Configuration TOC (Continued)*

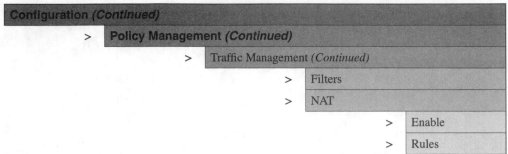

| Configuration *(Continued)* | | | | |
|---|---|---|---|---|
| > Policy Management *(Continued)* | | | | |
| | > Traffic Management *(Continued)* | | | |
| | | > Filters | | |
| | | > NAT | | |
| | | | > Enable | |
| | | | > Rules | |

# Complete Administration Table of Contents

Table 4-6 shows the complete administration table of contents (TOC).

**Table 4-6** *Complete Expansion of the Administration TOC*

| Administration | | | | |
|---|---|---|---|---|
| > Administer Sessions | | | | |
| > Software Update | | | | |
| | > Concentrator | | | |
| | > Clients | | | |
| > System Reboot | | | | |
| > Ping | | | | |
| > Monitoring Refresh | | | | |
| > Access Rights | | | | |
| | > Administrators | | | |
| | > Access Control List | | | |
| | > Access Settings | | | |
| | > AAA Servers | | | |
| | | > Authentication | | |
| > File Management | | | | |
| | > Swap Config File | | | |
| | > TFTP Transfer | | | |
| | > File Upload | | | |
| | > XML Export | | | |

**Table 4-6**    *Complete Expansion of the Administration TOC (Continued)*

| Administration *(Continued)* | | |
|---|---|---|
| > **Certificate Management** | | |
| | > | Enrollment |
| | > | Installation |

# Complete Monitoring Table of Contents

Table 4-7 shows the complete monitoring table of contents (TOC).

**Table 4-7**    *Complete Expansion of the Monitoring TOC*

| Monitoring | | | |
|---|---|---|---|
| > **Routing Table** | | | |
| > **Filterable Event Log** | | | |
| | > | Live Event Log | |
| > **System Status** | | | |
| > **Sessions** | | | |
| | > | Protocols | |
| | > | Encryption | |
| | > | Top Ten Lists | |
| | | > | Data |
| | | > | Duration |
| | | > | Throughput |
| > **Statistics** | | | |
| | > | PPTP | |
| | > | L2TP | |
| | > | IPSec | |
| | > | HTTP | |
| | > | Events | |
| | > | Telnet | |
| | > | DNS | |
| | > | Authentication | |
| | > | Accounting | |
| | > | Filtering | |

*continues*

**Table 4-7**    *Complete Expansion of the Monitoring TOC (Continued)*

| Monitoring *(Continued)* | | | | |
|---|---|---|---|---|
| | > Statistics *(Continued)* | | | |
| | | > VRRP | | |
| | | > SSL | | |
| | | > DHCP | | |
| | | > Address Pools | | |
| | | > SSH | | |
| | | > Load Balancing | | |
| | | > Compression | | |
| | | > Administrative AAA | | |
| | | > NAT | | |
| | | > MIP-II Stats | | |
| | | | > Interfaces | |
| | | | > TCP/UDP | |
| | | | > IP | |
| | | | > RIP | |
| | | | > OSPF | |
| | | | > ICMP | |
| | | | > ARP Table | |
| | | | > Ethernet | |

# Chapter Glossary

The following terms were introduced in this chapter or have special significance to the topics within this chapter.

**cookie**   A piece of information sent by a web server to a web browser that the browser is expected to save and send back to the web server whenever the browser makes additional requests of the web server.

**Extensible Markup Language (XML)**   A standard maintained by the World Wide Web Consortium (W3C). It defines a syntax that lets you create markup languages to specify information structures.

**JavaScript**   Interpreted programming language from Netscape. Used on websites for such things as pop-up windows and image change during mouse rollover.

**Network Time Protocol (NTP)**   Protocol built on top of TCP that ensures accurate local timekeeping with reference to radio and atomic clocks located on the Internet. This protocol is capable of synchronizing distributed clocks within milliseconds over long time periods.

**Remote Authentication Dial-In User Service (RADIUS)**   Database for authenticating dial-up users and for tracking connection time.

**Reverse Route Injection (RRI)**   Used to populate the routing table of an internal router running OSPF or RIP for remote VPN clients or LAN-to-LAN sessions.

**Scalable Encryption Processing (SEP)**   VPN concentrator modules that perform hardware-based cryptographic functions, including random number generation, hash transforms (MD5 and SHA-1) for authentication, and encryption and decryption (DES and Triple-DES).

**Security Dynamics International (SDI) authentication**   Third-party authentication services using token cards.

**Secure Shell (SSH)**   Sometimes called Secure Socket Shell, a UNIX-based command interface and protocol for gaining access to a remote computer securely.

**Secure Sockets Layer (SSL)**   Encryption technology for the web used to provide secure transactions, such as the transmission of credit card numbers for e-commerce.

**Virtual Router Redundancy Protocol (VRRP)**   In installations of two or more VPN concentrators in a parallel, redundant configuration, VRRP provides automatic switchover to a backup system in case the primary system is out of service, thus ensuring user access to the VPN.

**VPN concentrator**   Any of the Cisco VPN 3000 Series Concentrators.

**VPN Manager**   Cisco VPN 3000 Concentrator Manager.

# Q&A

As mentioned in Chapter 1, "All About the Cisco Certified Security Professional," these questions are more difficult than what you should experience on the CCSP exam. The questions do not attempt to cover more breadth or depth than the exam; however, the questions are designed to make sure you know the answer. Rather than allowing you to derive the answer from clues hidden inside the question itself, your understanding and recall of the subject are challenged. Questions from the "Do I Know This Already?" quiz from the beginning of the chapter are repeated here to ensure that you have mastered the chapter's topic areas. Hopefully, these questions will help limit the number of exam questions on which you narrow your choices to two options and guess!

You can find the answers to these questions in Appendix A, "Answers to the "Do I Know This Already" Quizzes and Q&A Sections."

**1** Where would you normally use unique preshared keys?

_____

_____

_____

**2** To use a web browser to access the VPN Manager application on VPN concentrators, what features must you enable on the browser?

_____

_____

_____

**3** What information is required to configure a LAN interface on the VPN concentrator?

_____

_____

_____

**4** What is the default administrator name and password for the GUI VPN Manager?

_____

_____

_____

**5** What options are available for addressing an IP interface on the IP Interfaces screen?

_____

_____

_____

**6** What is the maximum number of combined groups and users that can be supported on a VPN 3015 Concentrator?

_____

_____

_____

**7** What are the four subcategories under the Configuration option of the VPN Manager's TOC?

_____

_____

_____

**8** On the General tab of a group's Add screen, what options can you select for Access Hours?

_____

_____

_____

**9** What IPSec protocols are available from the default IPSec SA settings on the IPSec tab of the Group Add screen?

_____

_____

_____

**10** What are the nine subcategories under the Configuration | System option in the VPN Manager's table of contents?

_____

_____

_____

**11** Where does the VPN concentrator store system events?

_____

_____

_____

**12** What areas can be configured under the Traffic Management section of the Configuration | Policy Management section?

_____

_____

_____

**13** Where do you enter the preshared key so that a VPN Client can connect to a VPN concentrator?

_____

_____

_____

**14** What are the three types of preshared keys?

_____

_____

_____

**15** What types of interfaces are the Public and Private VPN interfaces?

_____

_____

_____

**16** Which interface do you need to configure using the browser-based VPN Manager?

_____

_____

_____

**17**  What would you do if you needed to re-enter the Quick Configuration mode after you have completed the initial configuration of the VPN concentrator?

_____

_____

_____

**18**  When the VPN Manager's Main window is displayed, how do you continue with the Quick Configuration that was started at the CLI?

_____

_____

_____

**19**  What methods can be selected for assigning IP addresses to the tunnel endpoints from the Quick Configuration Address Assignment screen?

_____

_____

_____

**20**  When using the VPN Manager, how can you tell that you have made changes to the active configuration?

_____

_____

_____

**21**  What is an external group in the VPN Manager system?

_____

_____

_____

**22**  What is the purpose of the SEP card assignment attribute on the General tab of the Group Add screen?

_____

_____

_____

**23** You would like to be able to pass DNS and WINS information from the VPN concentrator to the VPN Client. What Group option can you use to accomplish this?

_____

_____

_____

**24** What dynamic routing protocols are available on the VPN 3000 Concentrators?

_____

_____

_____

**25** What protocol does the VPN concentrator use to update software versions on Cisco VPN 3002 Hardware Clients?

_____

_____

_____

**26** How do you start the Cisco VPN Client installation process?

_____

_____

_____

**27** What methods can you use for user authentication on the Cisco VPN 3000 Series Concentrators?

_____

_____

_____

**28** What is a group preshared key?

_____

_____

_____

**29** When you boot up a Cisco VPN 3000 Concentrator with the default factory configuration, what happens?

_____

_____

_____

**30** If you supply an address of 144.50.30.24 and want to use a 24-bit subnet mask for the Private interface on a VPN concentrator, are you able to accept the default subnet mask offered by the VPN Manager?

_____

_____

_____

**31** What are the three major sections of the VPN Manager system?

_____

_____

_____

**32** The Quick Configuration system has displayed the System Info screen. What information, other than system date and time, can you enter on this screen?

_____

_____

_____

**33** What is the maximum number of combined groups and users that can be supported on a VPN 3060 Concentrator?

_____

_____

_____

**34** From where do users inherit attributes on the VPN concentrator?

_____

_____

_____

**35** What is the default number of simultaneous logins available to group members?

_____

_____

_____

**36** What is the purpose of IKE keepalives?

_____

_____

_____

**37** Where would you configure information for NTP and DHCP servers within the VPN Manager?

_____

_____

_____

**38** What is the most significant event severity level?

_____

_____

_____

**39** What Microsoft Windows operating systems can support the Cisco VPN Client?

_____

_____

_____

**40** What programs are available within the VPN Client installation?

_____

_____

_____

**41** What is a unique preshared key?

_____

_____

_____

**42**  What type of cable does the console port require on VPN concentrators?

_____

_____

_____

**43**  What is the default administrator name and password for VPN concentrators?

_____

_____

_____

**44**  How do you get your web browser to connect to the VPN concentrator's manager application?

_____

_____

_____

**45**  What is the first screen that appears when you click the **Click here to start Quick Configuration** option in the VPN Manager?

_____

_____

_____

**46**  If you select Internal Server as the method of user authentication, what additional screen does the Quick Configuration system give you?

_____

_____

_____

**47**  When do configuration changes become active on the Cisco VPN 3000 Series Concentrators?

_____

_____

_____

**48** When reviewing the list of attributes for a group, what does it mean when an attribute's Inherit? box is checked?

_____

_____

_____

**49** What is a realm in relation to user authentication?

_____

_____

_____

**50** What is split tunneling?

_____

_____

_____

**51** What management protocols can you configure on the VPN concentrator?

_____

_____

_____

**52** What is the process a VPN Client uses to connect to a VPN concentrator when load balancing is used between two or more VPN concentrators?

_____

_____

_____

**53** What variables can you supply during the installation process of the Cisco VPN Client?

_____

_____

_____

**54**  What methods can be used for device authentication between VPN peers?

_____

_____

_____

**55**  What is a wildcard preshared key?

_____

_____

_____

**56**  What information do you need to supply in the CLI portion of Quick Configuration?

_____

_____

_____

**57**  What is the last step you must take before moving from the CLI Quick Configuration mode to the browser-based Quick Configuration mode?

_____

_____

_____

**58**  What hot keys are available in the standard toolbar of the VPN Manager?

_____

_____

_____

**59**  What tunneling protocols does the VPN concentrator support?

_____

_____

_____

**60** When you select IPSec as the tunneling protocol, what screen does Quick Configuration present?

_____

_____

_____

**61** How many groups can a user belong to in the VPN concentrator's internal database?

_____

_____

_____

**62** What is the size range for user authentication passwords for internal users?

_____

_____

_____

**63** What does the Authentication option RADIUS with Expiry provide?

_____

_____

_____

**64** What tunneling protocol can be configured on the VPN concentrator to support the Microsoft Windows 2000 VPN client?

_____

_____

_____

**65** How does the VPN 3000 Concentrator handle software updates for VPN Software Clients?

_____

_____

_____

**66** How do you start the VPN Client on a Windows system?

_____

_____

_____

# Scenarios

The following scenarios and questions are designed to draw together the content of the chapter and exercise your understanding of the concepts. There might be more than one correct answer. The thought process and practice in manipulating each concept in the scenario are the goals of this section.

# Scenario 4-1

Users at one of your small branch facilities dial in to your corporate access server for access to the Internet, e-mail, and other network services. This four-user group is one of your research and development teams, and each of the four users dials in to the access server using 56-kbps modems for network services. Their work is considered top secret by upper management. Because of the sensitive nature of their communications, you want to establish a VPN for them using IPSec.

At the same time, other users at other branch sites—your sales staff and other key personnel—frequently use laptops and home computers to connect to the corporate network through the Internet or through the access server. These users discuss sales figures and development projects and also require IPSec protection on their MS Exchange messaging and MS SQL database traffic.

You had considered using your router as a VPN server, but decided to use a Cisco VPN Concentrator because of its ability to authenticate users internally. You don't anticipate ever having more than 50 VPN clients active in your user community at any given time, and your employee base is stable.

As the senior security architect for your organization, how would you answer these questions?

1  Which VPN 3000 Concentrator would you purchase and install?

2  Would you use preshared keys or digital certificates for device authentication?

3  Would you depend on the internal authentication services of the VPN device, or would you use some other user authentication method?

4  How would you assign VPN addresses?

5  Would you permit split tunneling?

6  Would you use multiple IPSec groups? If so, why?

7  Which IPSec protocol would you use?

8  Which encryption protocol would you use?

9  Would you allow unrestricted access hours?

10  What would you set for idle timeout and maximum connect time?

# Scenario 4-2

Your company sells donuts and has 60 shops located in a three-state area. These shops are each connected to the Internet using DSL circuits. You want to establish IPSec VPN connections from each shop through the Internet to the corporate network for sending/receiving e-mail, reporting sales, and ordering supplies.

You will be using a Cisco VPN 3030 Concentrator with no SEP modules. Device authentication is accomplished using preshared keys. User authentication is done through the NT Domain. The IP addresses of the DNS servers are 192.168.44.20 and 192.168.63.20. The IP addresses of the WINS servers are 192.168.44.25 and 12.168.63.25. No changes have been made to the default Base Group.

Create a group for the shops called DonutShops.

1   Indicate the settings that you would make on the group's General tab for each of the following attributes, and specify whether you would uncheck the Inherit? box.

- Access Hours
- Simultaneous Logins
- Minimum Password Length
- Allow Alphabetic-Only Passwords
- Idle Timeout
- Maximum Connect Time
- Filter
- Primary DNS
- Secondary DNS
- Primary WINS
- Secondary WINS
- SEP Card Assignment
- Tunneling Protocols
- Strip Realm

2   Indicate the settings that you would make on the group's IPSec tab for each of the following attributes, and specify whether you would uncheck the Inherit? box.

- IPSec SA
- IKE Peer Identity Validation
- IKE Keepalives

- Reauthentication on Rekey
- Tunnel Type
- Group Lock
- Authentication
- IPComp
- Mode Configuration

# Scenario Answers

The answers provided in this section are not necessarily the only correct answers. They merely represent one possibility for each scenario. The intention is to test your base knowledge and understanding of the concepts discussed in this chapter.

Should your answers be different (as they likely will be), consider the differences. Are your answers in line with the concepts of the answers provided and explained here? If not, reread the chapter, focusing on the sections that are related to the problem scenario.

# Scenario 4-1 Answers

1 Concentrator model? The Cisco VPN 3005 Concentrator is probably adequate for this installation. If your company were growing quickly, you might opt for the 3015. It has about the same capabilities but is expandable, all the way to a 3080, if you ever needed the additional capacity.

2 Type of device authentication? Because this is a chapter on preshared keys, you would opt to use preshared keys. For this small user base, the maintenance for preshared keys should not be a big concern.

3 Authentication? Internal authentication was one of the reasons for choosing the concentrator over the router. The internal database keeps authentication on the same device and is flexible enough to meet the needs of this application.

4 Address assignment? Set aside a pool of 100 IP addresses and let the VPN concentrator assign the IP addresses from the pool. You could use DHCP, but that brings another network device into the picture. Keep it simple.

5 Split tunneling? Yes. The R&D group is going to need the Internet for research and the 56-kbps modems are going to be killers. Eliminate the need for encryption on trivial traffic to help this group out.

6 Multiple IPSec groups? It would make sense to use multiple IPSec groups. Some of your users might not need split tunneling, and you could use different rules for access time, idle timeout, or maximum connect times. You might want to set up functional groups such as R&D, Sales, Engineering, Accounting, Execs, and so on. You are only constrained by the 100 combined users and groups limitation on the concentrator.

7 IPSec protocol? ESP. AH is authentication only with no encryption. You would want to encrypt some of these data, especially for the R&D group.

8 Encryption? Probably Triple-DES. You could choose DES, but the extra security does not cost that much more in performance.

9 Unlimited access? This would be a group-by-group decision. Does the R&D team work around the clock or just during business hours? Do you need to set aside a regular maintenance window for network upgrades? Do the execs need unlimited access?

10 Idle timeout and maximum connect time? You probably want to drop connections after they have been idle for 20 to 30 minutes. There is no overpowering reason to establish limits on connect time. If you close the connection when it is idle, you should not have to worry about lengthy connections.

# Scenario 4-2 Answers

1 General tab settings for the DonutShops group:

- **Access Hours**—No Restrictions
- **Simultaneous Logins**—1, uncheck Inherit?
- **Minimum Password Length**—8
- **Allow Alphabetic-Only Passwords**—No, uncheck Inherit?
- **Idle Timeout**—30
- **Maximum Connect Time**—0
- **Filter**—None
- **Primary DNS**—192.168.44.20, uncheck Inherit?
- **Secondary DNS**—192.168.63.20, uncheck Inherit?
- **Primary WINS**—192.168.44.25, uncheck Inherit?
- **Secondary WINS**—192.168.63.25, uncheck Inherit?
- **SEP Card Assignment**—You can leave these checked. Without SEP modules, this attribute has no effect.
- **Tunneling Protocols**—Check only IPSec, uncheck Inherit?
- **Strip Realm**—Leave unchecked. You will be using an external authentication service, so this field has no effect.

2 IPSec tab settings for the DonutShops group:

- **IPSec SA**—ESP-3DES-MD5
- **IKE Peer Identity Validation**—If supported by certificate
- **IKE Keepalives**—Enabled
- **Reauthentication on Rekey**—Enabled, uncheck Inherit?

- **Tunnel Type**—Remote access
- **Group Lock**—Disabled
- **Authentication**—NT Domain, uncheck Inherit?
- **IPComp**—None
- **Mode Configuration**—Enabled

# Exam Topics Discussed in This Chapter

This chapter covers the following topics, which you need to master in your pursuit of certification as a Cisco Certified Security Professional:

**15**  CA support overview

**16**  Certificate generation

**17**  Validating certificates

**18**  Configuring the Cisco VPN 3000 Concentrator Series for CA support

# Configuring Cisco VPN 3000 for Remote Access Using Digital Certificates

Chapter 4, "Configuring Cisco VPN 3000 for Remote Access Using Preshared Keys," discussed the opportunity of using preshared keys for device authentication between VPN peers, specifically between a remote access client and the VPN 3000 Concentrator. An IPSec group was defined on the VPN concentrator, and that group and its associated password were used as the preshared key for the VPN Client application.

While the process of using preshared keys is simple when using the Cisco VPN Concentrator and VPN Client, it is a process that does not scale well for large VPN applications. The Cisco application of preshared keys requires little work to implement initially. You just set up a group on the concentrator and supply the group name and password to your VPN user community. You could put everyone into one group to make it simple.

So where's the problem of scale? It's not with user authentication. The concentrator has finite limitations on the number of groups and users it can support for internal authentication. You will probably be using an external authentication service, and the per-user maintenance required for that does not change.

The official line is that as your user base grows, the number of passwords that you have to keep track of becomes unmanageable. But that's not really so. Cisco makes keeping track of passwords simple. You do not have to keep track of a unique key for each user, just for a group. If you only have a handful of groups, then that is how many passwords you have to keep track of. It's not a big problem.

The real problem of scale occurs because the passwords are compromised from time to time, and you have to change them. That is an easy task on the VPN concentrator, but you cannot change those passwords until you coordinate the change with all your users. These users might be using the Cisco VPN Client, but they are most likely also using a variety of operating systems. The logistics of changing device authentication passwords for a large user base would be difficult.

Security best practice says that you should be changing these passwords regularly, even if they are not compromised (in fact, that is one of the best ways to protect against compromised passwords). In this case, *regularly* means semiannually, quarterly, or better still, every 30 days.

What's the alternative to preshared keys? That's what this chapter is all about. The alternative to using preshared keys for device authentication is to use Certificate Authorities (CAs) and digital certificates.

# How to Best Use This Chapter

By taking the following steps, you can make better use of your time:

- Keep your notes and answers for all your work with this book in one place for easy reference.

- Take the "Do I Know This Already?" quiz, and write down your answers. Studies show retention is significantly increased through writing facts and concepts down, even if you never look at the information again.

- Use the diagram in Figure 5-1 to guide you to the next step.

**Figure 5-1**  *How to Use This Chapter*

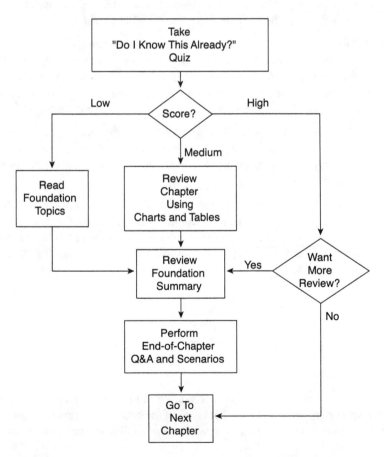

# "Do I Know This Already?" Quiz

The purpose of the "Do I Know This Already?" quiz is to help you decide what parts of the chapter to use. If you already intend to read the entire chapter, you do not need to answer these questions now.

This 16-question quiz helps you determine how to spend your limited study time. The quiz is sectioned into four smaller "quizlets," which correspond to the four major topic headings in the chapter. Figure 5-1 outlines suggestions on how to spend your time in this chapter based on your quiz score. Use Table 5-1 to record your scores.

**Table 5-1**    *Score Sheet for Quiz and Quizlets*

| Quizlet Number | Foundations Topics Section Covering These Questions | Questions | Score |
|---|---|---|---|
| 1 | CA support overview | 1–4 | |
| 2 | Certificate generation | 5–8 | |
| 3 | Validating certificates | 9–12 | |
| 4 | Configuring the Cisco VPN 3000 Concentrator Series for CA support | 13–16 | |
| All questions | | 1–16 | |

**1**  What Public Key Cryptography Standard (PKCS) is used to enroll with a CA?

_____

_____

_____

**2**  What field in the certificate request should match the IPSec group name on the VPN concentrator?

_____

_____

_____

**3**  What elements make up the X.500 distinguished name?

_____

_____

_____

**4** What default algorithm type and key size does the VPN concentrator use on the certificate request?

_____

_____

_____

**5** What entity is responsible for generating the Public Key Infrastructure (PKI) public/private key pair for a requesting host?

_____

_____

_____

**6** When are Secure Sockets Layer (SSL) certificates required on a VPN concentrator?

_____

_____

_____

**7** What is the first certificate that must be installed on a VPN concentrator before you can install any other certificates from a given CA?

_____

_____

_____

**8** What two enrollment methods are available on a VPN concentrator?

_____

_____

_____

**9** Where does a VPN concentrator obtain the root CA's public key?

_____

_____

_____

**10** During the authentication process, where does a VPN concentrator find the original hash that the CA calculated for an identity certificate?

_____

_____

_____

**11** When you select to cache Certificate Revocation Lists (CRLs) on the VPN concentrator, where are they stored?

_____

_____

_____

**12** With CRL caching disabled, how does a VPN concentrator check a certificate's serial number against a CRL?

_____

_____

_____

**13** Using the VPN Manager, where would you look to check the status of a certificate enrollment process?

_____

_____

_____

**14** When configuring digital certificate support on a VPN concentrator, where do you identify which certificate to use for Internet Key Exchange (IKE) Phase 1 negotiations?

_____

_____

_____

**15** What must be in place on a client's PC before you can configure the VPN Client for certificate support?

_____

_____

_____

**16** Which screen do you use to enable the use of digital certificates for device authentication during IKE Phase 1 negotiations?

_____

_____

_____

The answers to this quiz are listed in Appendix A, "Answers to the "Do I Know This Already?" Quizzes and Q&A Sections." The suggestions for your next steps, based on quiz results, are as follows:

- **2 or less score on any quizlet**—Review the appropriate sections of the "Foundation Topics" section of this chapter, based on Table 5-1. Proceed to the "Foundation Summary" section, the "Q&A" section, and then the scenarios at the end of the chapter.

- **8 or less overall score**—You should read the entire chapter, including the "Foundation Topics" and "Foundation Summary" sections, the "Q&A" section, and the scenarios at the end of the chapter.

- **9 to 12 overall score**—Begin with the "Foundation Summary" section, continue with the "Q&A" section, and then read the scenarios. If you are having difficulty with a particular subject area, read the appropriate section in the "Foundation Topics" section.

- **13 or more overall score**—If you feel you need more review on these topics, go to the "Foundation Summary" section, then to the "Q&A" section, then the scenarios. Otherwise, skip this chapter and go to the next chapter.

# Foundation Topics

## Digital Certificates and Certificate Authorities

**15**  CA support overview

Digital certificates are the basis of a strong Public Key Infrastructure (PKI) and provide an excellent tool for VPN device authentication. Digital certificates are the mechanism used to distribute and store public keys, and they usually take the form of X.509 certificates.

The PKI structure is based on the use of two keys, a public key and a private key. You can use these keys for a variety of functions, such as authentication, digital signatures, and encryption. The host holds the private key tightly but shares the public key with a variety of partners by sending them the host's digital certificate. The partner authenticates the certificate by using the public key of the CA.

This section covers the following topics:

- The CA architecture
- Simple Certificate Enrollment Process authentication methods
- CA vendors and products that support Cisco VPN products

### The CA Architecture

Certificate Authorities (CAs) are usually third-party agents such as VeriSign or Entrust, but you could also set up your own CA using applications, such as Windows 2000 (W2K) Certificate Services. If your organization already uses Windows, implementing a W2K CA is a simple matter and would allow you to completely manage the certificate process for your organization.

CAs provide the following services to an organization:

- **Device registration (enrollment)**—Each device is required to submit unique identifying information to the CA. For example, these items can include a common name, organization, and administrator's e-mail address and phone number. The CA verifies that all requested information has been supplied before issuing certificates.
- **Certification**—CAs issue certificates to requesting devices using a standard format. Three certificate types are important to the smooth operation of a PKI system:
  - **Root**—Identifies the overarching authority in the CA network, usually the issuing CA.

- **Identity**—Required by every device, these are signed by either the root CA or by a subordinate CA. The root CA must self-sign its own identity certificate.

- **Issuing (or subordinate)**—Serves the same purpose as the root certificate but is issued by a subordinate CA instead of the root CA. Subordinate CAs *do not* self-sign their own identity certificate.

- **Key generation**—Most Cisco devices generate their own public/private key pairs. Some devices do not have that capability and depend on the CA to generate key pairs. The private key is returned to the requesting device through some secure method, possibly even through some manual process.

- **Key recovery**—An optional service provided by some CAs is the ability to store private keys for devices that can be used in case the original key is lost.

- **Certificate revocation**—Another service that CAs render is the publication of lists of identity certificates that have been revoked prior to their expiration date. Revocation can occur for a variety of reasons, such as a name change, removal from service, or change of organization, or because of a suspected or real security compromise.

- **Cross-certification**—CAs in one organization might need to authenticate certificates issued by a second CA organization. This can be accomplished by using cross-certifications, which are a type of subordinate certificate.

The following sections review certificate requests, the enrollment process, the authentication process, CA hierarchies, and certificate revocation.

## Certificate Requests

When two hosts want to use digital certificates to secure communications between them, each host must contact the same CA and enroll its identity and public key with the CA. Enrollment is a multistep process on many systems. First, a host that wants to use digital certificates creates a pair of keys, one public and one private. Next, the host prepares a Public Key Cryptography Standards (PKCS) #10 certificate request. Finally, this PKCS #10 certificate request and the host's public key are then sent to the CA.

On the Cisco VPN 3000 Concentrator, the process is combined into one operation. The administrator simply fills out the PKCS #10 certificate request form, which includes a field to select the size of the key to generate. When the form is submitted, the VPN concentrator generates the key pair and then sends the certificate request and public key to the CA. Table 5-2 describes the fields that are contained on a VPN concentrator PKCS #10 certificate request.

**Table 5-2**    *Cisco VPN 3000 Concentrator PKCS #10 Certificate Request*

| Field Name and Abbreviation | Description | Examples |
|---|---|---|
| Common Name (CN) | The name for the host that identifies it in your organization. Spaces are allowed, but you must enter a name in this field. | Accounting 10<br>Sales_VA<br>Bridgeport_VPN |
| Organizational Unit (OU) | Must match the configured IPSec group name on VPN concentrators. Spaces are allowed. | vpngroup02<br>IPSECGRP1<br>SECUREVPN20 |
| Organization (O) | Enter the host's company name or organization. Spaces are allowed. | Cisco Systems<br>Parker Pumps<br>Jones Shoes |
| Locality (L) | Enter the city or town where this host is located. Spaces are allowed. | San Francisco<br>Detroit<br>Riverport |
| State/Province (SP) | Enter the state or province where this host is located. Spell out the name completely; do not abbreviate. Spaces are allowed. | North Carolina<br>Ohio<br>New Mexico |
| Country (C) | Enter the country where this host is located. Use two characters, no spaces, and no periods. This two-character code must conform to ISO 3166 country abbreviations. | US for United States<br>JP for Japan<br>CA for Canada<br>MX for Mexico<br>GB for United Kingdom |
| Subject Alternative Name (FQDN) | Enter the fully qualified domain name for this host. This field is optional. The alternative name is an additional data field in the certificate, and it provides interoperability with many Cisco IOS and PIX systems in LAN-to-LAN connections. | vpn3030.cisco.com<br>Sales10.parma.com<br>Mobile47.widgets.com |
| Key Size | The algorithm for generating the public-key/private-key pair, and the key size. Select from drop-down menu. | RSA 512 bits<br>RSA 768 bits<br>RSA 1024 bits<br>DSA 512 bits<br>DSA 768 bits<br>DSA 1024 bits |

| NOTE | In the Key Size field, RSA keys are generated using Rivest, Shamir, and Adelman (RSA) algorithms and are supported by almost all CAs. Directory System Agent (DSA) algorithms are backed by the U.S. Government but are not supported by as many CAs. The default, RSA 512 bits, is the most common, providing sufficient security and requiring the least processing by host systems. The 768-bit keys provide normal security but take 2 to 4 times more processing than 512-bit keys. The 1024-bit keys provide high security, but take 4 to 8 times more processing than 512-bit keys. |
|---|---|

The contents of the first six fields—CN, OU, O, L, SP, and C—make up a host's X.500 distinguished name. Using a mixture of the examples given in Table 5-2, for example, you could construct an X.500 distinguished name like this:

cn=Accounting 10, ou=vnpgroup02, o=Parker Pumps, l=Riverport, sp=New Mexico, c=US

## Enrollment Process

The CA computes a hash code of the unsigned PKCS #10 certificate request. The CA then takes that hash and encrypts it using the CA's private key. This encrypted hash is the digital signature, and the CA attaches it to the certificate and returns the signed certificate to the client. This certificate is called an *identity certificate* and is stored on the client device until it expires or is deleted. The CA also sends the client its own digital certificate, which becomes the root certificate for the client.

The client now has a signed digital certificate that it can send to any other peer partner. If the peer partner wants to authenticate the certificate, it decrypts the signature using the CAs public key.

The standard format for the identity and root certificates is the X.509 certificate.

The PKI is based on trust. In Figure 5-2, Alpha and Theta, a VPN concentrator and a VPN Client, for example, want to communicate, but they do not know or trust each other. However, they each know Omega, a CA, and trust its good judgment. Omega says that Alpha and Theta are okay and presents each of them with a certificate to that effect, the identity certificate. Additionally, Omega sends each of them a self-signed root certificate that Alpha and Theta can use to validate one another's identity.

Figure 5-2 shows the process of enrolling with a CA using the PKCS #10 certificate request and receiving the identity and root certificates in return.

**Figure 5-2**    *CA Enrollment Process*

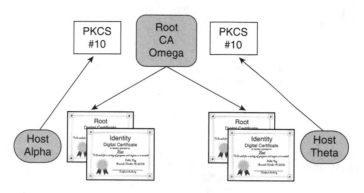

## Authentication Process

As part of the process of establishing the IPSec connection between Alpha and Theta, they each need to authenticate the identity of the other. Alpha sends its identity certificate to Theta. Theta performs a hashing algorithm on the certificate and calculates a hash value. Alpha's certificate says that Omega signed the certificate, so Theta then takes the CA's public key from the root certificate that Theta received from Omega and uses that public key to decrypt the signature of Alpha's identity certificate. The decryption process produces a hash of the certificate. If this hash matches the one that Theta calculated on its own, Theta can trust that Alpha is exactly who it says it is. This process is depicted in Figure 5-3 and would be repeated on Alpha using Theta's identity certificate.

Once Theta has authenticated Alpha's identity, Theta is now free to use the contents of Alpha's identity certificate. The most important element in the ID certificate is Alpha's public key. Theta can now use that key to authenticate digital signatures from Alpha or to encrypt data that are being sent to Alpha.

## CA Hierarchies

There are two basic types of CA structures: central and hierarchical. When the root CA creates and issues the identity certificate directly from PKCS #10 requests, as shown in Figure 5-2, that is called a *central CA structure*. The root CA generates all identity certificates in a central CA structure.

Hierarchical CA structures occur when subordinate CAs are involved in the process of issuing certificates. The subordinate CAs enroll with the root CA and receive identity and root certificates. The subordinate CAs then work directly with requesting hosts or subordinate CAs of their own and provide identity and subordinate CA certificates. Figure 5-4 shows a typical hierarchical CA structure and the certificates held at each level of the hierarchy.

**Figure 5-3** *Authentication Process on Theta*

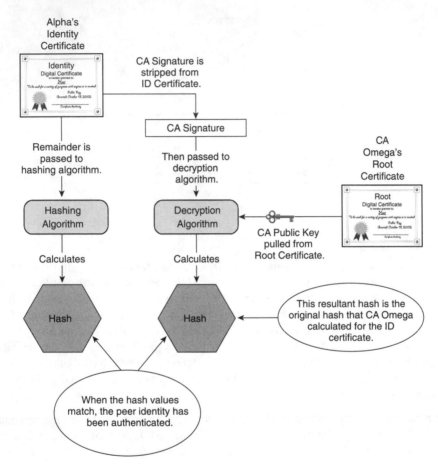

## Certificate Revocation

Whenever a VPN concentrator receives an identity certificate from a peer during IKE Phase 1, the concentrator performs three tests on the certificate before going through the authentication process shown in Figure 5-3. Those three tests are as follows:

- **Did a trusted CA sign the certificate?**—The concentrator must hold a root certificate from the CA before it can accept identity certificates that were created by that CA.

- **Has the certificate expired?**—The concentrator checks the Valid From date and time and the Valid To date and time. If the current date and time fall between those valid endpoints, the certificate has not expired.

- **Has the certificate been revoked?**—Many CAs issue CRLs periodically. VPN concentrators check the certificate's serial number against the CRLs.

**Figure 5-4**    *Hierarchical CA Organization*

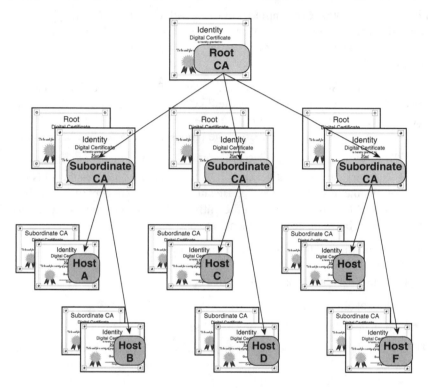

Changes occur frequently in organizations and can cause digital certificates to become invalid. This happens more often in the user community because of employees leaving the organization or due to something changing to affect the user's distinguished name, such as changing the last name when someone gets married. Less frequently, keys can become compromised, or hardware gets taken out of service.

For whatever reason, CAs have the responsibility of notifying their clientele when digital certificates become invalid and get revoked. CAs do that by issuing CRLs. CRLs contain an effective date and a list of identity certificate serial numbers that have been revoked. Associated with each serial number is a revocation date. The CA digitally signs the CRLs and distributes them to its clients.

Whenever a device receives its identity certificate or a CRL from the CA, the device performs an authentication check on the document. It does this by using the CAs public key from the root certificate to perform the authentication checking routine depicted in Figure 5-3.

# Simple Certificate Enrollment Process Authentication Methods

For Cisco VPN 3000 Concentrators to work with CAs, the CAs must support Cisco's Public Key Infrastructure (PKI) Protocol and the Simple Certificate Enrollment Process (SCEP). VPN concentrators support the use of SCEP to automate the exchange of certificates with a CA server.

Cisco sponsored SCEP as an Internet Engineering Task Force (IETF) draft as a way of managing the certificate life cycle. SCEP uses the PKCS #7 standard from RSA Security Inc. to encrypt and sign certificate enrollment messages. SCEP further uses PKCS #10 for standardizing certificate requests. PKCS #10 certificate requests were described in the section, "The CA Architecture."

SCEP is the mechanism that permits a CA to trust a host, such as the VPN concentrator, and that permits the host to trust the CA. Because the entire concept of CAs is built on this trust, it helps to be able to build this trust efficiently. SCEP provides the tool to do just that, enabling the CA and requesting host to authenticate one another.

You must first install the CA's root certificate onto the concentrator before you can request an identity certificate from that CA. SCEP provides the following two authentication methods to facilitate this certificate installation process:

- Manual authentication
- Authentication based on a preshared secret

The following sections describe both authentication methods in greater detail.

## Manual SCEP Authentication

In the manual mode, you, as the VPN administrator, submit a request to the CA using the Internet, e-mail, or a floppy disk. The CA operator then verifies your identity through some reliable out-of-band method. Upon verification, the CA returns a CA root certificate to you, which you then copy to your VPN Manager workstation. From there, you begin the process of installing the certificate on the concentrator using the Administration | Certificate Management option of the VPN Manager. Figure 5-5 shows the screen that is displayed by this option the first time you bring up this screen.

The **Click here to install a CA certificate** option only appears on this screen before you have installed any CA certificates. Clicking that option brings up the screen shown in Figure 5-6.

**Figure 5-5**    *Administration | Certificate Management*

| Administration | Certificate Management | | | | Friday, 21 June 2002 13:42:53 |

Refresh

This section lets you view and manage certificates on the VPN 3000 Concentrator. Installation of a CA certificate is required before identity and SSL certificates can be installed.

- Click here to install a CA certificate
- Click here to enroll with a Certificate Authority
- Click here to install a certificate

**Certificate Authorities** [ View All CRL Caches | Clear All CRL Caches ] (current: 0, maximum: 20)

| Subject | Issuer | Expiration | SCEP Issuer | Actions |
|---------|--------|------------|-------------|---------|
| No Certificate Authorities | | | | |

**Identity Certificates** (current: 0, maximum: 20)

| Subject | Issuer | Expiration | Actions |
|---------|--------|------------|---------|
| No Identity Certificates | | | |

**SSL Certificate** [ Generate ] *Note: The public key in the SSL certificate is also used for the SSH host key.*

| Subject | Issuer | Expiration | Actions |
|---------|--------|------------|---------|
| No SSL Certificates | | | |

**Enrollment Status** [ **Remove All:** Errored | Timed-Out | Rejected | Cancelled | In-Progress ] (current: 0 available: 20)

| Subject | Issuer | Date | Use | Reason | Method | Status | Actions |
|---------|--------|------|-----|--------|--------|--------|---------|
| No Enrollment Requests | | | | | | | |

**Figure 5-6**    *Administration | Certificate Management | Install | CA Certificate*

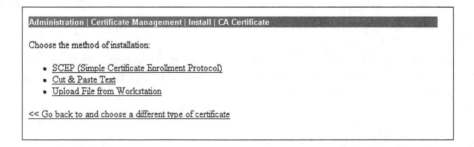

| Administration | Certificate Management | Install | CA Certificate |

Choose the method of installation:

- SCEP (Simple Certificate Enrollment Protocol)
- Cut & Paste Text
- Upload File from Workstation

<< Go back to and choose a different type of certificate

For the manual SCEP option, you have the following two choices: You can cut and paste the certificate from text, or you can upload the file from your management workstation. To install the file using the cut-and-paste method, open the CA certificate file in a text editor such as Notepad or WordPad and select and copy the contents of the file. Click the option **Cut & Paste Text** from the menu shown in Figure 5-6, and the VPN Manager displays the screen shown in Figure 5-7.

**Figure 5-7**    *Administration | Certificate Management | Install | CA Certificate | Cut & Paste Text*

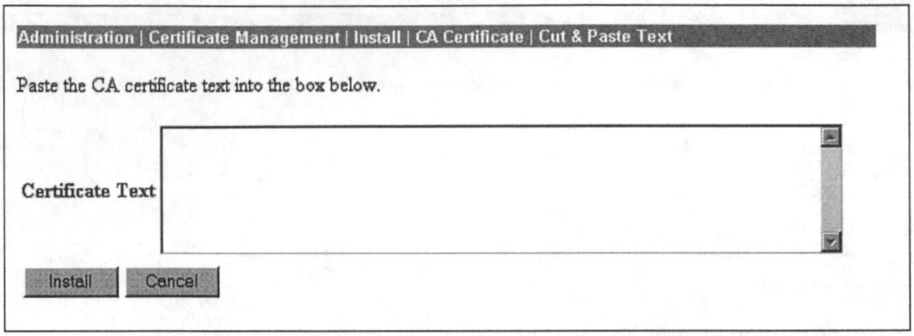

Paste the copied file into the Certificate Text area, and click **Install** to install the CA certificate.

You could also choose the **Upload File from Workstation** option, shown in Figure 5-6. When you do that, the screen shown in Figure 5-8 is displayed.

**Figure 5-8**    *Administration | Certificate Management | Install | CA Certificate | Upload File from Workstation*

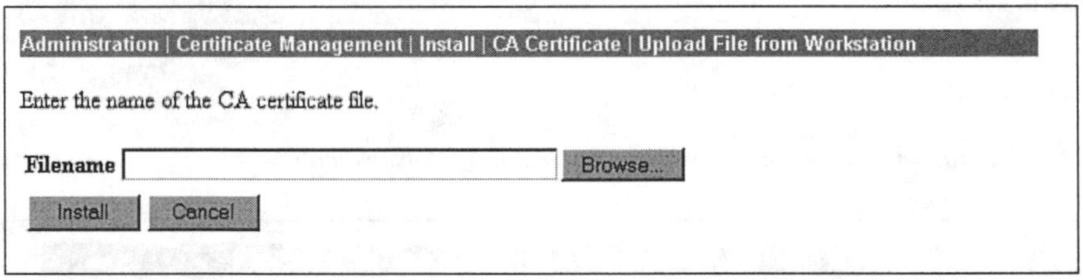

Certificate files usually have the cer extension. Insert the full path and name of the file in the Filename field using DOS notation; for example, c:\Certs\cacert.cer. Click **Install** to continue with the installation of the CA certificate.

## Preshared Key SCEP Authentication

The alternative to using manual SCEP authentication is to authenticate using preshared keys. When using preshared keys, the server distributes a shared key to the end entity that can uniquely associate the enrollment request with the given end entity. The distribution of the key must be private; only the end entity should know this key. When creating the enrollment request, the end entity is asked to provide a challenge password. When using preshared keys, the end entity must type in the preshared key as the password.

Choosing the SCEP option from the screen shown in Figure 5-6 allows you to install the CA certificate onto the VPN concentrator using the preshared key SCEP method. When you select this method, the screen shown in Figure 5-9 is displayed.

**Figure 5-9**   *Administration | Certificate Management | Install | CA Certificate | SCEP*

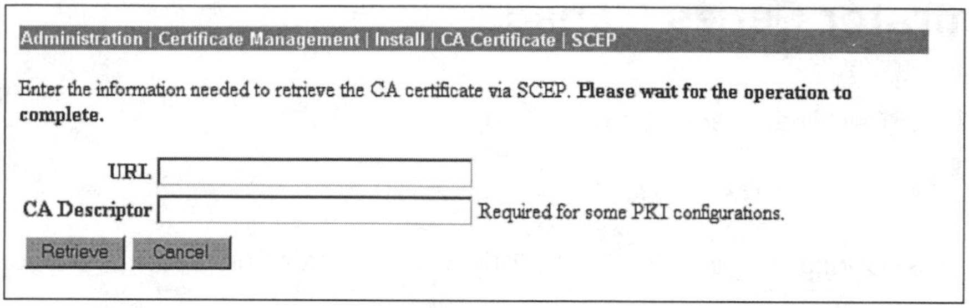

Enter the complete URL to the SCEP area of your CA's server. If you had your own Microsoft CA server whose IP address is 192.168.1.34, for example, you would enter the following URL:

> http://192.168.1.34/certsrv/mscep/mscep.dll

The CA Descriptor is just a single word used to describe the certificate.

At this point, the preshared key has not been used. The key is used during the enrollment with SCEP process, which is discussed in the upcoming section, "Enrolling Via SCEP."

## CA Vendors and Products that Support Cisco VPN Products

The Cisco VPN 3000 Concentrator Series works with the following Internet-based CAs:

- Entrust Technologies (www.entrust.com)
- VeriSign, Inc. (www.verisign.com)
- Baltimore Technologies (www.baltimoretechnologies.com)

These vendors provide digital certificates and all the associated management and maintenance support, for a fee. Well-established and reliable, these services can fill the needs of small- to mid-sized businesses without the need to set up internal CA support.

As your business grows, you will want to install your on CA server or servers. The following three products are available and are certified to work with the Cisco VPN Concentrator series:

- Microsoft Certificate Services for Windows 2000
- RSA Keon Certificate Authority for Solaris, Windows 2000, and Windows NT
- Netscape Certificate Management System for Solaris, Windows 2000, and Windows NT

# Digital Certificate Support Through the VPN 3000 Concentrator Series Manager

**16** Certificate generation

**17** Validating certificates

**18** Configuring the Cisco VPN 3000 Concentrator Series for CA support

The previous sections of this chapter have covered some of the VPN 3000 Concentrator Manager processes that support digital certificates. This section discusses the basic functions that you need to perform to support digital certificate authentication for IPSec VPNs on the Cisco VPN 3000 Concentrator Series, including the following:

- Generating and enrolling a certificate
- Validating a certificate
- Revoking certificates
- Configuring IKE

## Certificate Generation and Enrollment

CAs do not create public/private key pairs for hosts. CAs only provide a means to share public keys (digital certificate) and attest to the authenticity of the keys. The responsibility for generating the key pairs resides with the host, so the host software must be capable of generating the key pairs and storing the private key, root certificate, and identity certificate. Cisco VPN Concentrators and the Cisco VPN Client have that capability.

Normally, the process of generating the keys and then enrolling the public key with a CA are two separate functions. On VPN concentrators, that two-step process has been condensed into the single enrollment process. To begin the process, select **Administration | Certificate Management | Enroll** from the VPN Manager's table of contents. When you do that, the screen shown in Figure 5-10 is displayed.

You can enroll either an Identity certificate or an SSL certificate from this screen. SSL certificates are required when you want to establish secure communications between your browser and the VPN concentrator. The processes related to the identity and SSL certificates are similar. The following portions of this section of the chapter go through the processes that are related to the identity certificate and note any differences that can be required for SSL certificates.

**Figure 5-10**  *Administration | Certificate Management | Enroll*

**Administration | Certificate Management | Enroll**

This section allows you to create an SSL or identity certificate request. The identity certificate request allows the VPN 3000 Concentrator to be enrolled into the PKI. The certificate request can be sent to a CA, which will issue a certificate. *The CA's certificate **must** be installed as a Certificate Authority before installing the certificate you requested.*

Choose the type of certificate request to create:

- Identity certificate
- SSL certificate

<< Go back to Certificate Management

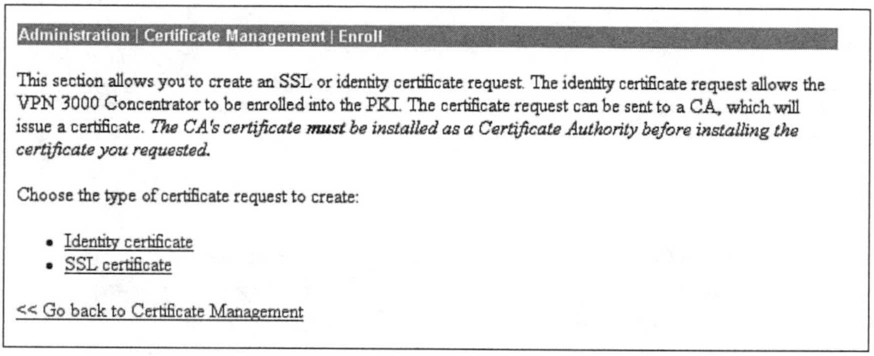

Notice the caveat in Figure 5-10 that states that the CA's certificate must be installed before installing any other certificates from that CA. To begin the process of enrolling an Identity certificate, click the **Identity certificate** option, which brings up the screen shown in Figure 5-11.

**Figure 5-11**  *Administration | Certificate Management | Enroll | Identity Certificate*

**Administration | Certificate Management | Enroll | Identity Certificate**

Select the enrollment method for the identity certificate. To install a certificate with SCEP, the issuing CA's certificate must also be installed with SCEP. Click here to install a new CA using SCEP before enrolling.

- Enroll via PKCS10 Request (Manual)
- Enroll via SCEP at MSCAsvr02
- Enroll via SCEP at MSCAsvr05

<< Go back and choose a different type of certificate

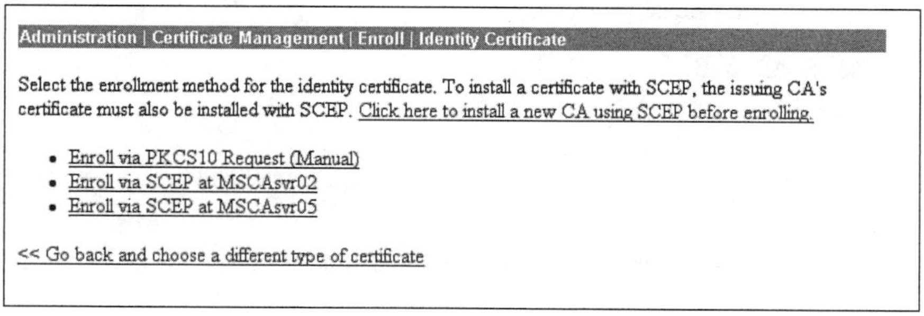

Enroll via SCEP. . . options are only available on this screen if you installed the CA certificate using SCEP. In this case, two CA certificates were installed using SCEP.

## Enrolling Via PKCS #10

Selecting **Enroll via PKCS10 Request (Manual)** from the Identity Certificate screen displays the screen shown in Figure 5-12. This is the same information that was shown in Table 5-2. Again, notice the caveat at the top of the screen, warning that the CA certificate must be installed first.

**Figure 5-12** *Administration | Certificate Management | Enroll | Identity Certificate | PKCS10*

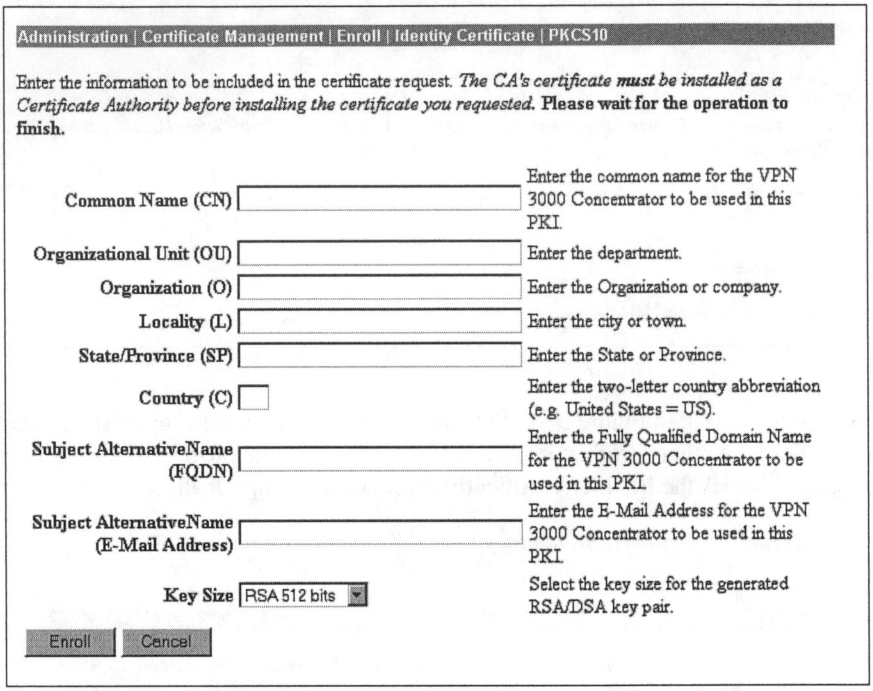

After you fill in the information on this screen, click **Enroll** and the concentrator performs the following steps:

**Step 1** Generates a public/private key pair and attaches the public key to the PKCS #10 request

**Step 2** Converts the PKCS #10 request to Privacy Enhanced Mail (PEM) format

**Step 3** Opens a browser window

**Step 4** Places the PEM-formatted request in the browser window

**Step 5** Presents the screen shown in Figure 5-13 to show the successful generation of the enrollment request

**NOTE**      PEM was an early standard for securing e-mail. Although never widely adopted as an Internet mail standard, it is used for CA correspondence. PEM takes the object (PKCS #10, PKCS #7, certificate, and so on), performs base64 encoding on it, and places the output in US-ASCII format between a standard PEM header and trailer.

**Figure 5-13** *Administration | Certificate Management | Enrollment | Request Generated*

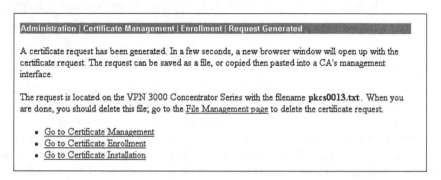

While the browser window shown in Figure 5-14 is opening to display the PEM-formatted certificate request, you can choose one of the following options from the Request Generated screen:

- If you feel you made a mistake in the PKCS #10 request, select **Go to Certificate Management** to view and manage the request.

- To enroll another certificate, select **Go to Certificate Enrollment**.

- To begin the manual process of installing the certificate, select **Go to Certificate Installation**.

**Figure 5-14** *PEM-Formatted Certificate Request*

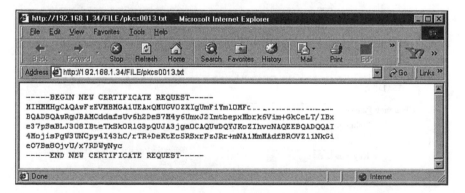

With the PEM version of the certificate request in hand, you now contact your CA operator and transmit the request. You could do that via HTTP, FTP, or e-mail, or by copying the request to a portable medium and physically transporting the request to the CA operator. Once the CA operator has accepted your request and enrolled it in the CA system, the CA operator returns the completed identity certificate to you in PEM format. Installation of the certificate is then completed in the same manner in which the CA certificate was handled in the previous section, "Manual SCEP Authentication" (see Figures 5-6, 5-7, and 5-8).

## Enrolling Via SCEP

The SCEP process of enrolling with the CA follows the same process as the PKCS #10 process, except that the concentrator contacts the CA, sends the request, receives the certificate, and installs the certificate automatically. The process starts by selecting one of the Enroll via SCEP. . . options shown in Figure 5-11. The screen shown in Figure 5-15 opens. Notice that this screen is similar to the PKCS #10 screen shown in Figure 5-12. The difference is that this screen asks for the challenge (preshared key) password to be used with the SCEP-capable CA.

**Figure 5-15** *Administration | Certificate Management | Enroll | Identity Certificate | SCEP*

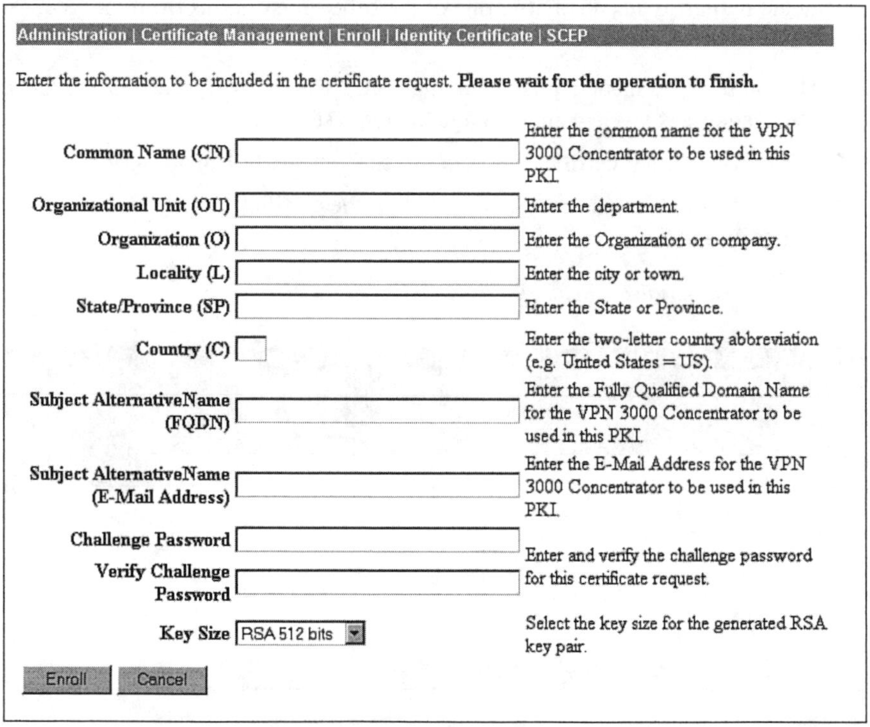

The process of contacting the CA, submitting the request, receiving the certificate, validating the certificate, and installing the certificate is completed for you when you complete the form and click **Enroll**. The VPN Manager returns the Request Generated screen shown in Figure 5-13. From there, you can go to the Certificate Management screen to verify the status of your identity certificate.

## Certificate Validation

Once the CA returns the identity certificate to the concentrator, the certificate must be validated before it can be installed. The concentrator does this for you by performing the authentication steps shown in Figure 5-3. To restate those steps, the concentrator calculates a hash of the certificate while decrypting the signature using the CA's public key to discover the hash created by the CA. If the two hash values match, the certificate has been authenticated as to origin.

Before performing the authentication process on the certificate, the concentrator must verify that a trusted CA signed the certificate, and that the current date and time fall within the validity window of the certificate. Additionally, the concentrator checks to see if the serial number of the certificate is listed on a CRL. Once the certificate passes these tests and has been authenticated, it can be used for further processing.

## Certificate Revocation Lists

The Administration | Certificate Management screen, shown in Figure 5-16, is a starting point for many certificate functions. As you study the screen, you can see that it is separated into four different sections, one for each of the three certificate types and one for pending certificates in the enrollment process. This screen provides a quick overview of the certificates, including the certificate expiration date.

The Certificate Management screen is the starting point for configuring CRL operability on a CA. Clicking the Configure hotlink in the Actions column for one of the CA certificates brings up the screen shown in Figure 5-17.

VPN concentrators use No CRL Checking as the default setting. This means that, by default, the VPN concentrator does not retrieve or check certificate revocation lists.

When you enable CRL checking for a certificate, every time the VPN concentrator uses the certificate for authentication during IKE Phase 1 negotiation, it also checks the CRL to ensure that the certificate being verified has not been revoked. If the certificate has been revoked, the tunnel is not established.

CRLs are stored at distribution points on external servers maintained by CAs. When verifying the revocation status of a certificate, a VPN concentrator retrieves the CRL from one of the distribution points and checks the serial number of the certificate against the list of serial numbers in the CRL. If there is a match, the certificate has been revoked and is invalidated by the concentrator. The VPN concentrator can be configured to retrieve the CRL from the distribution points specified in the certificate being checked, from a static list of CRL distribution points, or from a combination of these.

**Figure 5-16**  *Administration | Certificate Management*

| Administration | Certificate Management | | | | Tuesday, 8 October 2002 11:14:44 |
| | | | | | Refresh |

This section lets you view and manage certificates on the VPN 3000 Concentrator.

- Click here to enroll with a Certificate Authority
- Click here to install a certificate

**Certificate Authorities** [ View All CRL Caches | Clear All CRL Caches ] (current: 11, maximum: 20)

| Subject | Issuer | Expiration | SCEP Issuer | Actions |
|---|---|---|---|---|
| A Branch CA | Corp CA | 10/26/2004 | No | View | Configure | Delete<br>View CRL Cache | Clear CRL Cache |
| B Branch CA | Corp CA | 03/25/2004 | Yes | View | Configure | Delete | SCEP | Show RAs<br>View CRL Cache | Clear CRL Cache |
| Corp CA | Corp CA | 03/14/2021 | Yes | View | Configure | Delete | SCEP | Show RAs |
| CorpBakCA | Corp CA | 03/14/2021 | Yes | View | Configure | Delete | SCEP | Show RAs |
| Test CA | Test CA | 08/17/2002 | Yes | View | Configure | Delete | SCEP | Show RAs<br>View CRL Cache | Clear CRL Cache |

**Identity Certificates** (current: 4, maximum: 20)

| Subject | Issuer | Expiration | Actions |
|---|---|---|---|
| A Branch VPN 03 at The Corp | A Branch CA | 03/26/2003 | View | Renew | Delete |
| B Branch VPN 02 at The Corp | B Branch CA | 04/01/2003 | View | Renew | Delete |
| 192.168.1.99 identity sub 4 at The Corp | Corp CA | 04/01/2003 | View | Renew | Delete |
| 172.16.20.15 Tvpn at RnD The Corp | Test CA | 10/23/2004 | View | Renew | Delete |

**SSL Certificate** [ Generate ] *Note: The public key in the SSL certificate is also used for the SSH host key.*

| Subject | Issuer | Expiration | Actions |
|---|---|---|---|
| 192.168.14.34 at The Corp | 192.168.14.34 at The Corp | 11/01/2003 | View | Renew | Delete |

**Enrollment Status** [ Remove All: Errored | Timed-Out | Rejected | Cancelled | In-Progress ] (current: 0 available: 16)

| Subject | Issuer | Date | Use | Reason | Method | Status | Actions |
|---|---|---|---|---|---|---|---|
| No Enrollment Requests | | | | | | | |

You can also select to enable CRL caching from the Administration | Certificate Management | Configure CA Certificate screen. With caching enabled, the first time the VPN concentrator retrieves a CRL from a distribution point, it stores the CRL in volatile memory. The concentrator looks first in memory for the CRL it needs. If the CRL is found in memory, the concentrator checks for the subject certificate's serial number. The VPN concentrator looks for a new CRL if the cached CRL has expired or if the refresh time you established has elapsed. Caching can save network resources on busy networks and can minimize timeout problems during IKE negotiations while waiting to retrieve the latest CRL.

**Figure 5-17**  *Administration | Certificate Management | Configure CA Certificate*

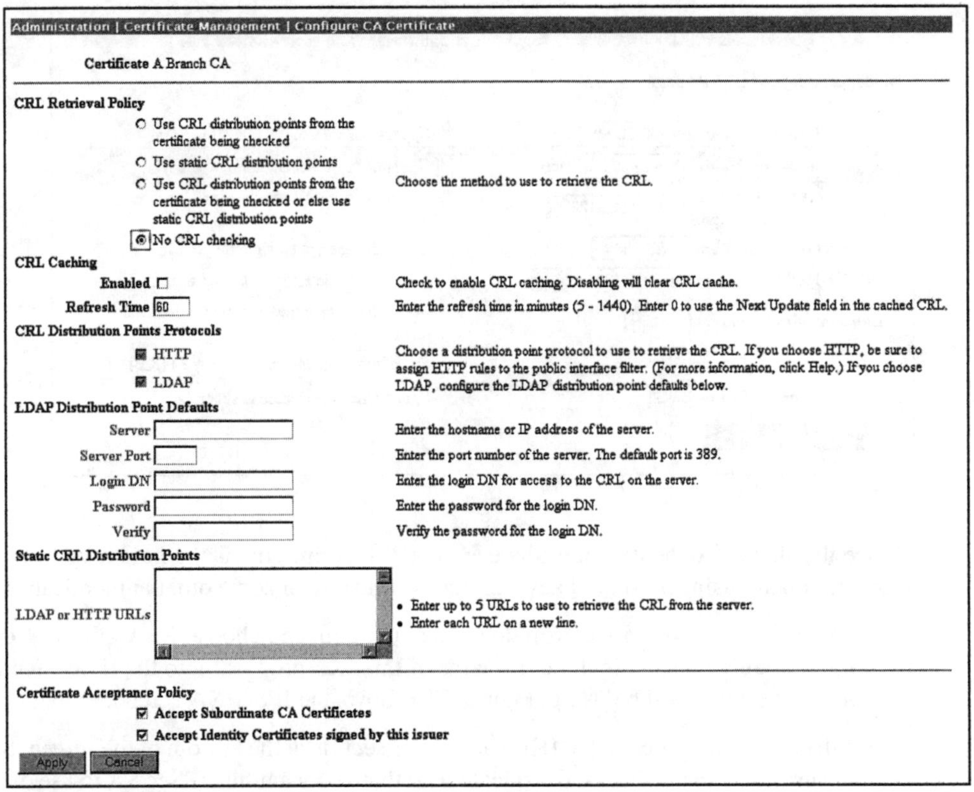

## IKE Configuration

Now that you have the digital certificate portion of the VPN concentrator configured, you must set up the concentrator to use the certificates during IKE negotiations. You need to tweak just two places to use digital certificates: the IKE proposal that you will use and the IPSec SA that you will use.

Figure 5-18 shows the screen used to modify IKE proposal configurations. You can modify an existing proposal, as is shown here, or create a new one.

**Figure 5-18**   *Configuration | System | Tunneling Protocols | IPSec | IKE Proposals | Modify*

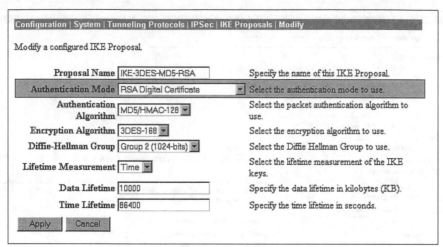

Notice the shaded Authentication Mode area on this form. That is the field used to determine whether you are using preshared keys, digital certificates, or some other authentication method.

Click the Authentication Mode drop-down menu button, and choose **RSA Digital Certificate** from the available options. Include the name of this IKE proposal into the IPSec Security Association that you will be using. Figure 5-19 shows the IPSec SA screen.

Notice the highlighted area in the IKE Parameters section at the bottom of the screen. Select the identity certificate in the Digital Certificate field that you want this IPSec SA to use during IKE Phase 1 negotiations. The drop-down box displays the certificates that you have installed on the VPN concentrator. You can then select from these certificates.

In this same area, enter the name of the IKE proposal that you modified on the IPSec IKE Proposals screen in Figure 5-18. You can select this proposal from the drop-down box.

You also have the option of which certificates to send to the peer during negotiations. You can select to send only the identity certificate (default action) or to send the entire certificate chain, which would be the identity, root, and any subordinate CA certificates the VPN concentrator holds.

That concludes the configuration of the VPN concentrator to support digital certificates. The next step is to configure the VPN Client for digital certificate support, as described in the next section.

**Figure 5-19**  *Configuration | Policy Management | Traffic Management | Security Associations | Modify*

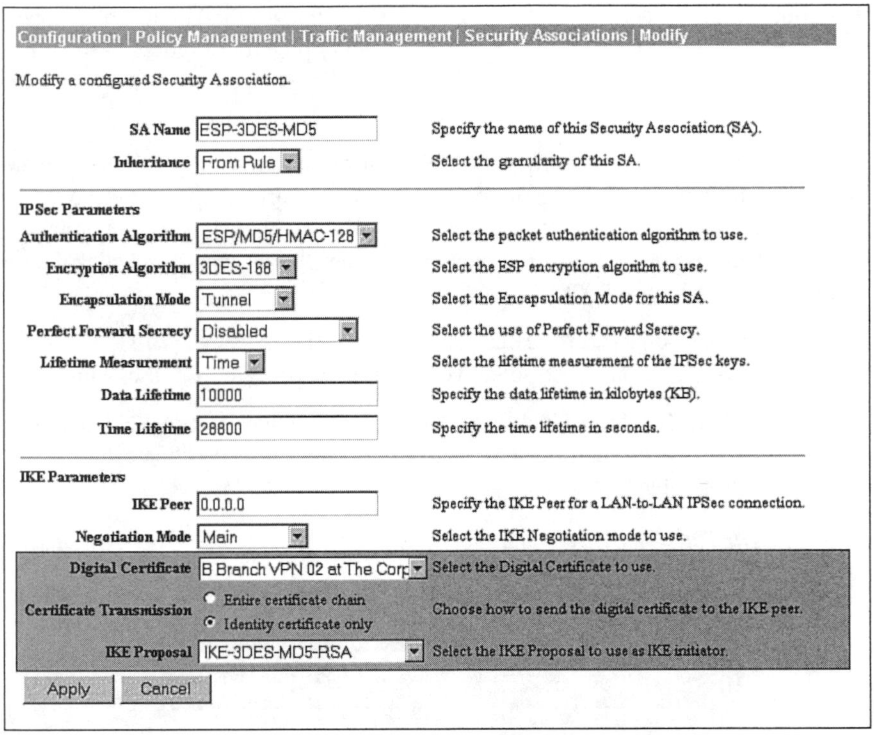

## Configuring the VPN Client for CA Support

**18**  Configuring the Cisco VPN 3000 Concentrator Series for CA support

Because you will now be using digital certificates for authentication on the VPN concentrator, you must modify the configuration of your user's VPN Client connection entries from using a preshared key to using a digital certificate. All your clients must have a root certificate and an identity certificate installed in the browser application of their VPN client system.

As the system administrator, you can manually enroll each of your users and copy the identity certificate and the issuing root CA certificate for them to floppy disk. These can then be imported into the browser. Figures 5-20 and 5-21 show the user's personal identity certificate and the root certificate in Microsoft's Internet Explorer.

**NOTE**    When you generate the PKCS #10 certificate request for your users, the OU field must match the group name you defined for them on the VPN concentrator. You might also need to mark the keys as exportable. The enrollment process is not depicted in Figures 5-20 and 5-21.

To complete the process, modify the VPN connection in the VPN Client software to use the identity certificate shown in Figure 5-20. To do that, start the VPN Client by choosing **Start**, **Programs**, **Cisco Systems VPN Client**, **VPN Dialer**. Select the correct connection entry, and click the **Options** button. Select **Properties** from the Options menu, and click the **Authentication** tab, as shown in Figure 5-22.

Now that you have digital certificates installed, the Certificate area is no longer grayed out. Select the **Certificate** button, and then select your identity certificate from the Name drop-down box.

You can check the **Send CA Certificate Chain** option to have your VPN Client send the identity, subordinate CA, and root certificates instead of just the identity certificate during IKE negotiations. This option is disabled by default.

**Figure 5-20**    *Personal Certificates—Internet Explorer*

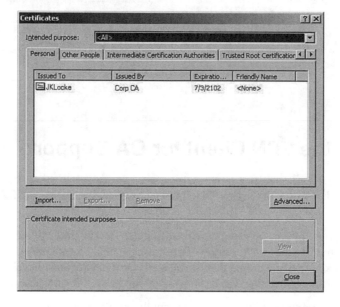

**Figure 5-21**  *Trusted Root Certification Authorities—Internet Explorer*

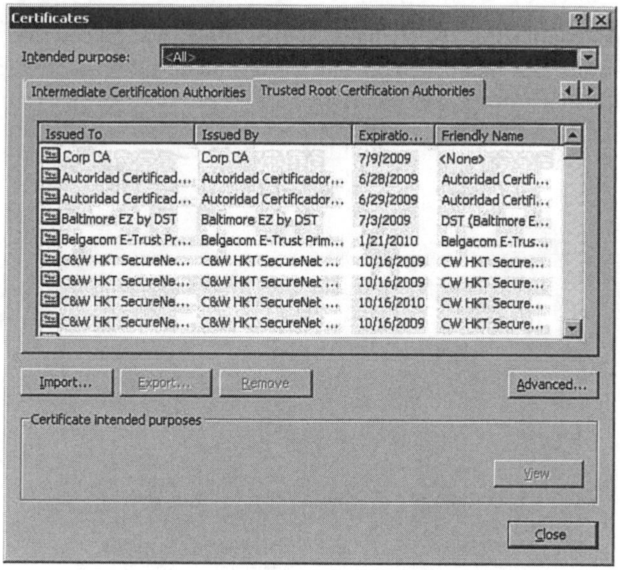

**Figure 5-22**  *Authentication Selection—VPN Client*

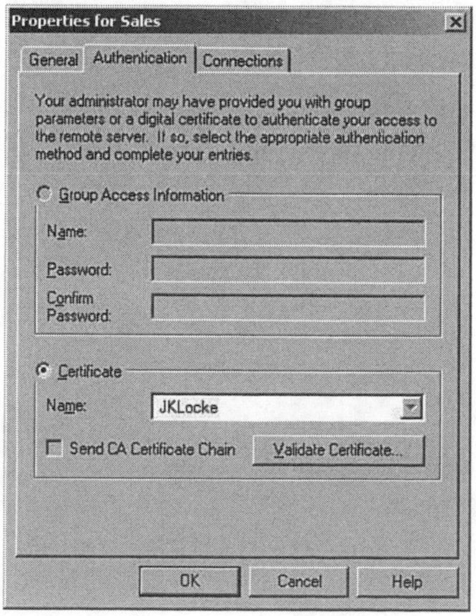

You can also check to see if the certificate is still valid by clicking the **Validate Certificate** button. A report is generated that lets you know if the certificate is still valid.

Once you have completed the changes on the Authentication tab, click **OK** to save the changes and return to the VPN Dialer screen, where you can now connect to the VPN concentrator using digital certificates instead of preshared keys.

## Foundation Summary

The Foundation Summary is a collection of tables and figures that provides a convenient review of many key concepts in this chapter. For those of you who are already comfortable with the topics in this chapter, this summary could help you recall a few details. For those who just read this chapter, this review should help solidify some key facts. For anyone doing his or her final preparation before the exam, these tables and figures can be a convenient way to review the material the day before the exam.

## PKCS #10 Certificate Request Fields

The following list outlines the VPN concentrator's PKCS #10 Certificate Request fields:

- Common Name (CN)
- Organization Unit (OU)
- Organization (O)
- Locality (L)
- State/Province (SP)
- Country (C)
- Subject Alternative Name (FQDN)
- Key Size

## X.509 Identity Certificate Fields

The following list outlines the X.509 Identity Certificate fields:

- Certificate Format Version
- Certificate Serial Number
- Signature Algorithm
- Issuer's X.500 Distinguished Name
- Validity Period
- Subject's X.500 Distinguished Name
- Subject's Public Key Information
- Extensions
- CA Signature

# Types of Digital Certificates

The types of digital certificates are as follows:

- **Root**—Identifies the overarching authority in the CA network.
- **Identity**—Required by every device, these are signed by either the root CA or by a subordinate CA. The root CA must self-sign its own identity certificate.
- **Issuing (or subordinate)**—Serves the same purpose as the root certificate, but is issued by a subordinate CA instead of the root CA. Subordinate CAs *do not* self-sign their own identity certificate.

# Types of CA Organization

The types of CA organizations are as follows:

- **Central CA**—The root CA issues certificates directly to all clients.
- **Hierarchical CA**—The root CA delegates signature authority to subordinate CAs. Subordinate CAs can further delegate signature authority to additional subordinates.

# Certificate Validation and Authentication Process

The following list outlines the certificate validation and authentication process:

**Step 1**    Certificate signed by trusted CA? Has a CA certificate been installed on the concentrator for this CA?

**Step 2**    Certificate still valid? Does the current date fall within the start and end dates of the certificate?

**Step 3**    Certificate revoked? Does the certificate's serial number exist on the CA's CRL?

**Step 4**    Certificate authenticated? Reasonable assurance that the certificate has not been altered.

   (a)  Calculate hash of signature.

   (b)  Retrieve CA's original hash of signature.

   - Decrypt digital signature on certificate.
   - Use root CA's key from root certificate.

   (c)  Do the two hash values match? Certificate authenticated.

# Internet-Based Certificate Authorities

The Cisco VPN 3000 Concentrator series works with the following Internet-based CAs:

- Entrust Technologies (www.entrust.com)
- VeriSign, Inc. (www.verisign.com)
- Baltimore Technologies (www.baltimoretechnologies.com)

# Certificate Management Applications

Certificate management applications are as follows:

- Microsoft Certificate Services for Windows 2000
- RSA Keon Certificate Authority for Solaris, Windows 2000, and Windows NT
- Netscape Certificate Management System for Solaris, Windows 2000, and Windows NT

## Chapter Glossary

The following terms were introduced in this chapter or have special significance to the topics within this chapter:

**Directory System Agent (DSA)**    Software that provides the X.500 Directory Service for a portion of the directory information base. Generally, each DSA is responsible for the directory information for a single organization or organizational unit.

**Public Key Cryptography Standards (PKCS)**    Series of specifications published by RSA Laboratories for data structures and algorithm usage for basic applications of asymmetric cryptography.

**Public Key Infrastructure (PKI)**    System of CAs (and optionally, RAs and other supporting servers and agents) that perform some set of certificate management, archive management, key management, and token management functions for a community of users in an application of asymmetric cryptography.

**Rivest, Shamir, and Adelman (RSA)**    The inventors of the technique of a public-key cryptographic system that can be used for encryption and authentication.

# Q&A

As mentioned in Chapter 1, these questions are more difficult than what you should experience on the CCSP exam. The questions do not attempt to cover more breadth or depth than the exam; however, the questions are designed to make sure you know the answer. Rather than allowing you to derive the answer from clues hidden inside the question itself, your understanding and recall of the subject are challenged. Questions from the "Do I Know This Already?" quiz from the beginning of the chapter are repeated here to ensure that you have mastered the chapter's topic areas. Hopefully, these questions will help limit the number of exam questions on which you narrow your choices to two options and guess!

**1**  What must be in place on a client's PC before you can configure the VPN Client for certificate support?

_____

_____

_____

**2**  What two methods are available on the VPN concentrator for installing certificates obtained through manual enrollment?

_____

_____

_____

**3**  What could cause a digital certificate to be revoked by the CA?

_____

_____

_____

**4**  What are the two types of CA structures?

_____

_____

_____

**5** During the authentication process, where does a VPN concentrator find the original hash that the CA calculated for an identity certificate?

_____

_____

_____

**6** During manual SCEP authentication, how is the request transmitted to the CA?

_____

_____

_____

**7** What Public Key Cryptography Standard is used to request enrollment with a CA?

_____

_____

_____

**8** What is the first certificate that must be installed on a VPN concentrator before you can install any other certificates from a given CA?

_____

_____

_____

**9** When configuring digital certificate support on a VPN concentrator, where do you identify which certificate to use for IKE Phase 1 negotiations?

_____

_____

_____

**10** After a VPN peer receives an identity certificate from its partner during IKE Phase 1, the peer calculates a hash of the certificate. What does the peer compare this hash against to verify that the certificate has not been altered?

_____

_____

_____

**11**  Where does a VPN concentrator obtain the root CA's public key?

_____

_____

_____

**12**  What entity is responsible for generating the PKI public/private key pair for a requesting host?

_____

_____

_____

**13**  In the VPN Manager, where do you identify that you want to use RSA Digital Certificates for IKE Phase 1 authentication?

_____

_____

_____

**14**  What three tests does a VPN concentrator perform on a partner's identity certificate before performing the authentication process?

_____

_____

_____

**15**  Which version of the X.509 standard identity certificate permits extensions?

_____

_____

_____

**16**  What is RSA Keon?

_____

_____

_____

**17** When does the **Click here to install a CA certificate** option appear on the Administration |
Certificate Management screen of the VPN Manager?

_____

_____

_____

**18** The VPN concentrator is certified to work with three Internet-based CAs. Which CAs are
they?

_____

_____

_____

**19** What elements make up the X.500 distinguished name?

_____

_____

_____

**20** Which screen do you use to enable the use of digital certificates for device authentication
during IKE Phase 1 negotiations?

_____

_____

_____

**21** What two enrollment methods are available on a VPN concentrator?

_____

_____

_____

**22** What field in the certificate request should match the IPSec group name on the VPN
concentrator?

_____

_____

_____

**23** When are SSL certificates required on a VPN concentrator?

_____

_____

_____

**24** What are the three types of certificates involved in the digital certificate process?

_____

_____

_____

**25** What is a CRL?

_____

_____

_____

**26** When you select to cache CRLs on the VPN concentrator, where are they stored?

_____

_____

_____

**27** What default algorithm type and key size does the VPN concentrator use on the certificate request?

_____

_____

_____

**28** Using the VPN Manager, where would you look to check the status of a certificate enrollment process?

_____

_____

_____

**29** What is a root certificate?

_____

_____

_____

**30** Where are you asked to supply a challenge password during the enrollment process?

_____

_____

_____

**31** How is the validity period of a digital certificate specified?

_____

_____

_____

**32** With CRL caching disabled, how does a VPN concentrator check a certificate's serial number against a CRL?

_____

_____

_____

**33** SCEP has two authentication methods available between a requester and the CA. What are those two methods?

_____

_____

_____

## Scenarios

The following scenarios and questions are designed to draw together the content of the chapter and exercise your understanding of the concepts. There might be more than one correct answer. The thought process and practice in manipulating each concept in the scenario are the goals of this section.

# Scenario 5-1

You have just configured a new Microsoft Windows 2000 Certificate Server in your network. You want to test the CA services before you roll out the service to your entire network. You are currently using a Cisco VPN 3005 Concentrator for remote access VPNs with 65 certificates installed. User authentication is handled through the NT domain. You will be using SCEP on the CA server. You will be using two laptop clients for testing. The laptops are using the Cisco VPN Client software.

1 Describe the steps you need to take to configure the VPN concentrator to use the new CA server.

2 Describe the steps you need to take to configure the clients to use the new CA server.

# Scenario 5-2

You have been using a Cisco VPN 3030 Concentrator for some time to manage VPN connections for remote access users. You want to use a CA server that does not support SCEP.

Describe the steps you need to take to configure the VPN concentrator to use the new CA server.

# Scenario Answers

The answers provided in this section are not necessarily the only correct answers. They represent one possibility for each scenario. The intention is to test your base knowledge and understanding of the concepts discussed in this chapter.

Should your answers be different (as they likely will be), consider the differences. Are your answers in line with the concepts of the answers provided and explained here? If not, reread the chapter, focusing on the sections that are related to the problem scenario.

## Scenario 5-1 Answers

1 The steps you need to take to configure the VPN concentrator to use the new CA server are as follows:

**Step 1** Install a CA certificate for the new CA onto the concentrator using SCEP.

**Step 2** Enroll the VPN concentrator with the CA server using SCEP.

**Step 3** Select the IKE proposal you will be using, and configure the authentication mode to use RSA digital certificates.

**Step 4** Select the IPSec SA you will be using, and identify the IKE proposal and certificate to use.

2 The steps required to configure the clients to use the new CA server are as follows:

**Step 1** From the VPN concentrator:

(a) Enroll the clients manually with the CA server to obtain their identity certificates.

(b) Copy the CA root certificate and the identity certificates to floppy disk.

**Step 2** From the VPN Client:

(a) Import the root and identity certificates into the browser on each client. Be sure to import only one identity certificate onto each client.

(b) Open the VPN Dialer, and select the connection to the VPN concentrator.

(c) Click **Options** and select **Properties**.

(d) Select the Authentication tab, and modify **Choose to use Certificates for authentication**. Select the name of the identity certificate from the drop-down menu.

(e) Test the connection.

# Scenario 5-2 Answers

The steps required to configure the VPN concentrator to use the new CA server are as follows:

**Step 1**  Install a CA certificate for the new CA onto the concentrator manually as follows:

(a) Copy the CA root certificate to your management workstation. You can do this from floppy disk or through file transfer from the CA.

(b) Install the CA certificate by choosing to upload the file from the workstation.

**Step 2**  Enroll the VPN concentrator with the CA server manually as follows:

(a) Prepare a PKCS #10 certificate request in PEM format.

(b) Transport the request to the CA server (electronically or physically).

(c) Receive the identity certificate from the CA server (electronically or physically).

(d) Select to install the identity certificate by uploading the file from the workstation.

**Step 3**  Select the IKE proposal you will be using, and configure the authentication mode to use RSA digital certificates.

**Step 4**  Select the IPSec SA you will be using, and identify the IKE proposal and certificate to use.

# Exam Topics Discussed in This Chapter

This chapter covers the following topics, which you need to master in your pursuit of certification as a Cisco Certified Security Professional:

**19** Overview of software client's firewall feature

**20** Software client's Are You There feature

**21** Software client's Stateful Firewall feature

**22** Software client's Central Policy Protection feature

**23** Client firewall statistics

**24** Customizing firewall policy

# CHAPTER 6

# Configuring the Cisco VPN Client Firewall Feature

This chapter deals with configuring the Cisco VPN Client firewall feature set. You learn about the Cisco VPN Client's basic configuration, how to create filters on the concentrator, and how to configure firewall features.

The VPN Client has an integrated Stateful Firewall feature as part of the client package. This client can be enabled to block all traffic coming into the user's system that does not originate from the head-end concentrator's network. This provides a good measure of security against intrusion from the Internet.

Cisco's VPN Client also works with third-party private firewalls from Zone Labs and Network ICE. These third-party firewalls provide additional features that are not found in the Stateful Firewall feature.

When connecting to a Cisco VPN 3000 Series Concentrator, the VPN Client receives instructions from the concentrator on how to configure and use the private firewall, if any, that can be installed with the VPN Client. The VPN concentrator can be configured to supply a firewall policy to the VPN Client so that every VPN Client connecting to the VPN concentrator has a centrally administered firewall policy for maximum protection of network resources.

This chapter discusses the various personal firewalls that can be used in conjunction with the VPN Client. The chapter also discusses the configuration steps necessary on the VPN concentrator and the VPN Client to make the best use of personal firewalls on VPN networks.

## How to Best Use This Chapter

By taking the following steps, you can make better use of your time:

- Keep your notes and answers for all your work with this book in one place for easy reference.

- Take the "Do I Know This Already?" quiz, and write down your answers. Studies show retention is significantly increased through writing facts and concepts down, even if you never look at the information again.

- Use the diagram in Figure 6-1 to guide you to the next step.

**Figure 6-1** *How to Use This Chapter*

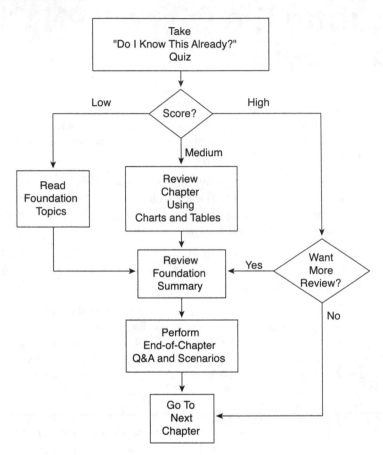

# "Do I Know This Already?" Quiz

The purpose of the "Do I Know This Already?" quiz is to help you decide what parts of the chapter to use. If you already intend to read the entire chapter, you do not need to answer these questions now.

This 18-question quiz helps you determine how to spend your limited study time. The quiz is sectioned into six smaller "quizlets," which correspond to the six major topic headings in the chapter. Figure 6-1 outlines suggestions on how to spend your time in this chapter based on your quiz score. Use Table 6-1 to record your scores.

**Table 6-1**     *Score Sheet for Quiz and Quizlets*

| Quizlet Number | Foundations Topics Section Covering These Questions | Question | Score |
|---|---|---|---|
| 1 | Overview of software client's firewall feature | 1–3 | |
| 2 | Software client's Are You There feature | 4–6 | |
| 3 | Software client's Stateful Firewall feature | 7–9 | |
| 4 | Software client's Central Policy Protection feature | 10–12 | |
| 5 | Client firewall statistics | 13–15 | |
| 6 | Customizing firewall policy | 16–18 | |

1   You have a number of clients running Windows 98 and a remote VPN 3002 Hardware Client assigned to the same group. Your supervisor wants you to force everyone on this group connecting to have a firewall running on his or her machine. Can you do this?

_____

_____

_____

2   How is the Always On option set on the VPN Client?

_____

_____

_____

3   In addition to IPSec, what tunneling protocols does the VPN Client support?

_____

_____

_____

4   How often does the VPN Client poll the personal firewall when using Are You There (AYT)?

_____

_____

_____

**5** You are using BlackICE as a client firewall. You are presently connected through the VPN. What happens if you stop the service running BlackICE? Does the VPN remain connected? If so, for how long? Can you connect again if BlackICE is not running?

_____

_____

_____

**6** Which two products from Zone Labs work with the VPN Client to enable the Are You There (AYT) capability?

_____

_____

_____

**7** What protocols are not automatically blocked when using the Stateful Firewall (Always On) feature?

_____

_____

_____

**8** You want to have secure VPN connections to the private network of the head-end concentrator and unsecured communications to the Internet. How would you configure the VPN Client's Stateful Firewall feature to support this split tunneling?

_____

_____

_____

**9** What is another name for the Stateful Firewall client that is a part of the Cisco VPN Client?

_____

_____

_____

**10** Where are the rules set for a client when using Central Protection Policy (CPP) with Zone AlarmPro?

_____

_____

_____

**11**  Why is CPP not used with the Tunnel Everything option?

_____

_____

_____

**12**  On what screen do you configure CPP?

_____

_____

_____

**13**  On the VPN Client, where do you see the current compression used for a VPN connection?

_____

_____

_____

**14**  From the VPN Client, where can you view the secured routes that are enabled to the client?

_____

_____

_____

**15**  What is meant by the term _Packets bypassed_ on the Statistics tab of the Connection Status screen?

_____

_____

_____

16 What debug classes do you use when creating a rule with the following options:

   a. Drop

   b. Drop and Log

   c. Forward

   d. Forward and Log

   e. Apply IPSec

   f. Apply IPSec and Log

   _____

   _____

   _____

17 How do you allow clients to use either of two firewalls? What is the only vendor you can do this with?

   _____

   _____

   _____

18 On the VPN 3000 Concentrator Series devices, you configure the client firewall properties on the Client FW tab of the Configuration | User Management | Groups | Add (or Modify) screen. You can only select one firewall policy from that screen. What are the three types of firewall policies that you can choose from on the Client FW tab?

   _____

   _____

   _____

The answers to this quiz are listed in Appendix A, "Answers to the "Do I Know This Already?" Quizzes and Q&A Sections." The suggestions for your next steps, based on quiz results, are as follows:

- **9 or less overall score**—Read the entire chapter, including the "Foundation Topics" and "Foundation Summary" sections, the "Q&A" section, and the scenarios at the end of the chapter.

- **10–15 overall score**—Begin with the "Foundation Summary" section, continue with the "Q&A" section, and then read the scenarios. If you are having difficulty with a particular subject area, read the appropriate section in the "Foundation Topics" section.

- **15–18 overall score**—If you feel you need more review on these topics, go to the "Foundation Summary" section, then to the "Q&A" section, then to the scenarios. Otherwise, skip this chapter and go to the next chapter.

# Foundation Topics

# Cisco VPN Client Firewall Feature Overview

**19** Overview of software client's firewall feature

The Cisco VPN Client version 3.6 is a software product that enables the use of secure tunnels from workstations to any Cisco Easy VPN Server. Currently, these servers include the Cisco PIX Firewall (version 6.0 and later), the Cisco IOS Software–based platforms (versions 12.2(8)T and later), and the Cisco VPN 3000 Series Concentrators (version 3.0 and later). The client is available for use on Windows-based workstations, including Windows 95 (OSR2+), 98, Me, 4.0, 2000, and XP. It is also available on Linux running the Intel chip set, Solaris UltraSparc (both 32- and 64-bit), and Macintosh computers running OS X 10.1. Table 6-2 highlights the abilities of the VPN Client.

**Table 6-2**   *VPN Client Abilities*

| Client Ability | Description |
| --- | --- |
| Tunneling protocols | Tunneling protocols supported are as follows:<br>• IP Security–Encapsulating Security Payload (IPSec-ESP)<br>• L2TP<br>• L2TP/IPSec<br>• NAT<br>• NAT Transparent IPSec<br>• Ratified IPSec/UDP<br>• IPSec/TCP<br>• PPTP |
| Encryption and authentication protocols | Encryption and authentication methods supported include the following:<br>• IPSec(ESP) with Data Encryption Standard (DES)/3DES(56/168 bits)<br>• AES(126/256-bit) with Message Digest (MD5) or SHA |

*continues*

**Table 6-2**   *VPN Client Abilities (Continued)*

| Client Ability | Description |
|---|---|
| Key management capabilities | Key management capabilities include the following:<br><br>• Internet Key Exchange (IKE)—Aggressive and Main mode (digital certificates)<br>• Diffie-Hellman (DH) Groups 1, 2, and 5<br>• PFS<br>• Rekeying |
| Compression method | LZS (Lempel-Ziv standard) |
| Authentication methods | Authentication methods include the following:<br><br>• XAUTH (eXtended AUTHentication)<br>• Remote Authentication Dial-In User Service (RADIUS) with the following:<br>   — MSCHAPv2 (NT password expiration)<br>   — State/Reply message attributes (token cards)<br>   — RSA SecurID (Security Dynamics)<br>   — Windows NT Domain Authentication<br>   — MX.509v3 digital certificates |
| Digital certificates | Digital certificates supported include the following:<br><br>• Simple Certificate Enrollment Protocol (SCEP)<br>• Entrust Entelligence<br>• Smartcards through MS CAPI:<br>   — Activcard<br>   — eAladdin<br>   — Gemplus<br>   — Datakey<br>• Internet Explorer Certificate Enrollment<br>• Authorities include the following:<br>   — Baltimore<br>   — Entrust<br>   — GTE Cybertrust<br>   — Microsoft<br>   — RSA Keon<br>   — VeriSign |

The VPN Client software is bundled with every Cisco VPN 3000 Series Concentrator, and customers can download upgrades from Cisco Systems if they have a maintenance (Smartnet) contract for their concentrator.

# Firewall Configuration Overview

**20**  Software client's Are You There feature

**21**  Software client's Stateful Firewall feature

**22**  Software client's Central Policy Protection feature

This section discusses two options on the firewall configuration: the optional and the required firewall. In essence, the VPN concentrator can require that the VPN Client use a particular configuration (required), or the VPN concentrator can allow a different configuration (optional).

When the VPN Client attempts to establish a connection, the concentrator looks at its own rules and acts accordingly. If the VPN concentrator has been set with a required configuration and the client's configuration is not correct, no tunnel is established. If the VPN concentrator uses the optional mode, it allows the client to connect and download the desired firewall with the correct configuration onto the client's PC.

The VPN concentrator does not permit a VPN tunnel to be established if the concentrator requires a firewall on the connecting device but one does not exist. The VPN concentrator does, however, allow the connecting device to run a firewall even when the concentrator does not require one. This permits the client's system to be protected in cases where communications might not be protected by a VPN tunnel. The next section discusses the VPN Client's Stateful Firewall feature.

This section covers the following topics:

- The Stateful Firewall (Always On) feature
- The Are You There feature

## The Stateful Firewall (Always On) Feature

The Stateful Firewall feature is configured on the VPN Client. The VPN concentrator does not control the Stateful Firewall feature. Enabling this feature prevents inbound connections from all other networks without regard to tunneling or encryption. In this mode, the PC does not respond to connection requests, with the following exceptions:

- **Traffic originating from the head-end network**—The purpose of the client is to allow secure communication with the head-end network.

- **DHCP requests**—Dynamic Host Configuration Protocol (DHCP) requests are sent from the client on one port to the DHCP server and received on a different port.

- **ESP**—Encapsulating Security Payload (ESP) is VPN data that are allowed from the secure gateway because ESP rules are always packet filters, as opposed to session-based filters.

Turning off the Always On option allows the user to have a secure VPN connection to the head-end network while still having nonsecured connections to other networks, such as the Internet. This merging of secured and nonsecured traffic on the same wire is called *split tunneling*. The Stateful Firewall (Always On) feature provides protection for nonsecured traffic when split tunneling is in use.

## Cisco Integrated Client

The VPN Client used on the Windows platforms includes a stateful firewall that is transparent to the user. Designed by Zone Labs, this firewall is called the Cisco Integrated Client (CIC). Although the Always On option of the VPN Client allows the user to choose whether to have basic firewall protection in place, the CIC can still be controlled by the concentrator using the Central Protection Policy (CPP). CPP allows the VPN concentrator to define rules for use during split-tunnel operation. Because the Tunnel Everything option already blocks all non-tunneled traffic, CPP is not used in this mode.

The Zone Labs Integrity Server, commonly refereed to as IS, is a stand-alone server that communicates with the VPN concentrator to maintain policies for the remote PCs. The IS also ensures policy enforcement by communicating with the concentrator to allow or drop connections, exchange session and user information, and report the status of connections.

## Centralized Protection Policy

CPP, which is also known as a *push policy* because it is pushed from the concentrator down to the client, allows you to define additional rules to allow or deny Internet traffic while the client is connected to the concentrator.

During the VPN connection negotiation, the concentrator sends a predefined policy to the VPN Client. The client then passes this policy to the CIC, which in turn enforces the policy. If the Always On option has been chosen on the client, more restrictive rules can be used regarding Internet traffic while the tunnel is established.

CPP can use a number of firewalls to enforce these rules, including CIC, Zone Alarm, and Zone AlarmPro. CPP allows finer tuning of the firewall than the Stateful Firewall feature because you can allow or deny specific ports and protocols.

## The Are You There Feature

An alternative to using the CPP method of defining policies on the personal firewall is where the VPN Client polls a firewall installed on the client PC every 30 seconds. This process is called Are You There (AYT). If the firewall does not answer these polls, the VPN Client drops the tunnel. Using this method, the VPN Client does not enforce a policy but rather ensures that a software firewall on the PC is running.

AYT is usable with BlackICE, Zone Alarm, or Zone AlarmPro. The only messages passed between the concentrator and the firewall are these AYT polls.

# Configuring Firewall Filter Rules

> **24** Customizing firewall policy

Before you can use filter rules from the concentrator, you must configure those rules. Although the concentrator's default configuration comes with some rules, these are not meant for production networks. The default rules are too open for a truly secure environment because they were designed merely to facilitate the building of rules for your individual network. Rules, which are specifications that allow or deny specific types of traffic, can be applied to either an interface or a VPN group. This section discusses how to build rules and filters for use with the VPN concentrator.

Rules are configured from the Configuration | Policy Management | Traffic Management | Rules screen, as shown in Figure 6-2.

**Figure 6-2**    *The Configuration | Policy Management | Traffic Management | Rules Screen*

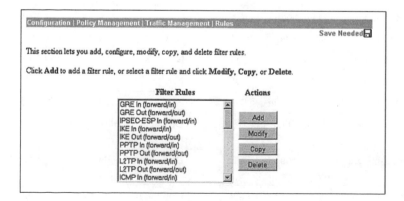

On this screen, you can add, modify, copy, or delete rules. The list shown consists of the default rules and those rules that the administrator has added, minus the deleted rules. Notice that each of these rules has text inside parentheses. The text within the parentheses describes the action and direction. The meaning of this action and direction text is discussed in the section describing the creation of a rule, "Name, Direction, and Action."

The default rules are listed in Table 6-3. For the default rules, the action is almost always forward and the source address is always Use IP Address/Wildcard mask, which is set to any address (0.0.0.0 255.255.255.255). The destination IP address is always Use IP Address/Wildcard mask, which is set to any address (0.0.0.0/255.255.255.255). The exceptions to these rules are with Virtual Router Redundancy Protocol (VRRP) In and VRRP Out, which use the Internet Assigned Numbers Authority (IANA)–assigned multicast IP address of 224.0.0.18/0.0.0.0.

**Table 6-3**   *Default Rules*

| Rule | Direction | Protocol | TCP Connection | TCP/UDP Source Port | TCP/UDP Connection Port | ICMP Packet Type |
|---|---|---|---|---|---|---|
| Any In | Inbound | Any | Don't care | 0–65535 | 0–65,535 | 0–255 |
| Any Out | Outbound | Any | Don't care | 0–65635 | 0–65,635 | 0–255 |
| Certificate Revocation List (CRL) checking over LDAP In | Inbound | TCP | Don't care | 389 | 0–65,535 | N/A |
| CRL checking over LDAP Out | Outbound | TCP | Don't care | 0–65535 | 389 | N/A |
| Generic Routing Encapsulation (GRE) In | Inbound | GRE | N/A | N/A | N/A | N/A |
| GRE Out | Outbound | GRE | N/A | N/A | N/A | N/A |
| ICMP In | Inbound | ICMP | N/A | N/A | N/A | 0–18 |
| ICMP Out | Outbound | ICMP | N/A | N/A | N/A | 0–18 |
| IKE In | Inbound | UDP | N/A | 0–65,535 | 500 | N/A |
| IKE Out | Outbound | UDP | N/A | 500 | 65,535 | N/A |
| Incoming HTTP In | Inbound | TCP | Don't care | 0–65,535 | 80 | N/A |
| Incoming HTTP Out | Outbound | TCP | Don't care | 80 | 65,535 | N/A |
| Incoming HTTPS In | Inbound | TCP | Don't care | 0–65,535 | 443 | N/A |

**Table 6-3**    *Default Rules (Continued)*

| Rule | Direction | Protocol | TCP Connection | TCP/UDP Source Port | TCP/UDP Connection Port | ICMP Packet Type |
|------|-----------|----------|----------------|---------------------|-------------------------|------------------|
| Incoming HTTPS Out | Outbound | TCP | Don't care | 443 | 0–65,535 | N/A |
| IPSec-ESP In | Inbound | ESP | N/A | N/A | N/A | N/A |
| L2TP In | Inbound | UDP | N/A | 0–65,535 | 1701 | N/A |
| L2TP Out | Outbound | UDP | N/A | 1701 | 0–65,535 | N/A |
| LDAP In | Inbound | TCP | Don't care | 0–65,535 | 389 | N/A |
| LDAP Out | Outbound | TCP | Don't care | 389 | 0–65,535 | N/A |
| OSPF In | Inbound | OSPF | N/A | N/A | N/A | N/A |
| OSPF Out | Outbound | OSPF | N/A | N/A | N/A | N/A |
| Outgoing HTTP In | Inbound | TCP | Don't care | 80 | 0–65,535 | N/A |
| Outgoing HTTP Out | Outbound | TCP | Don't care | 0–65,535 | 80 | N/A |
| Outgoing HTTPS In | Inbound | TCP | Don't care | 443 | 0–65,535 | N/A |
| Outgoing HTTPS Out | Outbound | TCP | Don't care | 0–65,535 | 443 | N/A |
| PPTP In | Inbound | TCP | Don't care | 0–65,535 | 1723 | N/A |
| PPTP Out | Outbound | TCP | Don't care | 1723 | 0–65,535 | N/A |
| RIP In | Inbound | UDP | N/A | 520 | 520 | N/A |
| RIP Out | Outbound | UDP | N/A | 520 | 520 | N/A |
| Secure Shell (SSH) In | Inbound | TCP | Don't care | 0–65,535 | 22 | N/A |
| SSH Out | Outbound | TCP | Don't care | 22 | 0–65,535 | N/A |
| Telnet/SSL In | Inbound | TCP | Don't care | 0–65,535 | 992 | N/A |
| Telnet/SSL Out | Outbound | TCP | Don't care | 992 | 0–65,535 | N/A |
| Virtual Cluster Agent (VCA) In | Inbound | UDP | N/A | 0–65,535 | 9023 | N/A |
| VCA Out | Outbound | UDP | N/A | 9023 | 0–65,535 | N/A |

*continues*

**Table 6-3** *Default Rules (Continued)*

| Rule | Direction | Protocol | TCP Connection | TCP/UDP Source Port | TCP/UDP Connection Port | ICMP Packet Type |
|------|-----------|----------|----------------|---------------------|-------------------------|------------------|
| VRRP In | Inbound | Other (112) | N/A | N/A | N/A | N/A |
| VRRP Out | Outbound | Other (112) | N/A | N/A | N/A | N/A |

To configure a new rule, click the Add button, which takes you to the Configuration | Policy Management | Traffic Management | Rules | Add screen, as shown in Figure 6-3. While configuring rules, remember that the rule is based on the viewpoint of the VPN concentrator. This means that if the rule is to be used on a VPN Client, you must verify that the rule is set for the client, not the head-end concentrator.

**Figure 6-3** *The Configuration | Policy Management | Traffic Management | Rules | Add Screen*

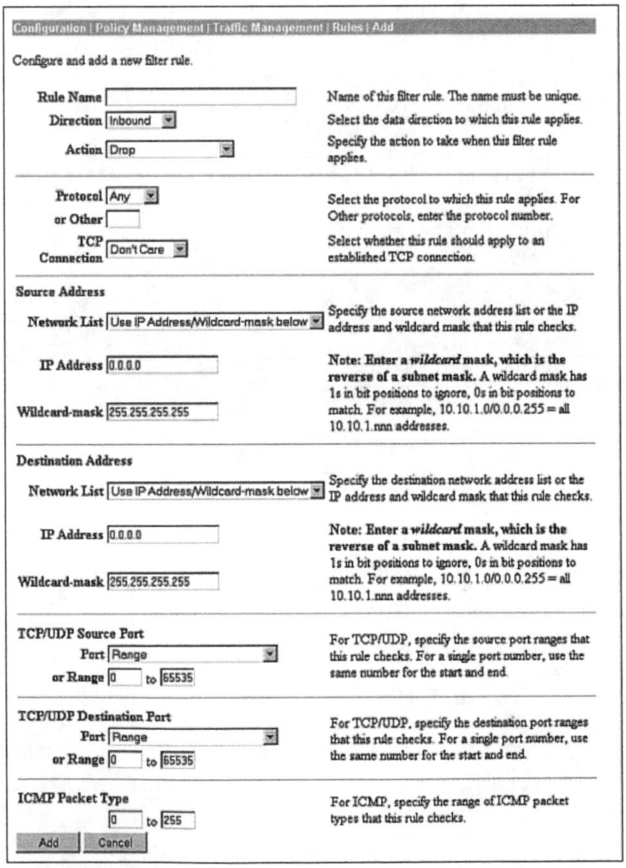

When you create a rule, the rule is read from the top of the screen down. Therefore, if one parameter does not match, the rest of the rule is not considered. Because this discussion focuses on configuring rules as applied to the VPN Client, the TCP Connection and Internet Control Message Protocol (ICMP) Packet Type are not relevant. The other relevant portions and fields within this screen are described in the following sections.

This section covers the following topics:

- Name, Direction, and Action
- Protocol and TCP connection
- Source address and destination address
- TCP/UDP source and destination ports
- ICMP packet type

## Name, Direction, and Action

In the Rule Name field, enter a unique rule name with a maximum of 48 characters. The Direction pull-down menu has two options: Inbound and Outbound. Remember that this rule is applied in reference to the VPN Client, not from the head-end concentrator.

The Action pull-down menu is used to determine how the concentrator deals with a packet that matches this rule. Only Drop and Forward are applicable when setting a filter for a VPN Client. The Action options are as follows:

- **Drop**—Discards the packet.
- **Drop and Log**—Discards the packet and logs a filtering event to the FILTERDBG event class.
- **Forward**—Allows the packet to leave the interface.
- **Forward and Log**—Allows the packet to leave the interface and logs a filtering event to the FILTERDBG event class.
- **Apply IPSec**—Applies IPSec to the packet. You must apply a Security Association (SA) to use this choice.
- **Apply IPSec and Log**—Applies IPSec to the packet and logs a filtering event to the FILTERDBG event class. You must apply an SA to use this choice.

## Protocol and TCP Connection

You either choose the protocol from the pull-down menu or place the IANA protocol number in the Other box. Table 6-4 shows the protocols, followed by the IANA-assigned number available from the pull-down menu.

**Table 6-4**    *Protocols*

| Protocol | IANA Number |
|---|---|
| Any Protocol | 255 |
| ICMP | 1 |
| TCP | 6 |
| EGP | 8 |
| IGP | 9 |
| UDP | 17 |
| ESP | 50 |
| AH | 51 |
| GRE | 47 |
| RSVP | 46 |
| IGMP | 2 |
| OSPF | 89 |
| Other protocols not listed | Appropriate IANA number |

The TCP Connection field is ignored for client firewall rules.

## Source Address and Destination Address

The source address and destination address sections work in the same manner. The pull-down menu lists all the network lists that are configured on the concentrator. Leaving the default of Use IP Address/Wildcard mask allows you to enter an IP address and wildcard mask combination to define the range of IP addresses to which this list applies.

## TCP/UDP Source and Destination Ports

The TCP/UDP source and destination ports sections work in a similar manner. You can choose to leave Range as the setting, in which case you enter two port numbers. If the port numbers are different, a range is used. If both port numbers are the same, that single port is used. The port numbers entered are the IANA-assigned port numbers. Otherwise, you can click the pull-down menu that brings up a list of the predefined ports with their associated IANA numbers, as shown in Table 6-5.

**Table 6-5**    *TCP and UDP Ports*

| Port | IANA Number |
|------|-------------|
| Echo | 7 |
| Discard | 9 |
| FTP-Data | 20 |
| FTP | 21 |
| SSH | 22 |
| Telnet | 23 |
| SMTP | 25 |
| DNS | 53 |
| TFTP | 69 |
| Finger | 79 |
| HTTP | 80 |
| POP3 | 110 |
| NNTP | 119 |
| NTP | 123 |
| NetBIOS Name Service | 137 |
| NetBIOS | 138 |
| NetBIOS Session | 139 |
| IMAP | 143 |
| SNMP | 161 |
| SNMP-TRAP | 162 |
| BGP | 179 |
| LDAP | 389 |
| HTTPS | 443 |
| SMTPS | 465 |
| IKE | 500 |
| SYSLOG | 514 |
| RIP | 520 |
| NNTPS | 563 |
| LDAP/SSL | 636 |

*continues*

**Table 6-5** *TCP and UDP Ports (Continued)*

| Port | IANA Number |
|------|-------------|
| Telnet/SSL | 992 |
| LapLink | 1547 |
| L2TP | 1701 |
| PPTP | 1723 |

## ICMP Packet Type

Finally, you configure the ICMP Packet Type if you are not using the client firewall. Make sure that you save the configuration, or you run the risk of losing your configuration due to loss of power. The VPN Client ignores any configurations that you make in this field.

# Configuring the Stateful Firewall

**21** Software client's Stateful Firewall feature

The Stateful Firewall feature is easily configured on the Cisco VPN Client. Open the client, as shown in Figure 6-4.

**Figure 6-4** *VPN Dialer*

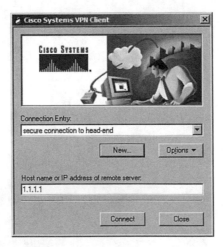

Choose the Options pull-down menu, as shown in Figure 6-5. If the Stateful Firewall (Always On) option does not have a check mark in front of it, click it once. Because the Options pull-down menu disappears, choose it again, and make sure that there is a check mark in front of the Stateful Firewall (Always On) option, as shown in Figure 6-5.

**Figure 6-5**    *VPN Client Options Menu*

# Configuring the VPN Concentrator for Firewall Usage

**24**  Customizing firewall policy

Configuration of the firewall for the VPN Client is done on the Configuration I User Management I Groups I Modify screen under the Client FW tab (see Figure 6-6). This screen is used for configuring all firewall options other than the Stateful (Always On) option, which is configured on the VPN Client itself. The following sections describe each of the options that are shown in the Client FW tab.

**Figure 6-6** *The Client FW Tab*

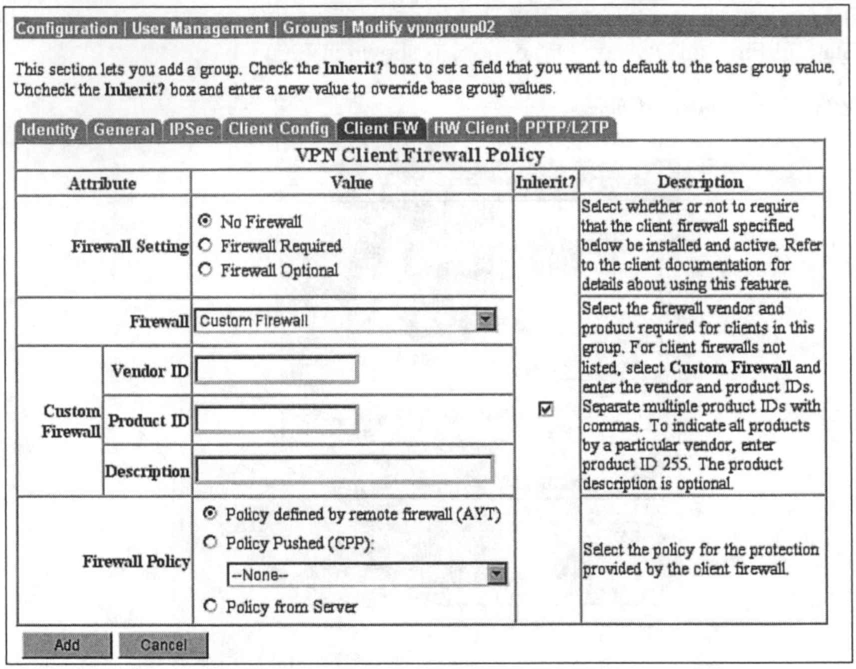

## Firewall Setting

The default setting is No Firewall, which means that there is no requirement for any firewall, including the Stateful Firewall (Always On) feature. The other two choices, Firewall Required and Firewall Optional, both work with the Firewall field discussed in the next section.

Choosing Firewall Required means that all the users within this group must use the specified firewall. Additionally, this firewall must be running during the time that the tunnel is active. Should the firewall software terminate, the tunnel is dropped. The VPN concentrator notifies the client that the firewall configuration does not match the required settings. Choose this option only when all the clients are Windows-based PCs. No other types of clients, including the VPN 3002 Hardware Client, can use this option and successfully connect.

Choosing Firewall Optional means that a client connecting with the specified firewall running can connect using that firewall. If the specified firewall is not installed or running, the client can still connect, but it receives a warning message. VPN 3002 Concentrators and non-Windows-based clients can also connect with this setting.

# Firewall

This Firewall pull-down menu allows you to choose the specified firewall for the group. The firewall specified determines the policy options that are supported. The options are listed in Table 6-6.

**Table 6-6**    *Firewall Options*

| Choice | Usage |
|--------|-------|
| Cisco Integrated Client Firewall | The Stateful Firewall feature built into the VPN Client. |
| Network ICE BlackICE Defender | A third-party personal firewall. |
| Zone Labs Zone Alarm | A third-party personal firewall. |
| Zone Labs Zone AlarmPro | The professional version of the Zone Labs Alarm personal firewall. |
| Zone Labs Zone Alarm or Zone Labs Zone AlarmPro | Allows the user to use either of the two firewalls. |
| Zone Labs Integrity Client | A policy pushed from a server to the client system that works with the Zone Labs Zone Alarm and Zone AlarmPro. |
| Custom Firewall | As of this writing, this feature is included for future use. This option will eventually allow the administrator to choose from any compliant firewall. Currently, this option allows you to choose only those firewalls previously listed, but you can use any combination of these firewalls by entering the associated numbers separated by commas in the product ID. You must have only a single vendor, although you can choose multiple products from that vendor. |

# Custom Firewall

Should you choose to use the Custom Firewall option when it becomes available, Table 6-7 provides you with the necessary codes to be input into the Vendor ID and Product ID fields.

**Table 6-7**    *Vendor and Product ID Codes*

| Vendor | Vendor ID | Product | Product ID |
|--------|-----------|---------|------------|
| Cisco Systems | 1 | Cisco Integrated Client (CIC) | 1 |
| Zone Labs | 2 | Zone Alarm | 1 |
| Zone Labs | 2 | Zone AlarmPro | 2 |
| Zone Labs | 2 | Integrity | 3 |
| Network ICE | 3 | BlackICE Defender/Agent | 1 |

Should you wish to combine, for example, Zone Alarm, Zone AlarmPro, and Integrity into a single firewall option, you would enter **2** into the Vendor ID field and **1,2,3** into the Product ID field. You cannot use multiple vendors.

You can enter an optional description if you are using a custom firewall.

# Firewall Policy

The Firewall Policy option allows you to select the firewall protection provided by the client firewall. The options are as follows:

- Policy defined by remote firewall (AYT)
- Policy Pushed (CPP)
- Policy from Server

The following sections describe each of these options in more detail.

## Policy Defined by Remote Firewall (AYT)

The Policy Defined by Remote Firewall (AYT) option allows policies defined by the remote firewall. The firewall must be running. A poll is sent from the VPN Client to the firewall service on the workstation every 30 seconds. If the firewall does not answer, the connection is dropped.

## Policy Pushed (CPP)

The Policy Pushed (CPP) option causes the concentrator to push the policy defined down to the client. The list shown depends on the filters you have defined on the concentrator. If the VPN Client has a firewall, these rules are added to the local firewall's rules. This means that the more restrictive of the two sets of rules applies. For example, if the VPN concentrator's rule allows web browsing but the client's firewall does not, no web browsing is allowed.

## Policy from Server

The Policy from Server option causes the users within the group to use a Zone Labs Integrity Server (IS) to mange their security settings on the firewall. If you choose this option, make sure that the Configuration I System I Servers I Firewall Server screen has the appropriate IP address of the IS and that the IS is reachable from the VPN concentrator.

# Monitoring VPN Client Firewall Statistics

> **23**  Client firewall statistics

Viewing the VPN Client firewall statistics is easy. When you first connected the client, an icon was placed in the Windows System tray. Click the icon shaped like a padlock on the lower-right side of your screen. This brings up the General screen. This should be similar to the screen shown in Figure 6-7.

**Figure 6-7**  *The Cisco Systems VPN Client Connection Status | General Screen*

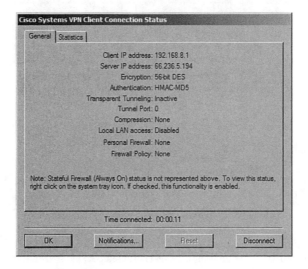

This screen shows the client IP address and the server IP address. Next, you see the encryption and authentication used for this connection. Then, you see whether transparent tunneling is active. If it is, the tunneling port number is shown. This is followed by the compression in use and a notation regarding the local LAN access. If a personal firewall were in effect, it would be listed here. Any firewall policy in use, such as AYT or CPP, is shown.

To look at the statistics for this connection, click the Statistics tab. An example of this screen is shown in Figure 6-8. On this screen, you can see the bytes in and out as well as the networks.

**Figure 6-8** *The Cisco Systems VPN Client Connection Status | Statistics Screen*

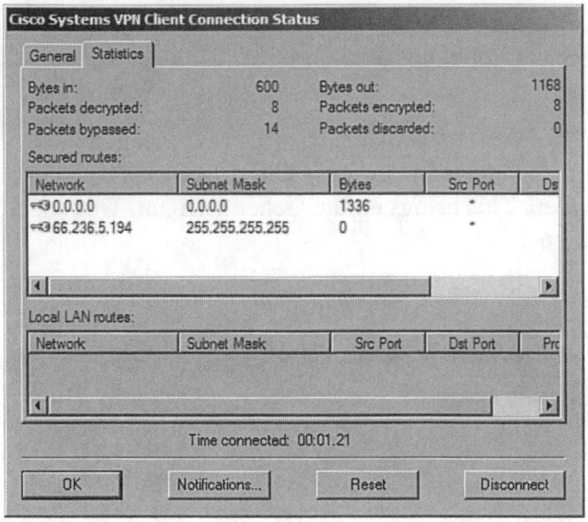

The top of the Statistics screen shows a number of items, as described in Table 6-8.

**Table 6-8** *Connection Statistics*

| Statistic | Meaning |
|---|---|
| Bytes in | The total amount of secure data received |
| Bytes out | The total amount of encrypted data transmitted through the tunnel |
| Packets decrypted | The total number of encrypted packets received and decrypted on the port |
| Packet encrypted | The total number of encrypted packets transmitted out the port |
| Packets bypassed | The total number of data packets that the VPN client did not process because they did not need to be encrypted |
| Packets discarded | The total number of data packets that the VPN client rejected because they did not originate from the gateway |

The Secured routes section of this screen lists the IPSec SAs. Notice the key icon that is on the left of the networks listed. This icon indicates that the network is protected. The lack of a key indicates no protection for that network. The Bytes column shows the total amount of data that this SA has processed.

# Enabling Automatic Client Update Through the Cisco VPN 3000 Concentrator Series Manager

One last topic needs to be discussed that does not fall under the firewall character of this chapter, but it does relate to the VPN Client. That topic is the Automatic Client Update feature of the Cisco VPN 3000 Concentrator Series, which can help ensure that all your users' systems are running the same client, making the implementation of firewall policies that much easier for you.

The CSVPN Client software can be upgraded by pushing the configuration from any of the devices in the VPN 3000 Concentrator Series. This means that the administrator needs to make a single change at the head-end VPN concentrator instead of manually upgrading each individual CSVPN from. This is especially efficient on large installations. Using the Automatic Client Update feature lets you control the version of the client that is used and control the initial configuration of the client.

The CSVPN Client is sent an ISAKMP message when it connects to the head-end concentrator, receiving notification that a software upgrade is pending. This ISAKMP message contains the IP address of a TFTP server, the directory path on the server, and filename to download.

Setting up the head-end VPN 3000 Series Concentrator for automatically updating CSVPN is simple through the GUI. Configuring the concentrator for Automatic Client Update consists of the following steps:

Step 1  Navigate to Configuration | User Management | Groups, and select the group. This example uses rtpvpn1 (Internally Configured).

Step 2  Choose **Modify Client Update** (see Figure 6-9).

Step 3  Choose **Add** from the Client Update screen to add a new client package.

Step 4  On the next screen, shown in Figure 6-10, enter **Windows** as the client type, enter *tftp://IP address of server/filename* as the URL, and enter the revision number.

Step 5  Select **Apply** to finish the setup at the head-end.

**Figure 6-9** *The Configuration | User Management | Groups Screen*

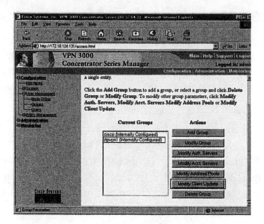

**Figure 6-10** *The Configuration | User Management | Groups | Client Update | Modify Screen*

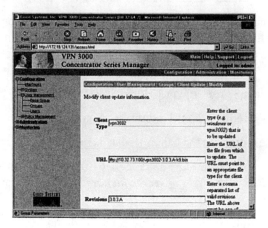

The next time that CSVPN connects, the user receives a message indicating that a software update is pending and prompting him/her through the process. When the user is notified, the user has the option to launch the install or cancel and perform the installation the next time the user connects to the concentrator.

# Foundation Summary

The Foundation Summary is a collection of tables and figures that provides a convenient review of many key concepts in this chapter. For those who are already comfortable with the topics in this chapter, this summary could help you recall a few details. For those who just read this chapter, this review should help solidify some key facts. For anyone doing final preparation before the exam, these tables and figures are a convenient way to review the day before the exam.

## Cisco VPN Client Firewall Feature Overview

Table 6-9 highlights the abilities of the VPN Client.

**Table 6-9**    *VPN Client Abilities*

| Client Ability | Description |
|---|---|
| Tunneling protocols | Tunneling protocols supported are as follows:<br>• IP Security–Encapsulating Security Payload (IPSec-ESP)<br>• L2TP<br>• L2TP/IPSec<br>• NAT<br>• NAT Transparent IPSec<br>• Ratified IPSec/UDP<br>• IPSec/TCP<br>• PPTP |
| Encryption and authentication protocols | Encryption and authentication methods supported include the following:<br>• IPSec(ESP) with Data Encryption Standard (DES)/3DES(56/168 bits)<br>• AES(126/256-bit) with Message Digest (MD5) or SHA |
| Key management | Key management capabilities include the following:<br>• Internet Key Exchange (IKE)—Aggressive and Main mode (digital certificates)<br>• Diffie-Hellman (DH) Groups 1, 2, and 5<br>• PFS<br>• Rekeying |

*continues*

**Table 6-9**   *VPN Client Abilities (Continued)*

| Client Ability | Description |
|---|---|
| Compression | LZS (Lempel-Ziv standard) |
| Authentication methods | Authentication methods include the following:<br><br>• XAUTH (eXtended AUTHentication)<br><br>• Remote Authentication Dial-In User Service (RADIUS) with the following:<br><br>  — MSCHAPv2 (NT password expiration)<br><br>  — State/Reply message attributes (token cards)<br><br>  — RSA SecurID (Security Dynamics)<br><br>  — Windows NT Domain Authentication<br><br>  — MX.509v3 digital certificates |
| Digital certificates | Digital certificates supported include the following:<br><br>• Simple Certificate Enrollment Protocol (SCEP)<br><br>• Entrust Entelligence<br><br>• Smartcards through MS CAPI:<br><br>  — Activcard<br><br>  — eAladdin<br><br>  — Gemplus<br><br>  — Datakey<br><br>• Internet Explorer Certificate Enrollment<br><br>• Authorities include the following:<br><br>  — Baltimore<br><br>  — Entrust<br><br>  — GTE Cybertrust<br><br>  — Microsoft<br><br>  — RSA Keon<br><br>  — VeriSign |

Table 6-10 describes the available products and the policies that are available on these products.

**Table 6-10**    *VPN Policies and Products*

| Policy/Product | Device | Purpose |
|---|---|---|
| Stateful Firewall (Always On) | VPN Client | Blocks all traffic except for the following:<br>• From the head-end network<br>• DHCP<br>• ESP |
| CPP with CIC | VPN concentrator | Centralized control:<br>• Concentrator defines the rules<br>• Pushed rules<br>Used with split tunnels |
| CPP with Zone Alarm and Zone AlarmPro | VPN concentrator | Centralized control:<br>• Concentrator defines the rules<br>• Pushed rules<br>Used with split tunnels |
| Personal Firewall Enforcement (AYT) | VPN Client | Used when you have a personal firewall<br>Rules are based on the personal firewall's rules<br>Tunnel is dropped if firewall does not answer polls<br>Used with the following:<br>• Zone Alarm<br>• Zone AlarmPro<br>• BlackICE |

# Stateful Firewall (Always On) Feature

Remember the following key points about the Stateful Firewall (Always On) feature:

- Uses only firewall with no control from the concentrator
- Configured at the client
- Split tunnel by turning off
- Allows DHCP and ESP in even when on

# Cisco Integrated Client

Remember the following key points about CIC:

- Defines rules for use with split tunnel
- Uses CPP

# Centralized Protection Policy

CPP functions as follows:

- Pushes policy
- Enforces pushed policy
- Sends client predefined policy
- Uses the following:
  - CIC
  - Zone Alarm
  - Zone AlarmPro
- Allows or denies specific ports

# Are You There Feature

Remember the following key points about the AYT feature:

- Is an alternative to CPP
- VPN Client polls firewall every 30 seconds
- Is also called "Are You There"
- Makes sure the client has a policy

# Configuring Firewall Filter Rules

Guidelines for configuring firewall filtering rules are as follows:

- Do not use the default rules in a real network.
- For default rules, the source and destination addresses are 0.0.0.0 255.255.255.255.
- VRRP uses 224.0.0.18/0.0.0.0.
- Rule for client is from the client's point of view.

- The filter is read from the top down until it finds a rule that matches the data and other conditions or until the end of the filter is reached.

- Configured on the Configuration | Policy Management | Traffic Management | Rules | Add (or Modify) screen. See Figure 6-11.

**Figure 6-11**  *The Configuration | Policy Management | Traffic Management | Rules | Add Screen*

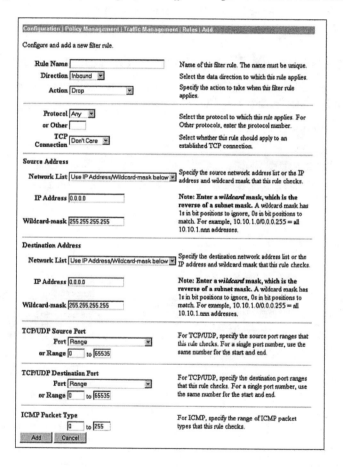

# Action

On the Action pull-down menu, only the Drop and Forward options are applicable when setting a filter for a VPN Client. The Action pull-down menu options are as follows:

- **Drop**—Discards the packet
- **Forward**—Allows the packet to leave the interface

# Configuring the Stateful Firewall

Configure the Stateful Firewall feature by following these steps:

**Step 1**   Open the client.

**Step 2**   Choose the **Options** menu.

**Step 3**   Choose **Stateful Firewall (Always On)**. This prevents split tunneling.

# Configuring the VPN Concentrator for Firewall Usage

Configuration is done on the Configuration | User Management | Groups | Modify screen under the Client FW tab, as shown in Figure 6-12.

**Figure 6-12**   *The Client FW Tab*

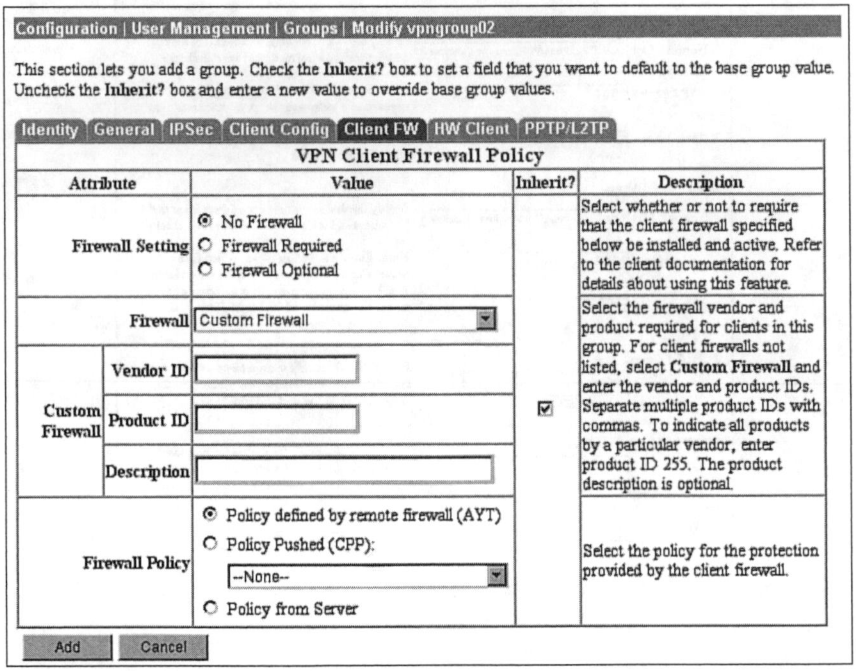

# Firewall

Table 6-11 describes firewall options.

**Table 6-11**    *Firewall Options*

| Choice | Usage |
|---|---|
| Cisco Integrated Client Firewall | The Stateful Firewall feature built into the VPN Client. |
| Network ICE BlackICE Defender | A third-party personal firewall. |
| Zone Labs Zone Alarm | A third-party personal firewall. |
| Zone Labs Zone AlarmPro | The professional version of the Zone Labs Zone Alarm personal firewall. |
| Zone Labs Zone Alarm or Zone Labs Zone AlarmPro | Allows the user to use either of the two firewalls. |
| Zone Labs Integrity Client | A policy pushed from a server to the client system that works with the Zone Labs Zone Alarm and Zone AlarmPro. |
| Custom firewall | As of this writing, this feature is included for future use. This will eventually allow the administrator to choose from any compliant firewall. Currently, this option allows you to choose only those firewalls listed above, but you can use any combination of these firewalls by entering the associated numbers separated by commas in the product ID. You must have only a single vendor, although you can choose multiple products within that vendor. |

# Firewall Policy

Firewall policy has the following options:

- Policy defined by remote firewall (AYT)
- Policy pushed (CPP)
- Policy from Server
- Always On/Stateful inspection

# Monitoring VPN Client Firewall Statistics

The General tab shows the following options:

- Your IP address
- VPN concentrator IP address
- Encryption used

- Authentication used
- Tunneling port
- Compression
- Local LAN access
- Firewall policy in use

Table 6-12 describes the Statistics tab.

**Table 6-12**  *Connection Statistics*

| Statistic | Meaning |
|---|---|
| Bytes in | The total amount of secure data received. |
| Bytes out | The total amount of encrypted data transmitted through the tunnel. |
| Packets decrypted | The total number of encrypted packets received and decrypted on the port. |
| Packet encrypted | The total number of encrypted packets transmitted out the port. |
| Packets bypassed | The total number of data packets that the VPN Client did not process because they did not need to be encrypted. |
| Packets discarded | The total number of data packets that the VPN Client rejected because they did not originate from the gateway. |

# Chapter Glossary

The following terms were introduced in this chapter or have special significance to the topics within this chapter.

**eXtended AUTHentication (XAUTH)**    XAUTH permits Cisco VPN Client systems to be authenticated by TACACS+ or RADIUS external servers during IKE Phase 1 negotiations when establishing an IPSec secure tunnel. When XAUTH is configured on the VPN Client, the user of that device is prompted for a username and password, which must be authenticated by the remote authentication server before the IPSec tunnel can be established.

**firewall**    Device or software package designated as a buffer between any connected public networks and a private network. A firewall uses access lists and other methods to ensure the security of the private network.

**Generic Routing Encapsulation (GRE)**    Tunneling protocol developed by Cisco that can encapsulate a variety of protocol packet types inside IP tunnels, creating a virtual point-to-point link to Cisco routers at remote points over an IP internetwork. By connecting multiprotocol subnetworks in a single-protocol backbone environment, IP tunneling using GRE allows network expansion across a single-protocol backbone environment.

**head-end**    End point of a broadband network. All stations transmit toward the head-end; the head-end then transmits toward the destination stations.

**Internet Assigned Numbers Authority (IANA)**    Organization operated under the auspices of the Internet Society (ISOC) as a part of the Internet Architecture Board (IAB). IANA delegates authority for IP address-space allocation and domain-name assignment to the InterNIC and other organizations. IANA also maintains a database of assigned protocol identifiers used in the TCP/IP stack, including autonomous system numbers.

**split tunneling**    The ability to direct packets over the Internet in clear text while simultaneously encrypting other packets through an IPSec tunnel. The VPN server provides either a list of networks whose traffic must be tunneled or a list of networks whose traffic must not be tunneled. You enable split tunneling on the VPN Client and configure the network list on the VPN server, such as the VPN concentrator.

**stateful firewall**    Denies or permits WAN traffic based on a session's state. Packets relating to dialogs initiated from within the firewall are permitted passage through the firewall, while those initiating from outside the firewall are denied passage through the firewall.

**Virtual Router Redundancy Protocol (VRRP)**    In installations of two or more VPN concentrators in a parallel (redundant configuration) VRRP provides automatic switchover to a backup system in case the primary system is out of service, thus ensuring user access to the VPN.

## Q&A

As mentioned in Chapter 1, "All About the Cisco Certified Security Professional," these questions are more difficult than what you should experience on the CCSP exam. The questions do not attempt to cover more breadth or depth than the exam; however, the questions are designed to make sure you know the answer. Rather than allowing you to derive the answer from clues hidden inside the question itself, your understanding and recall of the subject are challenged. Questions from the "Do I Know This Already?" quiz from the beginning of the chapter are repeated here to ensure that you have mastered the chapter's topic areas. Hopefully, these questions will help limit the number of exam questions on which you narrow your choices to two options and guess!

1  You have a number of clients running Windows 98 and a remote VPN 3002 Hardware Concentrator assigned to the same group. Your supervisor wants you to force everyone on this group connecting to have a firewall running on his or her machine. Can you do this?

_____

_____

_____

2  What firewalls can be used within the Custom Firewall option on the concentrator?

_____

_____

_____

3  Where are the rules set for a client when using CPP with Zone AlarmPro?

_____

_____

_____

4  What protocols are not automatically blocked when using the Stateful Firewall (Always On) feature?

_____

_____

_____

**5** Why is CPP not used with the Tunnel Everything option?

_____

_____

_____

**6** How often does the VPN Client poll the personal firewall when using AYT?

_____

_____

_____

**7** How is the Always On option set on the VPN Client?

_____

_____

_____

**8** Where is CPP configured?

_____

_____

_____

**9** What debug classes are used when creating a rule with the following options:

   a. Drop

   b. Drop and Log

   c. Forward

   d. Forward and Log

   e. Apply IPSec

   f. Apply IPSec and Log

_____

_____

_____

**10** By default, what IP address and wildcard mask does VRRP use?

_____.

_____

_____

**11** How do you allow clients to use either of two firewalls? What is the only vendor you can do this with?

_____

_____

_____

**12** You are using CPP and pushing a policy to a firewall at the client. The client's firewall allows FTP access. The concentrator's policy does not allow FTP access. Is FTP access allowed?

_____

_____

_____

**13** You are using BlackICE as a client firewall. You are presently connected through the VPN. What happens if you stop the service running BlackICE? Does the VPN remain connected? If so, for how long? Can you connect again if BlackICE is not running?

_____

_____

_____

**14** On the VPN Client, where do you see the current compression used for a VPN connection?

_____

_____

_____

**15** While configuring a filter, you want to apply this filter to all protocols. What number do you use?

_____

_____

_____

**16**  When using the VPN Client, what ICMP should be set?

_____

_____

_____

**17**  What authentication methods are allowed with the VPN Client?

_____

_____

_____

**18**  What types of key management can the VPN Client use?

_____

_____

_____

**19**  In addition to IPSec, what tunneling protocols does the VPN Client support?

_____

_____

_____

**20**  Which two products from Zone Labs work with the VPN Client to enable the Are You There (AYT) capability?

_____

_____

_____

**21**  You want to have secure VPN connections to the private network of the head-end concentrator and unsecured communications to the Internet. How would you configure the VPN Client's Stateful Firewall feature to support this split tunneling?

_____

_____

_____

**22** What is another name for the Stateful Firewall client that is a part of the Cisco VPN Client?

_____

_____

_____

**23** From the VPN Client, where can you view the secured routes that are enabled to the client?

_____

_____

_____

**24** What is meant by the term *Packets bypassed* on the Statistics tab of the Connection Status screen?

_____

_____

_____

**25** On the VPN 3000 Concentrator Series devices, you configure the client firewall properties on the Client FW tab of the Configuration I User Management I Groups I Add (or Modify) screen. You can only select one firewall policy from that screen. What are the three types of firewall policies that you can choose from the Client FW tab?

_____

_____

_____

# Scenarios

## Scenario 6-1

In Scenario 6-1, you connect a VPN Client to the VPN concentrator. You do this with and without a firewall installed on the client.

Your tasks are as follows:

1  Configure the concentrator to accept a VPN connection with an optional firewall on the client.

2  Configure the client with the Stateful Firewall feature off and then connect. Did you get a message stating that a firewall should be used?

3  Reconfigure the client with the Stateful Firewall feature on and retest the connection. Did you still get the message regarding the firewall usage? Why not?

4  Configure a filter on the concentrator.

5  Configure the concentrator to require a firewall and push the filter to the client. Test both configurations on the client. What happens? Why?

6  Reconfigure the concentrator to use AYT. Test both configurations on the client. What happens? Why?

## Scenario 6-1 Answers

The following answers pertain to the tasks presented in the previous section:

1  Configure the concentrator to accept a VPN connection with an optional firewall on the client in accordance with the text. Choose the Custom Firewall option on the Client FW tab on the Configuration | User Management | Groups | Modify screen to set the firewall option.

2  You should receive a message because the Firewall Optional configuration sends a message to the client stating that a firewall should be used if it is not there. However, you should be able to connect.

3  Setting the Stateful Firewall (Always On) feature to be enabled should have eliminated the message received from the concentrator.

4  See Number 5.

5 See the section "Configuring Firewall Filter Rules" for the procedures on these items. The key is to remember that if you are pushing the filter to the client, you must build the client from the filter's point of view. The filter has no effect on the client because the Stateful Firewall feature stands alone, and you cannot push a configuration from the concentrator to the client with a stateful firewall.

6 This configuration enables you to connect and remain connected only if the Stateful Firewall feature is enabled.

# Exam Topics Discussed in This Chapter

This chapter covers the following topics, which you need to master in your pursuit of certification as a Cisco Certified Security Professional:

**25** Monitoring the Cisco VPN 3000 Series Concentrator

**26** Administering the Cisco VPN 3000 Series Concentrator

# CHAPTER 7

# Monitoring and Administering the VPN 3000 Series Concentrator

This chapter deals with administering and monitoring the VPN 3000 Series Concentrator. Among these tasks are using preshared keys, configuring policies, and automatically updating the client, which are all tasks that you should master in order to pass the exam.

This text will guide you through most of the administering and monitoring options on the 3000 concentrators. Although every single screen is not examined, the vast majority of the screens and options are shown within this chapter. What have been skipped are those items with other screens that are so similar that their inclusion becomes redundant or of little value. One example of this is within the statistics section, where only a sample of the statistics screens available is shown; however, it will still benefit you in your daily activities to familiarize yourself with all of the available screens and options. The more thorough your knowledge of the system, the easier it becomes to use.

## How Best to Use This Chapter

By taking the following steps, you can make better use of your time:

- Keep your notes and answers for all your work with this book in one place for easy reference.

- Take the "Do I Know This Already?" quiz, and write down your answers. Studies show retention is significantly increased through writing facts and concepts down, even if you never look at the information again.

- Use the diagram in Figure 7-1 to guide you to the next step.

**Figure 7-1**  *How to Use This Chapter*

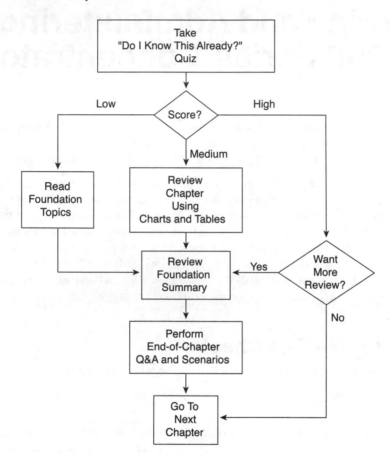

## "Do I Know This Already?" Quiz

The purpose of the "Do I Know This Already?" quiz is to help you decide what parts of the chapter to use. If you already intend to read the entire chapter, you do not necessarily need to answer these questions now.

This 10-question quiz helps you determine how to spend your limited study time. The quiz is sectioned into 2 smaller "quizlets," which correspond to the two major topic headings in the chapter. Figure 7-1 outlines suggestions on how to spend your time in this chapter based on your quiz score. Use Table 7-1 to record your scores.

**Table 7-1**   *Score Sheet for Quiz and Quizlets*

| Quizlet Number | Foundations Topics Section Covering These Questions | Question | Score |
|---|---|---|---|
| 1 | Administering the Cisco VPN 3000 Series Concentrator | 1–5 | |
| 2 | Monitoring the Cisco VPN 3000 Series Concentrator | 6–10 | |
| All questions | | 1–10 | |

1   What screen is used to set the password for the administrator?

_____

_____

_____

2   You wish to limit HTTP access to the concentrator to hosts on the same subnet as the inside interface of the concentrator. What is the format of the access control list?

_____

_____

_____

3   What types of AAA servers can the VPN 3000 Series Concentrator use for authenticating management sessions?

_____

_____

_____

4   What is the upper limit for a management session timeout?

_____

_____

_____

5   What form of encryption may be used on a configuration file?

_____

_____

_____

**6** On what screen can routes be cleared?

_____

_____

_____

**7** Where can you see the CPU utilization on a Cisco 3000 Series Concentrator?

_____

_____

_____

**8** Where can you troubleshoot an IPSec connection?

_____

_____

_____

**9** Where can you troubleshoot TCP/IP connections?

_____

_____

_____

**10** Where can you see the number of collisions on an Ethernet interface?

_____

_____

_____

The answers to this quiz are listed in Appendix A, "Answers to the "Do I Know This Already?" Quizzes and Q&A Sections." The suggestions for your next steps, based on quiz results, are as follows:

- **6 or less overall score**—Read the entire chapter, including the "Foundation Topics" and "Foundation Summary" sections, and the "Q&A" section.

- **7–8 overall score**—Begin with the "Foundation Summary" section, and continue with the "Q&A" section. If you are having difficulty with a particular subject area, read the appropriate section in "Foundation Topics" section.

- **9–10 overall score**—If you feel you need more review on these topics, go to the "Foundation Summary" section, and then to the "Q&A" section. Otherwise, skip this chapter and go to the next chapter.

# Administering the Cisco VPN 3000 Series Concentrator

**26**  Administering the Cisco VPN 3000 Series Concentrator

To administer the Cisco VPN Concentrator, set the URL of your web browser to the IP address of your concentrator. Alternatively, if your DNS server will resolve the host name, you may enter the host name of the concentrator. You will see a screen similar to that shown in Figure 7-2. Once this screen is shown, enter a username and password. Later in this chapter you learn how to administer users and passwords. Click the Login button to continue.

**Figure 7-2**  *Concentrator Login*

Once you have logged into the concentrator, you will be presented with the main screen, as shown in Figure 7-3. This screen allows you to configure, administrate, or monitor the concentrator. For purposes of this chapter, you will focus on the Administration and Monitoring options. Click the Administration link to start administering the concentrator.

**Figure 7-3**  *Main Screen*

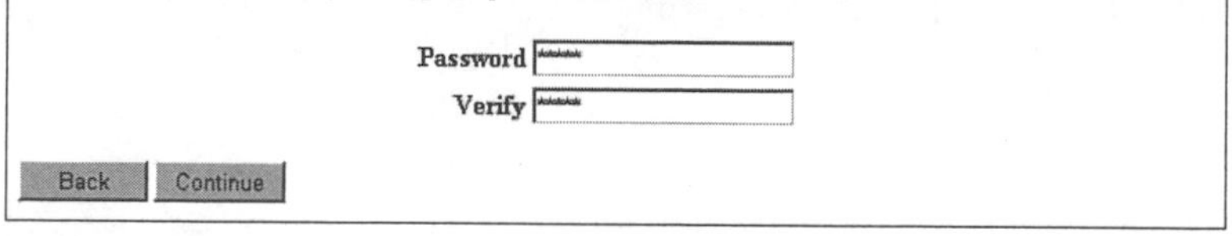

You should now be on the main administration screen, as shown in Figure 7-4. You will use this screen to navigate between all the administration options. From this point forward, with one general exception, in order to access a specific screen, you may choose to either click the link on the main part of the screen or to click one of the links shown in the menu system on the left. The general exception to this is when a parameter is being added or modified. For example, you cannot go directly to modifying an access list without first choosing the access list to modify. Therefore, there are no Modify submenus on the left side of the screen. The submenus shown on the left may be expanded by clicking on the + sign. Choosing the option from the left side of the screen or from the link on the main screen makes no difference because, either way, you will be brought to the same screen.

**Figure 7-4**  *Administration Screen*

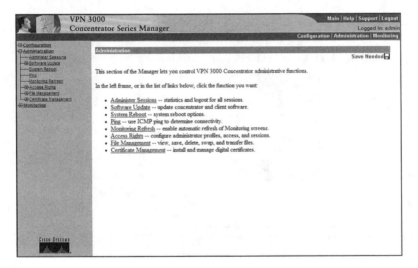

You are initially presented with eight options, each of which brings you to an associated screen as described in Table 7-2. Any of these screens may have subscreens associated with them. Take a moment to study Table 7-2, which lists all the menu and submenu options. Knowing how to navigate through the system will make administration easier. Knowing what options are controlled on individual screens will help you to pass the exam. After studying the table, continue to the next sections, which explore each individual item.

**Table 7-2**    *Administration Menu System*

| Menu Option | Level | Usage |
|---|---|---|
| Administration | 1 | Main screen for administering the VPN 3000 Concentrator. Enables all of the Administration submenus. |
| Administer Sessions | 2 | Shows all of the current sessions. Should you choose, you may filter the sessions shown by group. |
| Software Update | 2 | Enables submenu, allowing you to choose to update either the concentrator or clients. |
| Concentrator | 3 | Updates the concentrator to which you are currently logged on. |
| Clients | 3 | Updates all of the clients or clients based on groups. |
| System Reboot | 2 | Allows you to reboot the system either immediately or at a scheduled time. This is also the screen used to reboot without using the current configuration. |
| Ping | 2 | Allows you to check connectivity with a remote system by either name or IP address. |
| Monitoring Refresh | 2 | Sets if the screens should automatically refresh and, if so, how often. |
| Access Rights | 2 | Enables submenu used for setting username/password/rights combinations, access control lists for configuring the concentrator, setting session timeouts, and enables the submenu for AAA servers. |
| Administrators | 3 | Sets usernames, passwords, and rights. |
| Access Control List | 3 | Sets those IP addresses allowed to access the concentrator for administration and configuration. |
| Access Settings | 3 | Sets the session timeouts, limits the number of connections, and allows for encryption of the configuration file. |
| AAA Servers | 3 | Enables the submenu for setting the Authentication Servers. |
| Authentication | 4 | Allows the addition, modification, configuration, or deletion of TACACS+ servers. |
| File Management | 2 | Enables the submenu, allowing for swapping the backup and boot files, file transfers using TFTP, file uploads using HTTP, and exporting the configuration to an XML file. |
| Swap Config File | 3 | Allows swapping the boot and backup boot files. |
| TFTP Transfer | 3 | Allows uploading or downloading via a remote TFTP server. |
| File Upload | 3 | Allows uploading a file via HTTP. |
| XML Export | 3 | Allows a configuration file to be exported to an XML file. |

*continues*

**Table 7-2** *Administration Menu System (Continued)*

| Menu Option | Level | Usage |
|---|---|---|
| Certificate Manager | 2 | Enables the submenu, allowing enrollment and installation of certificates. |
| Enrollment | 3 | Enrolls certificates. |
| Installation | 3 | Installs certificates. |

## Administer Sessions

The Administration I Administer Sessions screen, shown in Figure 7-5, shows the session statistics for all connected sessions. You are able to filter the sessions by group using the Group pull-down menu. In this case, only those sessions belonging to the group chosen are shown.

**Figure 7-5** *Administration I Administer Sessions*

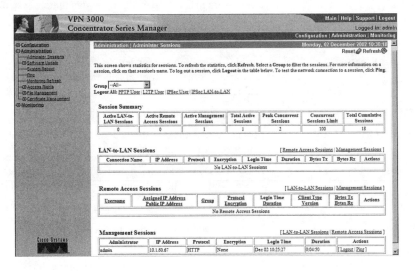

The Administer Session screen shows the peak connections by connection type as well as the limits on that connection type and the total number of sessions completed since the system was started. You are also able to log out sessions based on the session type. Clicking on a session's name will give more information regarding that session.

## Software Update

The Administration I Software Update screen consists of two submenu options. This is an intermediate screen that is used to navigate to the software update screens for the concentrator and clients. This screen is shown in Figure 7-6.

**Figure 7-6**    *Administration | Software Update*

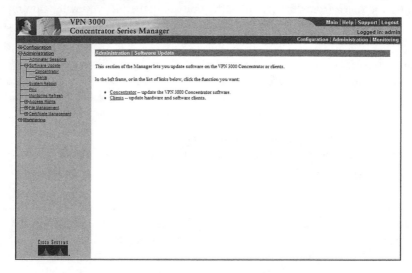

## Concentrator

The Administration | Software Update | Concentrator screen is shown in Figure 7-7. This screen shows the current version of the software and allows you to upload a new version to the concentrator.

**Figure 7-7**    *Administration | Software Update | Concentrator*

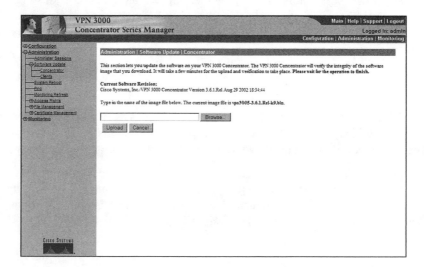

The Browse button is used to find the file you wish to upload on the workstation being used for configuration or from the network. After uploading the file, you will be prompted to move to the Administration | System Reboot screen shown later in Figure 7-9. The new software will not be activated until the system is rebooted.

During the download process, it is possible to corrupt the memory by failing to wait for the file transfer to complete. Therefore, you are advised to wait until the transfer is completed before doing any operations that can cause changes to the flash memory, such as listing, viewing, copying, deleting, or writing files.

Updating the software will not cause any disruption in current sessions, although rebooting the system will drop all sessions. Make sure that the current configuration is saved before rebooting, or it will be lost.

---

**NOTE**    Before loading any new software, it is wise to check for caveats and bugs related to the new software. This will help eliminate surprises caused by subtle differences between software versions. If you are loading new software in order to solve an existing problem, checking the notes on the new software lets you know in advance if the new software will fix your problem. Additionally, you are also cautioned to test any new software versions before deploying them throughout the enterprise. Features such as automatically downloading software to all clients may have disastrous effects if that software has not been tested within your organization.

---

After the new software is loaded, Cisco strongly urges that you clear the browser's cache, temporary files, and history files. This will ensure that the next update of software does not use an old copy. The authors prefer to clear these items both before and after updating software to ensure that there is absolutely no possibility that an old file is chosen, even if one of the clearings is forgotten.

## Clients

The Administration | Software Update | Clients screen is used to update hardware and software clients when they become connected to the concentrator. This screen is shown in Figure 7-8. The Group pull-down menu allows you to update all groups or any one group.

The process for updating the client is the same as on the concentrator. You choose a file using a Browse function. The requirement to update the client is controlled through the Configuration | User Management | Groups screen. This is discussed in Chapter 9, "Configuring Scalability Features of the Cisco VPN 3002 Hardware Client."

**Figure 7-8** *Administration | Software Update | Clients*

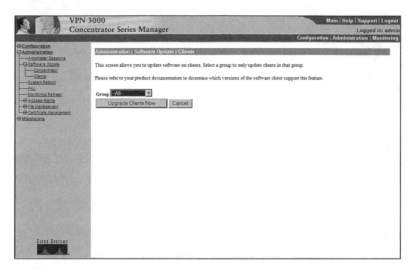

## System Reboot

The Administration | System Reboot screen allows you to reboot the system in a controlled manner. As shown in Figure 7-9, there are a number of rebooting options available, which are broken down into three sections:

- Action
- Configuration
- When to Reboot/Shutdown

Each of these is discussed in the following sections.

### Action

In the Action section, there are three straightforward choices:

- **Reboot**—Reboots the concentrator
- **Shutdown** —Shuts down without automatically rebooting
- **Cancel**—Cancels a pending shutdown or reboot

**Figure 7-9** *Administration | System Reboot*

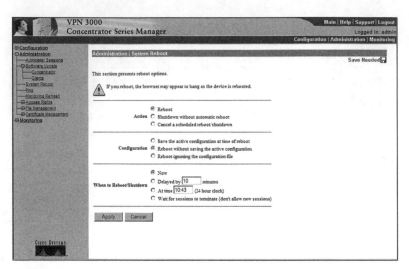

## Configuration

The configuration section allows you to control what happens during the shutdown and startup processes with the following three options:

- **Save the active configuration at time of reboot**—Is the most widely used because it saves the current configuration when the system is shut down

- **Reboot without saving the active configuration**—Usually used when you wish to revert to a previously saved configuration after attempting some unsuccessful configuration changes

- **Reboot ignoring the configuration file**—Allows you to bypass the configuration file upon rebooting, which is useful when you wish to change a very large amount of the configuration

## When to Reboot/Shutdown

The third section schedules a reboot or shutdown. You have four options:

- **Now**—Causes the concentrator to take the previously chosen action immediately with no considerations given for anyone who is presently connected to the concentrator

- **Delayed by minutes**—Allows the action to be delayed for a specific amount of time

- **At time**—Allows the action to be delayed until a specific time
- **Wait for session to terminate**—Takes the previously chosen action when the last connection becomes inactive, with no new connections allowed until the action has been taken, which allows for all users to disconnect in a normal manner before the action is taken

Clicking the Apply button enables the choices you have made.

## Ping

The Administration | Ping screen, shown in Figure 7-10, is used to test connectivity. You may enter the IP address of the remote device, or you may use the host name if you are using a DNS server. This device sends Internet Control Message Protocol (ICMP) echo requests to the remote device and shows the results of those requests.

**Figure 7-10** *Administration | Ping*

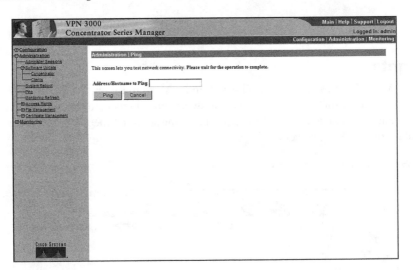

## Monitoring Refresh

The Administration | Monitoring Refresh screen is shown in Figure 7-11. There are only two options available on this screen. The first option, the Enable check box, sets whether the statistics screens should be refreshed. If this box is not checked, the statistics shown on a screen will remain the same despite the fact that the statistics are actually changing. Should the Enable check box be checked, the statistics screens will be refreshed at the time (in seconds) specified by the refresh period. The default for the refresh period is 30 seconds.

**Figure 7-11** *Administration | Monitoring Refresh*

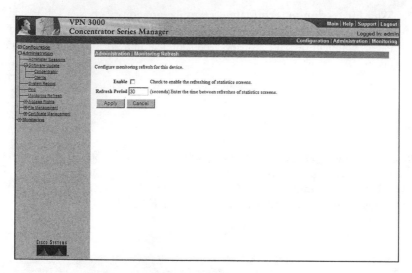

## Access Rights

The Administration | Access Rights screen is shown in Figure 7-12. This screen enables the submenu used for setting username, password, and rights combinations; configuring the concentrator with access control lists; and setting session timeouts. This screen also enables the submenu for AAA servers.

**Figure 7-12** *Administration | Access Rights*

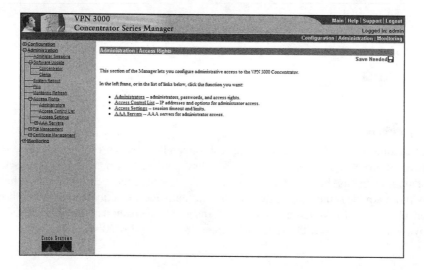

## Administrators

The Administration I Access Rights I Administrators screen, shown in Figure 7-13, is used to add those users who are allowed to access the concentrator's Configuration, Administration, and Monitoring functions. Up to five users may be allowed this type of access. To add a user, click the Modify button next to a username that is blank. Modifying a user is accomplished by clicking the Modify button next to a username that is not blank. Enabling the Administrator option gives the user full rights to the system. If the Enabled check box is not checked, the user will not be able to log on to the concentrator.

**Figure 7-13** *Administration I Access Rights I Administrators*

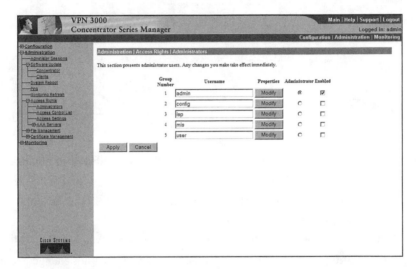

Once the Modify button is chosen, the Administration I Access Rights I Administrators I Modify Properties screen is shown, as shown in Figure 7-14. The username is entered, followed by the password. The password is also verified.

The Access Rights section of the Modify Properties screen contains four pull-down menus. These menus set the permissions for their associated titles as follows:

- **Authentication**—Sets the rights for the user regarding authentication
- **General**—Sets rights for most of the concentrator
- **SNMP**—Deals with SNMP-related issues
- **Files**—Sets rights regarding reading and writing of files

**Figure 7-14**  *Administration | Access Rights | Administrators | Modify Properties*

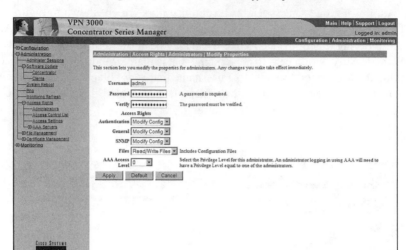

The pull-down menus for all of these options are the same. Shown in Figure 7-15, each of the pull-down menus has four options:

- **None**—The concentrator will not allow the user to access the section in any manner, including viewing and changing.

- **Stats Only**—This option restricts the user to those screens where statistics are displayed.

- **View Config** —This options allows the user to view, but not change, the current configuration.

- **Modify Config**—This option allows the user to change items within the section.

This system gives a great deal of flexibility with very little complexity. For example, imagine a user who has Modify Config access on Authentication, but None access on files. This user could change the configuration but would not be able to save that configuration. This would allow another administrator to review the changes made before committing those changes to the file system.

## Access Control List

The Administration I Access Rights I Access Control List screen allows for adding, modifying, and prioritizing access lists. These access lists are used to determine those IP addresses that may access the concentrator for management functions. It is important to note that this access is not limited to HTTP and Telnet access. The access lists are also used to define those IP addresses that may be used for SNMP, FTP, and TFTP purposes. If the list is empty, as shown in Figure 7-16, then all stations will be allowed all access.

**Figure 7-15**  *Access Rights Choices*

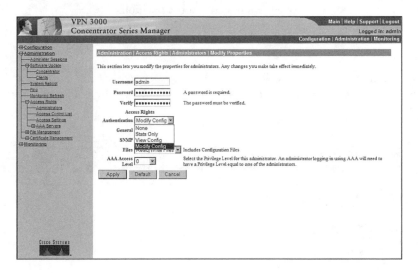

**Figure 7-16**  *Administration | Access Rights | Access Control List*

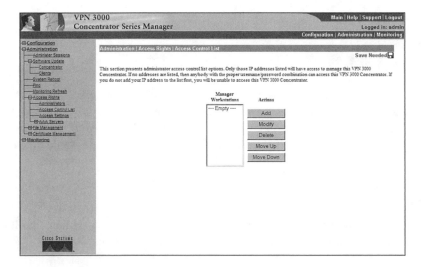

The access lists are very similar to the access lists used on the Cisco PIX firewall. That is, they rely on subnet masks, not on wildcard masks. Using 255.255.255.255 for the subnet mask specifies a single host, while using 0.0.0.0 for the subnet mask specifies all hosts. Choosing Add or Modify will bring up a screen where the IP address and subnet mask are entered. Additionally, the group that this access list is applied to is entered.

Moving an entry up or down will modify the order of the lists. This way, you may create lists in any order and then move them to their proper position.

## Access Settings

The Administration | Access Rights | Access Settings screen, shown in Figure 7-17, sets the session idle timeout, sets the session limit, and enables configuration file encryption.

**Figure 7-17** *Administration | Access Rights | Access Settings*

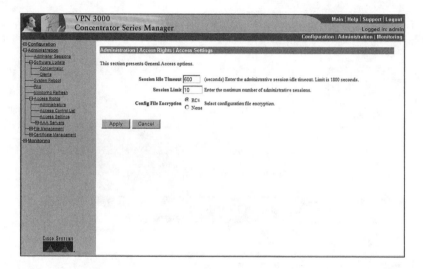

The Session Idle Timeout is entered in seconds. This specifies the amount of time that a connection is maintained without any activity on that session. After the timeout period without any activity, the session will be disconnected. The maximum allowable time is 1800 seconds, which calculates to 30 minutes. The default is 600 seconds (10 minutes).

The Session Limit is entered next. This option limits the number of concurrent management sessions. The default is 10 sessions.

The configuration file may also be encrypted using the RC4 encryption algorithm. This option is especially useful when storing configuration files on a remote server.

## AAA Servers

The Administration | Access Rights | AAA Servers screen, shown in Figure 7-18, is an entry screen used to navigate to the authentication screen. Click the Authentication link to continue.

**Figure 7-18** *Administration | Access Rights | AAA Servers*

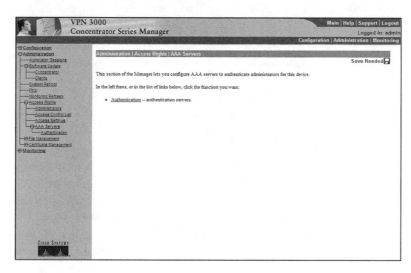

## Authentication

The Administration | AAA Servers | Authentication screen is used to add, modify, and test TACACS+ servers. A sample screen is shown in Figure 7-19.

**Figure 7-19** *Administration | AAA Servers | Authentication*

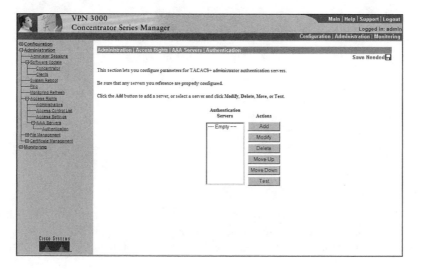

As with other screens of this type, choosing Add will allow you to add a new item, while Modify will allow changes to a chosen item. You may also move the order of the server entries and delete server entries, as well as test a connection to a TACACS+ server.

**NOTE**     Remember that the Cisco VPN 3000 Series Concentrators only use TACACS+ for administrator authentication. There are no provisions for these concentrators to use RADIUS or TACACS for the authentication.

Adding a new TACACS+ server is accomplished by clicking the Add button. You are taken to the Administration | Access Rights | AAA Servers | Authentication | Add screen, as shown in Figure 7-20. On this screen, you first enter the IP address or host name of the TACACS+ server. This is followed by the port, timeout (in seconds), and number of retries. Leaving the port number set to zero will use the default port. Finally, enter and verify the server secret.

**Figure 7-20**  *Administration | Access Rights | AAA Servers | Authentication | Add*

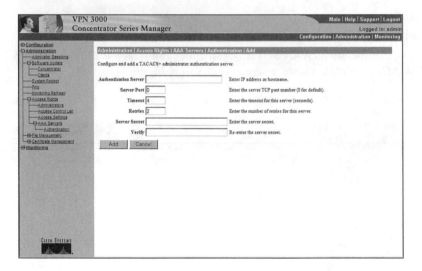

# File Management

The Administration | File Management screen is shown in Figure 7-21. This screen enables the submenu used to access the screens used for swapping the configuration file, TFTP transfers, file uploads using HTTP, and exporting the configuration to an XML file. You may also view, delete, or copy the configuration or log files.

**Figure 7-21** *Administration | File Management*

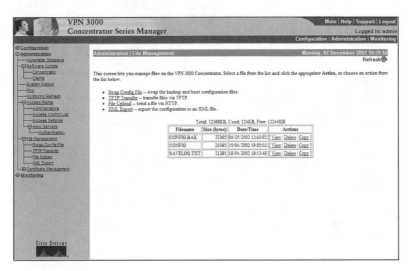

The VPN 3000 Series Concentrators merely need an IP address entered in order to transfer the files. Because multiple copies of the configuration file are available, you are able to move quickly between different configurations for testing purposes.

## Certificate Manager

The Administration | Certificate Management screen allows you to see all of your current certificates and enroll or install new certificates. Under this screen, you have an Enrollment and Installation screen. These comprise the final screens under the Administration section. As shown in Figure 7-22, the Certificate Manager screen will list all of your certificates. Chapter 5, "Configuring Cisco VPN 3000 for Remote Access Using Digital Certificates," provides a full explanation of working with certificates.

**Figure 7-22** *Administration | Certificate Management*

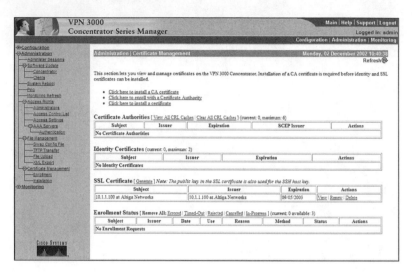

# Monitoring the Cisco VPN 3000 Series Concentrator

Assuming that you have logged into the concentrator, you will be presented with the main screen. For purposes of this section, you will be focusing on the Monitoring options. Click the Monitoring link to start monitoring the concentrator.

You should now be on the main monitoring screen, as shown in Figure 7-23. This screen will be used to navigate between all the monitoring options.

You are initially presented with six options, each of which brings you to an associated screen as described in Table 7-3. Any of these screens may have subscreens associated with them. Take a moment to study Table 7-3, which lists all of the menu and submenu options. Knowing how to navigate through the system will make administration easier. Knowing what options are controlled on individual screens will help you pass the exam. After studying the table, the next sections explore each individual item.

Next, you begin to explore some of the options available through the Monitoring menu system.

**Figure 7-23**  *Monitoring Screen*

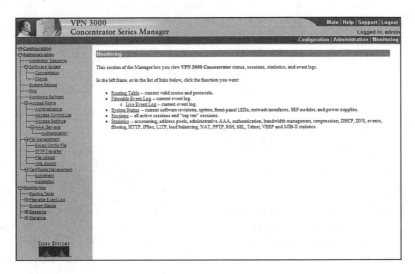

**Table 7-3**    *Monitoring Menu System*

| Menu Option | Level | Usage |
|---|---|---|
| Monitoring | 1 | Main screen for monitoring the VPN 3000 Concentrator. Enables all of the Monitoring submenus. |
| Routing Table | 2 | Shows the currently configured routes. |
| Filterable Event Log | 2 | Allows you to show events as defined by the debugging options set within the configuration. These events may be filtered. This screen is updated periodically based on the setting in the Administration \| Monitoring Refresh screen. |
| Live Event Log | 3 | Shows all events for which logging is enabled. These events are not filterable and show up in real time. |
| System Status | 2 | Shows the status and the serial number of the concentrator. |
| Sessions | 2 | Allows you to see the statistics for all the current sessions on the concentrator. This screen also enables the submenus for monitoring the sessions by protocol or encryption as well as the "top ten" list. |
| Statistics | 3 | Is similar to the Monitoring \| Protocols screen, but allows you to choose the protocol on which to filter the statistics. |
| Encryption | 3 | Is similar to the Monitoring \| Protocols screen, but allows you to choose the encryption on which to filter the statistics. |

*continues*

**Table 7-3**   *Monitoring Menu System (Continued)*

| Menu Option | Level | Usage |
|---|---|---|
| Top Ten Lists | 3 | Enables the submenu that allows you to see the statistics for the 10 most active sessions sorted by total bytes transmitted, total time connected, or average throughput. |
| Statistics | 2 | Enables the submenu for statistics. These statistics are divided into several submenus. |
| MIB-II Stats | 3 | Enables the submenu for those statistics that are reported through the MIB system. |

## Routing Table

The Monitoring | Routing Table screen, shown in Figure 7-24, shows your current routes and allows you to clear routing entries. Note that, after clearing the routes, those routes that are learned by routing protocols will eventually be learned again by those protocols. Static routes are not affected by clearing routes. Be aware that clearing routes may disrupt user connectivity.

**Figure 7-24**   *Monitoring | Routing Table*

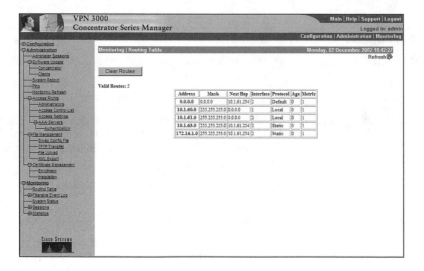

## Event Log Screen

The Filterable Event Log screen is used to see any events that have previously been defined as an event that should be logged. This screen, shown in Figure 7-25, allows you to filter these events by class and severity. You may also filter based upon the client's IP address. The output is shown in the bottom half of the screen. This screen is refreshed based on the values specified in the Administration | Monitoring Refresh screen.

**Figure 7-25**  *Monitoring | Filterable Event Log*

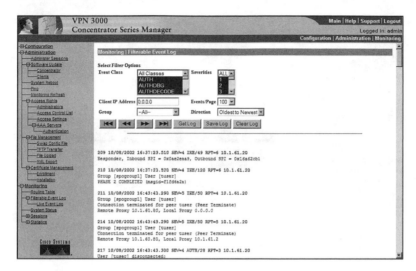

The Live Event Screen log, which is accessed by the link on the left side of the screen, does not allow for filtering but does have an advantage and a disadvantage when compared to the Filterable Event Log. The advantage is that events are shown immediately. The disadvantage is that monitoring these events, as in any debugging, may cause excessive CPU cycle utilization.

## System Status

The Monitoring | System Status screen is shown in Figure 7-26. This screen is the closest equivalent available on the concentrator to the **show version** command on a router. This screen shows the concentrator type, the serial number, and the software revisions being run. The time that the system has been active, the boot time, and the RAM size is also shown.

Similar to the graphical user interface (GUI) available for the Cisco switches, you may click on a module to find the details of the status for that module. The fan speeds, as well as the temperature for the interior of the concentrator, are shown. There are three graphs on the bottom of the screen, indicating the CPU utilization, the concentrator's throughput, and the number of active sessions.

**Figure 7-26**   *Monitoring | System Status*

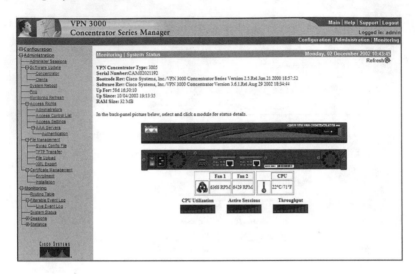

## Sessions

The Monitoring | Sessions screen, as seen in Figure 7-27, shows the statistics for the currently connected sessions. On this screen, you are able to limit the connections seen by group.

**Figure 7-27**   *Monitoring | Sessions*

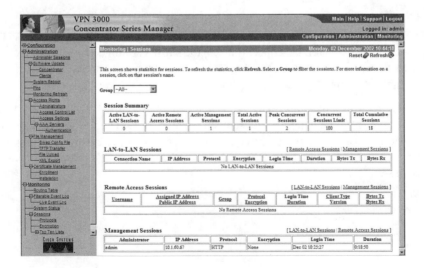

The screen is divided into four sections as follows. The following sections describe each in greater detail:

- Session Summary
- LAN-to-LAN Sessions
- Remote Access Sessions
- Management Sessions

This screen also provides you with a link to the top ten lists.

## Sessions Summary

The Session Summary section displays a summary of all the active sessions and the peak concurrent sessions. The sessions limit and cumulative sessions are also displayed. This information is useful when determining how heavily you are utilizing the concentrator.

## LAN-to-LAN Sessions

The LAN-to-LAN section allows you to see all the current LAN-to-LAN sessions. Noted in this section are the IP address and protocol used for connecting to the remote LAN as well as the encryption used. The time the tunnel was initiated and the duration the tunnel has been active are displayed next, followed by the bytes transmitted (Bytes Tx) and the bytes received (Bytes Rx). The Bytes Tx and Bytes Rx are useful when debugging a LAN-to-LAN connection. See Chapter 10, "Cisco VPN 3000 LAN-to-LAN with Preshared Keys," for more information.

## Remote Access Sessions

The Remote Access Sessions section shows the username, assigned IP address, and the public IP address for each of the connected remote access sessions.

The group to which this user belongs and the protocol encryption type are seen next. The duration of the connection, the client version, client type, and the Bytes Tx and Bytes Rx over the connection are shown.

## Management Sessions

The Management Sessions Section shows those users connected to the concentrator for management purposes. The IP address, protocol used, and encryption type are shown, as well as the login time and the duration of the connection.

## Top Ten Lists

The Top Ten Lists screen is shown in Figure 7-28. This screen enables the submenu system that allows you to see statistics for the top ten sessions. The choice of which sessions are included on these lists is based on data (the total amount of data sent and received), duration (the total time the session has been established), or throughput (the average amount of data throughput in bytes per second).

**Figure 7-28** *Monitoring | Sessions | Top Ten Lists*

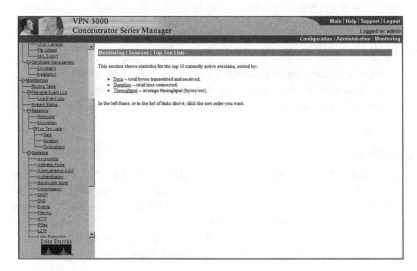

Choosing any of the three options brings you to the respective screen. All of these screens look virtually identical. The difference in them is merely the criteria for being selected for the list. As shown in Figure 7-29, groups may further filter the data. Choosing a group through the pull-down menu will show the top ten users for that individual group.

## Statistics

Shown in Figure 7-30, the Monitoring | Statistics screen is used to move further down the menu structure to an individual statistic.

**Figure 7-29**  *Monitoring | Sessions | Top Ten List | Data*

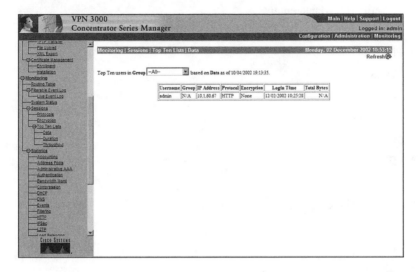

**Figure 7-30**  *Monitoring | Statistics*

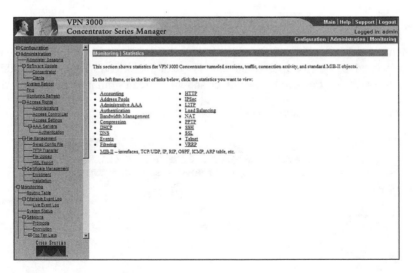

Following is a list of the Monitoring | Statistics submenu options:

- Accounting
- Address Pools
- Administrative AAA

- Authentication
- Bandwidth Management
- Compression
- DHCP
- DNS
- Events
- Filtering
- HTTP
- IPSec
- L2TP
- Load Balancing
- NAT
- PPTP
- SSH
- SSL
- Telnet
- VRRP

When you wish to view statistics based on any of the items shown in the preceding list, you merely need to click the appropriate link. For example, if you wish to see the address pools data, click the **Address Pools** link. You will be shown a screen similar to the one shown in Figure 7-31.

**Figure 7-31** *Monitoring | Statistics | Address Pools*

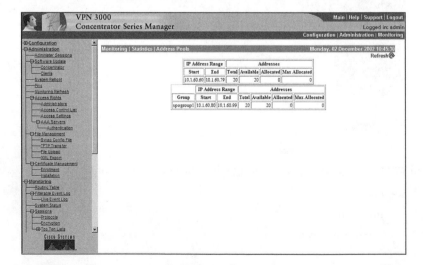

## Events

If you want to see what events have occurred since the last reboot, you would click the Events link. This causes the screen shown in Figure 7-32 to be displayed. This screen lists all of the events.

**Figure 7-32**  *Monitoring | Statistics | Events Screen*

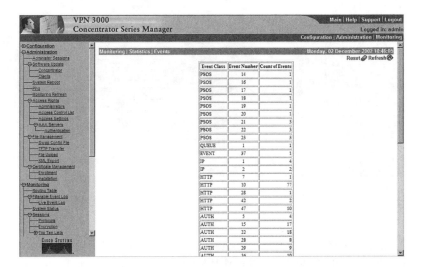

## IPSec

One of the most important screens for statistics is the Monitoring | Statistics | IPSec screen. As seen in Figure 7-33, this screen gives you a wealth of information regarding the IPSec protocol. This screen is split into two areas: IKE (Phase 1) Statistics and IPSec (Phase 2) Statistics.

The IPSec screen may be the most useful of all the statistics because of the amount the IPSec protocol is relied on to form connections to your concentrator. Notice that not only are the successful connections shown, but also items such as Failed Initiated Tunnels and Failed Inbound Authentications. Because these types of information are shown on this screen, you are able to quickly troubleshoot connection failures. For example, should you have a problem connecting from a remote device, watching how the counters on this screen change as connections are attempted will reveal to you the cause of the failure.

**Figure 7-33** *Monitoring | Statistics | IPSec*

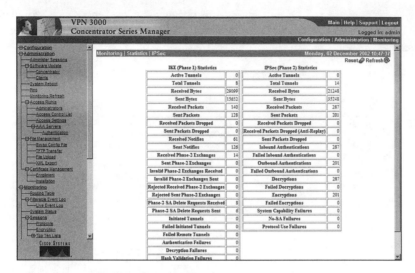

## MIB-II Statistics

The Monitoring | Statistics | MIB-II screen, as seen in Figure 7-34, is used to move further down the menu structure to an individual MIB statistics screen.

**Figure 7-34** *Monitoring | Statistics | MIB-II*

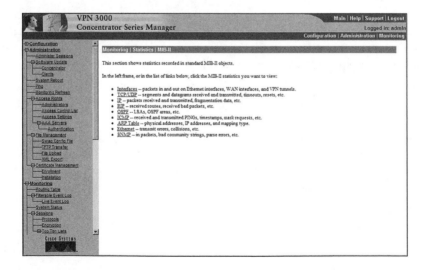

The MIB-II Statistics submenu system is shown in the following list so that you can familiarize yourself with the options available:

- Interfaces
- TCP/UDP
- IP
- RIP
- OSPF
- ICMP
- ARP Table
- Ethernet
- SNMP

Notice that the available options here refer to more fundamental aspects of the concentrator than those available within the Monitoring | Statistics screen. This is important for you to remember for both the exam and for your daily work. If, for example, you want to see the statistics on an interface port, you will look in the MIB-II section. However, if you want statistics regarding load balancing, you will look in the Statistics section. Basically, if you think in terms of the ISO layers, you will see all the Layer 1, Layer 2, Layer 3, and Layer 4 statistics here. You will also see your routing protocols and TCP/UDP and SNMP packets here. Virtually everything else is seen in the Statistics screen.

## Interfaces

A common task is to determine whether your interfaces are up. The Interfaces link allows you to see the state of your interfaces. As shown in Figure 7-35, this screen shows the state of your interface and the number of packets traversing the interface broken down by unicast, multicast, and broadcast types.

## IP

The IP screen is another critical screen on this submenu (see Figure 7-36). This screen shows IP packets sent, received, and discarded. You also see items such as fragmentation successes and failures.

**Figure 7-35** *Monitoring | Statistics | MIB-II | Interfaces*

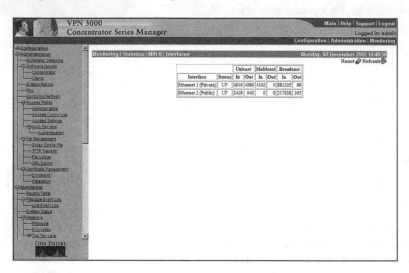

**Figure 7-36** *Monitoring | Statistics | MIB-II | IP*

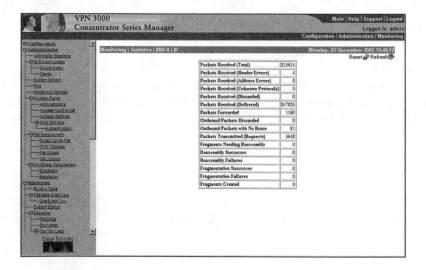

## RIP

Figure 7-37 shows the RIP screen. This screen shows you any errors regarding the RIP protocol. Should you experience issues regarding routes that should be known through RIP, refer to this screen when troubleshooting.

**Figure 7-37**  *Monitoring | Statistics | MIB-II | RIP*

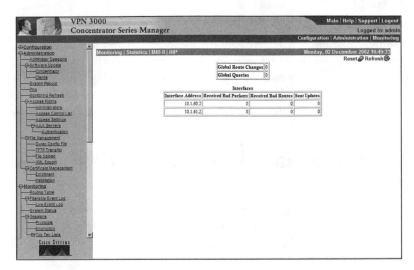

The whole of the Monitoring submenu system is used to find where issues in connectivity and performance lie. It is important for you to know where you can look to find that information. Take a few minutes and review Table 7-3 and the submenu lists for statistics and MIB II. Memorizing the contents of these tables will serve you well in quickly and efficiently troubleshooting connectivity.

# Foundation Summary

The Foundation Summary is a collection of tables and figures that provides a convenient review of many key concepts in this chapter. For those who are already comfortable with the topics in this chapter, this summary could help you recall a few details. For those who just read this chapter, this review should help solidify some key facts. For anyone doing final preparation before the exam, these tables and figures are a convenient way to review the day before the exam.

## Administering the Cisco VPN 3000 Series Concentrator

Figure 7-38 shows the main screen you will see after logging into the concentrator. This screen allows you to configure, administer, or monitor the concentrator.

**Figure 7-38** *Main Screen*

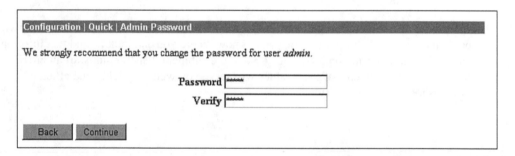

Figure 7-39 shows the main administration screen, which you use to navigate between all the administration options.

**Figure 7-39**  *Administration Screen*

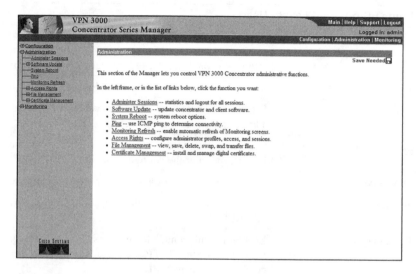

Table 7-4 details the administration menu options.

**Table 7-4**    *Administration Menu System*

| Menu Option | Level | Usage |
|---|---|---|
| Administration | 1 | Main screen for administering the VPN 3000 Concentrator. Enables all of the Administration submenus. |
| Administer Sessions | 2 | Shows all the current sessions. Should you choose, you may filter the sessions shown by group. |
| Software Update | 2 | Enables submenu, allowing you to choose to update either the concentrator or clients. |
| Concentrator | 3 | Is used to update the concentrator to which you are currently logged on. |
| Clients | 3 | Updates all the clients or clients based on groups. |
| System Reboot | 2 | Allows you to reboot the system either immediately or at a scheduled time. This is also the screen used to reboot without using the current configuration. |
| Ping | 2 | Allows you to check connectivity with a remote system by either name or IP address. |
| Monitoring Refresh | 2 | Sets if the screens should automatically refresh and, if so, how often. |

*continues*

**Table 7-4** *Administration Menu System (Continued)*

| Menu Option | Level | Usage |
|---|---|---|
| Access Rights | 2 | Enables submenu used for setting username/password/rights combinations, Access-Control lists for configuring the concentrator, setting session timeouts, and enables the submenu for AAA servers. |
| Administrators | 3 | Sets usernames, passwords, and rights. |
| Access Control List | 3 | Sets those IP addresses allowed to access the concentrator for administration and configuration. |
| Access Settings | 3 | Sets the session timeouts, limits the number of connections, and allows for encryption of the configuration file. |
| AAA Servers | 3 | Enables the submenu for setting the Authentication Servers. |
| Authentication | 4 | Allows the addition, modification, configuration, or deletion of TACACS+ Servers. |
| File Management | 2 | Enables the submenu, allowing for swapping the backup and boot files, file transfers using TFTP, file uploads using HTTP, and exporting the configuration to an XML file. |
| Swap Config File | 3 | Allows swapping the boot and backup boot files. |
| TFTP Transfer | 3 | Allows uploading or downloading via a remote TFTP server. |
| File Upload | 3 | Allows uploading a file via HTTP. |
| XML Export | 3 | Allows a configuration file to be exported to an XML file. |
| Certificate Manager | 2 | Enables the submenu, allowing enrollment and installation of Certificates. |
| Enrollment | 3 | Enrolls Certificates. |
| Installation | 3 | Installs Certificates. |

# Administer Sessions

Figure 7-40 presents the Administration | Administer Sessions screen, which shows the session statistics for all connected sessions. Filter the sessions by group using the Group pull-down menu.

**Figure 7-40**  *Administration | Administer Sessions*

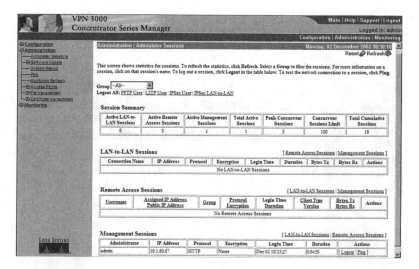

# Software Update

The Administration | Software Update screen, shown in Figure 7-41, consists of the submenu options.

**Figure 7-41**  *Administration | Software Update*

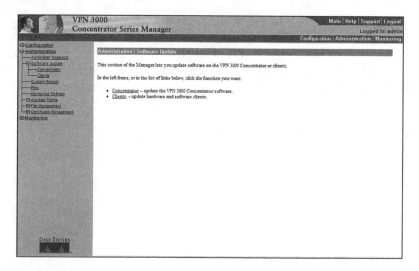

## Concentrator

The Administration | Software Update | Concentrator screen, seen in Figure 7-42, shows the current version of the software and allows you to upload a new version to the concentrator.

**Figure 7-42** *Administration | Software Update | Concentrator*

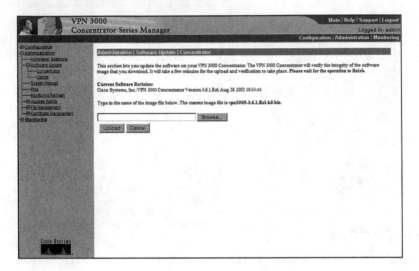

Cisco strongly urges that you clear the browser's cache, temporary files, and history files after updating.

## Clients

The Administration | Software Update | Clients screen, shown in Figure 7-43, is used to update hardware and software clients when they become connected to the concentrator.

**Figure 7-43**  *Administration | Software Update | Clients*

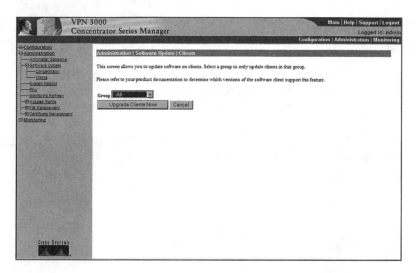

# System Reboot

The Administration | System Reboot screen, shown in Figure 7-44, allows you to reboot the system in a controlled manner.

**Figure 7-44**  *Administration | System Reboot*

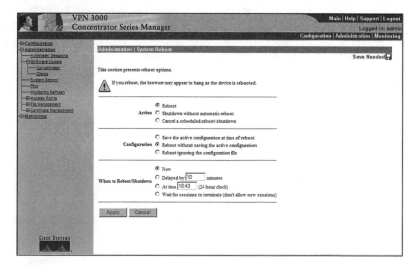

# Ping

The Administration | Ping screen, shown in Figure 7-45, is used to test connectivity.

**Figure 7-45** *Administration | Ping*

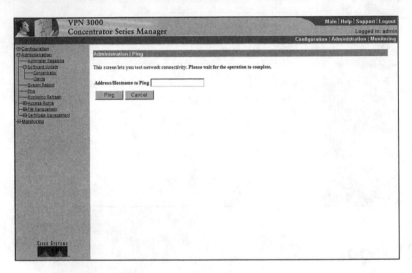

# Monitoring Refresh

The Administration | Monitoring Refresh screen is shown in Figure 7-46. The Enable check box sets whether the statistics screens should be refreshed. The statistics screens will be refreshed at the time (in seconds) specified by the refresh period. The default for the refresh period is 30 seconds.

**Figure 7-46**  *Administration | Monitoring Refresh*

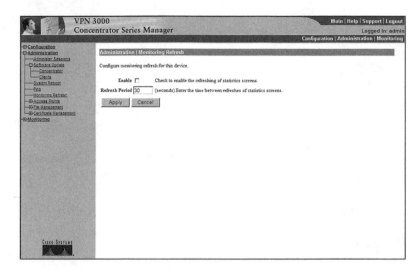

# Access Rights

The Access Rights screen enables the submenu used for setting username, password and rights combinations, access control lists for configuring the concentrator, setting session timeouts, and enables the submenu for AAA servers.

# Administrators

The Administration I Access Rights I Administrators screen is used to add those users who are allowed to access the concentrator's Configuration, Administration, and Monitoring functions (see Figure 7-47). Up to five users may be allowed this type of access.

**Figure 7-47**  *Administration | Access Rights | Administrators*

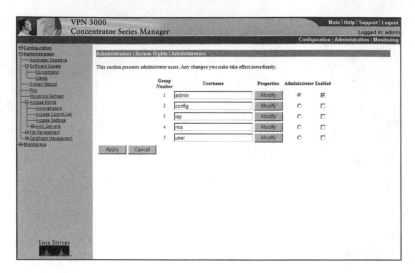

# Access Control List

The Administration | Access Rights | Access Control List screen allows for adding, modifying, and prioritizing access lists (see Figure 7-48). These access lists are used to determine those IP addresses that may access the concentrator for management functions.

**Figure 7-48**  *Administration | Access Rights | Access Control List*

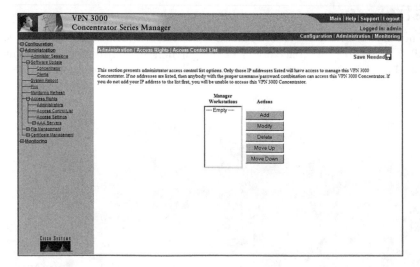

# Access Settings

The Administration I Access Rights I Access Settings screen sets the session idle timeout, sets the session limit, and enables configuration file encryption.

The Session Idle Timeout is entered in seconds. The maximum allowable time is 1800 seconds. The default is 600 seconds. The session limit default is 10 sessions. The configuration file may also be encrypted using the RC4 encryption algorithm.

# AAA Servers

The Administration I AAA Servers screen is an entry screen used to navigate to the authentication screen.

# Authentication

The Administration I AAA Servers I Authentication screen is used to add, modify, and test TACACS+ servers.

Remember that the Cisco VPN 3000 Series Concentrators only use TACACS+ for administrator authentication. There are no provisions for these concentrators to use RADIUS or TACACS for the authentication.

# File Management

The Administration I File Management screen enables the submenu.

The submenu options are

- Swap configuration files
- TFTP transfers
- File uploads
- Export to XML

# Certificate Manager

The Administration I Certificate Manager screen allows you to

- See current certificates
- Enroll certificates
- Install certificates

# Monitoring the Cisco VPN 3000 Series Concentrator

Figure 7-49 shows the Monitoring screen.

**Figure 7-49** *Monitoring Screen*

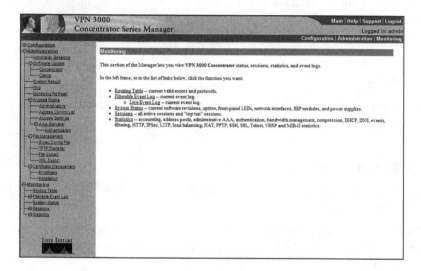

Table 7-5 describes the Monitoring screen menu options.

**Table 7-5** *Monitoring Menu System*

| Menu Option | Level | Usage |
|---|---|---|
| Monitoring | 1 | Main screen for monitoring the VPN 3000 Concentrator. Enables all of the Monitoring submenus. |
| Routing Table | 2 | Shows the currently configured routes. |
| Filterable Event Log | 2 | Allows you to show events as defined by the debugging options set within the configuration. These events may be filtered. This screen is updated periodically based on the setting in the Administration \| Monitoring Refresh screen. |
| Live Event Log | 3 | Shows all events for which logging is enabled. These events are not filterable and show up in real time. |
| System Status | 2 | Shows the status and the serial number of the concentrator. |
| Sessions | 2 | Allows you to see the statistics for all of the current sessions on the concentrator. This screen also enables the submenus for monitoring the sessions by protocol or encryption, as well as the "top ten" list. |
| Statistics | 3 | Is similar to the Monitoring \| Protocols screen but allows you to choose the protocol on which to filter the statistics. |

**Table 7-5**    *Monitoring Menu System (Continued)*

| Menu Option | Level | Usage |
|---|---|---|
| Encryption | 3 | Is similar to the Monitoring | Protocols screen, but allows you to choose the encryption on which to filter the statistics. |
| Top Ten Lists | 3 | Enables the submenu that allows you to see the statistics for the 10 most active sessions sorted by total bytes transmitted, total time connected, or average throughput. |
| Statistics | 2 | Enables the submenu for statistics. These statistics are divided into a great number of submenus. |
| MIB-II Stats | 3 | Enables the submenu for those statistics that are reported through the MIB system. |

# System Status

The System Status screen is the closest equivalent available on the concentrator to the **show version** command on a router. See Figure 7-50.

**Figure 7-50**  *System Status*

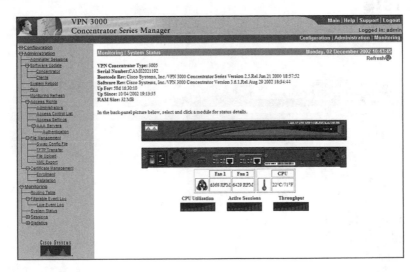

# Sessions

The Sessions screen shows the statistics for the currently connected sessions (see Figure 7-51).

**Figure 7-51**  *Sessions*

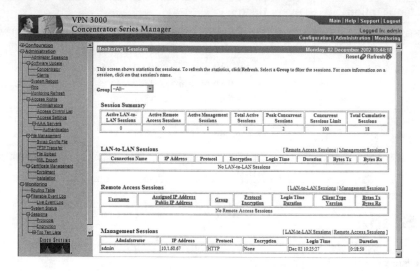

# Top Ten Lists

The Top Ten Lists screen is shown in Figure 7-52.

**Figure 7-52**  *Top Ten Lists*

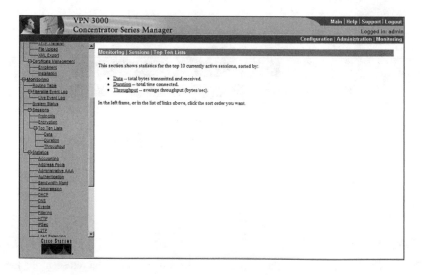

Figure 7-53 shows the Top Ten Lists Data screen.

**Figure 7-53**  *Top Ten Lists | Data*

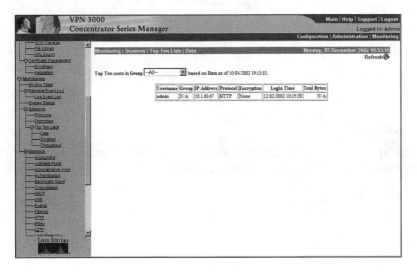

# Statistics

Following is a list of the Monitoring | Statistics submenu options:

- Accounting
- Address Pools
- Administrative AAA
- Authentication
- Bandwidth Management
- Compression
- DHCP
- DNS
- Events
- Filtering
- HTTP
- IPSec
- L2TP
- Load Balancing
- NAT

- PPTP
- SSH
- SSL
- Telnet
- VRRP

# MIB II Statistics

The MIB-II Statistics submenu system is shown in the following list in order for you to familiarize yourself with the options available:

- Interfaces
- TCP/UDP
- IP
- RIP
- OSPF
- ICMP
- ARP Table
- Ethernet
- SNMP

Basically, if you think in terms of the ISO layers, you will see all of the Layer 1, Layer 2, Layer 3, and Layer 4 statistics here. You will also see your routing protocols and TCP/UDP and SNMP packets here. Virtually everything else is seen in the Statistics screen.

# Q&A

As mentioned in Chapter 1, "All About the Cisco Certified Security Professional," these questions are more difficult than what you should experience on the CCSP exam. The questions do not attempt to cover more breadth or depth than the exam; however, the questions are designed to make sure you know the answer. Rather than allowing you to derive the answer from clues hidden inside the question itself, your understanding and recall of the subject are challenged. Questions from the "Do I Know This Already?" quiz from the beginning of the chapter are repeated here to ensure that you have mastered the chapter's topic areas. Hopefully, these questions will help limit the number of exam questions on which you narrow your choices to two options and guess!

1  What screen is used to set the password for the administrator?

2  You wish to limit HTTP access to the concentrator to hosts on the same subnet as the inside interface of the concentrator. What is the format of the access control list?

3  What types of AAA servers can the VPN 3000 Series Concentrator use for authenticating management sessions?

4  What is the upper limit for a management session timeout?

5  What form of encryption may be used on a configuration file?

**6** On what screen can routes be cleared?

_____

_____

_____

**7** Where can you see the CPU utilization on a Cisco 3000 Series Concentrator?

_____

_____

_____

**8** Where can you troubleshoot an IPSec connection?

_____

_____

_____

**9** Where can you troubleshoot TCP/IP connections?

_____

_____

_____

**10** Where can you see the number of collisions on an Ethernet interface?

_____

_____

_____

**11** What is the major difference between the Monitoring | Statistics and the Monitoring | Statistics | MIB II sections?

_____

_____

_____

**12** You wish to limit the number of concurrent management connections. Where is this done?

_____

_____

_____

**13** You wish to use a AAA server to authenticate management access to the concentrator. What must you use?

_____

_____

_____

**14** What are the differences between the Filterable Event Log screen and the Live Event Log screen?

_____

_____

_____

**15** On what screen can you see if a certificate has been requested but has not yet been received?

_____

_____

_____

**16** What section should you look in if you want to see the number of pings sent and received? From where on the concentrator do you send a ping?

_____

_____

_____

**17** Name two places that you can see the current software version on a concentrator.

_____

_____

_____

**18** What are the access control lists as defined in the Administration I Access Rights I Access Control Lists screen used for?

_____

_____

_____

**19** You find out that your assistant has changed the configuration and saved that new configuration. However, something was configured incorrectly. None of remote sites or remote users can connect to the concentrator. What is the quickest way to resolve the issue?

_____

_____

_____

**20** A remote client with a VPN 3002 Hardware Client calls you on the phone saying that he is unable to connect to your network. He says that he may have incorrectly configured the preshared key on his end. You have access through HTTP to your concentrator. Where is the first place you look to see if this is a preshared key issue?

_____

_____

_____

# Exam Topics Discussed in This Chapter

This chapter covers the following topics, which you need to master in your pursuit of certification as a Cisco Certified Security Professional:

**27** Cisco VPN 3002 Hardware Client remote access with preshared keys

**28** Overview of VPN 3002 interactive unit and user authentication feature

**29** Configuring VPN 3002 integrated unit authentication feature

**30** Configuring VPN 3002 user authentication

**31** Monitoring VPN 3002 user statistics

# CHAPTER 8

# Configuring Cisco 3002 Hardware Client for Remote Access

This chapter deals with configuring the VPN 3002 Hardware Client for remote access. These configuration tasks include using preshared keys, setting the VPN 3002 Hardware Client to use client and LAN Extension modes, and setting up individual authentication.

Chapter 3, "Cisco VPN 3000 Concentrator Series Hardware Overview," gave a brief overview of Cisco's VPN 3002 Hardware Client. From that discussion, you might remember that the VPN 3002 Hardware Client is a full-featured VPN client designed for a small office/home office (SOHO) environment, supports a single IPSec tunnel from its public interface, and can be purchased with an integral 8-port 10/100-Mbps auto-sensing switch.

The private interface supports standard Ethernet and Fast Ethernet and does not require a VPN software client on connecting user devices such as workstations and printers. That means that almost any device running any operating system that supports Ethernet can be used to connect to the VPN 3002 Hardware Client. This permits a small office to use a mixture of operating systems, such as Windows, MAC, Linux, Solaris, NetWare, or others, through a common Ethernet interface to transmit across a secure VPN tunnel. The VPN 3002 Hardware Client can support up to 253 concurrent users across the single VPN tunnel.

The VPN 3002 Hardware Client establishes the VPN tunnel with the head-end concentrator and performs all IPSec functions, relieving attached PCs of that processing load. This configuration simplifies administrative functions at the remote site because the individual user workstations do not need to be high-end machines and do not require an IPSec client. IPSec software or hardware updates need only to be accomplished on the VPN 3002 Hardware Client.

You can configure the VPN 3002 Hardware Client in one of two different operating modes: Client and Network Extension modes. In Client mode, all the end-user devices connecting to the VPN 3002 Hardware Client are invisible to the public network because their DHCP-acquired IP addresses are converted to a single IP address with Port Address Translation (PAT). The VPN 3002 Hardware Client acts as a software client when operating in Client mode.

In Network Extension mode, workstations attached to the VPN 3002 Hardware Client are each assigned an individual IP address. Network Address Translation (NAT) is not performed on the data in Network Extension mode. The addressing schemes on both sides of the secure tunnel are permitted to traverse the tunnel, simulating a connection via a private leased-line. This capability allows these devices to interact with network resources as though they were connected locally to those devices. The VPN 3002 Hardware Client acts as a site-to-site device when operating in Network Extension mode.

The following list is a quick look at some of the other capabilities of this handy device:

- Point-to-Point Protocol (PPP) over Ethernet (PPPoE) support for use with digital subscriber line (DSL) connections. This eliminates the need for PPPoE clients on the attached PCs.

- Auto-upgrade of the VPN 3002 Hardware Client's operating system from a central Trivial File Transfer Protocol (TFTP) server.

- Supports H.323 communications in Client mode, enabling the use of H.323 applications such as NetMeeting.

- Integral DHCP server for use in Client mode.

- Support for the major encryption, key management, and encryption algorithms used with IPSec. Protocols such as DES, 3DES, AES, MD5, SHA-1, HMAC with MD5, and HMAC with SHA-1 are all available on these devices.

# How to Best Use This Chapter

By taking the following steps, you can make better use of your time:

- Keep your notes and answers for all your work with this book in one place for easy reference.

- Take the "Do I Know This Already?" quiz, and write down your answers. Studies show retention is significantly increased through writing facts and concepts down, even if you never look at the information again.

- Use the diagram in Figure 8-1 to guide you to the next step.

**Figure 8-1** *How To Use This Chapter*

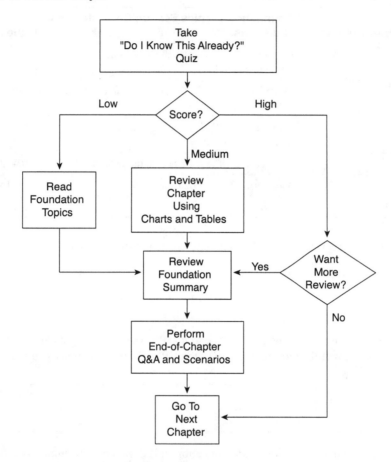

## "Do I Know This Already?" Quiz

The purpose of the "Do I Know This Already?" quiz is to help you decide what parts of the chapter to use. If you already intend to read the entire chapter, you do not need to answer these questions now.

This 15-question quiz helps you determine how to spend your limited study time. The quiz is sectioned into six smaller "quizlets," which correspond to the six major topic headings in this chapter. Figure 8-1 outlines suggestions on how to spend your time in this chapter based on your quiz score. Use Table 8-1 to record your scores.

**Table 8-1**    *Score Sheet for Quiz and Quizlets*

| Quizlet Number | Foundations Topics Section Covering These Questions | Questions | Score |
|---|---|---|---|
| 1 | Cisco VPN 3002 Hardware Client remote access with preshared keys | 1–3 | |
| 2 | Overview of VPN 3002 interactive unit and user authentication feature | 4–6 | |
| 3 | Configuring VPN 3002 integrated unit authentication feature | 7–9 | |
| 4 | Configuring VPN 3002 user authentication | 10–12 | |
| 5 | Monitoring VPN 3002 user statistics | 13–15 | |
| All questions | | 1–15 | |

1  What screen is used on the head-end concentrator to demand the use of preshared keys?

_____

_____

_____

2  You need to allow the main office to use PC Anywhere to connect to three separate machines at the remote office over the VPN. What mode must you use?

_____

_____

_____

3  You are using individual authentication in PAT mode. Your tunnel is established but the user cannot log in. What is the first item you should examine?

_____

_____

_____

4  What are the disadvantages in a large network (over 100 users) of using individual authentication with the internal authentication server in a VPN 3005 Concentrator?

_____

_____

_____

**5**  You are the second user to connect through a VPN 3002 Hardware Client for which interactive hardware client and individual user authentication have been configured. What authentication information will you be required to enter?

_____

_____

_____

**6**  You can use a static configuration for authenticating the VPN 3002 Hardware Client with the head-end concentrator. Why would you want to use interactive hardware client authentication?

_____

_____

_____

**7**  Where is interactive hardware client authentication configured?

_____

_____

_____

**8**  What authentication method is used for interactive hardware client authentication?

_____

_____

_____

**9**  What must you configure on the VPN 3002 Hardware Client in order to use interactive hardware client authentication?

_____

_____

_____

**10**  The HW Client tab of the Configuration | User Management | Groups | Modify (or Add) screen is used to configure individual user authentication. What other two attributes for individual user authentication can you set on this screen?

_____

_____

_____

**11** What is the default session idle timeout when using individual user authentication?

_____

_____

_____

**12** When individual user authentication is enabled, what initial screen are you directed to when you first try to establish a browser connection to an address in the private network of the head-end concentrator?

_____

_____

_____

**13** What VPN 3002 Hardware Client Manager screen can you use to quickly try to connect to the head-end concentrator?

_____

_____

_____

**14** What VPN 3002 Hardware Client Manager screen can you use when you want to view IKE Phase 1 and IPSec Phase 2 connection statistics?

_____

_____

_____

**15** What VPN 3002 Hardware Client Manager screen can you use if you suspect that DNS problems are interfering with user communications?

_____

_____

_____

The answers to this quiz are listed in Appendix A, "Answers to the "Do I Know This Already?" Quizzes and Q&A Sections." The suggestions for your next steps, based on quiz results, are as follows:

- **9 or less overall score**—Read the entire chapter, including the "Foundation Topics" and "Foundation Summary" sections, the "Q&A" section, and the scenarios at the end of the chapter.

- **10–11 overall score**—Begin with the "Foundation Summary" section, continue with the "Q&A" section, and then the scenarios. If you are having difficulty with a particular subject area, read the appropriate section in "Foundation Topics" section.

- **12–15 overall score**—If you feel you need more review on these topics, go to the "Foundation Summary" section, the "Q&A" section, and then the scenarios. Otherwise, skip this chapter and go to the next chapter.

# Foundation Topics

# Configure Preshared Keys

> **27** Cisco VPN 3002 Hardware Client remote access with preshared keys
>
> **31** Monitoring VPN 3002 user statistics

Setting the head-end concentrator and the VPN 3002 Hardware Client to use preshared keys is easy. Preshared keys must be at least 4 characters and no more than 32 characters in length and can contain a combination of letters and numbers, but not special characters. Start on the head-end concentrator. Navigate to the Configuration | System | Tunneling Protocols | IPSec LAN-to-LAN | Add screen, as shown in Figure 8-2. (Actually, you will go to either the Modify or the Add screen depending on whether you are modifying or creating a new connection. Both screens are identical except for the title.)

On this screen, name the connection **to_seattle**. Then, choose the interface, set the IP address of the peer, and choose to use preshared keys. Set the preshared key to mysharedkey. Choose to use ESP/MD5/HMAC-128 packet authorization and set the encryption to 168-bit 3DES.

On the VPN 3002 Hardware Client, navigate to the Configuration | System | Tunneling Protocols | IPSec screen, as shown in Figure 8-3. Here, you enter the remote server IP address and whether to use IPSec over TCP and the port to use. The default is to use IPSec over UDP. Make sure that the Use Certificate box is not checked, because you will be using preshared keys. The Certificate Transmission choices do not matter because you are not using certificates. Enter the group, password for the group, and verify the password. Next, enter the user, user password, and verify the password. This completes the configuration process.

**Figure 8-2** *Configuration | System | Tunneling Protocols | IPSec LAN-to-LAN | Add*

Configuration | System | Tunneling Protocols | IPSec LAN-to-LAN | Add

Add a new IPSec LAN-to-LAN connection.

|  |  |  |
|---|---|---|
| Name | to_seattle | Enter the name for this LAN-to-LAN connection. |
| Interface | Ethernet 2 (Public) (192.168.1.1) | Select the interface for this LAN-to-LAN connection. |
| Peer | 10.1.1.1 | Enter the IP address of the remote peer for this LAN-to-LAN connection. |
| Digital Certificate | None (Use Preshared Keys) | Select the digital certificate to use. |
| Certificate Transmission | ○ Entire certificate chain ● Identity certificate only | Choose how to send the digital certificate to the IKE peer. |
| Preshared Key | mysharedkey | Enter the preshared key for this LAN-to-LAN connection. |
| Authentication | ESP/MD5/HMAC-128 | Specify the packet authentication mechanism to use. |
| Encryption | 3DES-168 | Specify the encryption mechanism to use. |
| IKE Proposal | IKE-3DES-MD5 | Select the IKE Proposal to use for this LAN-to-LAN connection. |
| Filter | --None-- | Choose the filter to apply to the traffic that is tunneled through this LAN-to-LAN connection. |
| IPSec NAT-T | ☐ | Check to let NAT-T compatible IPSec peers establish this LAN-to-LAN connection through a NAT device. You must also enable IPSec over NAT-T under NAT Transparency. |
| Bandwidth Policy | ---None--- | Choose the bandwidth policy to apply to this LAN-to-LAN connection. |
| Reserved Bandwidth | 0   bps | Enter the reserved bandwidth for this LAN-to-LAN connection. |
| Routing | None | Choose the routing mechanism to use. **Parameters below are ignored if Network Autodiscovery is chosen.** |

Local Network: If a LAN-to-LAN NAT rule is used, this is the Translated Network address.

|  |  |  |
|---|---|---|
| Network List | MyLocalList | Specify the local network address list or the IP address and wildcard mask for this LAN-to-LAN connection. |
| IP Address | | **Note: Enter a *wildcard* mask, which is the reverse of a subnet mask. A wildcard mask has 1s in bit positions to ignore, 0s in bit positions to match. For example, 10.10.1.0/0.0.0.255 = all 10.10.1.nnn addresses.** |
| Wildcard Mask | | |

Remote Network: If a LAN-to-LAN NAT rule is used, this is the Remote Network address.

|  |  |  |
|---|---|---|
| Network List | MyRemoteList | Specify the remote network address list or the IP address and wildcard mask for this LAN-to-LAN connection. |
| IP Address | | **Note: Enter a *wildcard* mask, which is the reverse of a subnet mask. A wildcard mask has 1s in bit positions to ignore, 0s in bit positions to match. For example, 10.10.1.0/0.0.0.255 = all 10.10.1.nnn addresses.** |
| Wildcard Mask | | |

Add    Cancel

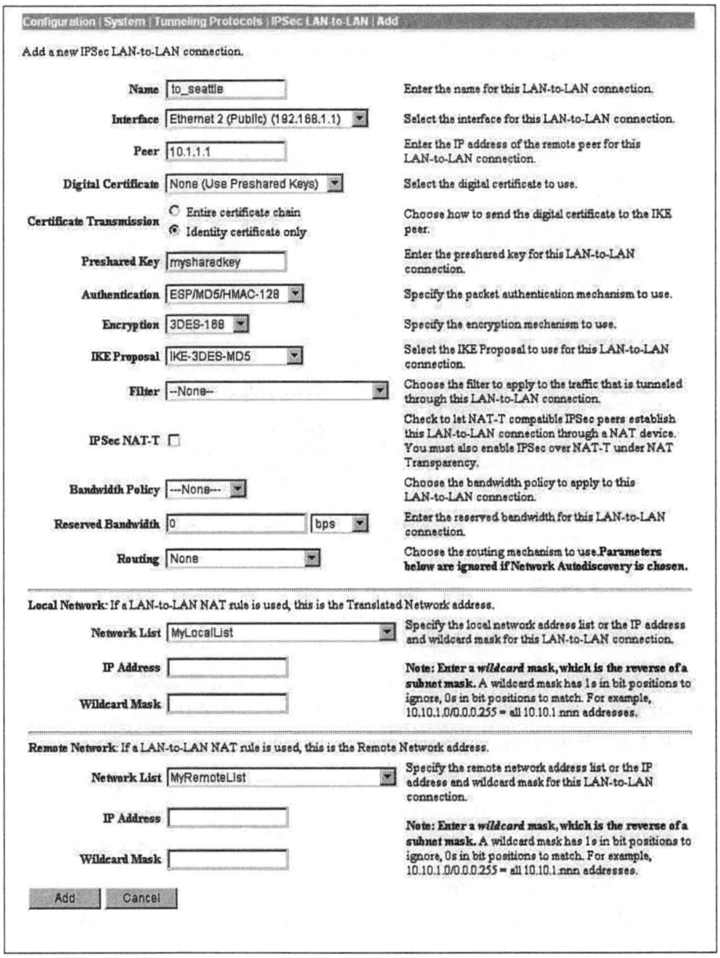

**Figure 8-3**  *Configuration | System | Tunneling Protocols | IPSec*

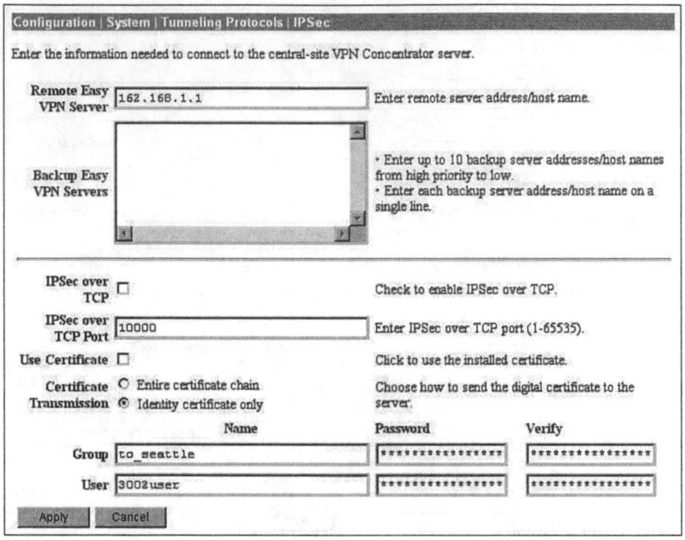

## Verify IKE and IPSec Configuration

Now that you have the IPSec tunnel created between the head-end VPN 3000 Series Concentrator and the VPN 3002 Hardware Client, you need to verify that the tunnel is operating correctly. The first step you should take is to ping the private interface of the VPN 3000 Series Concentrator from the VPN 3002 Hardware Client Manager's Administration | Ping screen. If this is successful, but you are unable to ping anything else, you might have an internal routing issue. In this case, make sure that the device you are attempting to ping knows how to reach your private network.

Another tool that you can use to verify that IKE and IPSec are functioning properly can be found in the VPN 3002 Hardware Client's Manager. Bring up the manager and proceed to the Monitoring | Statistics | IPSec screen, shown in Figure 8-4. This screen tells you if you have active IKE and IPSec tunnels and also provides statistics for these two protocols since the last time the VPN 3002 Hardware Client was booted up.

The VPN 3002 Hardware Client Manager monitors additional statistics for a variety of protocols. In addition to providing activity information since the last system was boot up or reset, these statistics also show active session information for any of these protocols that are currently in use on the VPN 3002 Hardware Client. If you are troubleshooting a problem, you can watch the counters for these protocols to help you identify what may be causing the problem. These additional screens are all found under Monitoring | Statistics, and were discussed in Chapter 7, "Monitoring and Administering the Cisco VPN 3000 Series Concentrator."

**Figure 8-4** *Monitoring | Statistics | IPSec*

| Monitoring | Statistics | IPSec | | Friday, 13 December 2002 15:21:19 Reset⏎Refresh⏎ | |
|---|---|---|---|
| **IKE (Phase 1) Statistics** | | **IPSec (Phase 2) Statistics** | |
| Active Tunnels | 1 | Active Tunnels | 1 |
| Total Tunnels | 2 | Total Tunnels | 4 |
| Received Bytes | 61358 | Received Bytes | 6536 |
| Sent Bytes | 7980 | Sent Bytes | 2104 |
| Received Packets | 775 | Received Packets | 44 |
| Sent Packets | 83 | Sent Packets | 13 |
| Received Packets Dropped | 1 | Received Packets Dropped | 0 |
| Sent Packets Dropped | 0 | Received Packets Dropped (Anti-Replay) | 0 |
| Received Notifies | 755 | Sent Packets Dropped | 0 |
| Sent Notifies | 132 | Inbound Authentications | 44 |
| Received Phase-2 Exchanges | 4 | Failed Inbound Authentications | 0 |
| Sent Phase-2 Exchanges | 0 | Outbound Authentications | 13 |
| Invalid Phase-2 Exchanges Received | 0 | Failed Outbound Authentications | 0 |
| Invalid Phase-2 Exchanges Sent | 0 | Decryptions | 44 |
| Rejected Received Phase-2 Exchanges | 0 | Failed Decryptions | 0 |
| Rejected Sent Phase-2 Exchanges | 0 | Encryptions | 13 |
| Phase-2 SA Delete Requests Received | 0 | Failed Encryptions | 0 |
| Phase-2 SA Delete Requests Sent | 3 | System Capability Failures | 0 |
| Initiated Tunnels | 0 | No-SA Failures | 0 |
| Failed Initiated Tunnels | 0 | Protocol Use Failures | 0 |
| Failed Remote Tunnels | 0 | | |
| Authentication Failures | 0 | | |
| Decryption Failures | 0 | | |
| Hash Validation Failures | 0 | | |
| System Capability Failures | 0 | | |
| No-SA Failures | 0 | | |

# Setting debug Levels

One of the tools that you can use when troubleshooting IPSec connections is debug, which can be implemented on both the VPN 3000 Series Concentrator and the VPN 3002 Hardware Client by modifying the way these devices handle events. Be careful when implementing debug on these devices because debug traffic can quickly fill up available memory and consume CPU cycles. Plan on short duration debug tests unless you are using a Syslog server, and even then the excess traffic generated could affect your network services. Cisco recommends that you only use debug under the guidance of a Cisco technical support representative.

If you do have a need to use debug, however, set the severity log to 1–13 on both devices for the following:

- **IKE**—ISAKMP/Oakley (IKE) subsystem
- **IKEDBG**—ISAKMP/Oakley (IKE) debugging
- **IPSEC**—IP Security subsystem
- **IPSECDBG**—IP Security debugging

These settings are made under the Configuration | System | Events series of screens on the VPN 3000 Concentrator Series and on the VPN 3002 Hardware Client. You can view the live event logs or filterable event logs using the Monitor portion of the managers of these devices.

After you have debug enabled, try to reestablish the VPN tunnel and then look at the logs. Here are a few of the items worth noting:

- IKE failures on Phase 1
- Incorrect group password
- Work group name incorrect
- Incorrect username
- Incorrect password
- Unable to ping with an established tunnel

The following sections describe each of these potential problems in more detail.

## IKE Failures on Phase 1

If you are experiencing failures during IKE Phase 1 negotiations, check the following issues:

- Xauth is required, but the proposal does not support Xauth.
- Check the priorities of IKE Xauth proposals in the IKE proposal list.
- Check the VPN 3002 Hardware Client group.
- Check the group on the VPN Concentrator.
- Check that all SA proposals are acceptable.

## Incorrect Group Password

On the VPN 3002 Hardware Client, you will see an error similar to the following:

```
Group [192.168.100.1]
Rxed Hash is incorrect:Pre-shared key or Digital Signature mismatch
```

## Work Group Name Incorrect

If the work group name is incorrect, the VPN Concentrator logs show a message similar to the following:

```
No Group found 3002group for Pre-shared key peer 192.168.100.1
```

## Incorrect Username

If the username is incorrect, the VPN Concentrator log will show a message similar to the following:

```
Authentication rejected: Reason = User was not found
```

### Incorrect User Password

If the password is incorrect, the VPN Concentrator log will show a message similar to the following:

```
Authentication rejected: Reason = Invalid password
```

### Unable to ping with an Established Tunnel

If you have an established tunnel and you are still unable to ping the private interface on the VPN Concentrator, you could have overlapping Security Associations (SAs) or you could be incorrectly filtering out the IPSec packets. In the VPN 3002 Hardware Client Manager, go to the Monitoring | System Status screen and note the Octets Out field. Next, go to the Monitoring | Statistics | IPSec screen shown in Figure 8-4 and note the Received Bytes counter. Attempt to ping the VPN Concentrator's inside interface again and recheck these counters. Based on this information, you will be able to see which of the two issues is causing the problem.

The first issue might be that there is an overlapping SA configured. An overlapping SA is where two or more VPN clients have the same network on the private side. For example, you might have a VPN 3002 Hardware Client with the 192.168.100.0/24 network and a VPN Software Client with an IP address of 192.168.100.4. If both of these counters are incrementing, this is the case. If only the Octets Out counter is incrementing on the VPN 3002 Hardware Client, but the Received Bytes is not, IPSec is being filtered. If UDP is enabled, make sure that the UDP port chosen, a default value of 10000, is not being blocked. If the VPN 3002 Hardware Client is behind a PAT device, make sure to enable **IPSec through NAT**.

## Configuring VPN 3002 Hardware Client and LAN Extension Modes

You can configure two different modes for the VPN 3002 Hardware Client to use. Client mode, also called Port Address Translation (PAT) mode, and LAN Extension mode (also called Network Extension mode) are useful depending upon what you are attempting to accomplish.

PAT mode, the default, is used to isolate all the clients behind the VPN 3002 Hardware Client (on the private side) from the corporate network. Enabling PAT mode disables LAN Extension mode. Disabling PAT mode enables LAN Extension mode. The mechanism used to select either of the two modes ensures that only one mode is enabled at any given time.

When using PAT mode, IPSec encapsulates all traffic traveling between the private network of the VPN 3002 Hardware Client to the network behind the IKE peer, usually a central-site VPN Concentrator. Utilizing NAT, the client's IP addresses on the private network are translated to the VPN 3002 Hardware Client's public interface IP address. Therefore, all traffic from the private network is seen at the head-end network with a single IP address. Because the VPN 3002 Hardware Client keeps track of the translations without advertising what these translations are, devices at the head-end cannot directly access the devices on the VPN 3002 Hardware Client's private network with utilities such as ping. However, there is no reason that a device on the VPN 3002 Hardware Client's private network cannot ping or otherwise connect to a device at the head-end.

The word *client* refers to the fact that the IPSec tunnel is not always active. The tunnel becomes active in one of the following two circumstances:

- When data attempts to travel from the private network (the client) to the head-end
- When the administrator purposefully brings up the tunnel by clicking the Connect Now button on the Monitoring I System Status screen

Configuring PAT is simple. Because enabling or disabling PAT is a traffic policy issue, start on the Configuration I Policy Management screen, shown in Figure 8-5. This is also the method used to disable PAT and move into LAN Extension mode. Choose **Traffic Management**. This brings you to the Configuration I Policy Management I Traffic Management screen, as shown in Figure 8-6.

**Figure 8-5**   *Configuration | Policy Management*

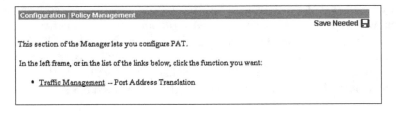

**Figure 8-6**   *Configuration | Policy Management | Traffic Management*

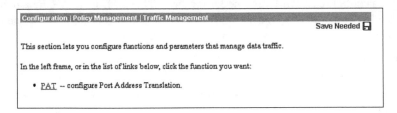

On the Configuration I Policy Management I Traffic Management screen, choose **PAT** to configure Port Address Translation. This brings you to the Configuration I Policy Management I Traffic Management I PAT screen, as shown in Figure 8-7. Choose **Enable** to enable (or disable) PAT.

**Figure 8-7**    *Configuration | Policy Management | Traffic Management | PAT*

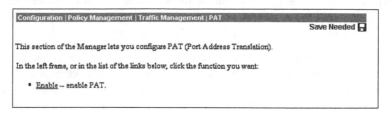

You are brought to the Configuration | Policy Management | Traffic Management | PAT | Enable screen, as shown in Figure 8-8. On this screen, checking the PAT Enabled box causes PAT to become enabled, whereas removing the check from the box causes your VPN 3002 Hardware Client to enter into Network Extension mode.

**Figure 8-8**    *Configuration | Policy Management | Traffic Management | PAT | Enable*

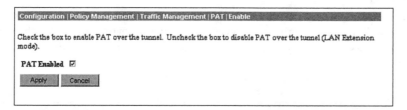

By default, a VPN Concentrator allows PAT connections only. If you choose to use Network Extension mode on the VPN 3002 Hardware Client, ensure that the head-end VPN Concentrator is configured to allow Network Extension mode. Failure to do so will cause the VPN 3002 Hardware Client to fail to connect. Because the VPN 3002 Hardware Client will attempt to connect every four seconds and be rejected every time, you will actually launch a minor form of a denial of service (DoS) attack on your own network.

There are some requirements for using both PAT and Network Extension modes. Table 8-2 outlines the requirements.

**Table 8-2**    *Requirements for PAT and LAN Extension Modes*

| PAT Mode | Network Extension Mode |
|---|---|
| The head-end concentrator must be running version 3.x or later. | The head-end concentrator must be running version 3.x or later. |
| You must configure a group, user, and password on the head-end concentrator. | You must configure a group, user, and password on the head-end concentrator. |
| You must enable addresses consistent with the head-end concentrator. For example, if one side runs DHCP, the other side must also run DHCP. | A static route or default route to the head-end concentrator must be configured. |

The Network Extension mode allows the VPN 3002 Hardware Client to present a single encrypted network over the tunnel to the head-end concentrator. In addition to removing the checkmark from the PAT Enabled box, the default IP address of the inside interface must also be changed from 192.168.10.1. Any other IP address will work.

Unlike PAT mode, the devices do not have NAT applied, and are, therefore, directly accessible from devices at the head-end with utilities such as ping. Only when you have not enabled split tunneling and are in Network Extension mode can the head-end concentrator send initial data. In all other circumstances, the VPN 3002 Hardware Client's network must send the initial data. These can be crucial considerations when deciding whether to use Network Extension or PAT mode.

In PAT mode, the VPN tunnel is created when data tries to travel to the IKE peer. The tunnel is dropped after the timeout period expires with no traffic over the tunnel. In Network Extension mode, the tunnel is always active.

# Split Tunneling

Split tunneling is where some traffic becomes encrypted while other traffic does not become encrypted. Specifically, the traffic headed for any destination other than those within the network lists is not encrypted while traffic destined for networks within the network lists is encrypted.

---

**NOTE**    Split tunneling creates a potential security issue if the client is not behind a firewall or does not support its own firewall. Because traffic is allowed outside of the secure VPN tunnel during split tunneling, that unsecured traffic path could be used to access client systems.

---

If you are in PAT mode, all devices on the private side have their addresses translated. In LAN Extension mode, NAT is applied only to those destinations not in the network lists.

Split tunneling is configured at the head-end concentrator. If the group to which the VPN 3002 Hardware Client belongs has split tunneling enabled, then split tunneling will be used. The following section gives you more information regarding how to set up split tunneling.

# Unit and User Authentication for the VPN 3002 Hardware Client

**28**  Overview of VPN 3002 interactive unit and user authentication feature

**29**  Configuring VPN 3002 integrated unit authentication feature

**30**  Configuring VPN 3002 user authentication

When two devices begin negotiations to establish an IPSec VPN connection between them, they must perform an authentication process during IKE Phase 1. This authentication process is structured around preshared keys or digital signatures. Additionally, the Cisco VPN 3000 Series Concentrators and the VPN 3002 Hardware Client require a unique username and password with the preshared key or digital signature as further security for the setup process. This username and password might be statically configured on the devices or you can choose to setup interactive hardware client authentication.

With interactive hardware client authentication, when a VPN 3002 Hardware Client tries to set up an IPSec tunnel with a VPN 3000 Concentrator, the user who initiated the request for VPN services will be prompted to enter a unique unit username and password. After the VPN 3002 Hardware Client is authenticated with this username and password, other users of the VPN 3002 Hardware Client can use the IPSec tunnel without being prompted for the username and password. You can choose to use internal authentication or external server authentication when you configure interactive hardware client authentication on the VPN 3000 Concentrator. This interactive process provides an extra layer of security when establishing VPN tunnels.

After the hardware devices have authenticated one another, the individual users must be authenticated before they will be permitted to access network resources. You can choose to set up individual user authentication when users enter the network through a VPN 3002 Hardware Client. With individual user authentication enabled, each user must open a web browser to enter a valid username and password. You can use the browser in two different ways to utilize this individual user authentication:

- Point the browser at a uniform resource locator (URL) on the private network of the head-end concentrator. The VPN 3002 Hardware Client will present the interactive individual user authentication screen requesting the user's username and password. After authentication is successfully accomplished, the browser will be directed to the original URL.

- Point the browser at the private interface of the head-end concentrator using the IP address of that interface. The user will be prompted to enter their username and password and, once authenticated, can utilize other network applications across the secure VPN tunnel.

Configuring interactive hardware authentication and individual user authentication for users connecting through a VPN 3002 Hardware Client requires configuration settings on the head-end concentrator as well as the VPN 3002 Hardware Client. The head-end concentrator settings for unit and user authentication are performed on the attributes of the VPN group. The next section discusses modifying a group on a VPN 3000 Concentrator to support communications with a VPN 3002 Hardware Client.

## Configuring the Head-End VPN Concentrator

Starting on the head-end VPN 3000 Series Concentrator, modify a group. This is done by going to the Configuration | User Management | Groups | Modify screen and choosing the VPN 3002 Hardware Client group you want to use. The group you use will eventually have individual users entered into it along with their respective passwords. This brings you to the Identity screen shown in Figure 8-9. Set the password and choose **Internal** as the authentication type. Click **Add** and select the **General** tab.

**Figure 8-9**   *Configuration | User Management | Groups | Modify > Identity*

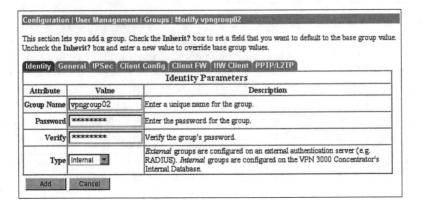

On the General tab screen, set the options as shown in Figure 8-10. You can see that most of the entries for the fields on this screen are inherited from the root group. You will need to make sure to set your WINS and DNS to entries that make sense on your own network. Also, make sure that you choose IPSec as the Tunneling Protocol. The only other entry that is modified from the root group's settings is the attribute to Allow Alphabetic-Only Passwords. In this case, it is disabled. Be sure to follow your own organization's security plan when making entries on these configuration screens. Click **Add** and then click the **IPSec** tab.

**Figure 8-10**  *Configuration | User Management | Groups | Modify > General*

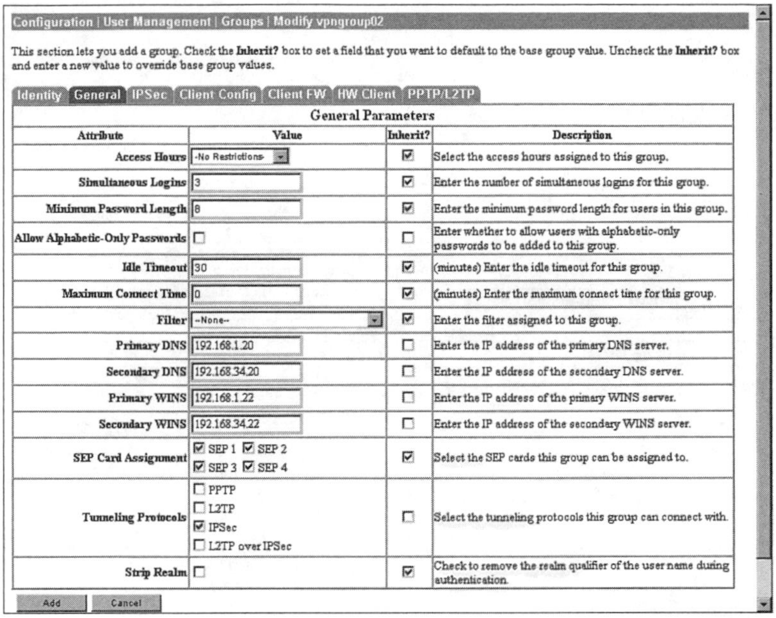

Figure 8-11 shows the IPSec tab screen. For this configuration, use ESP-3DES-MD5 for the IPSec Security Association. 3DES encryption is preferred when your data will be traversing the Internet. Ensure that the tunnel type is set to Remote Access and that the Mode Configuration box is checked. In this example, use the internal server. You could have used a RADIUS or other external server. If you choose to use an external server, you must also ensure that this external server contains the user's name and password.

Click **Add** and choose the **Mode Config** tab.

**Figure 8-11** *Configuration | User Management | Groups | Modify > IPSec*

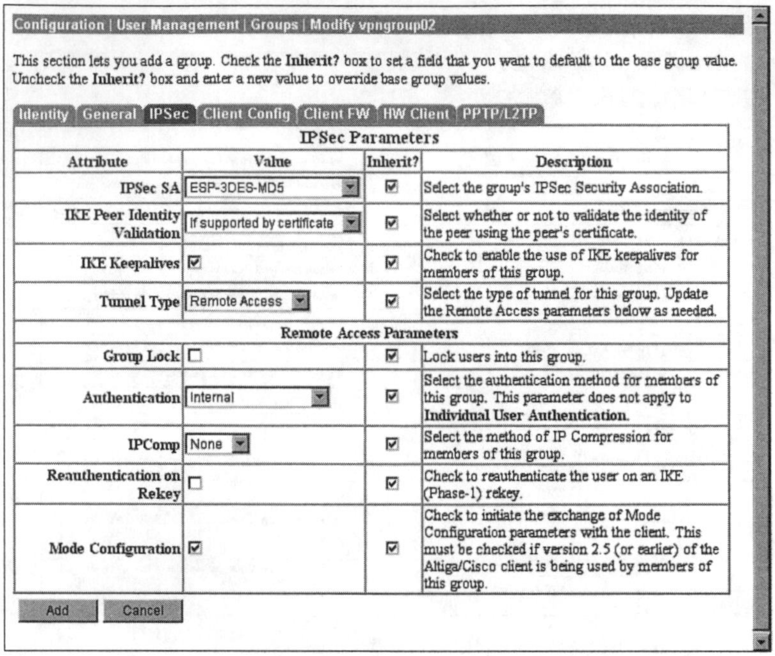

The Mode Config tab of previous versions of the VPN Manager has become the Client Config tab in the most recent release of the VPN Manager. On the Client Config tab screen shown in Figure 8-12, select the **Tunnel Everything** radio button. Earlier in this section, you learned that the VPN 3000 Concentrator is configured to either allow or disallow split tunneling. Use the Client Config screen to allow or disallow split tunneling. Here you have a few choices, as follows:

- **Tunnel everything**—This means that the VPN 3002 Hardware Client will encrypt all data to all destinations.

- **Allow the networks in the list to bypass the tunnel**—You can select this option to use the network list to define what is or is not tunneled. Checking the box means that those networks within the network list do not get tunneled.

- **Only tunnel networks in the list**—By selecting this option, you can use the network list to define where to tunnel your data.

**Figure 8-12**  *Configuration | User Management | Groups | Modify > Client Config*

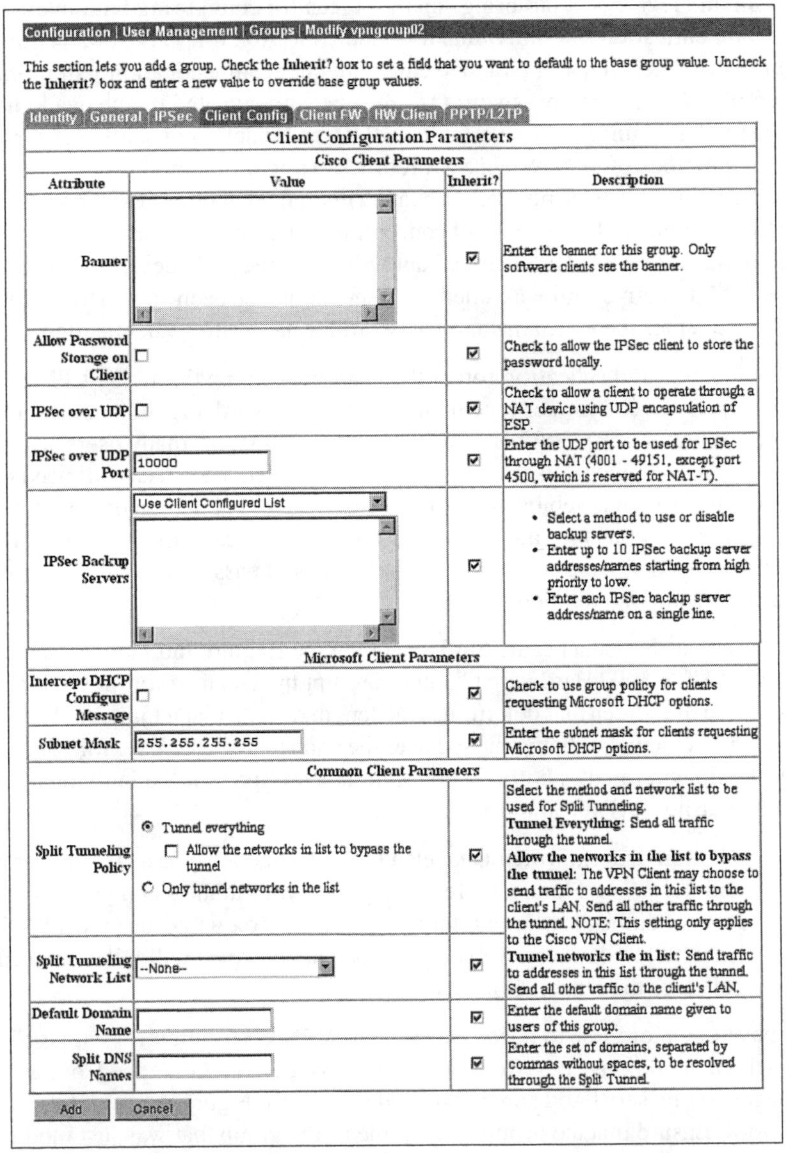

Configuration | User Management | Groups | Modify vpngroup02

This section lets you add a group. Check the Inherit? box to set a field that you want to default to the base group value. Uncheck the Inherit? box and enter a new value to override base group values.

Identity | General | IPSec | Client Config | Client FW | HW Client | PPTP/L2TP

## Client Configuration Parameters

### Cisco Client Parameters

| Attribute | Value | Inherit? | Description |
|---|---|---|---|
| Banner | | ☑ | Enter the banner for this group. Only software clients see the banner. |
| Allow Password Storage on Client | ☐ | ☑ | Check to allow the IPSec client to store the password locally. |
| IPSec over UDP | ☐ | ☑ | Check to allow a client to operate through a NAT device using UDP encapsulation of ESP. |
| IPSec over UDP Port | 10000 | ☑ | Enter the UDP port to be used for IPSec through NAT (4001 - 49151, except port 4500, which is reserved for NAT-T). |
| IPSec Backup Servers | Use Client Configured List | ☑ | • Select a method to use or disable backup servers.<br>• Enter up to 10 IPSec backup server addresses/names starting from high priority to low.<br>• Enter each IPSec backup server address/name on a single line. |

### Microsoft Client Parameters

| | | | |
|---|---|---|---|
| Intercept DHCP Configure Message | ☐ | ☑ | Check to use group policy for clients requesting Microsoft DHCP options. |
| Subnet Mask | 255.255.255.255 | ☑ | Enter the subnet mask for clients requesting Microsoft DHCP options. |

### Common Client Parameters

| | | | |
|---|---|---|---|
| Split Tunneling Policy | ⦿ Tunnel everything<br>☐ Allow the networks in list to bypass the tunnel<br>○ Only tunnel networks in the list | ☑ | Select the method and network list to be used for Split Tunneling.<br>**Tunnel Everything:** Send all traffic through the tunnel.<br>**Allow the networks in the list to bypass the tunnel:** The VPN Client may choose to send traffic to addresses in this list to the client's LAN. Send all other traffic through the tunnel. NOTE: This setting only applies to the Cisco VPN Client.<br>**Tunnel networks the in list:** Send traffic to addresses in this list through the tunnel. Send all other traffic to the client's LAN. |
| Split Tunneling Network List | --None-- | ☑ | |
| Default Domain Name | | ☑ | Enter the default domain name given to users of this group. |
| Split DNS Names | | ☑ | Enter the set of domains, separated by commas without spaces, to be resolved through the Split Tunnel. |

Add    Cancel

## Configuring Unit and User Authentication

Clicking the HW Client tab brings up the screen for configuring both interactive hardware client authentication and individual user authentication for VPN 3002 Hardware Clients (see Figure 8-13). Recall that interactive hardware client authentication will prompt the user for a specific username and password that must be authenticated by the head-end concentrator before the VPN tunnel will be established. IPSec tunnels are usually only maintained for specified periods of time. When SA lifetimes expire or tunnel time out values are reached, the IPSec tunnels are terminated. When a VPN tunnel does not exist between the VPN 3002 Hardware Client and the head-end concentrator, the first user that requires VPN services through the VPN 3002 Hardware Client will cause the VPN devices to begin establishing the tunnel. If interactive hardware client authentication has been specified, this initial user will be required to enter the username and password for hardware authentication.

Individual user authentication forces the users connecting through a VPN 3002 Hardware Client to use a web browser for initial VPN access in order to authenticate through the head-end concentrator. VPN 3002 Hardware Clients can support many users across a single IPSec tunnel. When individual user authentication is enabled, each user will need to establish their credentials through a web browser. In the case where both interactive hardware client authentication and individual user authentication are required, the initial user that brings up the VPN tunnel will need to enter two different username and password combinations: one for the hardware client, and one for themselves.

On the screen shown in Figure 8-13, checking the Require Individual User Authentication forces the VPN 3002 Hardware Client to prompt the end user for the username and password. This is also the screen that determines the length of time that a tunnel in PAT mode will remain active without any data being passed over the connection. The User Idle Timeout box is used to enter the time in minutes before a connection is dropped for the individual user or the remote site when using PAT mode.

Note the bottom button, which is labeled Cisco IP Phone Bypass. It is imperative that this box be checked if you want to use IP Telephony over your tunnels and you have chosen to require individual user authentication. Failure to check this box will cause the VPN 3002 Hardware Client to attempt to display a web page on the phone, which will fail anytime a user attempts to place a call over the tunnel. Click **Add**.

You have one more task to accomplish on the VPN Concentrator. That task is to set up your user with a valid name, password, and group assignment. Go to the Configuration | User Management | Users | Add screen and add a user (see Figure 8-14). Set the username and password. Ensure that the group is the same as the group that was just modified.

**Figure 8-13**  *Configuration | User Management | Groups | Modify > HW Client*

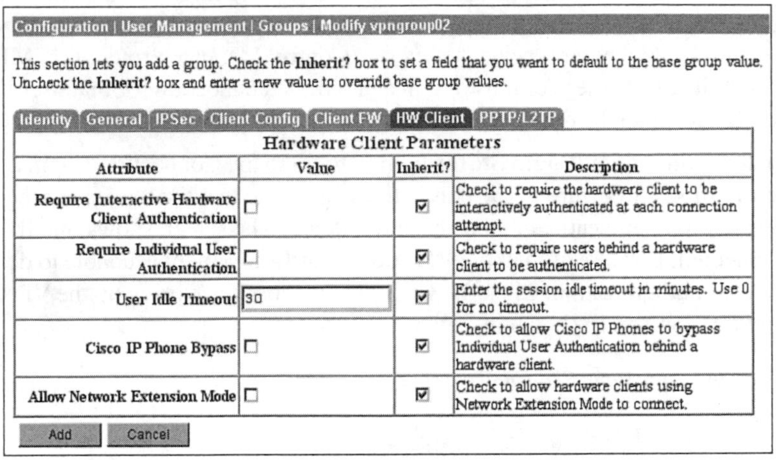

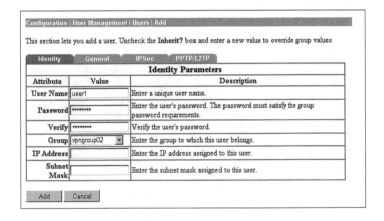

**Figure 8-14**  *Configuration | User Management | Users | Add*

# Interactive Hardware Client and Individual User Authentication

After you enable interactive hardware client authentication and/or individual user authentication, the next step is to test the system. From the private side of the VPN 3002 Hardware Client, open a web browser and point it to either the inside IP address of the VPN 3002 Hardware Client or to any IP address reachable through the tunnel. You will be redirected to the VPN 3002 Hardware Client Manager screen.

Because you have chosen to use individual authentication, anytime a user wants to access a remote network, they must first open the browser and log in. If the user attempts to, for example, ping a remote device through the tunnel without first opening the browser and logging in, the remote device will never receive the Internet Control Message Protocol (ICMP) packets and the ping will time out. The user must log in again if the connection for that user has been idle for a period longer than the timeout period defined for the group.

Click the **Connection/Login Status** hotlink to go to the Connection/Login Status screen. This screen is shown in Figure 8-15. This is the screen that the first user sees when interactive hardware client authentication has been requested. The screen shows that the VPN 3002 is disconnected. Because of that, the VPN 3002 Hardware Client is unable to determine the status of the user authentication. Click the **Connect Now** button to bring up the VPN 3002 Interactive Authentication screen shown in Figure 8-16.

**Figure 8-15**  *Connection/Login Status Showing Disconnected Status*

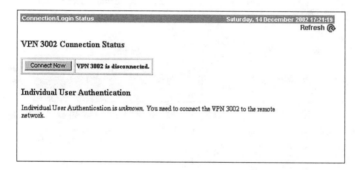

**Figure 8-16**  *VPN 3002 Interactive Authentication*

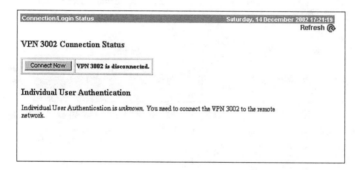

Enter the unique username and password that has been set up specifically for this hardware client authentication and click the **Connect** button. The head-end concentrator will authenticate the hardware client and the VPN 3002 Hardware Client and the head-end concentrator will now negotiate and establish the IPSec tunnel. The browser screen will change to that shown in Figure 8-17. Notice that the VPN 3002 is now connected but that the user is not logged in. Click the **Log In Now** button and the system will take you to the Individual User Authentication screen, as shown in Figure 8-18.

**Figure 8-17**  *Connection/Login Status with User Not Logged In*

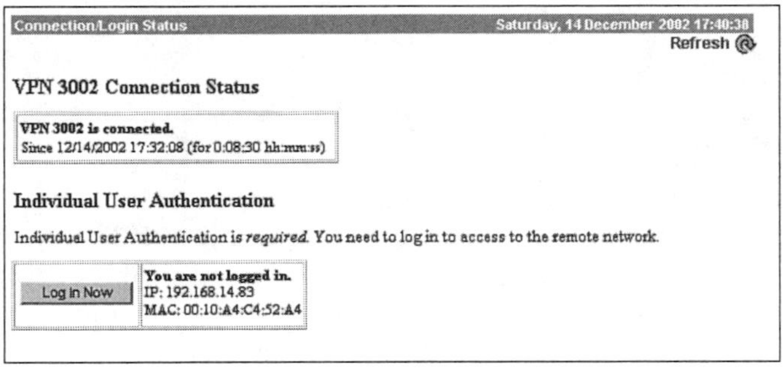

**Figure 8-18**  *Individual User Authentication*

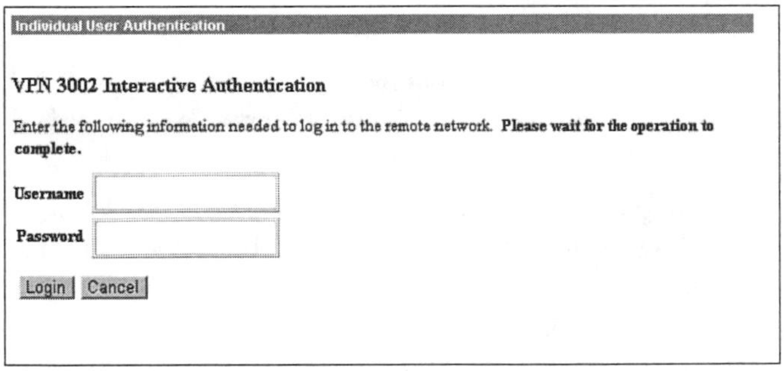

After you enter the username and password in this screen, click the **Login** button to authenticate the user through the head-end VPN 3000 Concentrator's internal user database. The system will now return a Connection/Login Status screen similar to that shown in Figure 8-19. The VPN 3002 Hardware Client and the user are now both connected.

**Figure 8-19** *Connection/Login Status*

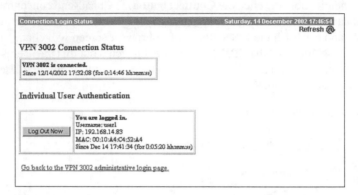

Attempt to ping the inside interface of the head-end concentrator. If you are successful, you have established a tunnel. If you are able to reach the network directly attached to the head-end concentrator's private interface, but are not able to reach anything beyond that network, the issue is probably related to routing. Make sure that any interior routers know about your IP addresses and that these addresses are reachable through the head-end concentrator.

Assume for a moment that the tunnel was not established. There are a few places you can check to determine where the problem resides. Because you are already on the VPN 3002 Hardware Client side, start there. Click the **Connection/Login Status** link.

There are three possible reasons why the tunnel was not established, as follows:

- The VPN Tunnel is connected but the user is not logged in. This is usually related to incorrect rights for the user or an incorrect username/password combination. An example of this condition was shown in Figure 8-17.

- The tunnel might not be connected and the user will not be logged in. This is usually an issue regarding connectivity between the head-end concentrator and the VPN 3002 Hardware Client. Go to the Monitoring | System Status screen, shown in Figure 8-20, to check this. You should see that a tunnel is established.

- The head-end concentrator and the VPN 3002 Hardware Client do not agree on a parameter. For example, the preshared keys may be different, or one side is expecting a certificate while the other side is expecting a preshared key. Go back through the configurations and make sure that everything is set the same on both sides.

  You will never see that the user is logged in but the tunnel is not connected unless there is a hardware error.

**Figure 8-20**  *Monitoring | System Status*

# Foundation Summary

The Foundation Summary is a collection of tables and figures that provides a convenient review of many key concepts in this chapter. For those aho are already comfortable with the topics in this chapter, this summary could help you recall a few details. For those who just read this chapter, this review should help solidify some key facts. For anyone doing final preparation before the exam, these tables and figures are a convenient way to review the day before the exam.

## Configure Preshared Keys

To configure preshared keys, follow these steps:

**Step 1** On the concentrator, go to the Configuration | System | Tunneling Protocols | IPSec LAN-to-LAN | Modify screen.

**Step 2** Set the IP address of the peer.

**Step 3** Set the preshared key.

**Step 4** On the VPN 3002 Hardware Client, go to the Configuration | System | Tunneling Protocols | IPSec screen.

**Step 5** Make sure that the Use Certificate box is not checked.

**Step 6** Enter the group and password.

**Step 7** Enter the user, username, and password.

## Troubleshooting IPSec

Follow these steps to troubleshoot IPSec:

**Step 1** Ping the private interface of the remote concentrator. If you can get there, IPSec works. If your ping fails, you should proceed to Steps 2 and 3.

**Step 2** Set the debug levels for 1–13 on both sides (IKE, IKEDBG, IPSEC, IPSECDBG).

**Step 3** Read and understand the log. It will tell you where the problem lies.

# Client and LAN Extension Modes

Table 8-3 compares Client mode and LAN Extension mode.

**Table 8-3**    *Client Versus LAN Extension Mode*

| Client (PAT) Mode | LAN Extension Mode |
|---|---|
| All devices appear at the head-end as one device with the IP address of the outside interface of the VPN 3002 Hardware Client. | Each device is seen at the head-end with its individual IP address. |
| This is the default on the head-end concentrator. | This must be configured at the head-end and on the VPN 3002 Hardware Client. |
| Tunnel is initiated by the administrator or when a device attempts to connect to the head-end. | Tunnel is always active. |
| Remote site must send initial data. | When not using split tunnel, head-end may send initial data. |

Table 8-4 describes the requirements for PAT mode and LAN Extension mode.

**Table 8-4**    *Requirements for Client and LAN Extension Modes*

| Client (PAT) Mode | Network Extension Mode |
|---|---|
| The head-end concentrator must be running version 3.x or later. | The head-end concentrator must be running version 3.x or later. |
| You must configure a group, user, and password on the head-end concentrator. | You must configure a group, user, and password on the head-end concentrator. |
| You must enable addresses consistent with the head-end concentrator. For example, if one side runs DHCP, the other side must also run DHCP. | A static route or default route to the head-end concentrator must be configured. |

# Split Tunnel

Remember the following key points about split tunneling:

- Configured on the head-end VPN 3000 Series Concentrator.
- Permits specific traffic to bypass the VPN tunnel.
- Options for split tunneling are
  - Tunnel all traffic.
  - Tunnel only traffic contained within a specified network list.
  - Do not tunnel traffic contained within a specified network list.

# Configuring Individual User Authentication on the VPN 3000 Concentrator

Follow these steps to configure individual user authentication on the VPN 3000 Series Concentrator:

**Step 1** Use the Configuration I User Management I Groups I Modify screen and choose the appropriate group.

**Step 2** Choose the General tab and set the WINS and DNS.

**Step 3** Choose the IPSec tab, set the tunnel type to Remote Access, and choose your authentication type.

**Step 4** Click the Mode Config tab and select what to tunnel.

**Step 5** Click the HW Client tab and check Require Individual User Authentication.

**Step 6** Go to the Configuration I User Management I Users I Modify screen and set the group, user, and passwords. Repeat for each user.

# Chapter Glossary

The following terms were introduced in this chapter or have special significance to the topics within this chapter.

**head-end**    End point of a broadband network. All stations transmit toward the head-end; the head-end then transmits toward the destination stations.

**LAN Extension mode**    A mode used on a concentrator that does not rely upon NAT. Each individual device behind the VPN 3002 Hardware Client retains its IP address when seen at the head-end network. This is the opposite of PAT mode.

**PAT mode**    A mode used on a concentrator where all the devices behind that concentrator have their IP addresses translated to the IP address of the outside interface of the VPN 3002 Hardware Client. This is the opposite of LAN Extension mode.

# Q&A

As mentioned in Chapter 1, these questions are more difficult than what you should experience on the CCSP exam. The questions do not attempt to cover more breadth or depth than the exam; however, the questions are designed to make sure you know the answer. Rather than allowing you to derive the answer from clues hidden inside the question itself, your understanding and recall of the subject are challenged. Questions from the "Do I Know This Already?" quiz from the beginning of the chapter are repeated here to ensure that you have mastered the chapter's topic areas. Hopefully, these questions will help limit the number of exam questions on which you narrow your choices to two options and guess!

1   What screen is used on the head-end concentrator to demand the use of preshared keys?

_____

_____

_____

2   Name five items to check when you are unable to connect a VPN tunnel and you are receiving IKE failures on Phase 1.

_____

_____

_____

3   You need to allow the main office to use PC Anywhere to connect to three separate machines at the remote office over the VPN. What mode must you use?

_____

_____

_____

4   You need to have a device behind the head-end concentrator to send data as soon as the VPN tunnel is established. Which mode should you use? Can you use split tunneling under these circumstances?

_____

_____

_____

5   What are the disadvantages in a large network (over 100 users) of using individual authentication with the internal server?

_____

_____

_____

6   You are using individual authentication in PAT mode. Your tunnel is established but the user cannot log in. What is the first item you should examine?

_____

_____

_____

7   What screen do you use on the VPN 3002 Hardware Client to configure preshared keys?

_____

_____

_____

8   You appear to be experiencing a DoS attack that is initiating from the IP address assigned to one of your VPN 3002 Hardware Clients. What is the problem?

_____

_____

_____

9   You need to allow the remote office to use PC Anywhere to connect to three separate machines at the main office over the VPN. What mode must you use?

_____

_____

_____

10  Some of your remote sites can use split tunneling and others cannot. How is this controlled?

_____

_____

_____

**11** Your remote site has an ISDN connection to the Internet. You are charged on a per-minute basis for connecting to the Internet. Which mode should you use?

_____

_____

_____

**12** What version of software must be running on the head-end concentrator to use PAT mode? What version is required for Network Extension mode?

_____

_____

_____

**13** You are the second user to connect through a VPN 3002 Hardware Client for which interactive hardware client and individual user authentication have been configured. What authentication information will you be required to enter?

_____

_____

_____

**14** You can use a static configuration for authenticating the VPN 3002 Hardware Client with the head-end concentrator. Why would you want to use interactive hardware client authentication?

_____

_____

_____

**15** Where is interactive hardware client authentication configured?

_____

_____

_____

**16** What authentication method is used for interactive hardware client authentication?

_____

_____

_____

**17** What must you configure on the VPN 3002 Hardware Client in order to use interactive hardware client authentication?

_____

_____

_____

**18** The HW Client tab of the Configuration I User Management I Groups I Modify (or Add) screen is used to configure individual user authentication. What other two attributes for individual user authentication can you set on this screen?

_____

_____

_____

**19** What is the default session idle timeout when using individual user authentication?

_____

_____

_____

**20** When individual user authentication is enabled, what initial screen are you directed to when you first try to establish a browser connection to an address in the private network of the head-end concentrator?

_____

_____

_____

**21** What VPN 3002 Hardware Client Manager screen can you use to quickly try to connect to the head-end concentrator?

_____

_____

_____

**22** What VPN 3002 Hardware Client Manager screen can you use when you want to view IKE Phase 1 and IPSec Phase 2 connection statistics?

_____

_____

_____

**23** What VPN 3002 Hardware Client Manager screen can you use if you suspect that DNS problems are interfering with user communications?

_____

_____

_____

# Scenarios

## Scenario 8-1

Your task in this scenario is to set up a VPN Concentrator and two VPN 3002 Hardware Clients as shown in Figure 8-22. Enable communications between the concentrators and the VPN 3002 Hardware Clients.

**Figure 8-21**  *Remote Access VPN Network*

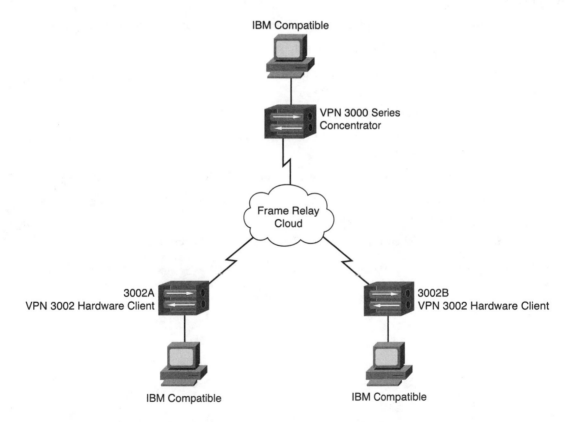

After you enable communications between the devices, you have seven tasks:

**Step 1**    Set up 3002A to use Client mode. Set the timeout to a low value, such as 5 or 10 minutes.

**Step 2**    Set up 3002B to use LAN Extension mode.

**Step 3**    Initiate the tunnels on both networks.

**Step 4**   Get a cup of coffee and relax for 10 or 20 minutes.

**Step 5**   Check the tunnels. Which one is still up? Why?

**Step 6**   From each remote side, ping a device behind the head-end concentrator. Can you see the device?

**Step 7**   From the head-end, ping a device at each remote site. Can you see devices at each site? Why?

# Scenario 8-2

Keep your existing configuration from Scenario 8-1 and complete the following tasks:

**Step 1**   Break the VPN tunnel on both sites.

**Step 2**   From the head-end, ping a device at each remote site. Can you see the devices? Why?

**Step 3**   Set both sites to use split tunneling.

**Step 4**   From the head-end, ping a device at each remote site. Can you see the devices? Why?

**Step 5**   Set up individual authentication for the 3002B sites. Do not log in.

**Step 6**   From each remote side, ping a device behind the head-end concentrator. Can you see the device? Why?

**Step 7**   Log in at each site and retry Step 6. What are the results?

# Scenario Answers

The following answers pertain to the tasks presented in the previous section.

## Scenario 8-1 Answers

The PAT (Client mode) tunnel should have dropped because the timeout has expired (assuming you didn't drink your coffee too fast). Because the LAN Extension mode always keeps the tunnel active, this tunnel will not drop.

You should be able to see individual devices at the head-end from each remote site. However, from the head-end, you should not be able to see any device on the site that is using PAT mode because the true IP address is hidden.

## Scenario 8-2 Answers

From the head-end, you will not be able to see anything at the remotes sites. The remote sites "bring up" the tunnel, not the head-end site. Split tunneling will not change this behavior. It is only after the tunnel is established and data flows from the remote site that the head-end can see anything at the remote sites. The exception to this is when LAN extension mode is enabled and split tunneling is *not* enabled.

A user should not be able to see the head-end if individual authentication is enabled and they have not logged in. If you can see something at the head-end, you are not using individual authentication. Only after you have logged in will you be able to see any devices at the head-end.

# Exam Topics Discussed in This Chapter

This chapter covers the following topics, which you need to master in your pursuit of certification as a Cisco Certified Security Specialist:

32  Overview of the VPN 3002 Reverse Route Injection feature

33  Configuring the VPN 3002 backup server feature

34  Configuring the VPN 3002 load balancing feature

35  Overview of the VPN 3002 Auto-Update Feature

36  Configuring the VPN 3002 Auto-Update Feature

37  Monitoring VPN 3002 Auto-Update Events

38  Overview of Port Address Translation

39  Configuring IPSec over UDP

40  Configuring IPSec over TCP

# CHAPTER 9

# Configuring Scalability Features of the VPN 3002 Hardware Client

A major issue on any network design is planning for the ability of the network to grow as the needs of the company grow. This chapter deals with some of the issues you will face when planning and implementing networks using the Cisco VPN 3002 Hardware Client.

By combining hardware and software, the VPN 3002 Hardware Client provides for the scalability of software while the hardware provides stability and reliability. This combination makes the VPN 3002 Hardware Client an ideal solution that will fit in environments where a large number of remote sites exist. The VPN 3002 Hardware Client has the capability to provide for 56-bit DES encryption or 168-bit 3DES (triple DES) encryption, also known as IPSec.

Reverse Route Injection, backup servers, load balancing and auto-update are all features that help you to easily administer large sites with the least amount of intervention. This chapter discusses these features.

## How to Best Use This Chapter

By taking the following steps, you can make better use of your time:

- Keep your notes and answers for all your work with this book in one place for easy reference.
- Take the "Do I Know This Already?" quiz, and write down your answers. Studies show retention is significantly increased through writing facts and concepts down, even if you never look at the information again.
- Use the diagram in Figure 9-1 to guide you to the next step.

**Figure 9-1** *How to Use This Chapter*

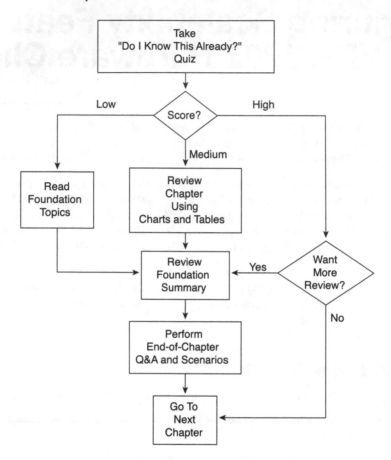

# "Do I Know This Already?" Quiz

The purpose of the "Do I Know This Already?" quiz is to help you decide what parts of the chapter to use. If you already intend to read the entire chapter, you do not necessarily need to answer these questions now.

This 27-question quiz helps you determine how to spend your limited study time. The quiz is sectioned into nine smaller "quizlets," which correspond to the nine major topic headings in the chapter. Figure 9-1 outlines suggestions on how to spend your time in this chapter based on your quiz score. Use Table 9-1 to record your scores.

**Table 9-1**    *Scoresheet for Quiz and Quizlets*

| Quizlet Number | Foundations Topics Section Covering These Questions | Question | Score |
|---|---|---|---|
| 1 | Overview of the VPN 3002 Reverse Route Injection Feature | 1–3 | |
| 2 | Configuring the VPN 3002 Backup Server Feature | 4–6 | |
| 3 | Configuring the VPN 3002 Load-Balancing Feature | 7–9 | |
| 4 | Overview of the VPN 3002 Auto-Update Feature | 10–12 | |
| 5 | Configuring the VPN 3002 Auto-Update Feature | 13–15 | |
| 6 | Monitoring VPN 3002 Auto-Update Events | 16–18 | |
| 7 | Overview of Port Address Translation (PAT) | 19–21 | |
| 8 | Configuring the Cisco VPN 3002 Series Concentrator for IPSec over UDP | 22–24 | |
| 9 | Configuring the Cisco VPN 3002 Series Concentrator for IPSec over TCP | 25–27 | |

1   What are the ramifications an administrator should consider when planning to use Virtual Router Redundancy Protocol (VRRP) along with Reverse Route Injection (RRI)?

_____

_____

_____

2   You wish to inject a route from the VPN concentrator to the VPN 3002 Hardware Client. What routing protocol must you use?

_____

_____

_____

3   You wish to use RIPv1 with Reverse Route Injection. Can this be done?

_____

_____

_____

**4** You are using a backup IPSec server because the primary server was down when the initial tunnel was initiated. The primary server is now up. Will the VPN 3002 Hardware Client restore a connection to the primary? If so, when?

_____

_____

_____

**5** What is the timeout period used when attempting to connect to the primary concentrator before a connection will be attempted to a secondary concentrator?

_____

_____

_____

**6** You tried to connect to your primary concentrator from your VPN 3002 Hardware Client but were unsuccessful. Your 3002 Hardware Client then attempted to connect to your backup concentrator without success. When will the VPN 3002 Hardware Client try again?

_____

_____

_____

**7** How is load balancing enabled on the VPN 3002 Hardware Client?

_____

_____

_____

**8** You have three VPN 3015 Concentrators on the same network. Assuming default priority settings, which one will be elected to balance the load?

_____

_____

_____

**9** What factors are considered for VPN 3000 Concentrator load balancing with VPN 3002 Hardware Clients or remote access VPN Clients?

_____

_____

_____

10 Which debug class or classes should you enable in order to debug an auto-update?

_____

_____

_____

11 What types of clients may use the auto-update feature?

_____

_____

_____

12 When a software update is pending, during the connection process, the concentrator sends a message indicating the IP address of the TFTP server and the software version to be downloaded. What type (protocol) is this message?

_____

_____

_____

13 What client type(s) are permissible to be set on the VPN concentrator for upgrading clients when using the VPN 3002 Hardware Client?

_____

_____

_____

14 On the VPN concentrator, what is the syntax used to specify the TFTP server and the filename used for updating the client software?

_____

_____

_____

15 You have configured auto-update to occur. Which device, the VPN concentrator or the VPN 3002 Hardware Client, recognizes that the software must be updated?

_____

_____

_____

**16** How is the VPN 3000 Concentrator configured to notify VPN 3002 Hardware Clients that a new software upgrade is available?

_____

_____

_____

**17** Your VPN 3002 Hardware Client attempts to auto-update. The system appears to "hang" and eventually times out on the download portion of the process. What are two likely causes?

_____

_____

_____

**18** You have tried to upgrade your VPN 3002 Hardware Client. However, the VPN 3002 Hardware Client keeps trying to upgrade without success. You know that you have connectivity. You can see in the logs that you have been downloading the file. What is the problem?

_____

_____

_____

**19** Why will some applications not work with either NAT or PAT?

_____

_____

_____

**20** Why will PAT cause problems with some applications whereas NAT does not cause these problems?

_____

_____

_____

**21** What are two main differences between NAT and PAT?

_____

_____

_____

**22** Why is UDP Transparent IPSec (IPSec over UDP) usable with either NAT or PAT when IPSec over TCP is not usable over PAT?

_____

_____

_____

**23** You are using UDP Transparent IPSec on your VPN 3002 Hardware Client. How are filters applied to inbound traffic? How are filters applied to outbound traffic?

_____

_____

_____

**24** What minimum version does the VPN concentrator have to be running in order to use UDP NAT Transparent IPSec? What version is required on the VPN 3002 Hardware Client?

_____

_____

_____

**25** What is the default port for IPSec over UDP?

_____

_____

_____

**26** When using IPSec over TCP, how are IKE and IPSec protocols handled in relation to NAT?

_____

_____

_____

**27** You are planning on terminating your VPN 3002 Hardware Client's VPN tunnel on a Microsoft Proxy Server. Should you use UDP NAT Transparent IPSec (IPSec over UDP) or IPSec over TCP?

_____

_____

_____

The answers to this quiz are listed in Appendix A, "Answers to the "Do I Know This Already?" Quizzes and Q&A Sections." The suggestions for your next steps, based on quiz results, are as follows:

- **2 or less overall score**—Review the appropriate sections of the "Foundation Topics" section of this chapter, based on Table 9-1. Then proceed to the "Foundation Summary" section, the "Q&A" section, and then the scenarios at the end of the chapter.

- **16 or less overall score**—Read the entire chapter, including the "Foundation Topics" and "Foundation Summary" sections, the "Q&A" section, and the scenarios at the end of the chapter.

- **17 to 22 overall score**—Begin with the "Foundation Summary" section, continue with the "Q&A" section, and then the scenarios. If you are having difficulty with a particular subject area, read the appropriate section in "Foundation Topics" section.

- **23 or more overall score**—If you feel you need more review on these topics, go to the "Foundation Summary" section, then to the "Q&A" section, and then the scenarios. Otherwise, skip this chapter and go to the next chapter.

# Foundation Topics

# VPN 3002 Hardware Client Reverse Route Injection

**32** Overview of the VPN 3002 Reverse Route Injection feature

Reverse Route Injection (RRI) is the process by which routes are added to a VPN concentrator and these routes are then advertised to remote clients, such as the VPN 3002 Hardware Client. Using either RIP or Open Shortest Path First (OSPF) while in network extension mode, the VPN 3002 Hardware Client automatically adds hosts on the private network to the VPN concentrator's routing table for redistribution. It is important to understand that, because the VPN 3002 Hardware Client is considered a client, it cannot advertise RRI, but it can inject network extensible routes back to the concentrator. The only device that can advertise RRI is the VPN concentrator.

There is no configuration requirement, other than being in Network Extension mode (NEM), on the VPN 3002 Hardware Client for RRI to occur. Therefore, this section will cover the configurations necessary on the VPN concentrator.

RRI will work only with RIP and OSPF. Using Virtual Routing Redundancy Protocol (VRRP) with RRI will probably cause routing loops because both the primary and the backup servers will advertise the same routes.

## Setting Up the VPN Concentrator Using RIPv2

In order for the VPN concentrator to advertise the routes learned through RRI, there must be at least outbound RIP (version 2) configured on the private interface. When using Autodiscovery, both inbound and outbound RIP will need to be configured. This is done through the Configuration | Interfaces screen (see Figure 9-2). Note that client RRI can be used by all VPN devices connected to the VPN concentrator.

**Figure 9-2** *Enabling RIP*

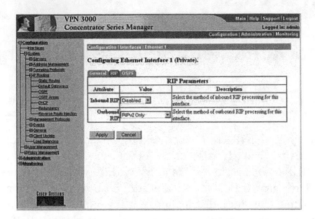

## Setting Up the VPN Concentrator Using OSPF

If you choose to use OSPF instead of RIP, go to the Configuration | System | IP Routing | OSPF screen (see Figure 9-3). There, you enable OSPF, place in the router ID or IP address, and specify if this is an Autonomous System Boundary Router (ASBR). The OSPF process on the VPN concentrator must be defined as an autonomous system. Specifying an ASBR when the router is not an ASBR or vice versa will generate unexpected results.

**Figure 9-3** *Configuration | System | IP Routing | OSPF*

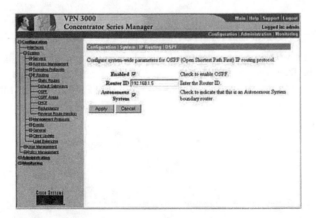

## Configuring VPN 3002 Hardware Client Reverse Route Injection

RRI can be configured in one of the following four ways:

- LAN-to-LAN remote network definitions are the injected routes as either a single network or a network list.
- The VPN 3002 Hardware Client connects using Network Extension mode, injecting its protected network address.
- VPN software clients inject their own IP address as host routes (Client RRI).
- RRI provides a hold-down route for the VPN client pool.

In addition to the preceding four options, the following sections also discuss configuring LAN-to-LAN with Autodiscovery.

### Configuring LAN-to-LAN Network RRI

After navigating to the Configuration | System | Tunneling Protocols | IPSec | LAN-to-LAN | Modify screen on the VPN concentrator, which is shown in Figure 9-4, configure RRI by following these steps:

**Step 1**  Fill in the name, interface, and peer.

**Step 2**  Choose the type of digital certificate.

**Step 3**  Enter the pre-shared key.

**Step 4**  Choose the authentication type, encryption, and IKE proposal.

**Step 5**  Choose **Reverse Route Injection** in the routing field. The VPN concentrator will advertise the learned routes to the interior routers.

This process is necessary to establish RRI on the VPN concentrator. Remember that RRI will only work with RIP or OSPF. When RIP is used, the remote network can only advertise routes to the VPN concentrator. Only when using OSPF can the VPN concentrator advertise routes to the VPN 3002 Hardware Client.

### Configuring LAN-to-LAN with Autodiscovery

The only configuration change necessary to enable Autodiscovery is made through the Configuration | System | Tunneling Protocols | IPSec | LAN-to-LAN | Modify screen. Here, you choose Autodiscovery instead of Network Lists. Remember that RIP is the only protocol available for use with Autodiscovery.

**Figure 9-4** *Configuration | System | Tunneling Protocols | IPSec | LAN-to-LAN | Modify*

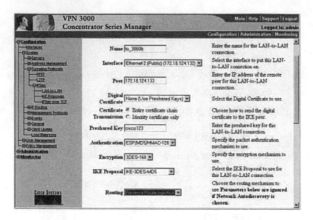

## Configuring Network Extension Mode RRI

The Network Extension mode RRI is configured on the Configuration | System | IP Routing | Reverse Route Injection screen (see Figure 9-5). Select the **Network Extension Reverse Route Injection** check box to add the RRI.

**Figure 9-5** *Configuration | System | IP Routing | Reverse Route Injection*

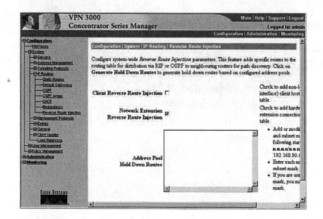

## Configuring Client RRI

Client RRI, where the client injects its routes into the VPN concentrator, is configured through the Configuration | System | IP Routing | Reverse Route Injection screen on the VPN concentrator (see Figure 9-6). Select the **Client Reverse Route Injection** checkbox to enable this feature.

**Figure 9-6**    *Configuration | System | IP Routing | Reverse Route Injection*

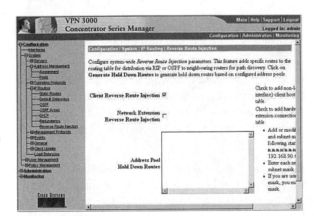

## Configuring Hold-Down Routes

Hold-down routes are used to make remote VPN connections appear as if they were active even when there is no VPN tunnel active. This way, the stability and speed of network topology calculations by the routing protocols is enhanced. Since the networks appear to be available at all times, the routing protocols do not have to recalculate the topology every time a VPN connection is established or dropped.

Hold-down routes are entered on the Configuration | System | IP Routing | Reverse Route Injection screen in the Address Pool Hold-Down Routes box on the VPN concentrator (see Figure 9-7). Double-click on an empty line on the box and enter the IP address/Subnet mask combination. Note that a backslash (/) should be used between the IP address and the subnet mask and that the subnet mask must be entered in standard octet notation.

**Figure 9-7**    *Address Pool Hold-Down Routes*

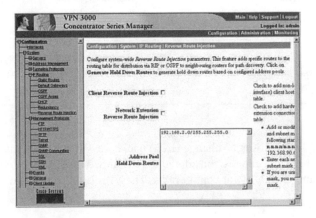

# VPN 3002 Hardware Client Backup Servers

**33**  Configuring the VPN 3002 backup server feature

Backup servers allow VPN 3002 Hardware Clients to connect to an alternative site when the primary site fails. You can configure backup servers either on a group basis at the central VPN concentrator or on an individual basis on the VPN 3002 Hardware Client. Configuration done on a group basis is pushed to the individual VPN 3002 Hardware Clients defined in the relevant group.

As an example, suppose that a company has two main offices and that each one has a VPN 3030 Concentrator. The IP address of the concentrator at the primary office is 161.44.246.15 and the IP address of the remote concentrator is 192.156.10.1, as shown in the configuration of a VPN 3002 Hardware Client's remote and backup servers in Figure 9-8. In the event that the VPN 3002 Hardware Client is unable to connect to 161.44.246.15, it will next attempt to connect to the concentrator at 192.156.10.1.

**Figure 9-8**    *The Configuration | System | Tunneling Protocols | IPSec screen*

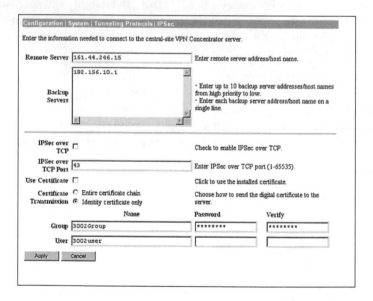

If the initial Internet Key Exchange (IKE) packet to 161.44.246.15 is not responded to within 8 seconds, the connection is considered to have timed out. The 8-second timeout period is a default parameter that is not configurable. The VPN 3002 Hardware Client will attempt to connect to the next server defined, in this case, Boston. If there are other servers on the list, the next server will be tried after 8 seconds without a connection. Up to 10 backup servers may be listed in the backup server list, each being tried in turn. If all of the servers are tried unsuccessfully, the attempts to connect are stopped without automatically retrying the list.

There are nine items you need to remember regarding backup servers:

- A backup server list can only be downloaded from a primary VPN concentrator, never from a backup.

- If the primary VPN concentrator is unavailable, a backup concentrator will be contacted ONLY if a backup list is already configured.

- The VPN 3002 Hardware Client will be unaware of changes made to servers unless that VPN 3002 Hardware Client is connected to the primary VPN concentrator.

- On the VPN 3002 Hardware Client, the backup servers are set on the Configuration | System | Tunneling Protocols | IPSec screen, which only applies if Use Client Configured List is set. The Configuration | System | Tunneling Protocols | IPSec screen is shown in Figure 9-8.

- On the VPN concentrator, the configuration of the backup servers is done through the Configuration | User Management | Base Group | Mode Configuration or the Configuration | User Management | Groups | Mode Configuration screens. An example of the Configuration | User Management | Base Group | Mode Config screen is shown in Figure 9-9.

- The group name, username, and password must be identical on the primary and backup servers.

- In Network Extension Mode, the VPN 3002 Hardware Client will attempt to connect to a backup server after the default of 4 seconds.

- In Client mode, the VPN 3002 Hardware Client only attempts a connection when the user clicks the Connect Now button on the Monitoring | System Status screen or when data passes through the VPN 3002 Hardware Client.

- VPN 3002 Hardware Clients have no knowledge of each other, only of the primary and backup servers.

**Figure 9-9** *Configuration | User Management | Base Group | Mode Config*

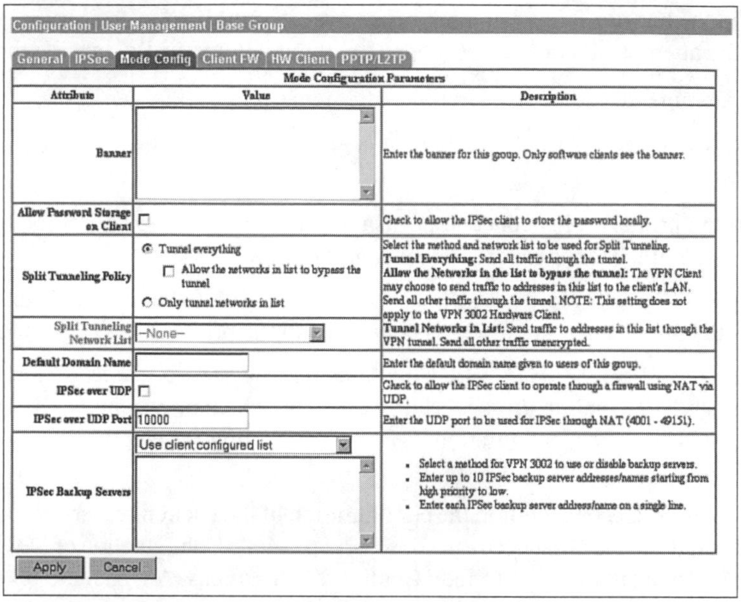

# VPN 3002 Hardware Client Load Balancing

**34** Configuring the VPN 3002 load balancing feature

The devices in the VPN 3000 Concentrator series have the ability to load balance connections from remote clients or VPN 3002 Hardware Clients. VPN 3002 Hardware Clients do not actually perform the load balancing function; they are merely beneficiaries of the results.

Load balancing and Virtual Router Redundancy Protocol (VRRP) cannot be used at the same time with the same concentrators. With VRRP, the backup device stays in an idle state until it is required to become active to assume the duties of the primary device. With load balancing, all of the devices in the virtual load balancing cluster are active.

Load balancing can occur between two or more VPN concentrators that are located on the same network to process remote access VPN connections. Load balancing only works with Cisco VPN Clients running version 3.0 or later, and with Cisco VPN 3002 Hardware Clients running version 3.5 or later. Other clients and LAN-to-LAN devices can still establish VPN connections to VPN concentrators participating in load balancing, but these clients and devices will not participate in load balancing by being directed away from their primary device.

In Cisco's implementation of load balancing on the VPN concentrators, the concentrators form a virtual load-balancing cluster with one of the devices acting as the virtual cluster master. The cluster is assigned a virtual IP address that is the peer address configured on software and hardware clients. When these clients attempt to connect to the cluster's address, the master concentrator intercepts the request, determines which concentrator in the cluster (including the master concentrator itself) is the least heavily loaded, and returns the physical IP address of that concentrator to the client. The client then takes the newly acquired IP address and reinitiates IKE negotiations with that concentrator. This process permits VPN activity to be distributed among the concentrators in the cluster.

The task of being the virtual cluster master is not tied to any specific concentrator. An election process based on a priority setting and time since last reboot occurs to determine which concentrator will be the master for the cluster. Each VPN concentrator model has a specific priority that can be overridden on the Configuration | System | Load Balancing screen. The device with the highest priority (the range is 0 to 10) becomes the virtual cluster master. In the case of a tie, the device that comes on line first acts as the master. The factory assigned priority settings are as follows:

- **VPN 3005 Concentrator**—Priority 1
- **VPN 3015 Concentrator**—Priority 3
- **VPN 3030 Concentrator**—Priority 5
- **VPN 3060 Concentrator**—Priority 7
- **VPN 3080 Concentrator**—Priority 9

There is some overhead involved with being the virtual cluster master, so the most capable device should take that responsibility. If the virtual cluster master should fail for any reason, the election process will occur among the remaining cluster participants to elect a new virtual cluster master. Any clients that were connected to the failed device will renegotiate their VPN tunnel by once again contacting the virtual IP address of the cluster.

Because the VPN 3002 Hardware Client series is a beneficiary of VPN concentrator load balancing, there is really nothing to configure on those devices except for using the virtual IP address of the cluster as the address of the peer. All of the configuration steps necessary for load balancing are done on the VPN concentrator using the Configuration | System | Load Balancing screen of the VPN 3000 Concentrator Series Manager. The fields on that screen are

- **Cluster Configuration**—This section is used to define the common elements of the load-balancing cluster. All of the devices in the cluster must have identical settings in this section and must all be on the same public and private IP networks.

  - **VPN Virtual Cluster IP Address**—A single IP address from the public subnet that will be used to represent the load-balancing cluster to potential clients.

  - **VPN Virtual Cluster UDP Port**—The default UDP port used for load balancing is 9023, but you can choose another port for the cluster if 9023 is in use by another application.

— **Encryption**—Virtual cluster communications are handled over LAN-to-LAN tunnels between VPN concentrators in the virtual cluster. Checking the encryption field forces that communication to be encrypted. The default setting is to have encryption enabled.

— **IPSec Shared Secret**—When you have selected to use encryption in the previous field, you will need to enter a password in this field that will be used as the preshared key when the cluster concentrators establish IPSec communication tunnels with their cluster peers.

— **Verify Shared Secret**—Re-enter the password in this field for verification of the entry.

• **Device Configuration**—This section is used to define device-specific parameters for VPN concentrators participating in load-balancing virtual clusters.

— **Load Balancing Enable**—This VPN concentrator will not participate in load balancing unless this field is checked. The default setting for this field is unchecked, disabling load balancing.

— **Priority**—This field is used to set the priority of the device. Election of the virtual cluster master uses this field as one of the determining factors in the election process. The default setting here is specific to the VPN concentrator model and was described in an earlier list within this section. The value can be a number from 1 to 10. The higher the value, the more likely the chance that the device will be selected as the virtual cluster master. When all the concentrators in the cluster are of the same model, set the priority to 10 on all of them to shorten the election process.

— **NAT Assigned IP Address**—The default setting for this field is 0.0.0.0, which indicates that the concentrator is not using NAT. Enter the NAT IP address here if the concentrator is protected by a firewall using NAT.

When a client attempts to connect to a load-sharing cluster, it will use the IPSec group settings to negotiate and establish the working VPN tunnel. Different clients might use different IPSec groups in order to provide different classes of service. Each VPN concentrator in the virtual load-balancing cluster must have a matching group for any potential client, and the settings for the group must be identical on every VPN concentrator in the cluster.

# Overview of Port Address Translation

**38** Overview of Port Address Translation

In order to understand the issues involved when using Port Address Translation (PAT), you first need to understand how Network Address Translation (NAT) works. NAT is the process of changing the source IP address on all packets sent out by a host and changing the destination

IP address of all incoming packets for that host. This prevents hosts outside of the LAN from knowing the true IP address of a local host. While not a true security method in itself, NAT may help security efforts through hiding the true IP address of the client. NAT may be configured in two differing ways. When NAT uses a specific global IP address for a given host, this is referred to as a *static NAT*. The other method of configuring NAT is to use a pool of IP addresses for all local hosts. Local hosts are assigned a global IP address on a first-come–first-served basis. The IP address of a specific local host will receive changes based on the availability of global IP addresses.

During the NAT process for a packet traveling outbound through the NAT device, the source IP within the IP packet is replaced with a global IP address. The NAT device tracks the inside IP address that is associated with the global IP address. For a packet traveling inbound through the NAT device, the destination address is replaced with the locally known IP address.

PAT is a form of NAT. When PAT is employed, not only does the source or destination address of an IP packet change, but the TCP or UDP source port is also changed. This way, the PAT device can allow multiple local devices to appear as a single global IP device with the differing source ports providing the unique identification necessary to translate the incoming packets to their respective local IP addresses. In essence, a NAT translation is a one-to-one translation of the IP address, where a PAT translation is a one-to-many translation of the IP address using the port to differentiate between the connections.

The first issue raised when using PAT is that some older programs will not work because the ports are translated. This is especially true when dealing with some Microsoft DOS programs. This can usually be overcome by upgrading the operating system and/or programs affected.

The second, and more severe issue is that traditional IPSec, discussed in the next section, relies heavily on the ports in use. As in some older DOS programs, IPSec will not work when combined with PAT. Cisco has come up with a solution when using the VPN 3002 Hardware Client that allows IPSec to run through a PAT connection. Cisco's solution is to use either IPSec over TCP/IP or UDP NAT Transparent IPSec. Both will be discussed shortly.

You usually have fewer global IP addresses that you can use than you have local hosts. The most common way of dealing with this is to assign static global addresses to those hosts that need to be reached from the Internet at a known IP address. Next, local hosts are assigned IP addresses from the global pool on a first-come–first-served basis. After all but one of the allotted global addresses have been assigned, you use PAT with the final global address for all the remaining local hosts.

# IPSec on the VPN 3002 Hardware Client

> **39** Configuring IPSec over UDP
>
> **40** Configuring IPSec over TCP

Internet Protocol Security (IPSec) is the standard that enables the VPN 3002 Hardware Client to connect securely to the centralized VPN concentrator. IPSec security methods include address data privacy, authentication, integrity, key management, and tunneling.

With the VPN 3002 Hardware Client, two IPSec options are available to you: IPSec over TCP/IP and IPSec over UDP. You may choose one of these, which will automatically disable the other option. The next sections describe both options in more detail.

## IPSec Over TCP/IP

The Cisco VPN Client and the Cisco VPN 3002 Hardware Client both fully support IPSec over TCP, encapsulating the encrypted data within the TCP packet. In this mode, the VPN 3002 Hardware Client is able to work where standard Encapsulating Security Payload (ESP) (protocol 50) or Internet Key Exchange (IKE) (UDP 500) cannot operate because of factors such as PAT. IPSec over TCP encapsulates both the IKE and IPSec protocols within the TCP packet, enabling the new packet to pass through NAT and PAT devices. This feature, however, will not work if the VPN termination on the other end is proxy based, such as in Microsoft Proxy Server.

There are three requirements for both the VPN concentrator and the VPN 3002 Hardware Client when using IPSec over TCP:

- Run version 3.5 or later software.
- IPSec over TCP must be enabled.
- The VPN concentrator and the VPN 3002 Hardware Client must use the same port.

To enable IPSec over TCP/IP, you must make configuration changes on both the VPN concentrator and the VPN 3002 Hardware Client. IPSec over TCP/IP is configured on the VPN 3002 Hardware Client under the Configuration I System I Tunneling Protocols I IPSec screen. On the VPN concentrator, configuration settings for IPSec over TCP/IP are made on the Configuration I System I Tunneling Protocols I IPSec I IPSec over TCP screen, as shown in Figure 9-10.

**Figure 9-10**  *Configuration | System | Tunneling Protocols | IPSec | IPSec over TCP*

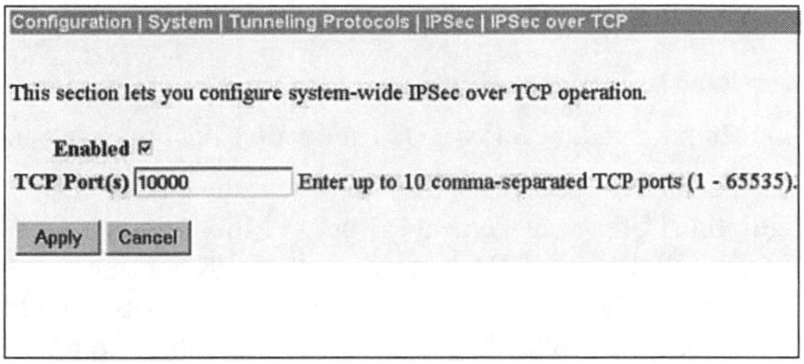

On either hardware client or concentrator, you simply check the box to enable IPSec over TCP and then select the TCP port to use between the devices. The default port is 10,000, but you can select any port between 1 and 65,635. If you select a well-known port, such as 80 for HTTP, the system will present a warning telling you that the protocol associated with the well-known port number will no longer be available on the public interface. On the VPN concentrator, you can enter up to 10 ports, separated by commas, so that you can use a different port for each hardware client that connects to the concentrator. The configuration screen for the VPN 3002 Hardware Client only permits you to enter one TCP port number.

## UDP NAT Transparent IPSec (IPSec Over UDP)

The VPN 3002 Hardware Client fully supports User Datagram Protocol Network Address Translation Transparent IPSec (UDP NAT Transparent IPSec). In this mode, the VPN 3002 Hardware Client encapsulates the data traffic within new UDP packets, bypassing the effects of NAT and PAT. This method sends keepalives on a regular basis to ensure the NAT mappings remain active. While this method does slightly increase the amount of bandwidth overhead, it is necessary because UDP is a connectionless protocol. There is a limitation on using UDP NAT Transparent IPSec; only a single VPN device may be behind the NAT device. In other words, you may have only a single VPN 3002 Hardware Client behind a PIX firewall.

Some of the workings of IPSec transparent mode are not readily visible to the administrator. For example, the VPN concentrator creates a filter rule, applying it to the public filter and passes this along to the VPN 3002 Hardware Client transparently. From the inbound side, the UDP traffic goes directly to the IPSec processing for decryption and deencapsulation before being routed. On the outbound side, the IPSec process encrypts, encapsulates, and then adds a new UDP header if required. These rules may be removed from the filter under one of three conditions:

- When a group is deleted
- When the last active IPSec over UDP Security Association (SA) for that group is deleted
- When IPSec over UDP is disabled for the group

UDP NAT Transparent IPSec, which disables IPSec over UDP, is the default configuration for the VPN 3002 Hardware Client, so no configuration is necessary. However, there are three requirements for running UDP NAT Transparent IPSec:

- Run version 3.0.3 or later software.

- The concentrator and the VPN 3002 Hardware Client must use the same port.

- You must configure IPSec over UDP for the group on the VPN concentrator through the Configuration | User Management | Groups | Modify screen, as shown in Figure 9-11. Clicking the **IPSec over UDP** box causes the VPN concentrator to expect IPSec over UDP (UDP NAT Transparent IPSec) instead of IPSec over TCP. The administrator may optionally change the default port of 10,000. Allowable port numbers for IPSec over UDP configurations are 4001 through 49,151. Be sure that IPSec over TCP has been disabled on the VPN 3002 Hardware Client's Configuration | System | Tunneling Protocols | IPSec screen.

**Figure 9-11** *Configuration | User Management | Groups | Modify*

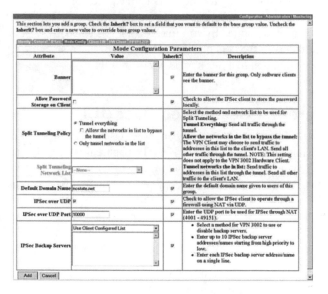

## Troubleshooting a VPN 3002 Hardware Client IPSec Connection

Testing the IPSec tunnel is fairly easy. The first step is to ping the private interface of the VPN concentrator from the Administration | Ping screen. If this is successful, but you are unable to ping anything else, the issue is internal routing. In this case, make sure that the device you are attempting to ping knows how to reach your private network. In other words, if you are not able to ping the inside interface of the VPN concentrator, the issue is probably within IPSec.

## Setting Debug Levels

The next action to be accomplished in debugging IPSec is to turn on debugging on both the VPN concentrator and the VPN 3002 Hardware Client. Set the severity log to 1-13 on both devices for the following:

- IKE
- IKEDBG
- IPSEC
- IPSECDBG

**NOTE**    The debugging levels may be set starting with Level 1-1 (Severe Error) through any of the levels up to Level 1-13 (Debugging Information). As with any Cisco logging, higher logging numbers give more detail than lower logging numbers. The reason you choose to log debugging information (Level 1–13) is that this level shows the most information available.

Try to reestablish the VPN tunnel and then look at the logs. Here are a few of the items worth noting:

- IKE failures on Phase 1
- Incorrect password
- Incorrect work name
- Incorrect username
- Incorrect password on the concentrator
- Unable to ping with an established tunnel

The following sections elaborate on each of these points.

## Errors on Phase 1

If you are experiencing failures during Phase 1, check these issues:

- XAUTH is required, but the proposal does not support XAUTH
- The priorities of IKE XAUTH proposals in the IKE proposal list
- The IPSec group
- The group on the VPN concentrator
- All SA proposals are acceptable

## Identifying an Incorrect Password at the VPN 3002 Hardware Client

On the VPN 3002 Hardware Client, you will see an error similar to the following if the password is incorrect:

```
Group [192.168.100.1]
Rxed Hash is incorrect:Preshared key or Digital Signature mismatch
```

## Identifying an Incorrect Work Group Name

If the work group name is incorrect, the VPN concentrator logs will show a message similar to the following:

```
No Group found 3002group for Preshared key peer 192.168.100.1
```

## Identifying an Incorrect Username

If the username given by the client is incorrect, the VPN concentrator log will show a message similar to the following:

```
Authentication rejected: Reason = User was not found
```

## Incorrect Password on the Concentrator

If the password is incorrect, the VPN concentrator log will show a message similar to the following:

```
Authentication rejected: Reason = Invalid password
```

## Unable to Ping with an Established Tunnel

If you have an established tunnel and you are still unable to ping the private interface on the VPN concentrator, there are two possibilities: overlapping SA or IPSec filtering. In the VPN 3002 Hardware Client, go to the Monitoring | System Status screen and note the Octets Out field. Next, go to the Monitoring | Sessions screen and note the Bytes Receiving counter. Attempt to ping the VPN concentrator's inside interface again and recheck these counters. Based on this information, you will be able to see which of two issues is causing the problem.

The first issue may be that there is an overlapping SA configured. An overlapping SA is where two or more VPN clients have the same network on the private side. For example, you may have a VPN 3002 Hardware Client with the 192.168.100.0/24 network and a VPN Software Client with an IP address of 192.168.100.4. If both of these counters are incrementing, this is the case.

If only the Octets Out counter is incrementing on the VPN 3002 Hardware Client, but the Bytes Received is not, then IPSec is being filtered. If UDP is enabled, make sure that the UDP port chosen, a default value of 10,000, is not being blocked. If the VPN 3002 Hardware Client is behind a PAT device, make sure to enable IPSec through NAT.

# Configuring Auto-Update for the VPN 3002 Hardware Client

**35** Overview of the VPN 3002 Auto-Update Feature

**36** Configuring the VPN 3002 Auto-Update Feature

Auto-update is a process by which the VPN concentrator requires that the connecting clients use a specific version of software. A client attempting to connect to the VPN concentrator with an incorrect software version will be denied access until after the software version becomes current. The VPN concentrator provides VPN Client users a link to the download server where the software can be obtained. Once the clients have the correct software version, they may once again connect in a normal fashion.

The VPN 3002 Hardware Client software can be upgraded automatically once the administrator copies the new version of the operating system to a TFTP server. The head-end VPN concentrator notifies the hardware client of the upgrade availability. Once the secure VPN tunnel has been established, the VPN 3002 Hardware Client copies the upgrade from the TFTP server and then performs a reload to activate the new version. This means that the administrator only needs to make changes at the head-end VPN concentrator instead of manually upgrading each individual VPN 3002 Hardware Client from the graphical user interface (GUI). This is especially efficient on large installations.

**NOTE**    The VPN 3000 Concentrator series client auto-update feature works only with the Windows-based VPN Client or with the VPN 3002 Hardware Client, not with any of the other VPN Clients, such as Linux or Macintosh.

The VPN 3002 Hardware Client is sent ISAKMP messages when it connects to the head-end concentrator, delivering notification that a software upgrade is pending. These ISAKMP messages contain the IP address of a TFTP server and filename to download, and they are sent in batches of 10 identical ISAKMP messages every 5 minutes. The VPN concentrator continues to send these messages until upgrade notification is disabled on the concentrator. VPN 3002 Hardware Clients that are already operating at the correct version level ignore the update messages.

VPN 3002 Hardware Clients store software images in two different locations, backup storage and active storage. During initial bootup, the hardware client copies the software image from backup storage into active storage. When the VPN 3002 Hardware Client copies the upgrade file from the TFTP server, it stores the file in backup storage. The update process then performs an integrity check of the copied file. If the file is damaged, the update process retries the file copy, performing this copy and check activity up to 20 times at 3-minute intervals until a good copy is received or the count of 20 is reached. Once a good file has been received, the update process issues a reload command to reboot the VPN 3002 Hardware Client and activate the new release.

VPN activities are not disturbed during the notification and download process. They are disrupted during the reboot, however, so the VPN tunnel to the head-end concentrator will need to be reestablished once the VPN 3002 Hardware Client as rebooted.

Setting up the head-end VPN 3000 Series Concentrator for automatically updating the VPN 3002 Hardware Client is accomplished through the VPN 3000 Concentrator Series Manager. The five steps follow:

**Step 1**  Navigate to the Configuration | User Management | Groups screen and select the group. Figure 9-12 shows that TCL Group (Internally Configured) was chosen.

**Step 2**  Choose **Modify Client Update**.

**Step 3**  Choose **Add** from the Client Update screen to add a new client package.

**Step 4**  On the next screen, enter **vpn3002** as the client type, enter **tftp://**{*IP address of server*}/{*filename*} as the URL, and enter the revision number (see Figure 9-13).

**Step 5**  Select **Add** to finish the setup at the head-end concentrator.

**Figure 9-12**  *Configuration | User Management | Groups*

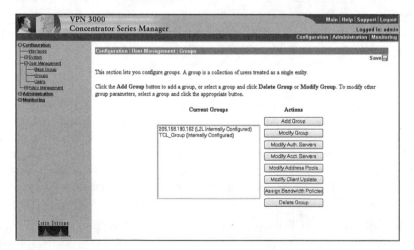

**Figure 9-13**  *Modifying Client Update Information*

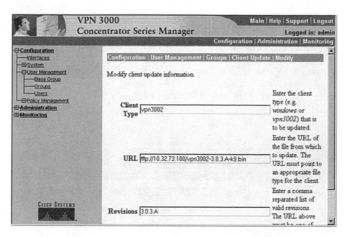

The Client Type has specific acceptable options and is case sensitive. The following list shows the available options:

- **Windows**—Provides update service to all Windows-based clients.

- **Win9X**—Provides update service to all Windows 95, Windows 98, and Windows ME clients.

- **WinNT**—Provides update service to Windows NT, Windows 2000, and Windows XP clients.

- **vpn3002**—Provides update service to VPN 3002 Hardware Clients.

The TFTP server must be located within the private network of the head-end VPN concentrator. The VPN 3002 Hardware Client reaches the TFTP server through the secure tunnel. In other words, the TFTP server IP address cannot be on the outside network of the public interface or routed in such a way that it needs to pull the image through the outside interface of the VPN concentrator without encryption.

The version number is derived from the filename you have specified to be downloaded. In this example, you used the file name vpn3002-3.0.3.A-k9.bin. The revision (3.0.3.A) is the part between the two dashes. Be sure you have entered the correct revision number. An incorrect or missing revision number will cause the VPN 3002 Hardware Client to enter an infinite cycle of attempting and failing to upgrade.

You may enter more than one revision number into the Revisions field, separating the entries by commas to indicate that you will support more than one client software release. The entry that you include in the URL field must be represented in the list of acceptable revisions. If the attaching client already operates with one of the versions listed in the revisions list, no action will be taken.

The next configuration step you need to do is to set up notification to VPN 3002 Hardware Clients (and software clients) about the upgrade. There are only three steps:

**Step 1** Using the VPN 3000 Concentrator Series Manager, go to **Administration | Software Update | Clients**.

**Step 2** Choose the group. In this example, the group is **rtpvpnl**.

**Step 3** Select **Upgrade Clients Now** (see Figure 9-14).

**Figure 9-14** *Updating Client Software*

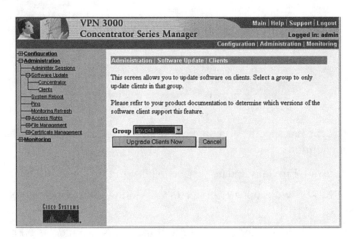

# Monitoring Auto-Update Events

**37** Monitoring VPN 3002 Auto-Update Events

In case the upgrade is not successful, debugging may be enabled to help determine the cause of failure. You should check the log file first to see if it contains any information on why the upgrade was unsuccessful. In the event that the log file does not provide enough information, configure debugging by following these steps:

**Step 1** Go to the **Configuration | System | Events | Classes | Add** screen, shown in Figure 9-15.

**Step 2** Choose the class named **AUTOUPDATE**.

**Step 3** Set the severity of the log to **1-13**.

**Step 4** Retrieve the log by going to the **Monitoring | Live Event Log** screen.

**Step 5** If you are also attached to the console, the console severity may also be set to **1-13**.

**Step 6** Likewise, the Syslog and Trap severities may be set if you are using a Syslog Server or an SNMP server such as CiscoWorks.

**Figure 9-15** *Configuration | System | Events | Classes | Add*

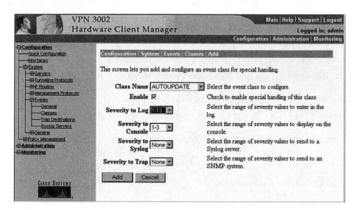

A sample output from the log is shown in Example 9-1. Table 9-2 explains the fields in the logs after this example.

**Example 9-1** *Sample Debugging Output*

```
12 08/21/2002 11:19:23.225 SEV=4 AUTOUPDATE/6 RPT=1
   Current version 3.0.2 does not match 3.0.3.A
13 08/21/2002 11:19:23.225 SEV=4 AUTOUPDATE/7 RPT=1
   Updating firmware to 3.0.3.A from 3.0.2
14 08/21/2002 11:19:23.225 SEV=4 AUTOUPDATE/12 RPT=1
   Update firmware will now begin using file
   vpn3002-3.0.3.A-k9.bin on server 192.268.101.3 [0A204964]
15 08/21/2002 11:35:00.700 SEV=4 AUTOUPDATE/5 RPT=1
   Current version 3.0.3.A is up to date
```

**Table 9-2** *Field Descriptions*

| Field | Definition |
|---|---|
| 12 | The first number in the list is the log number. |
| 08/21/2002 | The date is defined by the system date of the VPN 3002 Hardware Client. |
| 11:19:23.225 | The time of the log. |
| SEV=4 | The severity of the log. |
| AUTO-UPDATE/6 | The name of the event class. |
| RPT=1 | The description of the event. |

Notice that there are four steps in the automatic update process:

1  First, the VPN 3002 Hardware Client recognizes that the versions do not match.

2  Next, the update is started.

3  Then, a notice informs you that the new file will be used.

4  Finally, there is a log event showing that the current version is up to date.

Remember that configuring the wrong version number will cause an infinite loop attempting to upgrade. If you repeatedly see a message in the log that the current version does not match the new version but also see that the VPN 3002 Hardware Client will now be using a new file, the cause is almost certainly an incorrect version within the update screen.

A repeating attempt to update the firmware followed by a message indicating an inability to connect to the TFTP server may be explained by a few common issues, including the following:

- You do not have the correct IP address for the TFTP server.
- You do not have a route to the TFTP server.
- You do not have sufficient rights on the TFTP server.
- You do not have the ability to connect securely through a nontrusted interface to the server.

# Foundation Summary

The Foundation Summary is a collection of tables and figures that provides a convenient review of many key concepts in this chapter. For those who are already comfortable with the topics in this chapter, this summary could help you recall a few details. For those who just read this chapter, this review should help solidify some key facts. For anyone doing final preparation before the exam, these tables and figures are a convenient way to review the day before the exam.

## Table of RRI Configurations

Table 9-3 shows various RRI configurations.

**Table 9-3**    *RRI Configurations*

| RRI Type | Setup Screen | Things to Watch |
|---|---|---|
| RIPv2 | Configuration I Interfaces I RIP | Outbound RIP is configured. |
| OSPF | Configuration I System I IP Routing I OSPF | OSPF is defined as an autonomous system on the concentrator. ASBR is set correctly. |
| LAN-to-LAN | Configuration I System I Tunneling Protocols I IPSec | Use RIP or OSPF. |
| LAN-to-LAN Autodiscovery | Configuration I System I Tunneling Protocols I IPSec I LAN-to-LAN I Routing | Choose the Autodiscovery option. |
| NEM RRI | Configuration I System I IP Routing I Reverse Route Injection | Must have NEM enabled. |
| Client RRI | Configuration I System I IP Routing I Reverse Route Injection | Select check box. |
| Hold Down Routes | Configuration I System I IP Routing I Reverse Route Injection | Add *network/subnet mask*. |

## Backup Servers

There are nine items you need to remember regarding backup servers:

- A backup server list can only be downloaded from a primary VPN concentrator.
- A backup concentrator is contacted ONLY if the list already exists.
- The VPN 3002 Hardware Client must be connected to a primary VPN connector to know of changes.

- On a VPN 3002 Hardware Client, set the backup servers through Configuration | System | Tunneling Protocols | IPSec.

- On VPN concentrator, set through Configuration | User Management | Base Group | Mode Configuration or Configuration | User Management | Groups | Mode Configuration.

- The group name, username, and password must match on the primary and backup servers.

- In network extension mode, the VPN 3002 Hardware Client attempts connections after 4 seconds.

- In client mode, the VPN 3002 Hardware Client attempts connection when data is transferred or using Connect Now.

- VPN 3002 Hardware Clients have no knowledge of each other.

# Load Balancing

The following three points summarize load balancing:

- Automatic for VPN 3002.

- Must be on same private network.

- One VPN 3000 Series Concentrator acts as the master concentrator for the load-balancing cluster.

# Comparing NAT and PAT

Table 9-4 compares the characteristics of NAT and PAT.

**Table 9-4**    *NAT and PAT*

| NAT | PAT |
| --- | --- |
| Many-to-many relationship | One-to-many relationship |
| Changes source address outbound | Changes source address and source port |
| Changes destination address inbound | Changes destination address and port inbound |
| Works with almost any program | May not work with some older programs |

# IPSec Over TCP/IP

IPSec over TCP/IP has the following characteristics:

- Used with NAT and PAT

- Encapsulates IKE and IPSec in new TCP packet

- Must use version 3.5 or higher

- Both sides must use same port

- Must be enabled through the Configuration I System I Tunneling Protocols I IPSec I IPSec over TCP screen
- Will not work with proxy-based servers

# IPSec Over UDP

IPSec over UDP has the following characteristics:

- Used with NAT and PAT
- Encapsulates IKE and IPSec in new UDP packet
- Must use version 3.0.3 or higher
- Both sides must use same port
- Default port is 10,000
- Decreased available bandwidth caused by the amount of bandwidth used by keepalives
- A single VPN device behind a NAT device
- You may create a problem if
  - A group is deleted
  - The last SA is deleted
  - IPSec over UDP is disabled

# Troubleshooting IPSec

Remember the following when troubleshooting IPSec:

- Ping the inside interface of the remote concentrator. If you can get there, IPSec works.
- Set the debug levels for 1-13 on both sides (IKE, IKEDBG, IPSEC, IPSECDBG).
- Read and understand the log. It will tell you where the problem is.

# Auto-Update

Remember the following key points about auto-update:

- Pushes from central concentrator
- IPSec connection must exist
- Configure through Configuration I User Management I Groups
- Client type must be 3002
- The new version number must be precise
- Client is set up through Configuration I System I Events I Classes

# Chapter Glossary

The following terms were introduced in this chapter or have special significance to the topics within this chapter.

**Reverse Route Injection (RRI)** A process by which routes are added to a VPN concentrator, and then these routes are advertised back out to remote clients.

**head-end** Endpoint of a broadband network. All stations transmit toward the head-end; the head-end then transmits toward the destination stations.

**hold-down routes** Routes used to make a remote VPN connection appear to be active even when there is no current tunnel established.

**load balancing** In routing, the capability of a router to distribute traffic over all of its network ports that are the same distance from the destination address. Good load-balancing algorithms use both line speed and reliability information. Load balancing increases the use of network segments, thus increasing effective network bandwidth.

**Network Address Translation (NAT)** Mechanism for reducing the need for globally unique IP addresses. NAT allows an organization with addresses that are not globally unique to connect to the Internet by translating those addresses into globally routable address space. Also known as *Network Address Translator*.

**Port Address Translation (PAT)** Similar in nature to NAT. In PAT, the TCP or UDP port is translated in addition to the IP source or destination address. Also known as *Port Address Translator*.

# Q&A

As mentioned in Chapter 1, "All About the Cisco Certified Security Professional." these questions are more difficult than what you should experience on the CCSP exam. The questions do not attempt to cover more breadth or depth than the exam; however, the questions are designed to make sure you know the answer. Rather than allowing you to derive the answer from clues hidden inside the question itself, your understanding and recall of the subject are challenged. Questions from the "Do I Know This Already?" quiz from the beginning of the chapter are repeated here to ensure that you have mastered the chapter's topic areas. Hopefully, these questions will help limit the number of exam questions on which you narrow your choices to two options and guess!

1 What are the ramifications an administrator should consider when planning to use VRRP along with RRI?

_____

_____

_____

2 You wish to inject a route from the VPN concentrator to the VPN 3002 Hardware Client. What routing protocol must you use?

_____

_____

_____

3 You wish to use RIPv1 with Reverse Route Injection. Can this be done?

_____

_____

_____

4 Which screen on the VPN concentrator is used to configure RRI with OSPF?

_____

_____

_____

**5** You are using a backup IPSec server because the primary server was down when the initial tunnel was initiated. The primary server is now up. Will the VPN 3002 Hardware Client restore a connection to the primary? If so, when?

_____

_____

_____

**6** What is the timeout period used when attempting to connect to the primary concentrator before a connection will be attempted to a secondary concentrator.

_____

_____

_____

**7** You tried to connect to your primary concentrator from your VPN 3002 Hardware Client but were unsuccessful. Your 3002 Hardware Client then attempted to connect to your backup concentrator without success. When will the VPN 3002 Hardware Client try again?

_____

_____

_____

**8** What screen is used to configure backup servers on the VPN 3002 Hardware Client?

_____

_____

_____

**9** You have three VPN 3015 Concentrators on the same network. Assuming default priority settings, which one will be elected to balance the load?

_____

_____

_____

**10** What factors are considered for VPN 3000 Concentrator load balancing with VPN 3002 Hardware Clients or remote access VPN Clients?

_____

_____

_____

**11**  How is load balancing enabled on the VPN 3002 Hardware Client?

_____

_____

_____

**12**  What types of clients may use the auto-update feature?

_____

_____

_____

**13**  When a software update is pending, during the connection process, the concentrator sends a message indicating the IP address of the TFTP server and the software version to be downloaded. What type (protocol) is this message?

_____

_____

_____

**14**  What are two main differences between NAT and PAT?

_____

_____

_____

**15**  You are the administrator for a network using a single PAT address for connection to the Internet. You want to add two VPN 3002 Hardware Clients behind your PIX firewall. Which type of IPSec will you choose to use?

_____

_____

_____

**16**  What minimum version does the VPN concentrator have to be running in order to use IPSec over TCP/IP? What version is required on the VPN 3002 Hardware Client?

_____

_____

_____

**17** What minimum version does the VPN concentrator have to be running in order to use UDP NAT Transparent IPSec? What version is required on the VPN 3002 Hardware Client?

_____

_____

_____

**18** What is the default port for IPSec over UDP?

_____

_____

_____

**19** You have an established tunnel between two sites. From the remote site you are able to ping the inside interface of the VPN concentrator. However, you are unable to ping anything that lies beyond that point. What is wrong?

_____

_____

_____

**20** You are planning to upgrade your VPN 3002 Hardware Client. You have just received a file named vpn3002-3.0.3.A-k9.bin. What version is this?

_____

_____

_____

**21** You have tried to upgrade your VPN 3002 Hardware Client. However, the VPN 3002 Hardware Client keeps trying to upgrade without success. You know that you have connectivity. You can see in the logs that you have been downloading the file. What is the problem?

_____

_____

_____

**22** Why will some applications not work with either NAT or PAT?

_____

_____

_____

**23**  Why will PAT cause problems with some applications whereas NAT does not cause these problems?

_____

_____

_____

**24**  Which debug class or classes should you enable in order to debug an auto-update?

_____

_____

_____

**25**  On the VPN concentrator, what is the syntax used to specify the TFTP server and the filename used for updating the client software?

_____

_____

_____

**26**  You have configured auto-update to occur. Which device, the VPN concentrator or the VPN 3002 Hardware Client, recognizes that the software must be updated?

_____

_____

_____

**27**  What client type(s) are permissible to be set on the VPN concentrator for upgrading clients when using the VPN 3002 Hardware Client?

_____

_____

_____

**28**  How is the VPN 3000 Concentrator configured to notify VPN 3002 Hardware Clients that a new software upgrade is available?

_____

_____

_____

**29**  Your VPN 3002 Hardware Client attempts to auto-update. The system appears to "hang" and eventually times out on the download portion of the process. What are two likely causes?

_____

_____

_____

**30**  In Network Extension Mode, how long will the VPN 3002 Hardware Client wait before attempting to connect to a backup server if a connection to the primary server fails?

_____

_____

_____

**31**  Will a VPN 3002 Hardware Client connected to a backup server recognize that the primary server has added a new backup server?

_____

_____

_____

**32**  Does the VPN 3002 Hardware Client send keepalives to other VPN 3002 Hardware Clients connected to the same primary or backup server?

_____

_____

_____

**33**  Where are hold-down routes configured?

_____

_____

_____

**34**  What protocols may be used with LAN-to-LAN Autodiscovery?

_____

_____

_____

**35** When using IPSec over TCP, how are IKE and IPSec protocols handled in relation to NAT?

_____

_____

_____

**36** You are planning on terminating your VPN 3002 Hardware Client's VPN tunnel on a Microsoft Proxy Server. Should you use UDP NAT Transparent IPSec (IPSec over UDP) or IPSec over TCP?

_____

_____

_____

# Scenarios

## Scenario 9-1

Your task in this scenario is to set up a VPN concentrator and a VPN 3002 Hardware Client, as
shown in Figure 9-16. Enable communications between the concentrators and the VPN 3002
Hardware Client using IPSec over TCP/IP.

**Figure 9-16**  *Enabling RRI*

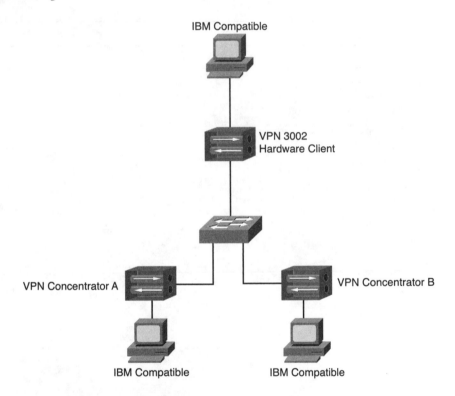

Once this is accomplished, you have four steps:

**Step 1**    Set up the VPN concentrator B as a backup and test.

**Step 2**    Update the VPN 3002 Hardware Client from the VPN concentrator A.

**Step 3**    Inject a route using OSPF from the VPN 3002 Hardware Client into the VPN
concentrator.

**Step 4**    Configure the VPN concentrators to use IPSec over UDP

# Scenario Answers

## Scenario 9-1 Answers

The following answers pertain to the tasks presented in the previous section:

**Step 1**    On the VPN 3002 Hardware Client, use the **Configuration | System | Tunneling Protocols | IPSec** screen and add the second concentrator. Ensure that **Use Client Configured List** is set.

To test, unplug the outside Ethernet interface on Concentrator A. Check that a VPN tunnel is established to Concentrator B.

**Step 2**    On the VPN concentrator:

(a)  Go to **Configuration | User Management | Groups**.

(b)  Select the group.

(c)  Choose **Modify Client Update**.

(d)  Choose **Add** from the Client Update screen.

(e)  On the next screen, enter **vpn3002** as the client type, enter the tftp address/filename, and enter the revision number.

(f)  Apply.

(g)  Go to **Administration | Software Update | Clients**.

(h)  Choose the group.

(i)  Select **Upgrade Client Now**.

**Step 3**    Reverse Route Injection is configured on the VPN concentrator. To do this, go to the **Configuration | System | IP Routing | Reverse Route Injection** screen. Check the **Client Reverse Route Injection** button.

**Step 4**    On the VPN 3002 Hardware Client, go to **Configuration | System | Tunneling Protocols | IPSec | IPSec over TCP**. The concentrator must also be configured using the **Configuration | System | Tunneling Protocols | IPSec | NAT Transparency | Enable IPSec over TCP** screen. Enable **IPSec over TCP/IP**.

# Exam Topics Discussed in This Chapter

This chapter covers the following topics, which you need to master in your pursuit of certification as a Cisco Certified Security Professional:

41 Cisco VPN 3000 IPSec LAN-to-LAN

42 LAN-to-LAN configuration

43 SCEP support overview

44 Root certificate installation

45 Identity certificate installation

# CHAPTER 10

# Cisco VPN 3000 LAN-to-LAN with Preshared Keys

One of the great benefits to using a VPN Concentrator is the ability to connect disparate LANs in a secure manner. For example, having your LAN in New York appear to be directly connected to the LAN in London makes administration of domains and user rights much easier for the systems administrator.

You accomplish this by creating a secure VPN from your concentrator to another concentrator, router, or PIX firewall at the remote site. Although it is certainly permissible — and sometimes advisable — to encrypt data through a VPN on a private frame network, it is much more common to use a VPN to reduce the need for dedicated connections by using the Internet as your long haul provider. One example of encrypting data over a private network occurs when you have a payroll department that is split between locations at two remote sites. Because you do not generally want the average administrator on your network to be able to find out salaries of other workers, you might want to encrypt this data between the two networks.

When you add the benefit of reducing the cost of these long distance connections through the use of VPNs over the Internet, the real benefits begin to show. This chapter deals with issues associated with connecting geographically separate LANs in a secure manner. Such connections will appear to the end user as if the network were next door, with one exception: latency. Because your VPN connections generally operate over the Internet, you will not be able to control how long it takes for a packet from one site to travel to the remote site.

You, as an administrator of private networks, have no real control over the Internet. You can control items such as your bandwidth to your ISP and are able to prioritize data within your own networks, but once your data reaches your ISP, you lose the ability to determine the priority of the data. When relying on the Internet for connectivity, you need to be aware that certain applications that are extremely time sensitive might lose connectivity even when your VPN connections are not directly affected. Always remember that using the Internet means that you rely upon a technology over which you have no control, and therefore, results cannot be guaranteed.

# How to Best Use This Chapter

By taking the following steps, you can make better use of your time:

- Keep your notes and answers for all your work with this book in one place for easy reference.

- Take the "Do I Know This Already?" quiz, and write down your answers. Studies show retention is significantly increased through writing facts and concepts down, even if you never look at the information again.

- Use the diagram in Figure 10-1 to guide you to the next step.

**Figure 10-1** *How to Use This Chapter*

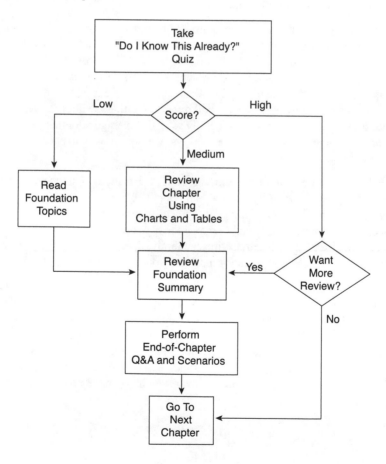

# "Do I Know This Already?" Quiz

The purpose of the "Do I Know This Already?" quiz is to help you decide what parts of the chapter to use. If you already intend to read the entire chapter, you do not necessarily need to answer these questions now.

This 15-question quiz helps you determine how to spend your limited study time. The quiz is sectioned into five smaller "quizlets," which correspond to the five major topic headings in the chapter. Figure 10-1 outlines suggestions on how to spend your time in this chapter based on your quiz score. Use Table 10-1 to record your scores.

**Table 10-1**    *Score Sheet for Quiz and Quizlets*

| Quizlet Number | Foundations Topics Section Covering These Questions | Questions | Score |
|---|---|---|---|
| 1 | Cisco VPN 3000 IPSec LAN-to-LAN | 1–3 | |
| 2 | LAN-to-LAN configuration | 4–6 | |
| 3 | SCEP support overview | 7–9 | |
| 4 | Root certificate installation | 10–12 | |
| 5 | Identity certificate installation | 13–15 | |
| All questions | | | |

1 What is a LAN-to-LAN connection?

_____

_____

_____

2 What equipment is required for a LAN-to-LAN connection?

_____

_____

_____

3 Where can a LAN-to-LAN connection be used?

_____

_____

_____

**4** When setting up network lists, how should the lists at each side of the LAN-to-LAN connection relate to each other?

_____

_____

_____

**5** You attempted to configure a LAN-to-LAN connection, but cannot see a specific network on one side of the connection. What is the most likely problem?

_____

_____

_____

**6** What routing protocol is used for Autodiscovery?

_____

_____

_____

**7** What is an identity certificate?

_____

_____

_____

**8** What is the advantage of using SCEP?

_____

_____

_____

**9** What are critical items when using any certificates?

_____

_____

_____

**10** Order the steps for using a certificate:

1. Issue an enrollment request.

2. Enroll with the CA.

3. The enrollment request is accepted.

4. Install the certificate.

5. Configure the concentrator to use the certificate.

_____

_____

_____

**11** You want to use SCEP to enroll an identity certificate. How must the associated CA certificate be obtained?

_____

_____

_____

**12** What are the default directory and file name for the DLL used with SCEP?

_____

_____

_____

**13** What are the three major steps involved in using digital certificates for a LAN-to-LAN connection?

_____

_____

_____

**14** When using an identity certificate, what is the affect of entering an incorrect name in the OU field?

_____

_____

_____

**15** What three key sizes may be used with DSA when installing certificates using SCEP?

_____

_____

_____

The answers to this quiz are listed in Appendix A, "Answers to the "Do I Know This Already?" Quizzes and Q&A Sections." The suggestions for your next steps, based on quiz results, are as follows:

- **1 on any quizlet**—Review the appropriate sections of the "Foundation Topics" section of this chapter, based on Table 10-1. Then proceed to the "Foundation Summary" section, the "Q&A" section, and then the scenarios at the end of the chapter.

- **9 or less overall score**—Read the entire chapter, including the "Foundation Topics" and "Foundation Summary" sections, the "Q&A" section, and the scenarios at the end of the chapter.

- **10–12 overall score**—Begin with the "Foundation Summary" section, continue with the "Q&A" section, and then the scenarios. If you have difficulty with a particular subject area, read the appropriate part in the "Foundation Topics" section.

- **13–15 overall score**—If you feel you need more review on these topics, go to the "Foundation Summary" section, the "Q&A" section, and then the scenarios. Otherwise, skip this chapter and go to the next chapter.

# Foundation Topics

## Overview of LAN-to-LAN VPN

**41**  Cisco VPN 3000 IPSec LAN-to-LAN

A LAN-to-LAN VPN is where two separate LANs are connected with a secure tunnel. This tunnel can use PPTP, L2TP, or IPSec. The purpose of the LAN-to-LAN VPN is to connect the two networks together seamlessly without compromising the integrity, authenticity, and confidentiality of the data. You can establish a LAN-to-LAN VPN through any combination of VPN Concentrators, routers, or firewalls.

LAN-to-LAN connections are designed to make each of the affected networks appear to be directly connected despite their physical distance from each other. Although this connection may travel through the Internet or a nontrusted network, you are assured of security because of the use of encryption on all packets traveling between these networks. The following section deals with the mechanics of configuring a LAN-to-LAN connection.

## LAN-to-LAN Configuration

**42**  LAN-to-LAN configuration

The LAN-to-LAN Wizard is an automated process that simplifies the task of connecting disparate LANs. However, to use the LAN-to-LAN Wizard, you must first have network lists configured. The following section provides the steps necessary to configure network lists before using the LAN-to-LAN Wizard.

### Configuring Network Lists

Generating network lists allows you to specify what traffic should be encrypted. The first task is to set the default gateway and the default tunnel gateway. In the example shown in Figure 10-2, the public interface is set to 192.168.1.2/24. The private interface is set to 172.16.1.2. Non-tunneled traffic will use the default gateway at 192.168.1.1. However, because you have checked the Override Default Gateway option, whenever you are using a tunnel, this will be your default gateway.

**Figure 10-2**  *Default Gateway*

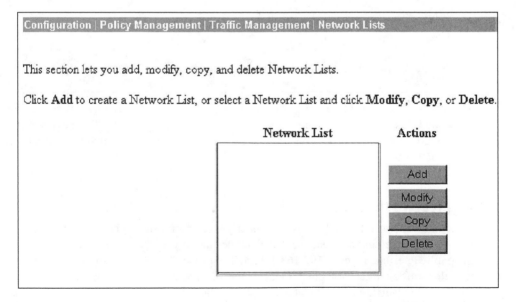

Next, set up your network list through the Configuration I Policy Management I Traffic
Management I Network Lists screen, shown in Figure 10-3. If you do not have any lists,
click **Add** to add a list. Otherwise, click the list and then click Modify, Copy, or Delete. You
must use a unique name for each list. You will need at least two networks lists: one for your
local network(s) and the other for the remote network(s).

**Figure 10-3**  *Configuration I Policy Management I Traffic Management I Network Lists*

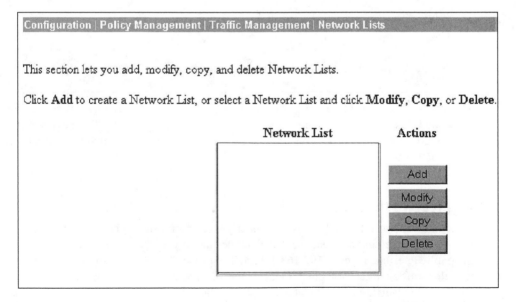

If you chose to modify an existing list, you will be taken to the Configuration I Policy Management I Traffic Management I Network Lists I Modify screen, as shown in Figure 10-4. Click a blank line within the Network List box. Next, enter the subnet and the wildcard mask in the following format: 192.168.1.0/0.0.0.255. The wildcard mask can be omitted if you want to use the default wildcard mask. Remember that a wildcard mask is different than a subnet mask. Enter as many networks as needed. Clicking the Generate Local List button on the bottom will create a list of all of the routing entries associated to the private interface. Make sure that you have at least two lists: one for the local networks and another for the remote networks.

**Figure 10-4** *Configuration | Policy Management | Traffic Management | Network Lists | Modify*

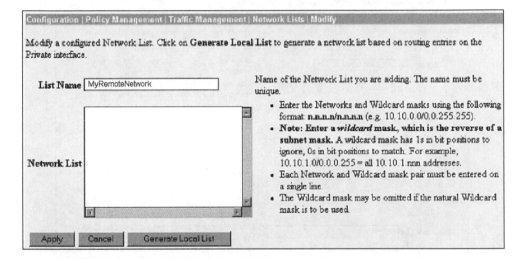

Network lists must be reflexive on opposite sides of the VPN connection. The networks listed as being "inside" on one concentrator should reflect those listed as "outside" on the other concentrator. Should a specific network be unreachable through a VPN connection, one of the first items to check is that the network lists on both sides show the "missing" network.

## Creating a Tunnel with the LAN-to-LAN Wizard

After you generate the network lists, you can use the LAN-to-LAN Wizard to create your tunnel. Modifying, adding, or deleting LAN-to-LAN connections is done through the Configuration I System I Tunneling Protocols I IPSec LAN-to-LAN I Modify screen, shown in Figure 10-5. (Actually, you are taken to either the Modify or the Add screen depending on whether you are modifying or creating a new connection. Both screens are identical except for the title.) Here, name the connection with the unique name **to_seattle**. Then, choose the interface, set the IP address of the peer, and choose to use preshared keys. You will send the entire certificate chain to the peer.

**Figure 10-5**   *Configuration | System | Tunneling Protocols | IPSec LAN-to-LAN | Modify*

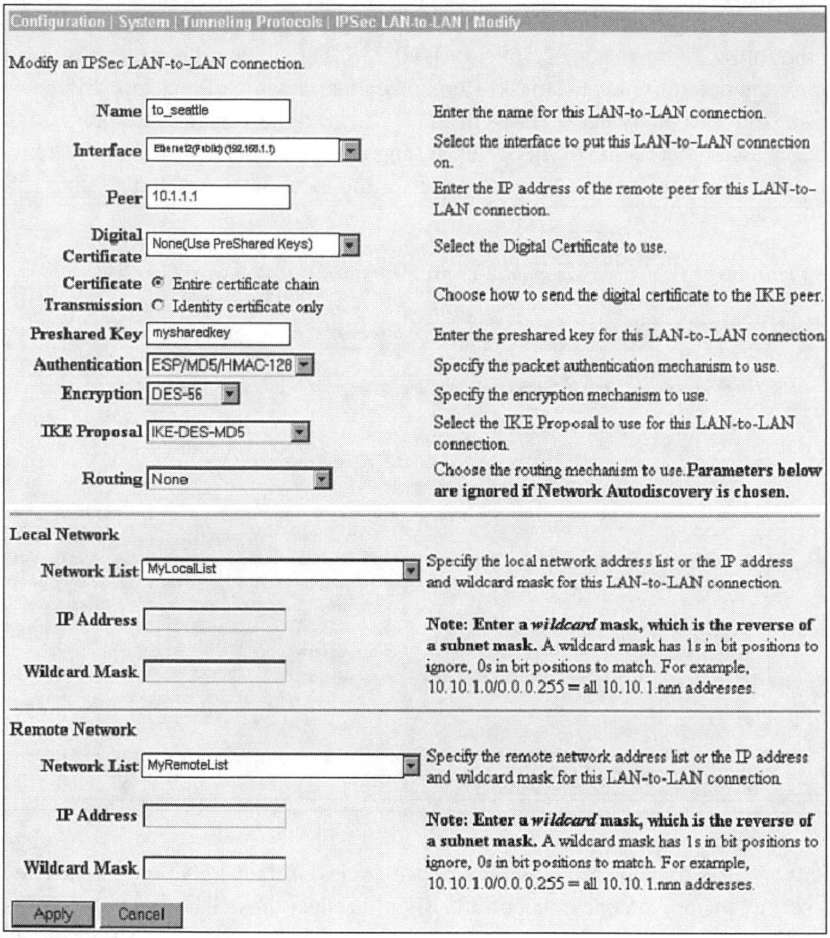

Set the preshared key to **mysharedkey**. Choose to use ESP/MD5/HMAC-128 packet authorization and set the encryption to DES-56. Use IKE-DES-MD5 for the IKE Proposal field and
choose None for the Routing field.

---

**NOTE**     The Configuration | System | Tunneling Protocols | IPSec LAN-to-LAN | Modify screen is one
of the most important screens within the VPN Concentrator configuration because you need to
make so many choices.

If you are using Certificates of Authority, discussed in the sections, "SCEP Support Overview"
and "Root Certificate Installation" later in this chapter, this screen is where you choose the
digital certificate to use. This example uses preshared keys. However, clicking the list on the
Digital Certificate field will show a list of existing certificates.

This screen is also where you choose whether to enable Network Auto discovery. Had you chosen Network Autodiscovery from the Network List drop-down menu, the system would have automatically generated a list of networks known by the remote peer. You still would see the bottom half of the screen, but any values within the bottom half would be ignored. Network Autodiscovery uses RIP to discover the networks attached to the Ethernet side of the concentrator. You must enable Inbound RIP RIPv2/v1 on the Ethernet interface on both concentrators. This is done on the Configuration | Interfaces screen.

The Configuration | System | Tunneling Protocols | IPSec LAN-to-LAN | Modify screen is also the "heart" of the connection process on the VPN Concentrator. You must access this screen any time a new connection is needed. You would do well to memorize the options on this screen.

---

On the bottom half of the screen, the local network list is shown, and then the remote network list is shown at the bottom. Alternatively, you could have used the IP address and wildcard mask for the local and remote connections. However, doing so means that only two single networks might be connected. If either side has more than a single network, the additional networks will not be reachable through this connection. Clicking the Apply button will bring you to a screen that verifies your configuration.

Using the menu system on the left, go to the Configuration | Policy Management | Traffic Management | Security Associations screen to see if you now have a new association. As shown in Figure 10-6, you should see the new association. This new association will appear at the bottom of the list. You can also use this screen to modify or delete an association.

**Figure 10-6**  *Configuration | Policy Management | Traffic Management | Security Associations*

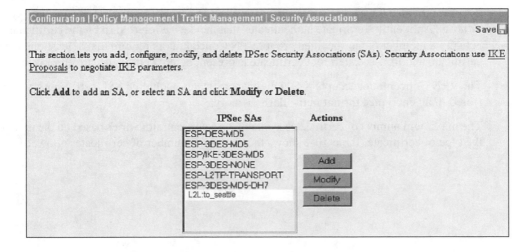

# SCEP Overview

**43** SCEP support overview

**44** Root certificate installation

**45** Identity certificate installation

Simple Certificate Enrollment Protocol (SCEP) is a protocol that eases your job as an administrator by enrolling devices with certificate authorities (CAs). The advantages of SCEP are that the job of the administrator are greatly simplified by removing much of the manual process previously required and added support for differing operating systems. Using SCEP enables the administrator to use certificates in much less time. Before you can understand SCEP, you first need to understand certificate management.

## Certificate Management

Digital certificates are used for authentication. Certificates are a form of identification issued by a CA. The role of a CA is to be the trusted authority who authenticates the certificates by "signing" the certificate.

A CA certificate is used to sign other certificates. A certificate signed by itself is called a *self-signing* or *root certificate*. When one certificate issues another, the issued certificate is referred to as a *subordinate certificate*.

A CA might also issue an identity certificate. Identity certificates are used on specific systems or hosts. An identity certificate authenticates that the device referred to by the certificate is actually a member of the specified group. VPN Concentrators require that at least one identity certificate and its associated root certificate is present before certificates are employed.

The VPN Concentrator accepts X.509 digital certificates, including SSL certificates, which are stored in an encrypted format in the flash memory.

The maximum number of certificates available on a concentrator varies based on the model and the type of certificate. Table 10-2 shows the maximum number of certificates allowed.

**Table 10-2**    *Maximum Certificates*

| Model | Certificate Limits |
|-------|--------------------|
| 3005 | Total of 6 root or subordinate certificates. |
| | Total of 2 identity certificates. |
| | Only a single SSL can be installed. |
| Other models | Total of 20 root or subordinate certificates. |
| | Total of 20 identity certificates. |
| | Only a single SSL can be installed. |

SCEP automates a number of the steps necessary under the manual process of enrolling a CA. Instead of manually specifying a large number of parameters, such as company name and IP address, SCEP sends the certificate server this information automatically after reading the data from within the concentrator's configuration.

SCEP can easily be used with the Cisco VPN Concentrators. SCEP allows administrators to easily obtain and maintain a CA. Since all CAs are sensitive to date and time, you should double-check that these are set correctly on both your server and your concentrator. NTP can be a valuable tool to overcome issues of disparate times and dates. IP connectivity is also required. Because filters and access lists can affect connections, ensure that the concentrator can communicate with the server before attempting to generate a certificate.

# Root Certificate Installation via SCEP

Three steps must be accomplished to use any certificate, as follows:

**Step 1**    Enroll the VPN Concentrator with the CA.

**Step 2**    A certificate server issues and accepts an enrollment request.

**Step 3**    Configure the concentrator to use the certificate.

The following sections elaborate on each step.

## Enrolling the Concentrator

The first step in generating a CA certificate via SCEP is to enroll the VPN Concentrator with a CA. If you want to use SCEP for enrolling identity or SSL certificates, the associated CA certificate must also be obtained by using SCEP.

To install a certificate on a VPN Concentrator, start off on the Administration I Certificate Management screen, as shown in Figure 10-7. On this screen, choose **Click here to install a CA certificate** to start the process of generating a certificate.

**Figure 10-7** *Administration | Certificate Management*

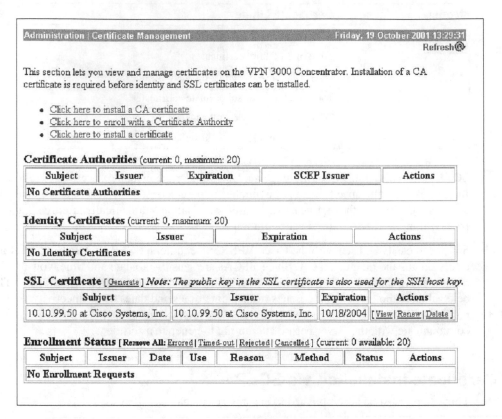

Should a certificate already be present on the concentrator, the option to install a CA certificate is not available. Instead, you will choose the **Click here to install a certificate** option. In either case, you will be brought to the Administration | Certificate Management | Install | CA Certificate screen, as shown in Figure 10-8.

Here, choose the SCEP (Simple Certificate Enrollment Protocol) option, which in turn brings you to the Administration | Certificate Management | Install | CA Certificate | SCEP screen, as shown in Figure 10-9.

**Figure 10-8**  *Administration | Certificate Management | Install | CA Certificate*

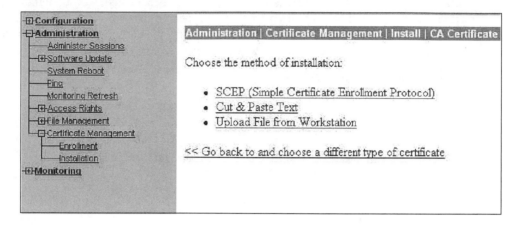

**Figure 10-9**  *Administration | Certificate Management | Install | CA Certificate | SCEP*

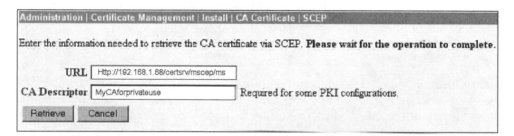

On the Administration | Certificate Management | Install | CA Certificate | SCEP screen, you first enter the URL address of the machine containing the Dynamic Link Library (DLL) in order to retrieve the certificate. This URL might be either a website containing the DLL or a certificate server containing the DLL. The URL consists of the IP address, followed by the directory name and the name of the DLL itself. By default, the directory is named certsrv/mscep and the DLL is named mscep.dll. You must have the certsrv directory shared and have sufficient rights to access this directory.

Next, enter the name you want the certificate to be called. In this case, myCAforprivateuse is the certificate name. Click the Retrieve button to install the CA certificate on the VPN Concentrator. You are automatically transferred back to the Administration | Certificate Management screen.

Check the Administration | Certificate Management screen to ensure that the certificate appears (see Figure 10-10). This might take a few minutes before being listed, so you might need to refresh the screen a number of times before it will appear. If the certificate does not get listed, make sure that there is connectivity to the server and that you have the correct permissions to access the DLL. Clicking the Click here to install a certificate option will install the certificate.

**Figure 10-10** *Administration | Certificate Management*

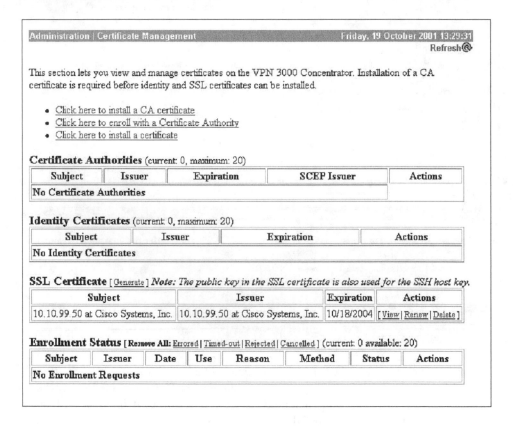

## Identity Certificate Installation Via SCEP

While on the Administration | Certificate Management screen, choose **Click here to enroll a with Certificate Authority**. You will be transferred to the Administration | Certificate Management | Enroll screen. Choose **Identity certificate**. As shown in Figure 10-11, this is also where you will go should you choose to use an SSL certificate.

**Figure 10-11**  *Administration | Certificate Management | Enroll*

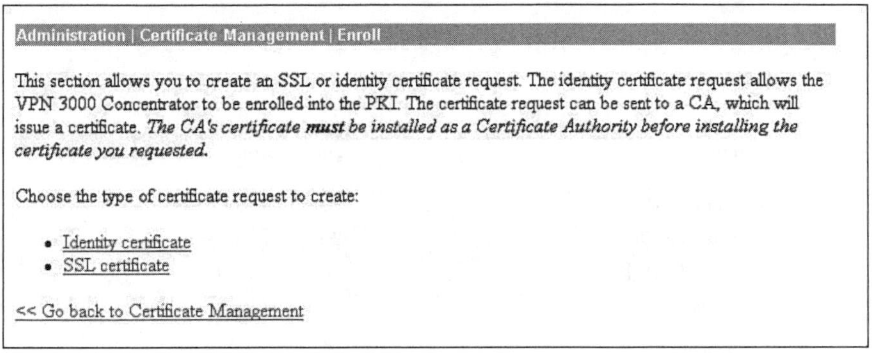

The Administration | Certificate Management | Enroll | Identity Certificate screen is next, shown in Figure 10-12. The title links shown in this screen are dependant upon the text entered in the previous screen. This screen will list all the SCEP certificates obtained. Choose the CA you want to install. This brings you to the Identity Certificate Screen.

**Figure 10-12**  *Administration | Certificate Management | Enroll | Identity Certificate*

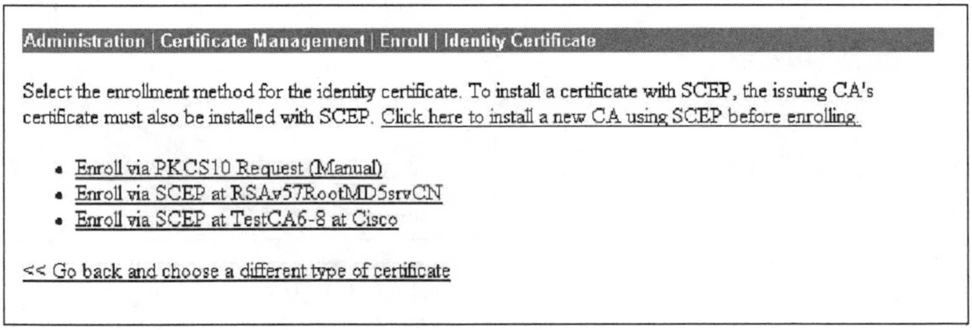

First, fill out the enrollment screen. As shown in Figure 10-13, a large number of variables exist. Table 10-3 addresses these variables.

**Figure 10-13**  *Administration | Certificate Management | Enroll | Identity Certificate | SCEP*

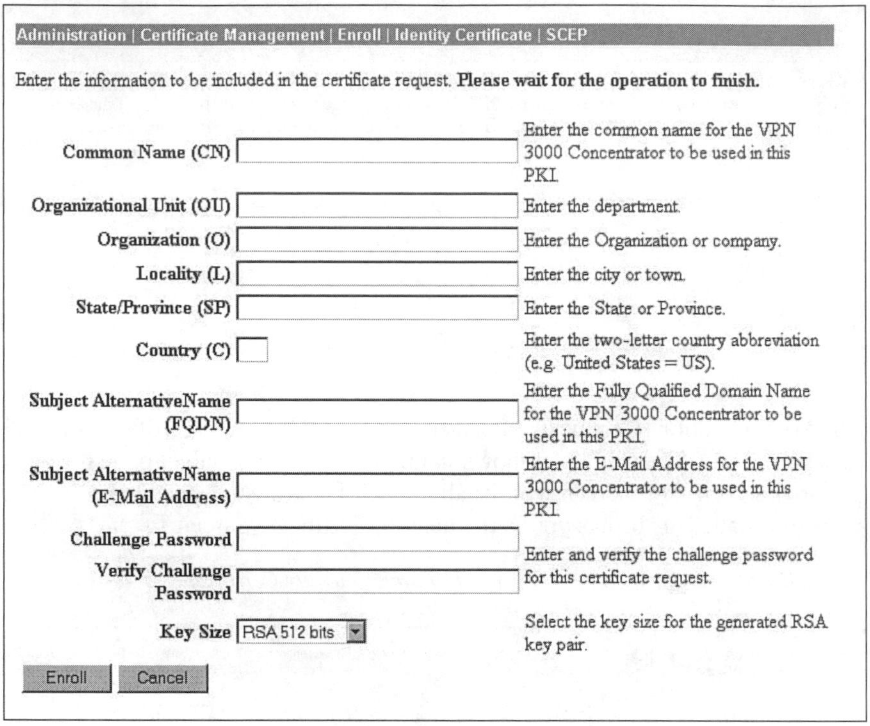

**Table 10-3**  *Enrollment Variables*

| Field | Explanation |
|---|---|
| Common Name (CN) | The identity associated with the certificate. This is a mandatory field. If you are using an SSL certificate, the IP address or domain name used to connect to the VPN Concentrator is entered. |
| Organizational Unit (OU) | The OU should match the IPSec group name. Using a different name than the IPSec group will mean that the IPSec group used will not have any access. |
| Organization (O) | Usually the organization's well-known and common name. Examples: Cisco Press and Widget Corporation of America. |
| Locality (L) | Where the VPN is physically located. Although there is not a specific requirement, by convention, the city name where the concentrator is located is entered. Example: London. |

**Table 10-3**    *Enrollment Variables (Continued)*

| Field | Explanation |
|---|---|
| State/Province (SP) | The state or province. You should spell out the entire state name. |
| Country (C) | The country is entered here. The two-character country code must conform to the ISO 3166 country codes. |
| Subject Alternative Name (FQDN) | Enter the FQDN (Fully Qualified Domain Name) here. For example: vpn3000.ciscopress.com. |
| Subject Alternative Name (E-mail Address) | Generally used for contacting the system administrator. This field is also used for connecting between the concentrator and a Cisco router or PIX firewall. |
| Challenge Password | Used when the certificate issuer requires a challenge password. |
| Verify Challenge Password | The password is entered twice to ensure that is was entered correctly. |
| Key Size | Sets the size of the key used by RSA with SCEP. Possible values are<br><br>• RSA 512 bits<br><br>• RSA 768 bits<br><br>• RSA 1024 bits<br><br>• RSA 2048 bits<br><br>The key sizes when using DSA are<br><br>• DSA 512 bits<br><br>• DSA 768 bits<br><br>• DSA 1024 bits |

Your concentrator will go into a polling state, waiting for the CA server to issue the certificate, as shown in Figure 10-14. On most certificate servers, issuing a certificate is a manual process. Therefore, contact the administrator for the certificate server and request that the certificate be issued.

After the certificate administrator has issued the certificate, check the Administration | Certificate Management screen. The certificate will appear under the Identity Certificates section.

**Figure 10-14** *SCEP Polling State*

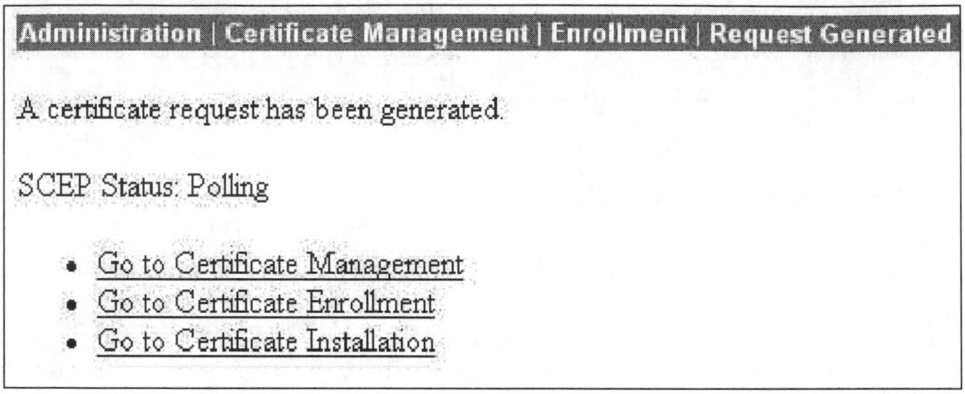

```
┌─────────────────────────────────────────────────────────────────────┐
│ Administration | Certificate Management | Enrollment | Request Generated │
│                                                                       │
│ A certificate request has been generated.                            │
│                                                                       │
│ SCEP Status: Polling                                                 │
│                                                                       │
│   • Go to Certificate Management                                     │
│   • Go to Certificate Enrollment                                     │
│   • Go to Certificate Installation                                   │
│                                                                       │
└─────────────────────────────────────────────────────────────────────┘
```

## Configuring VPN Concentrator for LAN-to-LAN with Digital Certificates

You have already learned how to set up a LAN-to-LAN connection and how to obtain digital certificates. This section discusses how to use digital certificates with a LAN-to-LAN connection.

Three basic steps are required for using digital certificates in a LAN-to-LAN connection:

**Step 1**   Activate an IKE proposal.

**Step 2**   Configure the LAN-to-LAN connection to use the IKE proposal.

**Step 3**   Configure the LAN-to-LAN connection to use the Identity Certificate.

Because you already have your digital certificates, configure your LAN-to-LAN connection and enable it to use your digital certificates. The first step is to go to the Configuration | System | Tunneling Protocols | IPSec LAN-to-LAN screen, as shown in Figure 10-15. Choose an existing connection or create a new connection.

**Figure 10-15** *Configuration | System | Tunneling Protocols | IPSec LAN-to-LAN*

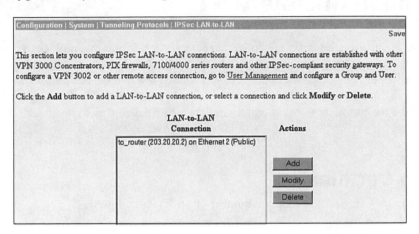

You are taken to the Configuration | System | Tunneling Protocols | IPSec LAN-to-LAN >Modify screen. In this screen, you click the **Digital Certificate** drop-down menu and choose **digital certificate**.

On the Certificate Transmission option, you have a choice. If you want to send only the Identity Certificate to the peer, choose Identity certificate only. Choosing Entire certificate chain sends the root and any subordinate certificates to the peer.

Click the **IKE Proposal** drop-down menu. You will receive a list of all the active IKE proposals. Choose the appropriate proposal. Click the **Modify** (or **Add**) button. You will be returned to the Configuration | System | Tunneling Protocols | IPSec LAN-to-LAN screen, as previously shown in Figure 10-15.

You are now using digital certificates for our LAN-to-LAN connection.

# Foundation Summary

The Foundation Summary is a collection of tables and figures that provides a convenient review of many key concepts in this chapter. For those who are already comfortable with the topics in this chapter, this summary could help you recall a few details. For those who just read this chapter, this review should help solidify some key facts. For anyone doing final preparation before the exam, these tables and figures are a convenient way to review the day before the exam.

## Maximum Certificates

Table 10-4 shows the maximum number of certificates allowed.

**Table 10-4**   *Maximum Certificates*

| Model | Certificate Limits |
|---|---|
| 3005 | Total of 6 root or subordinate certificates. Total of 2 identity certificates. Only a single SSL can be installed. |
| Other models | Total of 20 root or subordinate certificates. Total of 20 Identity Certificates. Only a single SSL can be installed. |

## Enrollment Variables

Table 10-5 explains the enrollment variables that you will see in the Enrollment screen.

**Table 10-5**   *Enrollment Variables*

| Field | Explanation |
|---|---|
| Common Name (CN) | The identity associated with the certificate. This is a mandatory field. If you are using an SSL certificate, the IP address or domain name used to connect to the VPN Concentrator is entered. |
| Organizational Unit (OU) | The OU should match the IPSec group name. Using a different name than the IPSec group will mean that the IPSec group used will not have any access. |
| Organization (O) | Usually the organization's well-known and common name. Examples: Cisco Press and Widget Corporation of America. |

**Table 10-5**    *Enrollment Variables (Continued)*

| Field | Explanation |
|---|---|
| Locality (L) | Where the VPN is physically located. Although there is not a specific requirement, by convention, the city name where the concentrator is located is entered. Example: London. |
| State/Province (SP) | The state or province. You should spell out the entire state name. |
| Country (C) | The country is entered here. The two-character country code must conform to the ISO 3166 country codes. |
| Subject Alternative Name (FQDN) | Enter the FQDN (Fully Qualified Domain Name) here. For example: vpn3000.ciscopress.com. |
| Subject Alternative Name (Email Address) | Generally used for contacting the system administrator. This field is also used for connecting between the concentrator and A Cisco router or PIX firewall. |
| Challenge Password | Used when the certificate issuer requires a challenge password. |
| Verify Challenge Password | The password is entered twice in order to ensure that is was entered correctly. |
| Key Size | Sets the size of the key used by RSA. Possible values are<br><br>• RSA 512 bits<br><br>• RSA 768 bits<br><br>• RSA 1024 bits<br><br>• RSA 2048 bits<br><br>The key sizes when using DSA are<br><br>• DSA 512 bits<br><br>• DSA 768 bits<br><br>• DSA 1024 bits |

## Chapter Glossary

The following term was introduced in this chapter or has special significance to the topics within this chapter.

**Network Autodiscovery**   A process used on VPN Concentrators to discover networks connected to the remote concentrator. Network Autodiscovery relies on RIP to discover networks.

# Q&A

As mentioned in Chapter 1, these questions are more difficult than what you should experience on the CCSP exam. The questions do not attempt to cover more breadth or depth than the exam; however, the questions are designed to make sure you know the answer. Rather than allowing you to derive the answer from clues hidden inside the question itself, your understanding and recall of the subject are challenged. Questions from the "Do I Know This Already?" quiz from the beginning of the chapter are repeated here to ensure that you have mastered the chapter's topic areas. Hopefully, these questions will help limit the number of exam questions on which you narrow your choices to two options and guess!

1  What is a LAN-to-LAN connection?

2  What equipment is required for a LAN-to-LAN connection?

3  Where can a LAN-to-LAN connection be used?

4  When setting up network lists, how should the lists at each side of the LAN-to-LAN connection relate to each other?

5  You attempted to configure a LAN-to-LAN connection, but cannot see a specific network on one side of the connection. What is the most likely problem?

**6** What routing protocol is used for Autodiscovery?

_____

_____

_____

**7** What is an identity certificate?

_____

_____

_____

**8** What is the advantage of using SCEP?

_____

_____

_____

**9** What are critical items when using any certificates?

_____

_____

_____

**10** Order the steps for using a certificate:

   1. Issue an enrollment request.

   2. Enroll with the CA.

   3. The enrollment request is accepted.

   4. Install the certificate.

   5. Configure the concentrator to use the certificate.

_____

_____

_____

**11** You want to use SCEP to enroll an identity certificate. How must the associated CA certificate be obtained?

_____

_____

_____

**12** What are the default directory and file name for the DLL used with SCEP?

_____

_____

_____

**13** What are the three major steps involved in using digital certificates for a LAN-to-LAN connection?

_____

_____

_____

**14** When using an identity certificate, what is the affect of entering an incorrect name in the OU field?

_____

_____

_____

**15** What three key sizes may be used with DSA when installing certificates using SCEP?

_____

_____

_____

**16** What screen is used to configure Network Autodiscovery?

_____

_____

_____

**17** You have two VPN Concentrators—one in Seattle, the other in London—used for connecting the two offices through VPNs. The Seattle office cannot reach one subnet attached to the London office. You have checked your network lists on the Seattle concentrator. You are sure that the "missing" network is properly configured. What is the most likely problem?

_____

_____

_____

18  You are using Network Autodiscovery. You do not see a single remote network that is connected through a series of routers to your remote concentrator. Where should your troubleshooting efforts be directed?

_____

_____

_____

19  You are using SCEP. Your junior assistant has configured the system. You have established a VPN connection to the remote site, but your remote group does not have access to your network. What is a probable cause?

_____

_____

_____

20  You are using SCEP. You are trying to enroll a certificate. Your concentrator shows that it is polling. It has been in this state for over an hour. What is the most likely cause?

_____

_____

_____

21  What screen is used to determine the IKE proposal used for a LAN-to-LAN connection?

_____

_____

_____

22  What is the purpose of the challenge password on the Administration | Certificate Management | Enroll | Identity Certificate | SCEP screen?

_____

_____

_____

23  You wish to use Network Autodiscovery because it sounds easier. How are the networks learned and how do you ensure that only specific networks are included?

_____

_____

_____

**24**  What are the differences between a root certificate, a subordinate certificate, and an identity certificate?

_____

_____

_____

**25**  What are the maximum numbers of certificates that may be used on concentrators?

_____

_____

_____

# CHAPTER 11

# Scenarios

The following scenarios and questions are designed to draw together the content of the book and exercise your understanding of the concepts. There might be more than one correct answer. The thought process and practice in manipulating each concept in the scenario are the goals of this chapter.

## Example Corporation

The Value-Packed Nutrition Corporation has a growing VPN infrastructure, as shown in Figure 11-1. The scenarios in this chapter are based on the elements shown in this diagram.

**Figure 11-1** *Value-Packed Nutrition Corporation*

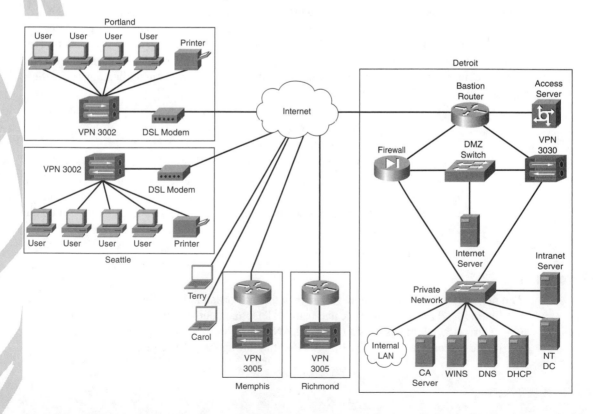

# Site Descriptions

The following sections describe the characteristics of the VPN environment at the Detroit, Portland, Seattle, Memphis, and Richmond sites and for the two user types represented by Terry and Carol.

## Detroit

Detroit is the central headquarters for Value-Packed Nutrition Corporation. All IPSec connections from branch offices and mobile users are through the Cisco VPN 3030 Concentrator in Detroit. VPN IPSec tunnels from remote sites and users all connect to the VPN 3030 Concentrator. A variety of corporate resources are available in Detroit's private network, including DHCP, DNS, CA (SCEP support), and Windows 2000 Directory Services. An access server is available to support employees when they come to Detroit for business meetings. DHCP is to be used to assign all IPSec endpoint IP addresses, with unique address ranges being used for each location. Detroit's private network IP addresses fall within the 172.16.0.0 subnet.

## Portland

Portland's four users connect to the network through a Cisco VPN 3002 Hardware Client equipped with an internal Ethernet 8-port switch. These users require numerous resources on the Internet as well as a local connection to a shared network printer. The VPN connection to Detroit is a remote access connection using digital signatures. Detroit has chosen to perform user authentication for the Portland office using the 3030's internal authentication server. Set up the 3002 for Network Extension mode.

## Seattle

Seattle is much like Portland, except that the users in Seattle do not use resources on the Internet. The users also require access to local LAN resources. The 3002 Hardware Client here also has an internal 8-port switch, but the remote access connection is authenticated using preshared keys. Seattle users are also authenticated using the 3030's internal server. Set up the 3002 for Client Extension mode.

## Memphis

The network at Memphis is more robust than that at Portland or Seattle. Users require use of the Internet and must be authenticated using NT Domain authentication. The VPN 3005 Concentrator at Memphis uses a LAN-to-LAN connection and is authenticated with digital certificates. Secure all traffic except HTTP traffic through the IPSec tunnel.

## Richmond

Richmond is the same as Memphis, with the exception that the LAN-to-LAN connection's authentication is through preshared keys.

## Terry and Carol

Terry and Carol represent 30 salespeople that connect through a national ISP. These salespersons use the Cisco VPN Client, and a mixture of digital certificates and preshared keys is used for device authentication. User authentication for the preshared key users is through the 3030's internal authentication server. Detroit is converting these users to digital certificates, Zone Labs' ZoneAlarm Pro client firewall, and NT Domain authentication; to date, 20 users have been converted, including Terry. Original system users, such as Carol, are currently using the Cisco Integrated Client (CIC) firewall. Terry will use Are You There (AYT) firewall policy. Carol will use Central Protection Policy (CPP) firewall policy.

Use the information contained in the descriptions of the various locations and users to complete the requirements of the following scenarios.

# Scenario 11-1—The Basics

Determine the additional information that you need to configure the systems based on the information provided in the following sections.

## IKE Policy

Identify the parameters that you need to configure the IKE policy required for each site and user type. These parameters are as follows:

- 168-bit encryption
- 128-bit hashing algorithm
- VPN peer and user authentication as described for each branch or user:
    - Portland
    - Seattle
    - Memphis
    - Richmond
    - Terry
    - Carol
- 1024-bit key exchange
- Default IKE SA lifetime

## IPSec Policy

Identify the parameters that you need to configure the IPSec policy required for each site and user type. These parameters are as follows:

- The IPSec protocol, which provides encryption
- 128-bit hashing algorithm
- 168-bit encryption
- SA to be established by IKE
- Identify the traffic to be protected for each site:
  - Portland
  - Seattle
  - Memphis
  - Richmond
  - Terry
  - Carol
- Select a unique IP address subnet for each site for DHCP address assignment:
  - Portland
  - Seattle
  - Memphis
  - Richmond
  - Terry and other digital certificate users
  - Carol and other preshared key users

# Scenario 11-2—Portland

Configure the Detroit VPN 3030 Concentrator and the Portland VPN 3002 Hardware Client to support the Portland users.

# Scenario 11-3—Seattle

Configure the Detroit VPN 3030 Concentrator and the Seattle VPN 3002 Hardware Client to support the Seattle users.

# Scenario 11-4—Memphis

Configure the Detroit and Memphis VPN concentrators to support the Memphis users.

# Scenario 11-5—Richmond

Configure the Detroit and Richmond VPN concentrators to support the Richmond users.

# Scenario 11-6—Terry and Carol

Configure the Detroit VPN concentrator and Terry and Carol's VPN Client to provide the required access.

# Scenario Answers

The answers provided in this section are not necessarily the only correct answers. They merely represent one possibility for each scenario. The intention is to test your basic knowledge and understanding of the concepts that were discussed in this chapter.

Should your answers be different (as they likely will be), consider the differences. Are your answers in line with the concepts of the answers provided and explained here? If not, reread the chapter, focusing on the sections that are related to the problem scenario.

# Scenario 11-1 Answers

The additional information that you need to configure the systems is described in the following sections.

## IKE Policy

The parameters that are needed to configure the IKE policy required for each site and user type are as follows:

- **3DES**—168-bit encryption
- **MD5**—128-bit hashing algorithm (use the HMAC variant)
- VPN peer and user authentication as described for each branch or user:
  - **Portland**—RSA signatures for VPN peer authentication and VPN 3030 internal authentication for users
  - **Seattle**—Preshared keys for VPN peer authentication and VPN 3030 internal authentication for users
  - **Memphis**—RSA signatures for VPN peer authentication and NT Domain for user authentication
  - **Richmond**—Preshared keys for VPN peer authentication and NT Domain for user authentication
  - **Terry**—RSA signatures for VPN peer authentication and NT Domain for user authentication
  - **Carol**—Preshared keys for VPN peer authentication and VPN 3030 internal authentication for users
- **Diffie-Hellman 2**—1024-bit key exchange
- **86,400 seconds** for IKE SA lifetime

## IPSec Policy

The parameters needed to configure the IPSec policy required for each site and user type are as follows:

- **ESP**—The IPSec protocol that provides encryption
- **MD5**—128-bit hashing algorithm
- **3DES**—168-bit encryption
- SA established by IKE
- Traffic to be protected for each site:
    - **Portland**—Only traffic destined for internal network addresses
    - **Seattle**—All traffic
    - **Memphis**—All traffic except HTTP
    - **Richmond**—All traffic except HTTP
    - **Terry**—Only traffic destined for internal network addresses
    - **Carol**—Only traffic destined for internal network addresses
- Possible unique IP address subnets for each site for DHCP address assignment are as follows:
    - **Portland**—192.168.20.1 to 192.168.20.20
    - **Seattle**—192.168.30.1 to 192.168.30.20
    - **Memphis**—192.168.40.1 to 192.168.40.200
    - **Richmond**—192.168.50.1 to 192.168.50.200
    - **Terry and other digital certificate users**—192.168.60.1 to 192.168.60.50
    - **Carol and other preshared key users**—192.168.70.1 to 192.168.70.50

# Scenario 11-2 Answers

The configurations required to support the Portland users are described in the following sections.

## Detroit VPN 3030 Concentrator and Router (Generic for All)

Configure the following settings and attributes on the Detroit router and VPN 3030 Concentrator to support all the sites and users:

1    On the Detroit Bastion router, configure an ACL that permits the IPSec ports and protocols, specifically UDP port 500 for ISAKMP, protocol 50 for ESP, and protocol 51 for AH.

2 On the 3030, obtain the root CA certificate from the Detroit CA using SCEP. Remember that you must install the root CA certificate first and that you must use SCEP to do that if you want to use SCEP for subsequent identity or SSL certificates from that CA.

3 Enroll the 3030 with the Detroit CA server using SCEP to install the 3030's identity certificate.

4 On the Configuration I System I Servers I Authentication screen, add Internal and SDI server types, using the IP address of Detroit's CA server for the address of the SDI server.

5 On the Configuration I System I Address Management I Assignment screen, select Use DHCP for client IP address assignment.

6 Change the password for the admin user.

7 Configure the 3030's base group as follows:

— No restrictions on access hours.

— 1 simultaneous login.

— 8 characters for a minimum password length.

— Disable alphabetic-only passwords.

— Establish 60 minutes as the idle timeout.

— Enter the DNS and WINS servers' IP addresses.

— Select IPSec for the tunneling protocol.

— If the VPN 3030 Concentrator has SEP modules (not specified for these scenarios), identify which SEP modules this group can use.

— Select **ESP/IKE-3DES-MD5** for the IPSEC SA.

— Ensure that IKE Keepalives are enabled.

— Select **Required** for IKE Peer Identity Validation.

## Detroit VPN 3030 Concentrator for Portland

Configure these attributes on Detroit's VPN 3030 Concentrator to support the Portland users:

1 Create a new group specifically for Portland:

— Use a descriptive name for the group such as Portland-LAN-to-LAN.

— Use a generic password.

— Select Internal authentication for remote access users.

— Select tunnel type Remote Access.

— Enable split tunneling and only tunnel addresses in the Detroit network.

2  Add Portland's users to the internal database. All of these users should be in the Portland-LAN-to-LAN group.

3  Configure a static route to point 192.168.20.0 toward the Portland VPN 3002 Hardware Client.

# Portland VPN 3002 Hardware Client

Configure the following attributes on Portland's VPN 3002 Hardware Client to support the Portland users:

1  Configure the public interface for a static address or a DHCP address, depending on the requirements of the Portland ISP.

2  Because Portland uses a digital subscriber line (DSL) modem, configure the Point-to-Point Protocol (PPP) over Ethernet (PPPoE) username and password on the public interface. You can obtain these from the Portland ISP.

3  Configure a default route from the 3002 to the 3030. This can be the same address as the default gateway for the VPN 3002 Hardware Client.

4  Change the default IP address of the private interface from 192.168.10.1 to 192.168.20.100 (or some other address outside of the DHCP range of addresses for this subnet).

5  Disable PAT under Configuration | Policy Management. Disabling PAT enables Network Extension mode. You cannot disable PAT until you have changed the IP address of the private interface.

6  On the Configuration | System | IP Routing | DHCP screen, verify that DHCP is disabled on the private interface.

7  On the Configuration | System | Tunneling Protocols | IPSec screen, enter the IP address of Detroit's VPN 3030 Concentrator. Check the **Use Certificate** box. You only need to send the identity certificate because both VPN devices use the same root CA server. You do not need to enter a group or username because you will be using digital certificates for authentication.

8  Install root and identity certificates from Detroit's CA server (after you have configured the public interface on the VPN 3002 Hardware Client).

9  Because the 3002 has an internal switch, you do not need to do anything to share the local printer.

10  Change the password for the admin user.

# Scenario 11-3 Answers

The configurations required to support the Seattle users are described in the following sections.

## Detroit VPN 3030 Concentrator for Seattle

Configure these attributes on Detroit's VPN 3030 Concentrator to support the Seattle users:

1 Create a new group specifically for Seattle, as follows:

— Use a descriptive name for the group, such as Seattle-LAN-to-LAN.

— Use a generic password.

— Select Internal Authentication.

— Select tunnel type Remote Access.

— Enable split tunneling and only tunnel addresses in the Detroit network.

2 Add Seattle's users to the internal database. All of these users should be in the Seattle-LAN-to-LAN group.

3 Create a separate user to be used by the VPN 3002 Hardware Client during IKE Phase 1 negotiations with the VPN 3030 Concentrator. This user should also be in the Seattle-LAN-to-LAN group.

4 Configure a static route to point 192.168.30.0 toward the Seattle VPN 3002 Hardware Client.

## Seattle VPN 3002 Hardware Client

Configure the following attributes on Seattle's VPN 3002 Hardware Client to support the Seattle users:

1 Configure the public interface for a static address or a DHCP address, depending on the requirements of the Seattle ISP.

2 Because Seattle uses a DSL modem, configure the Point-to-Point Protocol over Ethernet (PPPoE) username and password on the public interface. You can obtain these from the Seattle ISP.

3 Configure a default route from the 3002 to the 3030. This can be the same address as the default gateway for the VPN 3002 Hardware Client.

4 Change the default IP address of the private interface from 192.168.10.1 to 192.168.30.100 (or some other address outside of the DHCP range of addresses for this subnet).

5 Enable PAT under Configuration | Policy Management. Enabling PAT enables Client Extension mode.

**6** On the Configuration I System I IP Routing I DHCP screen, verify that DHCP is disabled on the private interface.

**7** On the Configuration I System I Tunneling Protocols I IPSec screen, enter the IP address of Detroit's VPN 3030 Concentrator. Be sure to uncheck the Use Certificate box. Enter the Seattle-LAN-to-LAN group name and password (this combination becomes the preshared key for authentication purposes). Enter the username and password of the unique user you created on the VPN 3030 Concentrator for IKE Phase 1 negotiations.

**8** Because the 3002 has an internal switch, you do not need to do anything to share the local printer.

**9** Change the password for the admin user.

# Scenario 11-4 Answers

The configurations required to support the Memphis users are described in the following sections.

## Detroit VPN 3030 Concentrator for Memphis

Configure the following attributes on Detroit's VPN 3030 Concentrator to support the Memphis users:

**1** Assign a static IP for the Memphis 3005 Concentrator.

**2** On the Configuration I System I Tunneling Protocols I IPSec LAN-to-LAN screen, add a connection to Memphis using the IP address of the Memphis VPN 3005 Concentrator. Select to use digital certificates, and select the VPN 3030's identity certificate to use for authentication.

**3** Configure a static route to point 192.168.40.0 toward the Memphis VPN 3005 Concentrator.

## Memphis VPN 3005 Concentrator and Router

Configure the following attributes on Memphis's VPN 3005 Concentrator and router to support the Memphis users:

**1** On the Memphis router, configure an ACL that permits the IPSec ports and protocols, specifically UDP port 500 for ISAKMP, protocol 50 for ESP, and protocol 51 for AH.

**2** On the Memphis VPN 3005 Concentrator, install root and identity certificates.

**3** Assign a static IP for Detroit's 3030 Concentrator.

484 Chapter 11: Scenarios

4 Configure IPSec LAN-to-LAN under Tunneling Protocols. Be sure to set this to use digital certificates using only the identity certificate of the Memphis 3005 Concentrator. Use the IP address of the Detroit VPN 3030 Concentrator for the peer address.

# Scenario 11-5 Answers

The configurations required to support the Richmond users are described in the following sections.

## Detroit VPN 3030 Concentrator for Richmond

Configure the following attributes on Detroit's VPN 3030 Concentrator to support the Richmond users:

1 Assign a static IP for Richmond's 3005 Concentrator.

2 On the Configuration | System | Tunneling Protocols | IPSec LAN-to-LAN screen, add a connection to Richmond using the IP address of the Richmond VPN 3005 Concentrator and selecting a preshared key to use for authentication.

3 Configure a static route to point 192.168.50.0 toward the Richmond VPN 3005 Concentrator.

## Richmond VPN 3005 Concentrator and Router

Configure the following attributes on Richmond's VPN 3005 Concentrator and router to support the Richmond users:

1 On the Richmond router, configure an ACL that permits the IPSec ports and protocols, specifically UDP port 500 for ISAKMP, protocol 50 for ESP, and protocol 51 for AH.

2 On the Richmond VPN 3005 Concentrator, assign a static IP for Detroit's 3030 Concentrator.

3 Configure IPSec LAN-to-LAN under Tunneling Protocols. Be sure to set this to use preshared keys, using the key you created on Detroit's VPN 3030 Concentrator.

# Scenario 11-6 Answers

The configurations required to support Terry and Carol are described in the following sections.

## Detroit VPN 3030 Concentrator for Terry and Similar Users

Configure the following attributes on Detroit's VPN 3030 Concentrator to support Terry and similar users:

1 Create a new group for users like Terry who will be using digital certificates.

— Use a descriptive name for the group, such as Remote-Digital-Certificates.

— Use a generic password.

— Select NT Domain authentication.

2 Select tunnel type Remote Access.Select **Firewall Required**, and select **Zone Labs ZoneAlarm Pro** as the firewall type.

3 Select AYT firewall policy.

4 Create a floppy disk for Terry with root and identity certificates. (You must enroll Terry's system.)

5 Configure a static route to point 192.168.60.0 out toward the Internet cloud.

## Terry VPN Client and Browser

Configure the following attributes on Terry's VPN Client and browser:

1 Install the root and identity certificates into the browser.

2 Configure the connection to Detroit to use the newly installed identity certificate.

## Detroit VPN 3030 Concentrator for Carol and Similar Users

Configure the following attributes on Detroit's VPN 3030 Concentrator to support Carol and similar users:

1 Create a new group for users like Carol, who will be using preshared keys.

— Use a descriptive name for the group, such as Remote-Preshared-Keys.

— Use a generic password.

— Select Internal authentication.

2 Select tunnel type Remote Access. Select **Firewall Required**, and select **Cisco Client Integrated Firewall** as the firewall type.

3 Select CPP firewall policy and define the policy.

4 Add Carol as a user to the internal authentication database by supplying a username and password. You must do this for all users like Carol.

5 Configure a static route to point 192.168.70.0 out toward the Internet cloud.

## Carol VPN Client and Browser

Configure the following attributes on Carol's VPN Client and browser:

1 Configure the VPN Client on Carol's system to use the Remote-Preshared-Keys group and password as the preshared key for establishing the VPN connection to Detroit's VPN 3030 Concentrator.

# Answers to the "Do I Know This Already?" Quizzes and Q&A Sections

## Chapter 2—Do I Know This Already?

**1** Which Cisco hardware product families support IPSec VPN technology?

**Cisco IOS routers, PIX Firewalls, and VPN 3000 Series Concentrators, including the VPN 3002 Hardware Client, support IPSec VPN technology.**

**2** What are the two IPSec protocols?

**The two IPSec protocols are Authentication Header (AH) and Encapsulating Security Payload (ESP).**

**3** Which type of VPNs use a combination of the same infrastructures that are used by the other two types of VPNs?

**Business-to-business, or extranet, VPNs use a combination of the same infrastructures that are used by remote access and intranet VPNs.**

**4** Which of the Cisco VPN 3000 Series Concentrators is a fixed-configuration device?

**The Cisco VPN 3005 Concentrator is a fixed-configuration system that supports up to 100 simultaneous sessions.**

**5** What key element is contained in the AH or ESP packet header?

**The key element contained in each protocol's header is the Security Parameters Index (SPI), giving the destination peer the information that it needs to authenticate and decrypt the packet.**

**6** What are the two modes of operation for AH and ESP?

**AH and ESP use Transport and Tunnel modes. In Transport mode, the original IP packet header is left intact and is not protected by IPSec. In Tunnel mode, the original IP packet header is copied and the entire original IP packet is then protected by AH or ESP.**

**7** How many Security Associations (SAs) does it take to establish bidirectional IPSec communications between two peers?

**It takes three SAs to establish bidirectional IPSec communications between two peers. IPSec SAs are simplex, so it takes one for each direction for IKE Phase 2. IKE SAs are bidirectional, so you only need one of those to complete IKE Phase 1.**

**8** What is a message digest?

**A message digest is a condensed representation of a message of a fixed length, which depends on the hashing algorithm used.**

**9** Which current RFCs define the IPSec protocols?

**There are two IPSec protocols, AH and ESP. AH is now defined by RFC 2402. ESP is now defined by RFC 2406. Their original RFCs were 1826 and 1827, respectively.**

**10** What message integrity protocols does IPSec use?

**IPSec uses Message Digest 5 (MD5), Secure Hash Algorithm-1 (SHA-1), and Hash-Based Message Authentication Code (HMAC) as hashing protocols to provide message integrity.**

**11** What is the triplet of information that uniquely identifies a security association?

**The combination of the destination IP address, the IPSec protocol, and the SPI uniquely identifies a security association.**

**12** You can select to use both authentication and encryption when using the ESP protocol. Which is performed first when you do this?

**If you select to use both ESP authentication and encryption, encryption is performed first. This allows authentication to be done with the assurance that the sender does not alter the datagram before transmission and the receiver can authenticate the datagram before decrypting the package.**

**13** What five parameters are required by IKE Phase 1?

**IKE Phase 1 needs to know the following five parameters:**

  **a. Encryption algorithm**

  **b. Hashing algorithm**

  **c. Authentication method**

  **d. Key exchange method**

  **e. IKE SA lifetime**

14  What is the difference between the **deny** keyword in a crypto Access Control List (ACL) and the **deny** keyword in an access ACL?

**In an access ACL, the deny keyword tells the network device to drop the packet. In a crypto ACL, the deny keyword tells the network device to pass the traffic in the clear without the benefit of IPSec security.**

15  What transform set would allow SHA-1 authentication of both AH and ESP packets and would also provide Triple Data Encryption Standard (3DES) encryption for ESP?

**The transform set that would allow 3DES for ESP and SHA-1 for both is ah-sha-hmac esp-3des esp-sha-hmac.**

16  What are the five steps of the IPSec process?

**The five steps of the IPSec process are as follows:**

a.  **Interesting traffic triggers IPSec process.**

b.  **Authenticate peers and establish IKE SAs (IKE Phase 1).**

c.  **Establish IPSec SAs (IKE Phase 2).**

d.  **Allow secured communications.**

e.  **Terminate VPN.**

# Chapter 2—Q&A

1  What are the Cisco hardware product families that support IPSec VPN technology?

**Cisco IOS Software routers, PIX Firewalls, and VPN 3000 Series Concentrators, including the VPN 3002 Hardware Client, support IPSec VPN technology.**

2  What are the two IPSec protocols?

**The two IPSec protocols are Authentication Header (AH) and Encapsulating Security Payload (ESP).**

3  What are the three major VPN categories?

**The three major VPN categories are remote access, intranet (site-to-site), and extranet (business-to-business).**

4  What is an SEP module used for?

**Scalable Encryption Processing (SEP) modules are used with Cisco VPN 3030, 3060, and 3080 Concentrators to provide hardware-based encryption services.**

**5**  What are the primary reasons cited for choosing VPN technology?

**Security and reduced cost are most often cited as the reasons for selecting VPN technology.**

**6**  Why are remote access VPNs considered ubiquitous?

**Remote access VPNs are considered ubiquitous because they can be established any time from practically anywhere over the Internet.**

**7**  What types of VPNs are typically built across service provider shared network infrastructures?

**Site-to-site, or intranet, VPNs are typically built across service provider shared network infrastructures, such as Frame Relay, ATM, or point-to-point circuits.**

**8**  Which type of VPNs use a combination of the same infrastructures that are used by the other two types of VPNs?

**Business-to-business, or extranet, VPNs use a combination of the same infrastructures that are used by remote access and intranet VPNs.**

**9**  What hardware would you use to build intranet and extranet VPNs?

**Cisco IOS Software routers are the best choice for intranet and the site-to-site portion of extranet VPNs. VPN encryption modules in these devices can provide powerful platforms for supporting VPNs between sites.**

**10**  Which Cisco routers provide support for Cisco EzVPN Remote?

**The Cisco router models that support Cisco EzVPN Remote include Models 827H, uBR905, 806, 1710, and 1700. Of these, the 827H and the 806 offer support only for EzVPN Remote. The others also provide support for EzVPN Server.**

**11**  Which Cisco router series supports VAMs?

**The Cisco 7200 Router Series supports VPN Acceleration Modules (VAMs) to enhance VPN support characteristics on the router.**

**12**  Which Cisco router series supports ISMs?

**The Cisco 7100 Router Series supports Integrated Services Modules (ISMs) to expand the VPN capabilities of the router.**

**13**  Which of the Cisco PIX Firewall models are fixed-configuration devices?

**The Cisco PIX 501 Firewall and the Cisco PIX 506E Firewall models are fixed-configuration devices.**

**14** Which Cisco PIX Firewall models offer a failover port for high availability and support VACs?

**The three high-end models of the PIX Firewall have a failover port and support VPN Accelerator Cards (VACs). Those models are the Cisco PIX 515E Firewall, the Cisco PIX 525 Firewall, and the Cisco PIX 535 Firewall.**

**15** Which series of Cisco hardware devices are purpose-built remote access VPN devices?

**The Cisco VPN 3000 Series Concentrators were designed specifically to support remote access VPN services.**

**16** Which of the Cisco VPN 3000 Series Concentrators is a fixed-configuration device?

**The Cisco VPN 3005 Concentrator is a fixed-configuration system that supports up to 100 simultaneous sessions.**

**17** Which of the Cisco VPN 3000 Series Concentrators can accept SEP modules?

**The three high-end concentrators support SEP modules. These systems are the Cisco VPN 3030 Concentrator, the 3060 Concentrator, and the 3080 Concentrator.**

**18** What feature of the Cisco Unity Client makes it scalable?

**The client version updates can be pushed to the user's system from a central network site when the user makes the initial login attempt. This scalability feature relieves the burden of having to configure numerous client systems and enables a managed growth path for VPN deployment.**

**19** Which of Cisco's VPN clients can be used with any operating system that communicates in IP?

**The Cisco VPN 3002 Hardware Client enables any user device that communicates in IP to access an IPSec tunnel. Operating systems such as Windows, Solaris, MAC, and Linux can all participate in IPSec secure communications using these devices.**

**20** What protocol enables IP-enabled wireless devices such as PDAs and Smart Phones to participate in VPN communications?

**The Elliptic Curve Cryptosystem (ECC) Protocol permits IP-enabled wireless devices to participate in VPN communications. All Cisco VPN 3000 Series Concentrators support ECC, which is a new Diffie-Hellman group that allows faster processing of keying information.**

**21** What are the three phases of Cisco Mobile Office?

**The three phases of Cisco Mobile Office are On The Road, At Home, and At Work.**

**22** What is the distinctive characteristic of Cisco VPN Device Manager?

**Cisco VPN Device Manager is an embedded device manager that is installed directly into a supporting router's flash memory.**

**23** What is Cisco's AAA server, and what AAA systems does it support?

**The Cisco Secure Access Control Server (ACS) is Cisco's Authentication, Authorization, and Accounting (AAA) server. This device supports both Terminal Access Controller Access Control System Plus (TACACS+) and Remote Authentication Dial-In User Service (RADIUS).**

**24** Which web-based management tool can display a physical representation of each managed device?

**CiscoView is the web-based management tool that displays a physical representation of each managed device. Modules, ports, and indicators are depicted with color coding to indicate the current, dynamically updated status of the element.**

**25** What are the current RFCs that define the IPSec protocols?

**There are two IPSec protocols, Authentication Header (AH) and Encapsulating Security Payload (ESP). AH is defined by RFC 2402. ESP is defined by RFC 2406. Their original RFCs were 1826 and 1827, respectively.**

**26** What are three shortcomings of IPSec?

**Any of the following are shortcomings of IPSec:**

**a. IPSec does not support DLSw or SRB.**

**b. IPSec does not support multipoint tunnels.**

**c. IPSec works strictly with unicast IP datagrams only. It does not work with multicast or broadcast IP datagrams.**

**d. IPSec is slower than Cisco Encryption Technology (CET) because IPSec provides per-packet data authentication.**

**e. IPSec provides packet expansion that can cause fragmentation and reassembly of IPSec packets, creating another reason that IPSec is slower than CET.**

**27** What message encryption protocols does IPSec use?

**IPSec uses Data Encryption Standard (DES) and Triple DES (3DES) encryption protocols.**

**28** What message integrity protocols does IPSec use?

**IPSec uses Message Digest 5 (MD5), Secure Hash Algorithm-1 (SHA-1), and Hash-based Message Authentication Code (HMAC) as hashing protocols to provide message integrity.**

**29** What methods does IPSec use to provide peer authentication?

**Three methods are available to IPSec for peer authentication: preshared keys, RSA digital signatures, and RSA encrypted nonces.**

**30** What methods does IPSec use for key management?

**IPSec uses Certificate Authorities (CAs) and the Diffie-Hellman key exchange process for key management.**

**31** What is the key element contained in the AH or ESP packet header?

**The key element contained in each protocol's header is the SPI, giving the destination peer the information it needs to authenticate and decrypt the packet.**

**32** Which IPSec protocol does not provide encryption services?

**Authentication Header (AH) does not provide encryption services. AH packets are sent as clear text.**

**33** What is the triplet of information that uniquely identifies a Security Association?

**The combination of the destination IP address, the IPSec protocol, and the Security Parameters Index (SPI) uniquely identifies a Security Association (SA).**

**34** What is an ICV?

**An Integrity Check Value (ICV) is a calculated representation of the immutable contents of an IPSec packet. Each peer calculates this value for the packet independently. If the values do not match, the packet is considered as having been altered in transit and the packet is discarded.**

**35** What IPSec protocol must you use when confidentiality is required in your IPSec communications?

**You must use ESP when confidentiality is required in your IPSec communications. ESP provides encryption; AH does not.**

**36** What is the primary difference between the mechanisms used by AH and ESP to modify an IP packet for IPSec use?

**AH inserts an IPSec header into the packet containing the SPI and other related information. ESP encapsulates the original IP packet or the data portion of that packet by surrounding it with both a header and a trailer.**

**37** What are the two modes of operation for AH and ESP?

**AH and ESP use Transport and Tunnel modes. In Transport mode, the original IP packet header is left intact and is not protected by IPSec. In Tunnel mode, the original IP packet header is copied and the entire original IP packet is then protected by AH or ESP.**

**38** Which IPSec protocol should you use if your system is using NAT?

**AH does not support Network Address Translation (NAT) because changing the source IP address in the IP header causes authentication to fail.**

**39** You can select to use both authentication and encryption when using the ESP protocol. Which is performed first when you do this?

**If you select to use both ESP authentication and encryption, encryption is performed first. This allows authentication to be done with assurance that the sender does not alter the datagram before transmission and the receiver can authenticate the datagram before decrypting the package.**

**40** How many SAs does it take to establish bidirectional IPSec communications between two peers?

**It takes three SAs to establish bidirectional IPSec communications between two peers. IPSec SAs are simplex, so it takes one for each direction for IKE Phase 2. IKE SAs are bidirectional, so you only need one of those to complete IKE Phase 1.**

**41** Which encryption protocol was considered unbreakable at the time of its adoption?

**The Data Encryption Standard (DES) holds this distinction. DES was once considered such a strong encryption technique that it was barred from export from the continental United States.**

**42** What process does 3DES use to obtain an aggregate 168-bit key?

**Triple DES performs an encryption process, a decryption process, and then another encryption process, each with a different 56-bit key. This triple process produces an aggregate 168-bit key, providing strong encryption.**

**43** What is a message digest?

**A message digest (MD) is a condensed representation of a message of a fixed length, which depends on the hashing algorithm used.**

**44** What does HMAC-MD5-96 mean?

**HMAC-MD5-96 is a variant of MD5 that uses a 128-bit secret key to produce a 128-bit MD. AH and ESP-HMAC only use the left-most 96 bits, placing them into the authentication field. The destination peer then calculates a complete 128-bit message digest but then only uses the left-most 96 bits to compare with the value stored in the authentication field.**

**45** What does HMAC-SHA1-96 mean?

**HMAC-SHA1-96 is a variant of SHA-1 that produces a 160-bit message digest using a 160-bit secret key. Cisco's implementation of HMAC-SHA1-96 truncates the 160-bit MD to the left-most 96 bits and sends those in the authentication field. The receiving peer recreates the entire 160-bit message digest using the same 160-bit secret key but then only compares the leading 96 bits against the MD fragment in the authentication field.**

**46** How are preshared keys exchanged?

**Preshared keys are exchanged manually, severely impacting the scalability of their use.**

**47** What does the Diffie-Hellman key agreement protocol permit?

**The Diffie-Hellman (D-H) key agreement protocol allows two peers to exchange a secret key without having any prior secrets. This protocol is an example of an asymmetrical key exchange process in which peers exchange different public keys to generate identical private keys.**

**48** Why is D-H not used for symmetric key encryption processes?

**Asymmetric key encryption processes like Diffie-Hellman are much too slow for the bulk encryption required in high-speed VPN circuits.**

**49** What is a CRL?

**A Certificate Revocation List (CRL) is a list of expired or voided digital certificates that a CA makes available to its customers. Clients use these CRLs during the process of authenticating a peer.**

**50** What are the five parameters required by IKE Phase 1?

**IKE Phase 1 needs to know the following parameters:**

**a. Encryption algorithm**

**b. Hashing algorithm**

**c. Authentication method**

**d. Key exchange method**

**e. IKE SA lifetime**

**51** What are the valid AH authentication transforms?

**There are only three valid AH authentication transforms: ah-md5-hmac, ah-sha-hmac, and ah-rfc1828.**

**52** What transform set would allow for SHA-1 authentication of both AH and ESP packets and would also provide 3DES encryption for ESP?

**The transform set that would allow for 3DES for ESP and SHA-1 for both is ah-sha-hmac esp-3des esp-sha-hmac.**

53 What steps should you take before you begin the task of configuring IPSec on a Cisco device?

**The five preconfiguration steps are as follows:**

**Step 1   Establish an IKE policy.**

**Step 2   Establish an IPSec policy.**

**Step 3   Examine the current configuration.**

**Step 4   Test the network before IPSec.**

**Step 5   Permit IPSec ports and protocols.**

54 What are the five steps of the IPSec process?

**The five steps of the IPSec process are as follows:**

**Step 1   Interesting traffic triggers IPSec process.**

**Step 2   Authenticate peers and establish IKE SAs (IKE Phase 1).**

**Step 3   Establish IPSec SAs (IKE Phase 2).**

**Step 4   Allow secured communications.**

**Step 5   Terminate VPN.**

55 What is the difference between the **deny** keyword in a crypto ACL and the **deny** keyword in an access ACL?

**In an access ACL, the deny keyword tells the network device to drop the packet. In a crypto ACL, the deny keyword tells the network device to pass the traffic in the clear without the benefit of IPSec security.**

# Chapter 3—Do I Know This Already?

1 What models are available in the Cisco VPN 3000 Concentrator Series?

**Five models are available in the Cisco VPN 3000 Concentrator Series: VPN 3005, VPN 3015, VPN 3030, VPN 3060, and VPN 3080.**

2 What is the maximum number of simultaneous sessions that can be supported on the Cisco VPN 3015 Concentrator?

**The Cisco VPN 3015 Concentrator supports up to 100 simultaneous sessions.**

3 What is the maximum number of simultaneous sessions that can be supported on the Cisco VPN 3080 Concentrator?

**The Cisco VPN 3080 Concentrator supports up to 10,000 simultaneous sessions.**

**4** On a Cisco VPN 3005 Concentrator, what does a blinking green system LED indicate?

**On a Cisco VPN 3005 Concentrator, a blinking green system LED indicates that the system is in a shutdown (halted) state and is ready to be powered off.**

**5** What is the maximum encryption throughput rate for the VPN 3000 series?

**The VPN 3000 series of concentrators can sustain a maximum encryption throughput of 100 Mbps.**

**6** What tunneling protocols do Cisco VPN 3000 Concentrators support?

**The Cisco VPN 3000 Concentrators support the following tunneling protocols: Internet Protocol Security (IPSec), Point-to-Point Tunneling Protocol (PPTP), Layer 2 Tunneling Protocol (L2TP), L2TP/IPSec, and Network Address Translation (NAT) Transparent IPSec.**

**7** How do VPN concentrators reduce communications expenses?

**VPN concentrators reduce communications expenses by allowing remote users to connect to the corporate network through the Internet by dialing into local ISP connections rather than by using expensive long-distance or 800 numbers. Digital subscriber line (DSL) or cable modem users can also use broadband connections with VPN concentrators to gain security for their high-speed data circuits.**

**8** What other authentication capability exists if standard authentication servers are not available?

**When authentication servers are not available, the VPN concentrators have the ability to authenticate users from an internal database.**

**9** What routing protocols do the Cisco VPN 3000 Concentrators support?

**The Cisco VPN 3000 Concentrators support Routing Information Protocol 1 (RIP1), RIP2, and Open Shortest Path First (OSPF). In addition to these dynamic routing protocols, the concentrators also support static routing.**

**10** What protocol permits multichassis redundancy and failover?

**The Virtual Router Redundancy Protocol (VRRP) permits multichassis redundancy and failover support.**

**11** List some of the methods that can be used to interface with the embedded Cisco VPN Manager software on VPN concentrators?

**You can access the Cisco VPN Manager through the console port, Telnet, SSH, HTTP, and Secure HTTP.**

**12** What four options are available under the Configuration menu of the VPN Manager?

**The four options on the Configuration menu are Interfaces, System, User Management, and Policy Management.**

**13** What mechanism is used by Cisco VPN Clients to monitor firewall activity between the client and the concentrator?

**The Cisco VPN Clients use the Are You There (AYT) mechanism to monitor firewall activity.**

**14** What optional feature on the Cisco VPN 3002 Hardware Client allows you to connect Ethernet devices to the client?

**The Cisco VPN 3002 Hardware Client can be configured with an optional 8-port Ethernet switch.**

**15** During large-scale implementations, how can VPN 3000 Concentrators be configured to simplify client configuration?

**Cisco VPN 3000 Concentrators can push the client policies and configurations to the clients upon initial login to the system.**

**16** Which of Cisco's client offerings has no limitations with regard to the types of client operating systems it can support?

**The Cisco VPN 3002 Hardware Client works with every type of client operating system, as long as the system speaks TCP/IP.**

**17** What two operating modes can a Cisco VPN 3002 Hardware Client be configured to support?

**The Cisco VPN 3002 Hardware Client can be configured to support either Client mode or Network Extension mode.**

**18** What operating systems does the Cisco VPN Client support?

**The Cisco VPN Client supports the full range of Microsoft Windows operating systems, including Windows 95, 98, Me, NT 4.0, 2000, and XP. The Cisco VPN Client also supports Linux (Intel), Solaris (UltraSparc-32bit), and MAC OS X 10.1.**

# Chapter 3—Q&A

**1** How do VPN concentrators reduce communications expenses?

**VPN concentrators reduce communications expenses by allowing remote users to connect to the corporate network through the Internet by dialing into local ISP connections rather than by using expensive long-distance or 800 numbers. Digital subscriber line (DSL) or cable modem users can also use broadband connections with VPN concentrators to gain security for their high-speed data circuits.**

**2**  What are two of the standard authentication servers that Cisco VPN 3000 Concentrators can use for authentication?

**These concentrators can work with existing RADIUS, TACACS+, NT Domain, internal authentication, digital certificates, or Security Dynamics servers, which are also known as RSA Security International (SDI) servers. You could choose any two of these for the correct answer.**

**3**  What other authentication capability exists if standard authentication servers are not available?

**When authentication servers are not available, the VPN concentrators have the ability to authenticate users from an internal database.**

**4**  With respect to firewalls, where can you install Cisco VPN 3000 Concentrators?

**These powerful concentrators can be installed in front of, behind, or in parallel with existing firewalls, or even in the DMZ when the firewall provides one.**

**5**  What routing protocols do the Cisco VPN 3000 Concentrators support?

**The Cisco VPN Concentrators support RIP1, RIP2, and OSPF. In addition to these dynamic routing protocols, the concentrators also support static routing.**

**6**  During large-scale implementations, how can Cisco VPN 3000 Concentrators be configured to simplify client configuration?

**Cisco VPN 3000 Concentrators can push the client policies and configurations to the clients upon initial login to the system.**

**7**  What is the maximum encryption throughput rate for the VPN 3000 Concentrator Series?

**The Cisco VPN 3000 Concentrator Series can sustain a maximum encryption throughput of 100 Mbps.**

**8**  What hardware device is required to achieve maximum encryption throughput on the Cisco VPN 3000 Concentrators?

**When Cisco VPN 3000 Concentrators use Scalable Encryption Processors (SEPs), they can attain maximum encryption throughput.**

**9**  What element on SEPs permits them to be so fast and flexible?

**SEPs are designed around digital signal processors (DSPs), which are programmable, high-speed processors.**

**10**  Why are Cisco VPN Concentrators so good at supporting VPN communications?

**These VPN concentrators were purposely designed to provide only VPN support. They do not perform any other major network functions. Additionally, Scalable Encryption Processor (SEP) modules can be installed in most models to perform encryption routines, providing further support for VPN processes.**

**11** What tunneling protocols do Cisco VPN 3000 Concentrators support?

**The Cisco VPN 3000 Concentrators support the following tunneling protocols: Internet Protocol Security (IPSec), Point-to-Point Tunneling Protocol (PPTP), Layer 2 Tunneling Protocol (L2TP), L2TP/IPSec, and Network Address Translation (NAT) Transparent IPSec.**

**12** In addition to RIP and OSPF, what other routing capabilities do Cisco VPN Concentrators have?

**Cisco VPN Concentrators also support static routes, automatic endpoint discovery, Network Address Translation (NAT), and classless interdomain routing (CIDR).**

**13** What encryption and authentication protocols do Cisco VPN 3000 Concentrators support?

**Cisco VPN 3000 Concentrators support IPSec Encapsulating Security Payload (ESP) using DES/3DES (56/168-bit) with MD5 or SHA, or MPPE using 40/128-bit RC4.**

**14** What protocol permits multichassis redundancy and failover?

**The Virtual Router Redundancy Protocol (VRRP) permits multichassis redundancy and failover support.**

**15** What hardware items can be made redundant on Cisco VPN 3000 Concentrators?

**Cisco VPN 3000 Concentrators support redundant fans and can have redundant SEP modules and power supplies.**

**16** What are some of the methods that can be used to interface with the embedded Cisco VPN Manager software on VPN concentrators?

**You can access the Cisco VPN Manager through the console port, Telnet, SSH, HTTP, and Secure HTTP.**

**17** What are the most secure forms of authentication that can be used with Cisco VPN 3000 Series Concentrators?

**Digital certificates and tokens are the most secure form of authentication that can be used with Cisco VPN 3000 Series Concentrators.**

**18** What mechanism is used by Cisco VPN Clients to monitor firewall activity between the client and the concentrator?

**The Cisco VPN Clients use the Are You There (AYT) mechanism to monitor firewall activity.**

**19** What is the rated mean time between failure (MTBF) for Cisco VPN 3000 Concentrators?

**Cisco VPN 3000 Concentrators have an MTBF of 200,000 hours.**

20  You have installed two Cisco VPN 3000 Concentrators in parallel on your network. Both devices have redundant power supplies, fans, and SEPs. You need to ensure 99.9% uptime. How can you achieve this rate of fault tolerance?

**Configure both VPN concentrators into the same VRRP group, permitting one of the devices to become the active unit and the other to take a role as a hot standby concentrator.**

21  During the initial configuration of the VPN concentrators, what management interface must you use?

**You must use the command-line interface (CLI) to configure initial network settings on the concentrator.**

22  What do you need to do to activate configuration changes to Cisco VPN Concentrators that are made through the Cisco VPN Manager?

**Configuration changes are stored within the memory of the VPN concentrator and take effect immediately.**

23  What four options are available under the Configuration menu of the VPN Manager?

**The four available options on the Configuration menu are Interfaces, System, User Management, and Policy Management.**

24  What is the hierarchical order of property inheritance on Cisco VPN Concentrators?

**The Base Group is the root element in the property inheritance hierarchy. Next come specific groups, which inherit default properties from the Base Group. After specific groups come users, who inherit default properties from specific groups or from the Base Group if the user has not been assigned to a specific group.**

25  What options are available on the Administration menu of the Cisco VPN Manager?

**The options available from the Administration menu are Administer Sessions, Software Update, System Reboot, Ping, Monitoring Refresh, Access Rights, File Management, and Certificate Management.**

26  What options are available on the Monitoring menu of the Cisco VPN Manager?

**The options available from the Monitoring menu are Routing Table, Filterable Event Log, System Status, Sessions, and Statistics.**

27  Where in the Cisco VPN Manager could you go to view the current IP address for the private interface on a Cisco VPN 3000 Concentrator?

**To view the current IP settings for all Cisco VPN 3000 Concentrator interfaces, click the Interfaces option from the Configuration menu of the Cisco VPN Manager.**

**28** What models are available in the Cisco VPN 3000 Concentrator Series?

**Five models are available in the Cisco VPN 3000 Concentrator Series: VPN 3005, VPN 3015, VPN 3030, VPN 3060, and VPN 3080.**

**29** Which of the Cisco VPN 3000 Series Concentrators is a fixed configuration that is not upgradeable?

**The Cisco VPN 3005 Concentrator is a fixed configuration that is not upgradeable.**

**30** How can purchasers of a Cisco VPN 3000 Series Concentrator obtain a license for the Cisco VPN Client?

**The Cisco VPN Client configured for unlimited installations is shipped with every Cisco VPN 3000 Series Concentrator sold. Additionally, customers with access to Cisco.com can download upgrades from the CCO website without cost.**

**31** What is the maximum number of simultaneous sessions that can be supported on the Cisco VPN 3005 Concentrator?

**The Cisco VPN 3005 Concentrator supports up to 100 simultaneous sessions.**

**32** What is the maximum number of simultaneous sessions that can be supported on the Cisco VPN 3015 Concentrator?

**The Cisco VPN 3015 Concentrator supports up to 100 simultaneous sessions.**

**33** What is the maximum number of simultaneous sessions that can be supported on the Cisco VPN 3030 Concentrator?

**The Cisco VPN 3030 Concentrator supports up to 1500 simultaneous sessions.**

**34** What is the maximum number of simultaneous sessions that can be supported on the Cisco VPN 3060 Concentrator?

**The Cisco VPN 3060 Concentrator supports up to 5000 simultaneous sessions.**

**35** What is the maximum number of simultaneous sessions that can be supported on the Cisco VPN 3080 Concentrator?

**The Cisco VPN 3080 Concentrator supports up to 10,000 simultaneous sessions.**

**36** Which of the Cisco VPN 3000 Series Concentrators is only available in a fully redundant configuration?

**The Cisco VPN 3080 Concentrator is the only one of the series that is only available in a fully redundant configuration.**

**37** On a Cisco VPN 3005 Concentrator, what does a blinking green system LED indicate?

**On a Cisco VPN 3005 Concentrator, a blinking green system LED indicates that the system is in a shutdown (halted) state and is ready to be powered off.**

**38** On a Cisco VPN 3000 Concentrator, what does a blinking amber system LED indicate?

**On any of the Cisco VPN 3000 Concentrators, a blinking amber system LED indicates that the system has crashed and halted.**

**39** What does a blinking green Ethernet link status LED indicate on a Cisco VPN Concentrator?

**A blinking green Ethernet link status LED indicates that the interface is connected to the network and configured, but the interface has been disabled.**

**40** What does an amber SEP status LED indicate?

**An amber SEP status LED indicates that the module failed during operation.**

**41** Which of Cisco's client offerings has no limitations with regard to the types of client operating systems it can support?

**The Cisco VPN 3002 Hardware Client works with every type of client operating system, as long as the system speaks TCP/IP.**

**42** What optional feature on the Cisco VPN 3002 Hardware Client allows you to connect Ethernet devices to the client?

**The Cisco VPN 3002 Hardware Client can be configured with an optional 8-port Ethernet switch.**

**43** What two operating modes can a Cisco VPN 3002 Hardware Client be configured to support?

**The Cisco VPN 3002 Hardware Client can be configured to support either Client mode or Network Extension mode.**

**44** What operating systems does the Cisco VPN Client support?

**The Cisco VPN Client supports the full range of Microsoft Windows operating systems, including Windows 95, 98, Me, NT 4.0, 2000, and XP. The Cisco VPN Client also supports Linux (Intel), Solaris (UltraSparc-32bit), and MAC OS X 10.1.**

# Chapter 4—Do I Know This Already?

**1** What methods can you use for user authentication on the Cisco VPN 3000 Series Concentrators?

**You can configure the VPN concentrators to use RADIUS, NT Domain, Security Dynamics International (SDI), and internal user authentication.**

**2** What methods can you use for device authentication between VPN peers?

**You can accomplish device authentication between VPN peers by using either preshared keys or digital certificates.**

3 What are the three types of preshared keys?

   **Preshared keys can be unique, group, or wildcard.**

4 What is a unique preshared key?

   **A unique preshared key is one that is associated with a specific IP address.**

5 When you boot up a Cisco VPN 3000 Concentrator with the default factory configuration, what happens?

   **The default factory configuration causes the VPN concentrator to boot up into Quick Configuration mode.**

6 What information do you need to supply in the command-line interface (CLI) portion of Quick Configuration?

   **The CLI portion of the Quick Configuration requests system time, date, and time zone as well as the private interface IP address, subnet mask, speed, and duplex mode.**

7 Which interface do you need to configure using the browser-based VPN Manager?

   **You need to configure the Public interface with the VPN Manager. If you have other interfaces, you also need to configure those. The Private interface was configured using the CLI portion of Quick Configuration.**

8 What is the default administrator name and password for VPN concentrators?

   **The default VPN concentrator administrator name and password is admin/admin.**

9 How do you get your web browser to connect to the VPN concentrator's Manager application?

   **To connect to the VPN Manager, enter the IP address of the concentrator's Private interface in the Address box of the browser.**

10 What is the default administrator name and password for the GUI VPN Manager?

   **The administrator name and password are the same for the CLI and the GUI systems: admin/admin.**

11 What are the three major sections of the VPN Manager system?

   **The three major sections of the VPN Manager system are Configuration, Administration, and Monitoring.**

12 What hot keys are available in the standard toolbar of the VPN Manager?

   **The standard hot keys are Main, Help, Support, Logout, Configuration, Administration, and Monitoring.**

**13**  From where do users inherit attributes on the VPN concentrator?

**VPN concentrator users inherit their attributes from their groups. If a user is not a member of a group, the user inherits attributes from the Base Group.**

**14**  How many groups can a user belong to in the VPN concentrator's internal database?

**A VPN concentrator user can belong to only one group.**

**15**  What is an external group in the VPN Manager system?

**An external group is a group from an external authentication server such as RADIUS or NT Domain.**

**16**  When reviewing the list of attributes for a group, what does it mean when an attribute's Inherit? box is checked?

**Checking the Inherit? box for an attribute means that the attribute is always inherited from the Base Group.**

**17**  What are the nine subcategories under the Configuration | System option in the VPN Manager's table of contents?

**The Configuration | System subcategories are Servers, Address Management, Tunneling Protocols, IP Routing, Management Protocols, Events, General, Client Update, and Load Balancing Cisco VPN Clients.**

**18**  Where would you configure information for Network Time Protocol (NTP) and Dynamic Host Configuration Protocol (DHCP) servers within the VPN Manager?

**NTP, DHCP, and other servers are configured in the Configuration | System | Servers section of the VPN Manager.**

**19**  What tunneling protocol can you configure on the VPN concentrator to support the Microsoft Windows 2000 VPN Client?

**L2TP over IPSec is the protocol required to support Microsoft Windows 2000 VPN clients. This option is available on the VPN concentrators.**

**20**  What dynamic routing protocols are available on the VPN 3000 Concentrators?

**The Cisco VPN 3000 Concentrators support RIP and OSPF routing protocols. RIP is configured on the interface.**

**21**  What Microsoft Windows operating systems can support the Cisco VPN Client?

**The Cisco VPN Client can operate on Microsoft Windows 95, 98, 98 SE, Me, NT, 2000, and XP operating systems.**

**22**  How do you start the Cisco VPN Client on a Windows system?

**From the Windows Desktop, choose Start, Programs, Cisco Systems VPN Client, VPN Dialer.**

**23** How do you start the Cisco VPN Client installation process?

**You start the Cisco VPN Client installation process by inserting the CD-ROM into the PC and allowing Autorun to bring up the CD's menu. Select Install Cisco VPN Client from the menu.**

**24** What variables can you supply during the installation process of the Cisco VPN Client?

**The only options, other than when to reboot the system, are to select the location in which to store files and the location in which to place the application.**

# Chapter 4—Q&A

**1** Where would you normally use unique preshared keys?

**You would normally use unique preshared keys in site-to-site VPNs.**

**2** To use a web browser to access the VPN Manager application on VPN concentrators, what features must you enable on the browser?

**You must enable both JavaScript and cookies on the browser to access the VPN Manager.**

**3** What information is required to configure a LAN interface on the VPN concentrator?

**You must supply the IP address, subnet mask, speed, and duplex mode to configure a VPN concentrator LAN interface.**

**4** What is the default administrator name and password for the GUI VPN Manager?

**The administrator name and password are the same for the CLI and the GUI systems: admin/admin.**

**5** What options are available for addressing an IP interface on the IP Interfaces screen?

**The IP Interfaces screen gives you the option to disable the interface, obtain an address from DHCP, or assign a static IP address.**

**6** What is the maximum number of combined groups and users that can be supported on a VPN 3015 Concentrator?

**The 3015 Concentrator can support a maximum of 100 combined groups and users.**

**7** What are the four subcategories under the Configuration option of the VPN Manager's TOC?

**The four subcategories under the Configuration option are Interfaces, System, User Management, and Policy Management.**

**8**  On the General tab of a group's Add screen, what options can you select for Access Hours?

**On the General tab of the Group Add screen, you can select No Restrictions, Never, or Business Hours as the access hours for the system.**

**9**  What IPSec protocols are available from the default IPSec SA settings on the IPSec tab of the Group Add screen?

**The only IPSec protocol available by default on the IPSec tab of the Group Add screen is the ESP Protocol. Authentication Header (AH) is not an option. ESP provides encryption and authentication, whereas AH provides only authentication.**

**10**  What are the nine subcategories under the Configuration | System option in the VPN Manager's table of contents?

**The Configuration | System subcategories are Servers, Address Management, Tunneling Protocols, IP Routing, Management Protocols, Events, General, Client Update, and Load Balancing Cisco VPN Clients.**

**11**  Where does the VPN concentrator store system events?

**The VPN concentrator stores system events in nonvolatile memory.**

**12**  What areas can be configured under the Traffic Management section of the Configuration | Policy Management section?

**Under the Configuration | Policy Management | Traffic Management section of the VPN Manager, you can configure Network Lists, Rules, SAs, Filters, and NAT.**

**13**  Where do you enter the preshared key so that a VPN Client can connect to a VPN concentrator?

**During the creation of a connection in the VPN Client, you are presented with a screen that allows you to enter Group Access Information. Enter the group name and the group's password in that screen. The group's password is the preshared key.**

**14**  What are the three types of preshared keys?

**Preshared keys can be unique, group, or wildcard.**

**15**  What types of interfaces are the Public and Private VPN interfaces?

**On the VPN concentrators, the Public and Private interfaces are each 10/100-Mbps Ethernet interfaces.**

**16**  Which interface do you need to configure using the browser-based VPN Manager?

**You need to configure the Public interface with the VPN Manager. If you have other interfaces, you need to configure those as well. The Private interface was configured using the CLI portion of Quick Configuration.**

**17** What would you do if you needed to re-enter the Quick Configuration mode after you have completed the initial configuration of the VPN concentrator?

**To re-enter the Quick Configuration mode, you need to select the system reboot option to Reboot with Factory/Default Configuration.**

**18** When the VPN Manager's Main window is displayed, how do you continue with the Quick Configuration that was started at the CLI?

**To start the VPN Manager's version of Quick Configuration, select Click here to start Quick Configuration. This option is only available the first time the VPN Manager opens.**

**19** What methods can be selected for assigning IP addresses to the tunnel endpoints from the Quick Configuration Address Assignment screen?

**The Quick Configuration Address Assignment screen allows you to select from Client Specified, Per User, DHCP, or Configured Pool as the method used to assign IP addresses for the tunnel endpoint. You can select multiple methods.**

**20** When using the VPN Manager, how can you tell that you have made changes to the active configuration?

**You can tell that changes have been made to the active configuration when the Save Needed icon appears in the upper-right corner of the main window.**

**21** What is an external group in the VPN Manager system?

**An external group is a group from an external authentication server such as RADIUS or NT Domain.**

**22** What is the purpose of the SEP card assignment attribute on the General tab of the Group Add screen?

**The SEP card assignment attribute of the Group Add screen's General tab is used to manage load sharing across the SEP devices within a VPN concentrator.**

**23** You would like to be able to pass DNS and WINS information from the VPN concentrator to the VPN Client. What Group option can you use to accomplish this?

**You would need to enable Mode Configuration to permit the concentrator to share this information with the client.**

**24** What dynamic routing protocols are available on the VPN 3000 Concentrators?

**The Cisco VPN 3000 Concentrators support RIP and OSPF routing protocols. RIP is configured on the interface.**

**25**  What protocol does the VPN concentrator use to update software versions on Cisco VPN 3002 Hardware Clients?

**The VPN concentrator uses TFTP to update the operating system of VPN 3002 Hardware Clients.**

**26**  How do you start the Cisco VPN Client installation process?

**You start the Cisco VPN Client installation process by inserting the CD-ROM into the PC and allowing Autorun to bring up the CD's menu. Select Install Cisco VPN Client from the menu.**

**27**  What methods can you use for user authentication on the Cisco VPN 3000 Series Concentrators?

**You can configure the VPN concentrators to use RADIUS, NT Domain, SDI, and internal user authentication.**

**28**  What is a group preshared key?

**A group preshared key is one that is associated with a specific user group.**

**29**  When you boot up a Cisco VPN 3000 Concentrator with the default factory configuration, what happens?

**The default factory configuration causes the VPN concentrator to boot up into Quick Configuration mode.**

**30**  If you supply an address of 144.50.30.24 and want to use a 24-bit subnet mask for the Private interface on a VPN concentrator, are you able to accept the default subnet mask offered by the VPN Manager?

**The VPN Manager offers the default subnet mask for the class of address you assign. Because this is a Class B address and the default mask for that class is 16 bits, you would not be able to accept the mask offered by the VPN Manager.**

**31**  What are the three major sections of the VPN Manager system?

**The three major sections of the VPN Manager system are Configuration, Administration, and Monitoring.**

**32**  The Quick Configuration system has displayed the System Info screen. What information, other than system date and time, can you enter on this screen?

**Other than system date and time, the System Info screen allows you to enter a system name, DNS server, domain name, and default gateway.**

**33**  What is the maximum number of combined groups and users that can be supported on a VPN 3060 Concentrator?

**The 3060 Concentrator can support a maximum of 1000 combined groups and users.**

**34** From where do users inherit attributes on the VPN concentrator?

**VPN concentrator users inherit their attributes from their groups. If a user is not a member of a group, the user inherits attributes from the Base Group.**

**35** What is the default number of simultaneous logins available to group members?

**Group members are allowed three simultaneous logins by default.**

**36** What is the purpose of IKE keepalives?

**IKE keepalives keep tabs on peers. If a peer does not respond to IKE keepalives, then the VPN concentrator drops the connection. This helps to prevent hung connections.**

**37** Where would you configure information for NTP and DHCP servers within the VPN Manager?

**NTP, DHCP, and other servers are configured in the Configuration | System | Servers section of the VPN Manager.**

**38** What is the most significant event severity level?

**Level 1 is the most significant event severity level on the Cisco VPN 3000 Concentrator.**

**39** What Microsoft Windows operating systems can support the Cisco VPN Client?

**The Cisco VPN Client can operate on Microsoft Windows 95, 98, 98 SE, Me, NT, 2000, and XP operating systems.**

**40** What programs are available within the VPN Client installation?

**The VPN Client installs the following applications: Certificate Manager, Help, Log Viewer, Set MTU, Uninstall VPN Client, and VPN Dialer.**

**41** What is a unique preshared key?

**A unique preshared key is one that is associated with a specific IP address.**

**42** What type of cable does the console port require on VPN concentrators?

**VPN concentrator console cables are straight-through RS-232 serial cables with a female DB-9 connector.**

**43** What is the default administrator name and password for VPN concentrators?

**The default VPN concentrator administrator name and password is admin/admin.**

**44** How do you get your web browser to connect to the VPN concentrator's manager application?

**To connect to the VPN Manager, simply enter the IP address of the concentrator's Private interface in the Address box of the browser.**

**45** What is the first screen that appears when you click the **Click here to start Quick Configuration** option in the VPN Manager?

**The first screen of the VPN Manager's Quick Configuration is the IP Interfaces screen.**

**46** If you select Internal Server as the method of user authentication, what additional screen does the Quick Configuration system give you?

**When you select Internal Server as the method of user authentication, you must then configure the users and their passwords, so the VPN Manager provides the User Database screen.**

**47** When do configuration changes become active on the Cisco VPN 3000 Series Concentrators?

**Configuration changes take effect immediately on the VPN concentrators.**

**48** When reviewing the list of attributes for a group, what does it mean when an attribute's Inherit? box is checked?

**Checking the Inherit? box for an attribute means that the attribute will always be inherited from the Base Group.**

**49** What is a realm in relation to user authentication?

**The Internal authentication server can use a qualified username for authentication. The qualified name takes the form of *username@group*. The @*group* portion is called the realm. You can set a group's attribute to not use the realm portion for authentication.**

**50** What is split tunneling?

**Split tunneling allows some traffic to pass over the connection to the concentrator that is unprotected by IPSec.**

**51** What management protocols can you configure on the VPN concentrator?

**VPN Manager allows you to configure FTP, HTTP/HTTPS, TFTP, Telnet, SNMP, SNMP Community Strings, SSL, SSH, and XML.**

**52** What is the process a VPN Client uses to connect to a VPN concentrator when load balancing is used between two or more VPN concentrators?

**The VPN Client initially tries to connect to the virtual IP address of the cluster. The cluster master intercepts the call and sends the client the public IP address of the least-loaded available concentrator. The client then uses that address to negotiate an IPSec session.**

**53** What variables can you supply during the installation process of the Cisco VPN Client?

**The only options, other than when to reboot the system, are to select the location to store files and the location to place the application.**

**54** What methods can be used for device authentication between VPN peers?

**Device authentication can be accomplished between VPN peers by using either preshared keys or digital certificates.**

**55** What is a wildcard preshared key?

**A wildcard preshared key is one that is not associated with either an IP address or user group. These keys can be used by any device holding the key.**

**56** What information do you need to supply in the CLI portion of Quick Configuration?

**The CLI portion of the Quick Configuration requests system time, date, and time zone as well as the Private interface IP address, subnet mask, speed, and duplex mode.**

**57** What is the last step you must take before moving from the CLI Quick Configuration mode to the browser-based Quick Configuration mode?

**Before leaving the CLI Quick Configuration mode, select the option to Save changes to Config file.**

**58** What hot keys are available in the standard toolbar of the VPN Manager?

**The standard hot keys are Main, Help, Support, Logout, Configuration, Administration, and Monitoring.**

**59** What tunneling protocols does the VPN concentrator support?

**The VPN concentrator supports L2TP, PPTP, IPSec, and L2TP over IPSec.**

**60** When you select IPSec as the tunneling protocol, what screen does Quick Configuration present?

**When you select IPSec as the tunneling protocol, Quick Configuration provides the IPSec Group screen so that you can supply a group name and password to be used by those devices connecting through preshared keys.**

**61** How many groups can a user belong to in the VPN concentrator's internal database?

**A VPN concentrator user can belong to only one group.**

**62** What is the size range for user authentication passwords for internal users?

**Internal user passwords can range from 1 to 32 characters. The allowable length is controlled by the group that the users belong to.**

**63**  What does the Authentication option RADIUS with Expiry provide?

**RADIUS with Expiry lets the user know that his password has expired and permits the user to select a new password.**

**64**  What tunneling protocol can be configured on the VPN concentrator to support the Microsoft Windows 2000 VPN client?

**L2TP over IPSec is the protocol that is required to support Microsoft Windows 2000 VPN clients. This option is available on the VPN concentrators.**

**65**  How does the VPN 3000 Concentrator handle software updates for VPN Software Clients?

**The VPN 3000 Concentrator provides a message to the clients during login. The message provides a location for downloading the updated software version.**

**66**  How do you start the VPN Client on a Windows system?

**From the Windows Desktop, choose Start, Programs, Cisco Systems VPN Client, VPN Dialer.**

# Chapter 5—Do I Know This Already?

**1**  What Public Key Cryptography Standard (PKCS) is used to enroll with a CA?

**PKCS #10 is the standard form generally used to request certificate enrollment with a CA.**

**2**  What field in the certificate request should match the IPSec group name on the VPN concentrator?

**The Organization Unit (OU) should match the IPSec group name on the VPN concentrator.**

**3**  What elements make up the X.500 distinguished name?

**Six fields make up the X.500 distinguished name: Common Name (CN), Organizational Unit (OU), Organization (O), Locality (L), State/Province (SP), and Country (C).**

**4**  What default algorithm type and key size does the VPN concentrator use on the certificate request?

**The VPN concentrator uses RSA 512 keys as the default on the certificate request.**

**5**  What entity is responsible for generating the Public Key Infrastructure (PKI) public/ private key pair for a requesting host?

**The host itself must generate the PKI public/private key pair and include the public key with the enrollment request sent to the CA.**

**6**  When are Secure Sockets Layer (SSL) certificates required on a VPN concentrator?

**SSL certificates are required on a VPN concentrator when you want to establish secure communications between the concentrator and the browser on the administrator's workstation.**

**7**  What is the first certificate that must be installed on a VPN concentrator before you can install any other certificates from a given CA?

**You must install the root certificate from a CA before you can install any other certificates from that CA on a VPN concentrator.**

**8**  What two enrollment methods are available on a VPN concentrator?

**The VPN concentrator allows you to perform a manual enrollment using a PKCS #10 request or an automated enrollment using the Simple Certificate Enrollment Process (SCEP).**

**9**  Where does a VPN concentrator obtain the root CA's public key?

**The VPN concentrator obtains the root CA's public key from the root certificate.**

**10**  During the authentication process, where does a VPN concentrator find the original hash that the CA calculated for an identity certificate?

**The VPN concentrator extracts the original hash that the CA calculated for an identity certificate from the digital signature on the certificate. This signature is decrypted using the CA's public key from the root certificate.**

**11**  When you select to cache Certificate Revocation Lists (CRLs) on the VPN concentrator, where are they stored?

**Enabling CRL caching on the VPN concentrator permits the concentrator to store CRLs in volatile memory.**

**12**  With CRL caching disabled, how does a VPN concentrator check a certificate's serial number against a CRL?

**When caching is disabled, the VPN concentrator must request a CRL from one of the CA's distribution points each time it needs to check a certificate's serial number.**

13 Using the VPN Manager, where would you look to check the status of a certificate enrollment process?

**To check the status of a certificate enrollment process using the VPN Manager, select Administration | Certificate Management from the table of contents. The last section on this screen displays enrollment status.**

14 When configuring digital certificate support on a VPN concentrator, where do you identify which certificate to use for Internet Key Exchange (IKE) Phase 1 negotiations?

**When configuring digital certificate support on a VPN concentrator, the certificate to use is identified on the Configuration | Policy Management | Traffic Management | Security Associations | Add/Modify screen.**

15 What must be in place on a client's PC before you can configure the VPN Client for certificate support?

**Before you can configure the VPN Client for certificate support, you must install a root certificate and an identity certificate in the browser.**

16 Which screen do you use to enable the use of digital certificates for device authentication during IKE Phase 1 negotiations?

**The Authentication tab on the Properties page for a defined connection permits you to select between using preshared keys and digital certificates for IKE Phase 1 authentication.**

# Chapter 5—Q&A

1 What must be in place on a client's PC before you can configure the VPN Client for certificate support?

**Before you can configure the VPN Client for certificate support, you must install a root certificate and an identity certificate in the browser.**

2 What two methods are available on the VPN concentrator for installing certificates obtained through manual enrollment?

**To install certificates on the VPN concentrator that were obtained through manual enrollment, you can either cut and paste the text from the PEM-configured file or upload the file from your workstation.**

3 What could cause a digital certificate to be revoked by the CA?

**The CA might revoke a certificate if something changed to affect the user's distinguished name, if a certificate's keys became compromised, or if the hardware owner of the key gets taken out of service.**

**4**  What are the two types of CA structures?

**The two types of CA structures are the central CA structure and the hierarchical CA structure.**

**5**  During the authentication process, where does a VPN concentrator find the original hash that the CA calculated for an identity certificate?

**The VPN concentrator extracts the original hash that the CA calculated for an identity certificate from the digital signature on the certificate. This signature is decrypted using the CA's public key from the root certificate.**

**6**  During manual SCEP authentication, how is the request transmitted to the CA?

**During manual SCEP authentication, the certificate request is transmitted to the CA using the Internet, e-mail, a floppy disk, or some other means.**

**7**  What Public Key Cryptography Standard is used to request enrollment with a CA?

**PKCS #10 is the standard form generally used to request certificate enrollment with a CA.**

**8**  What is the first certificate that must be installed on a VPN concentrator before you can install any other certificates from a given CA?

**You must install the root certificate from a CA before you can install any other certificates from that CA on a VPN concentrator.**

**9**  When configuring digital certificate support on a VPN concentrator, where do you identify which certificate to use for IKE Phase 1 negotiations?

**When configuring digital certificate support on a VPN concentrator, the certificate to use is identified on the Configuration | Policy Management | Traffic Management | Security Associations | Add/Modify screen.**

**10**  After a VPN peer receives an identity certificate from its partner during IKE Phase 1, the peer calculates a hash of the certificate. What does the peer compare this hash against to verify that the certificate has not been altered?

**After calculating a hash of the certificate, the peer decrypts the signature on the certificate with the public key of the root CA taken from the root certificate. This decryption process reveals the hash that the root calculated on the certificate. If the two hash values match, there is a high degree of certainty that the certificate has not been altered.**

**11**  Where does a VPN concentrator obtain the root CA's public key?

**The VPN concentrator obtains the root CA's public key from the root certificate.**

**12**  What entity is responsible for generating the PKI public/private key pair for a requesting host?

**The host itself must generate the PKI public/private key pair and include the public key with the enrollment request sent to the CA.**

**13**  In the VPN Manager, where do you identify that you want to use RSA Digital Certificates for IKE Phase 1 authentication?

**In the VPN Manager, you can select RSA Digital Certificates as the method for IKE Phase 1 authentication from the IKE Proposals screen.**

**14**  What three tests does a VPN concentrator perform on a partner's identity certificate before performing the authentication process?

**The VPN concentrator validates the partner's identity certificate before authentication by verifying that the certificate was signed by a trusted CA, that the certificate has not expired, and that the certificate has not been revoked.**

**15**  Which version of the X.509 standard identity certificate permits extensions?

**X.509 version 3 permits extensions.**

**16**  What is RSA Keon?

**RSA Keon is a CA application that runs on Solaris, Windows 2000, and Windows NT.**

**17**  When does the **Click here to install a CA certificate** option appear on the Administration | Certificate Management screen of the VPN Manager?

**The Click here to install a CA certificate option appears on the Administration | Certificate Management screen until you have installed the first CA certificate.**

**18**  The VPN concentrator is certified to work with three Internet-based CAs. Which CAs are they?

**The VPN concentrator is certified to work with these Internet-based CAs: Entrust, VeriSign, and Baltimore.**

**19**  What elements make up the X.500 distinguished name?

**Six fields make up the X.500 distinguished name: Common Name (CN), Organizational Unit (OU), Organization (O), Locality (L), State/Province (SP), and Country (C).**

**20**  Which screen do you use to enable the use of digital certificates for device authentication during IKE Phase 1 negotiations?

**The Authentication tab on the Properties page for a defined connection permits you to select between using preshared keys and digital certificates for IKE Phase 1 authentication.**

21  What two enrollment methods are available on a VPN concentrator?

**The VPN concentrator allows you to perform a manual enrollment using a PKCS #10 request or an automated enrollment using SCEP.**

22  What field in the certificate request should match the IPSec group name on the VPN concentrator?

**The Organization Unit (OU) should match the IPSec group name on the VPN concentrator.**

23  When are SSL certificates required on a VPN concentrator?

**SSL certificates are required on a VPN concentrator when you want to establish secure communications between the concentrator and the browser on the administrator's workstation.**

24  What are the three types of certificates involved in the digital certificate process?

**The three types of certificates involved in the digital certificate process are the root, identity, and issuing certificates.**

25  What is a CRL?

**A CRL is a Certificate Revocation List. It contains the serial numbers of digital certificates with the date the certificate became invalid. CRLs are issued by the CA and contain only information about certificates that were issued by the CA.**

26  When you select to cache CRLs on the VPN concentrator, where are they stored?

**Enabling CRL caching on the VPN concentrator permits the concentrator to store CRLs in volatile memory.**

27  What default algorithm type and key size does the VPN concentrator use on the certificate request?

**The VPN concentrator uses RSA 512 keys as the default on the certificate request.**

28  Using the VPN Manager, where would you look to check the status of a certificate enrollment process?

**To check the status of a certificate enrollment process using the VPN Manager, select Administration | Certificate Management from the table of contents. The last section on this screen displays enrollment status.**

29  What is a root certificate?

**A root certificate is a special form of the identity certificate that is self-signed by the root CA and contains the public key of the root CA. This certificate is used by VPN peers to authenticate their partner's identity certificate.**

**30** Where are you asked to supply a challenge password during the enrollment process?

**The enrollment of an identity certificate through SCEP requests that you enter the challenge password.**

**31** How is the validity period of a digital certificate specified?

**The validity period of a digital certificate is specified with a starting date and time and an ending date and time.**

**32** With CRL caching disabled, how does a VPN concentrator check a certificate's serial number against a CRL?

**When caching is disabled, the VPN concentrator must request a CRL from one of the CA's distribution points each time it needs to check a certificate's serial number.**

**33** SCEP has two authentication methods available between a requester and the CA. What are those two methods?

**The two SCEP authentication methods are manual authentication and preshared key authentication.**

# Chapter 6—Do I Know This Already?

**1** You have a number of clients running Windows 98 and a remote VPN 3002 Hardware Client assigned to the same group. Your supervisor wants you to force everyone on this group connecting to have a firewall running on his or her machine. Can you do this?

**No. The Firewall Required option cannot be used with the VPN 3002 Hardware Client.**

**2** How is the Always On option set on the VPN Client?

**The Always On option is set under the Options pull-down menu. The default setting is to have Always On disabled.**

**3** In addition to IPSec, what tunneling protocols does the VPN Client support?

**The VPN Client supports the tunneling protocols IPSec, PPTP, L2TP, and L2TP over IPSec.**

**4** How often does the VPN Client poll the personal firewall when using Are You There (AYT)?

**The VPN Client polls the personal firewall every 30 seconds when using AYT.**

5 You are using BlackICE as a client firewall. You are presently connected through the VPN. What happens if you stop the service running BlackICE? Does the VPN remain connected? If so, for how long? Can you connect again if BlackICE is not running?

**The answer depends on two configuration choices. The first choice is the Are You There (AYT) configuration. If AYT is off, no noticeable difference is seen.**

**If AYT is on, the connection reacts differently depending on other choices made. If you configure the Firewall setting as Firewall Optional or No Firewall, you do not see a noticeable difference during this connection. However, if you choose the Firewall Required option, the connection is dropped after there is no response from the concentrator's poll. With the Firewall Required option, you cannot connect until you start BlackICE again. If you set the Firewall Optional option, you receive a message indicating that a firewall should be running when you connect.**

6 Which two products from Zone Labs work with the VPN Client to enable the Are You There (AYT) capability?

**Zone Alarm and Zone AlarmPro are the personal firewalls that work with the Cisco VPN Client to enable the AYT capability. The other product that works with the VPN Client is BlackICE Defender from Network ICE.**

7 What protocols are not automatically blocked when using the Stateful Firewall (Always On) feature?

**Dynamic Host Control Protocol (DHCP) and Encapsulating Security Payload (ESP) are not automatically blocked when using the Stateful Firewall (Always On) feature. Additionally, traffic from the concentrator's network is not blocked.**

8 You want to have secure VPN connections to the private network of the head-end concentrator and unsecured communications to the Internet. How would you configure the VPN Client's Stateful Firewall feature to support this split tunneling?

**To enable split tunneling, you must disable the VPN Client's Stateful Firewall feature. If enabled, the Stateful Firewall blocks all traffic coming from the Internet.**

9 What is another name for the Stateful Firewall client that is a part of the Cisco VPN Client?

**The Stateful Firewall client that is part of the Cisco VPN Client is also called the Cisco Integrated Client (CIC).**

10 Where are the rules set for a client when using Central Protection Policy (CPP) with Zone AlarmPro?

**Using Centralized Protection Policy (CPP) means that the concentrator controls all rules for the clients. This applies to CIC as well as Zone Alarm and Zone AlarmPro.**

**11**  Why is CPP not used with the Tunnel Everything option?

**CPP is designed to be used with split tunneling because the Tunnel Everything option already blocks all nontunneled traffic.**

**12**  On what screen do you configure CPP?

**CPP is configured on the Client FW tab of the Configuration | User Management | Groups | Modify screen within the VPN concentrator.**

**13**  On the VPN Client, where do you see the current compression used for a VPN connection?

**You see the current compression used for a VPN connection under the General tab of the Connection Status dialog box on the client software. You can also view the current compression method by using the client CLI command** vpnclient stat.

**14**  From the VPN Client, where can you view the secured routes that are enabled to the client?

**You can view a list of secured routes that are enabled to the VPN Client from the Statistics tab of the Connection Status screen.**

**15**  What is meant by the term *Packets bypassed* on the Statistics tab of the Connection Status screen?

**The Packets bypassed field on the Statistics tab of the Connection Status screen shows the number of packets that did not need to be encrypted but which were still sent out over the wire in unencrypted form.**

**16**  What debug classes do you use when creating a rule with the following options:

a. Drop

b. Drop and Log

c. Forward

d. Forward and Log

e. Apply IPSec

f. Apply IPSec and Log

**The FILTERDBG event class is used with the Drop and Log option, Apply IPSec and Log option, and the Forward and Log option. The other three options do not use a debug class.**

**17** How do you allow clients to use either of two firewalls? What is the only vendor you can do this with?

**To allow clients to use either of two firewalls, choose the Custom Firewall option on the Client FW tab on the Configuration | User Management | Groups | Modify screen. Enter the Vendor ID and the Product IDs separated by commas. Because Zone Labs is the only vendor with more than one product, this vendor must be used.**

**18** On the VPN 3000 Concentrator Series devices, you configure the client firewall properties on the Client FW tab of the Configuration | User Management | Groups | Add (or Modify) screen. You can only select one firewall policy from that screen. What are the three types of firewall policies that you can choose from on the Client FW tab?

**You can select to enable a Policy defined by remote firewall (AYT), a Policy Pushed (CPP), or a Policy from Server on the Client FW tab.**

# Chapter 6—Q&A

**1** You have a number of clients running Windows 98 and a remote VPN 3002 Hardware Client assigned to the same group. Your supervisor wants you to force everyone on this group connecting to have a firewall running on his or her machine. Can you do this?

**No. The Firewall Required option cannot be used with the VPN 3002 Hardware Client.**

**2** What firewalls can be used within the Custom Firewall option on the concentrator?

**The acceptable firewalls are as follows:**

**a. CIC**

**b. Zone Alarm**

**c. Zone AlarmPro**

**d. Zone Labs Integrity**

**e. BlackICE Defender/Agent**

**3** Where are the rules set for a client when using CPP with Zone AlarmPro?

**Using CPP means that the concentrator controls all rules for the clients. This applies to CIC as well as Zone Alarm and Zone AlarmPro.**

**4** What protocols are not automatically blocked when using the Stateful Firewall (Always On) feature?

**DHCP and ESP are not automatically blocked when using the Stateful Firewall (Always On) feature. Additionally, traffic from the concentrator's network is not blocked.**

**5** Why is CPP not used with the Tunnel Everything option?

**CPP is designed to be used with split tunneling because the Tunnel Everything option already blocks all nontunneled traffic.**

**6** How often does the VPN Client poll the personal firewall when using AYT?

**The VPN Client polls the personal firewall every 30 seconds.**

**7** How is the Always On option set on the VPN Client?

**The Always On option is set in the Options pull-down menu. The default setting is to have Always On disabled.**

**8** Where is CPP configured?

**CPP is configured on the Client FW tab of the Configuration | User Management | Groups | Modify screen within the VPN concentrator.**

**9** What debug classes are used when creating a rule with the following options:

   a. Drop

   b. Drop and Log

   c. Forward

   d. Forward and Log

   e. Apply IPSec

   f. Apply IPSec and Log

**The FILTERDBG event class is used with the Drop and Log option, the Apply IPSec and Log option, and the Forward and Log option. The other three options do not use a debug class.**

**10** By default, what IP address and wildcard mask does VRRP use?

**By default, VRRP uses 224.0.0.18/0.0.0.0.**

**11** How do you allow clients to use either of two firewalls? What is the only vendor you can do this with?

**To allow clients to use either of two firewalls, choose the Custom Firewall option on the Client FW tab on the Configuration | User Management | Groups | Modify screen. Enter the Vendor ID and the Product IDs separated by commas. Because Zone Labs is the only vendor with more than one product, this vendor must be used.**

**12** You are using CPP and pushing a policy to a firewall at the client. The client's firewall allows FTP access. The concentrator's policy does not allow FTP access. Is FTP access allowed?

**No, FTP access is not allowed. When using CPP and pushing to a firewall, the more restrictive of the policies pertains. Therefore, because one of these limits FTP traffic, the FTP traffic is limited.**

**13** You are using BlackICE as a client firewall. You are presently connected through the VPN. What happens if you stop the service running BlackICE? Does the VPN remain connected? If so, for how long? Can you connect again if BlackICE is not running?

**The answer depends on two configuration choices. The first choice is the Are You There (AYT) configuration. If AYT is off, no noticeable difference is seen.**

**If AYT is on, the connection reacts differently depending on other choices made. If you configured the firewall setting as Firewall Optional or No Firewall, no noticeable difference is seen during this connection. However, if you choose the Firewall Required option, the connection is dropped after there is no response from the concentrator's poll. With Firewall Required, you cannot connect until you start BlackICE again. If you set the Firewall Optional option, you receive a message indicating that a firewall should be running when you connect.**

**14** On the VPN Client, where do you see the current compression used for a VPN connection?

**You see the current compression used for a VPN connection under the General tab of the Connection Status dialog box on the client software. You can also view the current compression method by using the client CLI command** vpnclient stat.

**15** While configuring a filter, you want to apply this filter to all protocols. What number do you use?

**Using 255 applies the filter to all protocols.**

**16** When using the VPN Client, what ICMP should be set?

**None. The VPN Client cannot be filtered based on the ICMP protocol.**

**17** What authentication methods are allowed with the VPN Client?

**The following authentication methods are allowed with the VPN Client:**

**a. XAUTH (eXtended AUTHentication)**

**b. RADIUS with:**

**MSCHAPv2**

**State/Reply message attributes (token cards)**

**RSA SecurID**

**Windows NT Domain Authentication**

**MX.509v3 digital certificates**

**18**  What types of key management can the VPN Client use?

**The VPN Client can use the following types of key management:**

a. **XAUTH**

b. **IKE—Aggressive and Main mode (digital certificates)**

c. **Diffie-Hellman Groups 1, 2, and 5**

d. **PFS**

e. **Rekeying**

**19**  In addition to IPSec, what tunneling protocols does the VPN Client support?

**The VPN Client supports the tunneling protocols IPSec, PPTP, L2TP, and L2TP over IPSec.**

**20**  Which two products from Zone Labs work with the VPN Client to enable the Are You There (AYT) capability?

**Zone Alarm and Zone AlarmPro are the personal firewalls that work with the Cisco VPN Client to enable the AYT capability. The other product that works with the VPN Client is BlackICE Defender from Network ICE.**

**21**  You want to have secure VPN connections to the private network of the head-end concentrator and unsecured communications to the Internet. How would you configure the VPN Client's Stateful Firewall feature to support this split tunneling?

**To enable split tunneling, you must disable the VPN Client's Stateful Firewall feature. If enabled, the Stateful Firewall blocks all traffic coming from the Internet.**

**22**  What is another name for the Stateful Firewall client that is a part of the Cisco VPN Client?

**The Stateful Firewall client that is part of the Cisco VPN Client is also called the Cisco Integrated Client (CIC).**

**23**  From the VPN Client, where can you view the secured routes that are enabled to the client?

**You can view a list of secured routes that are enabled to the VPN Client from the Statistics tab of the Connection Status screen.**

**24**  What is meant by the term *Packets bypassed* on the Statistics tab of the Connection Status screen?

**The Packets bypassed field on the Statistics tab of the Connection Status screen shows the number of packets that did not need to be encrypted but which were still sent out over the wire in unencrypted form.**

25 On the VPN 3000 Concentrator Series devices, you configure the client firewall properties on the Client FW tab of the Configuration | User Management | Groups | Add (or Modify) screen. You can only select one firewall policy from that screen. What are the three types of firewall policies that you can choose from the Client FW tab?

**You can select to enable a Policy defined by remote firewall (AYT), a Policy Pushed (CPP), or a Policy from Server on the Client FW tab.**

# Chapter 7—Do I Know This Already?

1 What screen is used to set the password for the administrator?

**Administration | Access Rights | Administrators**

2 You wish to limit HTTP access to the concentrator to hosts on the same subnet as the inside interface of the concentrator. What is the format of the Access Control List?

**Use the network IP address of the interface's base network and the proper subnet mask.**

3 What types of AAA servers can the VPN 3000 Series Concentrator use for authenticating management sessions?

**TACACS+**

4 What is the upper limit for a management session timeout?

**30 minutes**

5 What form of encryption may be used on a configuration file?

**RC4**

6 On what screen can routes be cleared?

**Monitoring | Routing Table**

7 Where can you see the CPU utilization on a Cisco 3000 Series Concentrator?

**Monitoring | System Status**

8 Where can you troubleshoot an IPSec connection?

**Monitoring | Statistics | IPSec**

9 Where can you troubleshoot TCP/IP connections?

(Note that the keyword in this question is "connection," which requires TCP):

**Monitoring | Statistics | MIB II | TCP/UDP**

10 Where can you see the number of collisions on an Ethernet Interface?

**Monitoring | Statistics | Interface | MIB II-> | Statistics**

# Chapter 7—Q&A

1    What screen is used to set the password for the administrator?

**Administration | Access Rights | Administrators**

2    You wish to limit HTTP access to the concentrator to hosts on the same subnet as the inside interface of the concentrator. What is the format of the Access Control List?

**Use the network IP address of the interface's base network and the proper subnet mask.**

3    What types of AAA servers can the VPN 3000 Series Concentrator use for authenticating management sessions?

**TACACS+**

4    What is the upper limit for a management session timeout?

**30 minutes**

5    What form of encryption may be used on a configuration file?

**RC4**

6    On what screen can routes be cleared?

**Monitoring | Routing Table**

7    Where can you see the CPU utilization on a Cisco 3000 Series Concentrator?

**Monitoring | System Status**

8    Where can you troubleshoot an IPSec connection?

**Monitoring | Statistics | IPSec**

9    Where can you troubleshoot TCP/IP connections?

(Note that the keyword in this question is "connection," which requires TCP):

**Monitoring | Statistics | MIB II | TCP/UDP**

10    Where can you see the number of collisions on an Ethernet Interface?

**Monitoring | Statistics | Interface | MIB II-> | Statistics**

11    What is the major difference between the Monitoring | Statistics and the Monitoring | Statistics | MIB II sections?

**The MIB II section works on the first four layers of the OSI model, while the Statistics section works at higher levels.**

**12** You wish to limit the number of concurrent management connections. Where is this done?

**To limit the number of concurrent management connections, go to the Administration | Access Rights | Access Settings screen.**

**13** You wish to use a AAA server to authenticate management access to the concentrator. What must you use?

**You must use a TACACS+ server. Also, you will need connectivity to the server.**

**14** What are the differences between the Filterable Event Log screen and the Live Event Log screen?

**There are two major differences between the Filterable Event Log screen and the Live Event Log screen. First, the Filterable Event Log screen allows you to limit logs seen. Second, the Live Event Log updates as events occur instead of by the refresh value set in the Administration | Monitoring Refresh screen.**

**15** On what screen can you see if a certificate has been requested but has not yet been received?

**The Administration | Certificate Management screen is used to see certificates that have been requested, but have not yet been received.**

**16** What section should you look in if you want to see the number of pings sent and received? From where on the concentrator do you send a ping?

**The number of pings sent and received is shown under the Monitoring | Statistics | MIB II | ICMP screen. Pings are sent from the Administration | Ping screen.**

**17** Name two places that you can see the current software version on a concentrator.

**The current software in use can be seen on the Monitoring | System Status and the Administration | Software Update | Concentrator screens.**

**18** What are the access control lists as defined in the Administration | Access Rights | Access Control Lists screen used for?

**These access control lists are only used for access to the concentrator for management purposes.**

**19** You find out that your assistant has changed the configuration and saved that new configuration. However, something was configured incorrectly. None of remote sites or remote users can connect to the concentrator. What is the quickest way to resolve the issue?

**The quickest way to resolve this is to go to the Administration | File Management | Swap Config File screen and swap the backup configuration with the current configuration. Then, go to the Administration | System Reboot screen and reboot the concentrator. Because no users are connected, the reboot may be set to happen immediately.**

**20** A remote client with a VPN 3002 hardware client calls you on the phone saying that he is unable to connect to your network. He says that he may have incorrectly configured the preshared key on his end. You have access through HTTP to your concentrator. Where is the first place you look to see if this is a preshared key issue?

**The first place you should look is on the Monitoring | Statistics | IPSec screen. This screen will quickly show whether the issue is with an incorrect preshared key.**

# Chapter 8—Do I Know This Already?

**1** What screen is used on the head-end concentrator to demand the use of preshared keys?

**The Configuration | System | Tunneling Protocols | IPSec LAN-to-LAN | Modify screen is used to demand preshared keys from a VPN 3000 Series Concentrator.**

**2** You need to allow the main office to use PC Anywhere to connect to three separate machines at the remote office over the VPN. What mode must you use?

**You must use Network Extension mode because all the machines at the remote office will appear as a single IP address at the corporate office if you use Port Address Translation (PAT) mode.**

**3** You are using individual authentication in PAT mode. Your tunnel is established but the user cannot log in. What is the first item you should examine?

**First, check if the username and password are correct. You know that PAT mode only connects when data is sent to the head-end. If the tunnel is up, but the user cannot connect, this is usually an issue caused by an incorrect password or username.**

**4** What are the disadvantages in a large network (over 100 users) of using individual authentication with the internal authentication server in a VPN 3005 Concentrator?

**There are two main disadvantages to using individual authentication in a large network. The first issue is that each user must be individually assigned a username and password. This takes a large amount of time. The second issue is that an external authentication server must be used because the internal database on a VPN 3005 Concentrator only allows a maximum of 100 combined users and groups.**

**5** You are the second user to connect through a VPN 3002 Hardware Client for which interactive hardware client and individual user authentication have been configured. What authentication information will you be required to enter?

**You will only be required to enter your individual username and password. The VPN tunnel would have already been established by the previous user who would have been required to enter the hardware client's username and password, as well as the individual username and password.**

6   You can use a static configuration for authenticating the VPN 3002 Hardware Client with the head-end concentrator. Why would you want to use interactive hardware client authentication?

**Interactive hardware client authentication provides another layer of security to the system. The device authentication username and password are not stored on the VPN 3002 Hardware Client but are entered by the first user that brings up the VPN connection. The password can be quickly changed on the head-end device and communicated to the users connecting to the VPN 3002 Hardware Client. The head-end concentrator pushes the policies you set for authentication out to the VPN 3002 Hardware Client. You can also use both individual user and interactive hardware client authentication simultaneously.**

7   Where is interactive hardware client authentication configured?

**You configure interactive hardware client authentication on the head-end VPN 3000 Series Concentrator on the HW Client tab of the Configuration | User Management | Groups | Modify (or Add) screen.**

8   What authentication method is used for interactive hardware client authentication?

**The authentication method used is governed by the method you selected to use for the VPN group. You can use either internal or external authentication.**

9   What must you configure on the VPN 3002 Hardware Client in order to use interactive hardware client authentication?

**There are no special configuration steps required on the VPN 3002 Hardware Client to enable interactive hardware client authentication. This function is driven completely from the head-end concentrator.**

10  The HW Client tab of the Configuration | User Management | Groups | Modify (or Add) screen is used to configure individual user authentication. What other two attributes for individual user authentication can you set on this screen?

**Along with enabling individual user authentication, the HW Client tab lets you establish User Idle Timeout and Cisco IP Phone Bypass.**

11  What is the default session idle timeout when using individual user authentication?

**The default session idle timeout for individual user authentication is 30 minutes.**

12  When individual user authentication is enabled, what initial screen are you directed to when you first try to establish a browser connection to an address in the private network of the head-end concentrator?

**You will be redirected to the VPN 3002 Hardware Client Manager login screen. From this screen you will select the Connection/Login Status hotlink, which will permit you to log in to the network.**

**13** What VPN 3002 Hardware Client Manager screen can you use to quickly try to connect to the head-end concentrator?

**The Monitoring | System Status screen of the VPN 3002 Hardware Client Manager has two buttons: Disconnect Now and Connect Now. Simply click the Connect Now button to try to establish the connection.**

**14** What VPN 3002 Hardware Client Manager screen can you use when you want to view IKE Phase 1 and IPSec Phase 2 connection statistics?

**The Monitoring | Statistics | IPSec screen of the VPN 3002 Hardware Client Manager provides information on IKE and IPSec connections.**

**15** What VPN 3002 Hardware Client Manager screen can you use if you suspect that DNS problems are interfering with user communications?

**The Monitoring | Statistics | DNS screen of the VPN 3002 Hardware Client Manager provides information DNS requests, responses, timeouts, and other data that may help you diagnose a DNS problem on your system.**

# Chapter 8—Q&A

**1** What screen is used on the head-end concentrator to demand the use of preshared keys?

**The Configuration | System | Tunneling Protocols | IPSec LAN-to-LAN | Modify screen is used to demand preshared keys from the VPN 3002 Hardware Client.**

**2** Name five items to check when you are unable to connect a VPN tunnel and you are receiving IKE failures on Phase 1.

**The five items to check when receiving Phase 1 errors are**

- **Xauth is required, but the proposal does not support Xauth.**
- **Check the priorities of IKE Xauth proposals in the IKE proposal list.**
- **Check the VPN 3002 Hardware Client group.**
- **Check the group on the VPN Concentrator.**
- **Check that all SA proposals are acceptable.**

**3** You need to allow the main office to use PC Anywhere to connect to three separate machines at the remote office over the VPN. What mode must you use?

**You must use Network Extension mode because all the machines at the remote office will appear as a single IP address at the corporate office if you use PAT mode.**

**4** You need to have a device behind the head-end concentrator to send data as soon as the VPN tunnel is established. Which mode should you use? Can you use split tunneling under these circumstances?

**You must use Network Extension mode. You cannot use split tunneling. In Network Extension mode without split tunneling, a device at the head-end can initiate data transfer. In either PAT mode or Network Extension mode without split tunneling the VPN 3002 Hardware Client's network must initiate data transfer.**

**5** What are the disadvantages in a large network (over 100 users) of using individual authentication with the internal server?

**There are two main disadvantages to using individual authentication in a large network. The first issue is that each user must be individually assigned a username and password. This takes a large amount of time. The second issue is that an external authentication server must be used because the internal database only allows 100 users.**

**6** You are using individual authentication in PAT mode. Your tunnel is established but the user cannot log in. What is the first item you should examine?

**First, check if the username and password are correct. You know that PAT mode only connects when data is sent to the head-end. If the tunnel is up, but the user cannot connect, this is usually an issue caused by an incorrect password or username.**

**7** What screen do you use on the VPN 3002 Hardware Client to configure preshared keys?

**You use the Configuration | System | Tunneling Protocols | IPSec screen on the VPN 3002 Hardware Client to configure preshared keys.**

**8** You appear to be experiencing a DoS attack that is initiating from the IP address assigned to one of your VPN 3002 Hardware Clients. What is the problem?

**The problem is that the VPN 3002 Hardware Client has been set to Network Extension mode but the head-end concentrator has not been changed from the default PAT mode.**

**9** You need to allow the remote office to use PC Anywhere to connect to three separate machines at the main office over the VPN. What mode must you use?

**You can use either PAT or Network Extension mode. It is only when going from the main office to the remote office that there is an issue of whether to use Network Extension or PAT mode.**

**10** Some of your remote sites can use split tunneling and others cannot. How is this controlled?

**The decision to allow split tunneling is controlled on a group-by-group basis by the VPN 3002 Hardware Client.**

**11**  Your remote site has an ISDN connection to the Internet. You are charged on a per-minute basis for connecting to the Internet. Which mode should you use?

**Other than changing ISPs, the best move here is to use PAT mode because the tunnel will disconnect after a specified amount of time, reducing the charges for your connection. Using Network Extension mode means that the tunnel is always active.**

**12**  What version of software must be running on the head-end concentrator to use PAT mode? What version is required for Network Extension mode?

**Both require version 3.x.**

**13**  You are the second user to connect through a VPN 3002 Hardware Client for which interactive hardware client and individual user authentication have been configured. What authentication information will you be required to enter?

**You will only be required to enter your individual username and password. The VPN tunnel would have already been established by the previous user who would have been required to enter the hardware client's username and password, as well as their individual username and password.**

**14**  You can use a static configuration for authenticating the VPN 3002 Hardware Client with the head-end concentrator. Why would you want to use interactive hardware client authentication?

**Interactive hardware client authentication provides another layer of security to the system. The device authentication username and password are not stored on the VPN 3002 Hardware Client but are entered by the first user that brings up the VPN connection. The password can be quickly changed on the head-end device and communicated to the users connecting to the VPN 3002 Hardware Client. The head-end concentrator pushes the policies you set for authentication out to the VPN 3002 Hardware Client. You can also use both individual user and interactive hardware client authentication simultaneously.**

**15**  Where is interactive hardware client authentication configured?

**You configure interactive hardware client authentication on the head-end VPN 3000 Series Concentrator on the HW Client tab of the Configuration | User Management | Groups | Modify (or Add) screen.**

**16**  What authentication method is used for interactive hardware client authentication?

**The authentication method used is governed by the method you selected to use for the VPN group. You can use either internal or external authentication.**

**17** What must you configure on the VPN 3002 Hardware Client in order to use interactive hardware client authentication?

**There are no special configuration steps required on the VPN 3002 Hardware Client to enable interactive hardware client authentication. This function is driven completely from the head-end concentrator.**

**18** The HW Client tab of the Configuration | User Management | Groups | Modify (or Add) screen is used to configure individual user authentication. What other two attributes for individual user authentication can you set on this screen?

**Along with enabling individual user authentication, the HW Client tab lets you establish User Idle Timeout and Cisco IP Phone Bypass.**

**19** What is the default session idle timeout when using individual user authentication?

**The default session idle timeout for individual user authentication is 30 minutes.**

**20** When individual user authentication is enabled, what initial screen are you directed to when you first try to establish a browser connection to an address in the private network of the head-end concentrator?

**You will be redirected to the VPN 3002 Hardware Client Manager login screen. From this screen you will select the Connection/Login Status hotlink, which will permit you to log in to the network.**

**21** What VPN 3002 Hardware Client Manager screen can you use to quickly try to connect to the head-end concentrator?

**The Monitoring | System Status screen of the VPN 3002 Hardware Client Manager has two buttons: Disconnect Now and Connect Now. Simply click the Connect Now button to try to establish the connection**

**22** What VPN 3002 Hardware Client Manager screen can you use when you want to view IKE Phase 1 and IPSec Phase 2 connection statistics?

**The Monitoring | Statistics | IPSec screen of the VPN 3002 Hardware Client Manager provides information on IKE and IPSec connections.**

**23** What VPN 3002 Hardware Client Manager screen can you use if you suspect that DNS problems are interfering with user communications?

**The Monitoring | Statistics | DNS screen of the VPN 3002 Hardware Client Manager provides information DNS requests, responses, timeouts, and other data that might help you diagnose a DNS problem on your system.**

# Chapter 9—Do I Know This Already?

**1** What are the ramifications an administrator should consider when planning to use Virtual Router Redundancy Protocol (VRRP) along with reverse route injection (RRI)?

**VRRP (Virtual Router Redundancy Protocol) and RRI (Reverse Route Injection) are incompatible and should not be used together.**

**2** You wish to inject a route from the VPN Concentrator to the VPN 3002 Hardware Client. What routing protocol must you use?

**You must use OSPF if you wish to use the VPN Concentrator to advertise a route to the VPN 3002 Hardware Client.**

**3** You wish to use RIPv1 with Reverse Route Injection. Can this be done?

**You must use RIPV2.**

**4** You are using a backup IPSec server because the primary server was down when the initial tunnel was initiated. The primary server is now up. Will the VPN 3002 Hardware Client restore a connection to the primary? If so, when?

**The connection to the primary server will only be reestablished after a connection to the backup server is terminated.**

**5** What is the timeout period used when attempting to connect to the primary concentrator before a connection will be attempted to a secondary concentrator?

**The timeout period is 8 seconds.**

**6** You tried to connect to your primary concentrator from your VPN 3002 Hardware Client but were unsuccessful. Your 3002 Hardware Client then attempted to connect to your backup concentrator without success. When will the VPN 3002 Hardware client try again?

**Once a VPN 3002 Hardware Client goes through its list of backup concentrators, it will not attempt any more connections until the Connect Now button on the Monitoring | System Status screen is clicked.**

**7** How is load balancing enabled on the VPN 3002 Hardware Client?

**The load-balancing feature is automatic on the VPN 3002 Hardware Client.**

**8** You have three VPN 3015 Concentrators on the same network. Assuming default priority settings, which one will be elected to balance the load?

**The first VPN 3015 Concentrators on the network will balance the load.**

9  What factors are considered for VPN 3000 Concentrator load balancing with VPN 3002 Hardware Clients or remote access VPN clients?

**Total number of connections, the number of connections on each VPN Concentrator, and the total number of connecting clients are the factors considered during load balancing.**

10  Which debug class or classes should you enable in order to debug an auto-update?

**The auto-update class is all that is necessary for debugging an auto-update.**

11  What types of clients may use the auto-update feature?

**Only Windows-based clients and the VPN 3002 Hardware Client can use the auto-update feature.**

12  When a software update is pending, during the connection process, the concentrator sends a message indicating the IP address of the TFTP server and the software version to be downloaded. What type (protocol) is this message?

**This is an ISAKMP message.**

13  What client type(s) are permissible to be set on the VPN Concentrator for upgrading clients when using the VPN 3002 Hardware Client?

**Because only the VPN 3002 Hardware Client is able to be upgraded, the only permissible value is vpn3002.**

14  On the VPN Concentrator, what is the syntax used to specify the TFTP server and the filename used for updating the client software?

**The syntax is tftp://{IP address of server}/{filename}**

15  You have configured auto-update to occur. Which device, the VPN Concentrator or the VPN 3002 Hardware Client, recognizes that the software must be updated?

**The VPN 3002 Hardware Client recognizes that the software needs to be updated and starts the update process.**

16  How is the VPN 3000 Concentrator configured to notify VPN 3002 Hardware Clients that a new software upgrade is available?

**Using the VPN 3000 Concentrator Series Manager, go to Administration | Software Update | Clients.**

**Choose the group**

**Select Upgrade Clients Now**

**17**  Your VPN 3002 Hardware Client attempts to auto-update. The system appears to "hang" and eventually times out on the download portion of the process. What are two likely causes?

**The two most likely causes are that your VPN 3002 Hardware Client either cannot connect to the TFTP server or the Client does not have sufficient permissions on the server to download the software.**

**18**  You have tried to upgrade your VPN 3002 Hardware Client. However, the VPN 3002 Hardware Client keeps trying to upgrade without success. You know that you have connectivity. You can see in the logs that you have been downloading the file. What is the problem?

**The problem is that you have entered an incorrect version number in the VPN Concentrator. If you can see that the file has been downloaded but it still tries to update the software, this is the only explanation.**

**19**  Why will some applications not work with either NAT or PAT?

**Some applications, especially very old DOS applications, were written before the OSI model was fully accepted. These applications embed the workstation address within the data instead of relying on TCP/IP to carry the IP address. These programs will fail using either NAT or PAT because the message will be sent back to the workstation address within the data, not the workstation address that was translated.**

**20**  Why will PAT cause problems with some applications whereas NAT does not cause these problems?

**Some applications expect to use specific ports. Because PAT changes the ports used, this can cause problems with this type of application.**

**21**  What are two main differences between NAT and PAT?

**The first difference between NAT and PAT is that NAT is a one-to-one translation while PAT is a one-to-many translation. The second major difference is that PAT translates ports (either TCP or UDP) as well as source or destination addresses.**

**22**  Why is UDP Transparent IPSec (IPSec over UDP) usable with either NAT or PAT when IPSec over TCP is not usable over PAT?

**UDP Transparent IPSec bypasses the effects of NAT and PAT by encapsulating the data traffic within new UDP packets.**

**23**  You are using UDP Transparent IPSec on your VPN 3002 Hardware Client. How are filters applied to inbound traffic? How are filters applied to outbound traffic?

**Traffic inbound is decrypted before routing. Traffic outbound is routed and then encrypted.**

24  What minimum version does the VPN Concentrator have to be running in order to use UDP NAT Transparent IPSec? What version is required on the VPN 3002 Hardware Client?

**Both the VPN Concentrator and the VPN 3002 Hardware Client must be running version 3.0.3 or later software.**

25  What is the default port for IPSec over UDP?

**The default port is 10000.**

26  When using IPSec over TCP, how are IKE and IPSec protocols handled in relation to NAT?

**The whole packet is encapsulated within a new IP packet. This allows the new packet to have its source address changed by NAT and the source address and port changed by PAT without worrying about encryption or decryption of the original data.**

27  You are planning on terminating your VPN 3002 Hardware Client's VPN tunnel on a Microsoft Proxy Server. Should you use UDP NAT Transparent IPSec (IPSec over UDP) or IPSec over TCP?

**You must use UDP NAT Transparent IPSec because IPSec over TCP will not work with a proxy server.**

# Chapter 9—Q&A

1  What are the ramifications an administrator should consider when planning to use VRRP along with RRI?

**VRRP (Virtual Router Redundancy Protocol) and RRI (Reverse Route Injection) are incompatible and should not be used together.**

2  You wish to inject a route from the VPN Concentrator to the VPN 3002 Hardware Client. What routing protocol must you use?

**You must use OSPF if you wish to use the VPN Concentrator to advertise a route to the VPN 3002 Hardware Client.**

3  You wish to use RIPv1 with Reverse Route Injection. Can this be done?

**No. You must use RIPV2.**

4  Which screen on the VPN Concentrator is used to configure RRI with OSPF?

**The Configuration | System | IP Routing | OSPF screen is used for configuring RRI with OSPF.**

**5** You are using a backup IPSec server because the primary server was down when the initial tunnel was initiated. The primary server is now up. Will the VPN 3002 Hardware Client restore a connection to the primary? If so, when?

**The connection to the primary server will only be reestablished after a connection to the backup server is terminated.**

**6** What is the timeout period used when attempting to connect to the primary concentrator before a connection will be attempted to a secondary concentrator.

**The timeout period is 8 seconds.**

**7** You tried to connect to your primary concentrator from your VPN 3002 Hardware Client but were unsuccessful. Your 3002 Hardware Client then attempted to connect to your backup concentrator without success. When will the VPN 3002 Hardware Client try again?

**Once a VPN 3002 Hardware Client goes through its list of backup concentrators, it will not attempt any more connections until the Connect Now button on the Monitoring | System Status screen is clicked.**

**8** What screen is used to configure backup servers on the VPN 3002 Hardware Client?

**The Configuration | System | Tunneling Protocols | IPSec screen is used to configure backup servers on the VPN 3002 Hardware Client.**

**9** You have three VPN 3015 Concentrators on the same network. Assuming default priority settings, which one will be elected to balance the load?

**The first VPN 3015 Concentrator on the network will balance the load.**

**10** What factors are considered for VPN 3000 Concentrator load balancing with VPN 3002 Hardware Clients or remote access VPN Clients?

**Total number of connections, the number of connections on each VPN concentrator, and the total number of connecting clients are the factors considered during load balancing.**

**11** How is load balancing enabled on the VPN 3002 Hardware Client?

**The load-balancing feature is automatic on the VPN 3002 Hardware Client.**

**12** What types of clients may use the auto-update feature?

**Only Windows-based VPN Clients and the VPN 3002 Hardware Client can use the auto-update feature.**

**13** When a software update is pending, during the connection process, the concentrator sends a message indicating the IP address of the TFTP server and the software version to be downloaded. What type (protocol) is this message?

**This is an ISAKMP message.**

**14** What are two main differences between NAT and PAT?

**The first difference between NAT and PAT is the NAT is a one-to-one translation while PAT is a one-to-many translation. The second major difference is that PAT translates ports (either TCP or UDP), as well as the source or destination address.**

**15** You are the administrator for a network using a single PAT address for connection to the Internet. You want to add two VPN 3002 Hardware Clients behind your PIX firewall. Which type of IPSec will you choose to use?

**You must use IPSec over TCP/IP because IPSec over UDP will not work if you are using PAT and you attempt to have more than one VPN 3002 Hardware Client translated to the same ad.**

**16** What minimum version does the VPN Concentrator have to be running in order to use IPSec over TCP/IP? What version is required on the VPN 3002 Hardware Client?

**Both the VPN Concentrator and the VPN 3002 Hardware Client must be running version 3.5 or later software.**

**17** What minimum version does the VPN Concentrator have to be running in order to use UDP NAT Transparent IPSec? What version is required on the VPN 3002 Hardware Client?

**Both the VPN Concentrator and the VPN 3002 Hardware Client must be running version 3.0.3 or later software.**

**18** What is the default port for IPSec over UDP?

**The default port is 10000.**

**19** You have an established tunnel between two sites. From the remote site you are able to ping the inside interface of the VPN Concentrator. However, you are unable to ping anything that lies beyond that point. What is wrong?

**If you can ping the inside interface of the VPN Concentrator, but cannot get beyond that point, the issue is that the interior routing is incorrect. Make sure that the interior routers know that the remote LAN can be reached through the inside Interface of the VPN Concentrator.**

**20** You are planning to upgrade your VPN 3002 Hardware Client. You have just received a file named vpn3002-3.0.3.A-k9.bin. What version is this?

**This is version 3.0.3.A. The area between the dashes is the version number.**

**21** You have tried to upgrade your VPN 3002 Hardware Client. However, the VPN 3002 Hardware Client keeps trying to upgrade without success. You know that you have connectivity. You can see in the logs that you have been downloading the file. What is the problem?

**The problem is that you have entered an incorrect version number in the VPN Concentrator. If you can see that the file has been downloaded but it still tries to update the software, this is the only explanation.**

**22** Why will some applications not work with either NAT or PAT?

**Some applications, especially very old DOS applications, were written before the OSI model was fully accepted. These applications embed the workstation address within the data instead of relying on TCP/IP to carry the IP address. These programs will fail using either NAT or PAT because the message will be sent back to the workstation address within the data, not the workstation address that was translated.**

**23** Why will PAT cause problems with some applications whereas NAT does not cause these problems?

**Some applications expect to use specific ports. Because PAT changes the ports used, this can cause problems with this type of application.**

**24** Which debug class or classes should you enable in order to debug an auto-update?

**The AUTOUPDATE class is all that is necessary for debugging an auto-update.**

**25** On the VPN Concentrator, what is the syntax used to specify the TFTP server and the filename used for updating the client software?

**The syntax is tftp://{IP address of server}/{filename}.**

**26** You have configured auto-update to occur. Which device, the VPN Concentrator or the VPN 3002 Hardware Client, recognizes that the software must be updated?

**The VPN 3002 Hardware Client recognizes that the software needs to be updated and starts the update process.**

**27** What client type(s) are permissible to be set on the VPN Concentrator for upgrading clients when using the VPN 3002 Hardware Client?

**Because only the VPN 3002 Hardware Client is able to be upgraded, the only permissible value is vpn3002.**

**28** How is the VPN 3000 Concentrator configured to notify VPN 3002 Hardware Clients that a new software upgrade is available?

**Using the GUI, go to Administration | Software Update | Clients**

**Choose the group**

**Select Upgrade Clients Now.**

**29** Your VPN 3002 Hardware Client attempts to auto-update. The system appears to "hang" and eventually times out on the download portion of the process. What are two likely causes?

**The two most likely causes are that your VPN 3002 Hardware Client either cannot connect to the TFTP server or the Client does not have sufficient permissions on the server to download the software.**

**30** In Network Extension mode, how long will the VPN 3002 Hardware Client wait before attempting to connect to a backup server if a connection to the primary server fails?

**In Network Extension mode, the VPN 3002 Hardware Client will wait 4 seconds before attempting to connect to a backup server.**

**31** Will a VPN 3002 Hardware Client connected to a backup server recognize that the primary server has added a new backup server?

**No. The VPN 3002 Hardware Client will only recognize a new backup server if it is connected to the primary server.**

**32** Does the VPN 3002 Hardware Client send keepalives to other VPN 3002 Hardware Clients connected to the same primary or backup server?

**No. VPN 3002 Hardware Clients have no knowledge of other VPN 3002 Hardware Clients unless their inside interfaces are on the same LAN. In this case, this is only used for load balancing.**

**33** Where are hold-down routes configured?

**Hold-down routes are configured on the concentrator from the Configuration | System | IP Routing | Reverse Route Injection screen.**

**34** What protocols may be used with LAN-to-LAN Autodiscovery?

**RIP is the only protocol currently available for use with LAN-to-LAN autodiscovery.**

**35** When using IPSec over TCP, how are IKE and IPSec protocols handled in relation to NAT?

**The entire packet is encapsulated within a new IP packet. This allows the new packet to have its source address changed by NAT and the source address and port changed by PAT without worrying about encryption or decryption of the original data.**

**36** You are planning on terminating your VPN 3002 Hardware Client's VPN tunnel on a Microsoft Proxy Server. Should you use UDP NAT Transparent IPSec (IPSec over UDP) or IPSec over TCP?

**You must use UDP NAT Transparent IPSec because IPSec over TCP will not work with a proxy server**

# Chapter 10—Do I Know This Already?

1 What is a LAN-to-LAN connection?

**A LAN-to-LAN connection is a secure connection between two LANs.**

2 What equipment is required for a LAN-to-LAN connection?

**A LAN-to-LAN connection requires any combination of concentrators, routers and firewalls.**

3 Where can a LAN-to-LAN connection be used?

**You can use a LAN-to-LAN connection**

- **Across the Internet**
- **Between two networks connected through a trusted network**
- **Between two networks connected through a non-trusted network**

4 When setting up network lists, how should the lists at each side of the LAN-to-LAN connection relate to each other?

**They must be reflective of each other. The network lists reflect the networks that are coming into the concentrator therefore referencing the network on the opposite side of where the network list is configured.**

5 You attempted to configure a LAN-to-LAN connection, but cannot see a specific network on one side of the connection. What is the most likely problem?

**Most likely, the network is missing from the network list on one of the concentrators.**

6 What routing protocol is used for Autodiscovery?

**RIP is used for Autodiscovery.**

7 What is an identity certificate?

**The identity certificate is used to uniquely identify a specific network device.**

8 What is the advantage of using SCEP?

**SCEP simplifies the process of obtaining and installing certificates.**

9 What are critical items when using any certificates?

**The date and time on the device are the most critical items when using any certificates.**

10 Order the steps for using a certificate:

1. Issue an enrollment request

2. Enroll with the CA

3. The enrollment request is accepted

4. Install the Certificate

5. Configure the concentrator to use the Certificate

**2, 1, 3, 4, 5**

11  You want to use SCEP to enroll an identity certificate. How must the associated CA certificate be obtained?

**The CA certificate must be obtained using SCEP.**

12  What are the default directory and filename for the DLL used with SCEP?

**The default filename is mscep.dll; The default directory is certserv.**

13  What are the three major steps involved in using digital certificates for a LAN-to-LAN connection?

**Configure the LAN-to-LAN connection to use the identity certificate. Configure the LAN-to-LAN connection to use the IKE proposal. Activate the IKE proposal.**

14  When using an identity certificate, what is the affect of entering an incorrect name in the OU field?

**The group will have no access.**

15  What three key sizes may be used with DSA when installing certificates using SCEP?

**512 bits; 1024 bits; 768 bits.**

# Chapter 10—Q&A

1  What is a LAN-to-LAN connection?

**A LAN-to-LAN connection is a secure connection between two LANs.**

2  What equipment is required for a LAN-to-LAN connection?

**A LAN-to-LAN connection requires any combination of concentrators, routers and firewalls.**

3  Where can a LAN-to-LAN connection be used?

**You can use a LAN-to-LAN connection**

- **Across the Internet**
- **Between two networks connected through a trusted network**
- **Between two networks connected through a non-trusted network**

**4** When setting up network lists, how should the lists at each side of the LAN-to-LAN connection relate to each other?

**They must be reflective of each other. The network lists reflect the networks that are coming into the concentrator therefore referencing the network on the opposite side of where the network list is configured.**

**5** You attempted to configure a LAN-to-LAN connection, but cannot see a specific network on one side of the connection. What is the most likely problem?

**Most likely, the network is missing from the network list on one of the concentrators.**

**6** What routing protocol is used for Autodiscovery?

**RIP is used for Autodiscovery.**

**7** What is an identity certificate?

**The identity certificate is used to uniquely identify a specific network device.**

**8** What is the advantage of using SCEP?

**SCEP simplifies the process of obtaining and installing certificates.**

**9** What are critical items when using any certificates?

**The date and time on the device are the most critical items when using any certificates.**

**10** Order the steps for using a certificate:

1. Issue an enrollment request

2. Enroll with the CA

3. The enrollment request is accepted

4. Install the Certificate

5. Configure the concentrator to use the Certificate

**2, 1, 3, 4, 5**

**11** You want to use SCEP to enroll an identity certificate. How must the associated CA certificate be obtained?

**The CA certificate must be obtained using SCEP.**

**12** What are the default directory and filename for the DLL used with SCEP?

**The default filename is mscep.dll; The default directory is certserv.**

**13** What are the three major steps involved in using digital certificates for a LAN-to-LAN connection?

**Configure the LAN-to-LAN connection to use the identity certificate. Configure the LAN-to-LAN connection to use the IKE proposal. Activate the IKE proposal.**

**14** When using an identity certificate, what is the affect of entering an incorrect name in the OU field?

**The group will have no access.**

**15** What three key sizes may be used with DSA when installing certificates using SCEP?

**512 bits; 1024 bits; 768 bits.**

**16** What screen is used to configure Network Autodiscovery?

**The Configuration | System | Tunneling Protocols | IPSec LAN-to-LAN | Modify is used to set Network Autodiscovery.**

**17** You have two VPN Concentrators—one in Seattle, the other in London—used for connecting the two offices through VPNs. The Seattle office cannot reach one subnet attached to the London office. You have checked your network lists on the Seattle concentrator. You are sure that the "missing" network is properly configured. What is the most likely problem?

**Because the network lists must be reflexive, both sets of network lists must be checked. The next item to check is the network lists on the London concentrator.**

**18** You are using Network Autodiscovery. You do not see a single remote network that is connected through a series of routers to your remote concentrator. Where should your troubleshooting efforts be directed?

**Because Network Autodiscovery relies on the RIP protocol, the first place to look is in the RIP tables. Is RIP enabled on the interface? Is this network advertised? Are you filtering the RIP Protocol somewhere along the way? Is the network so far away that it exceeds the RIP hop count limit?**

**19** You are using SCEP. Your junior assistant has configured the system. You have established a VPN connection to the remote site, but your remote group does not have access to your network. What is a probable cause?

**The OU (Organizational Unit) must match your IPSec group name. If they are different, the VPN will be established, but the group that connects over this connection will be different than the expected group. The connected group will not have any access.**

**20** You are using SCEP. You are trying to enroll a certificate. Your concentrator shows that it is polling. It has been in this state for over an hour. What is the most likely cause?

**Because enrolling certificates is a manual process on most systems, the most probable cause is that the administrator on the certificate server has failed to issue the certificate. Contact the administrator to find out the status of the certificate.**

**21** What screen is used to determine the IKE proposal used for a LAN-to-LAN connection?

**The Configuration | System | Tunneling Protocols | IPSec LAN-to-LAN | Modify screen is used to determine which IKE proposal is used for a LAN-to-LAN connection.**

**22** What is the purpose of the challenge password on the Administration | Certificate Management | Enroll | Identity Certificate | SCEP screen?

**The challenge password may be required by the certificate server. The server uses this password to ensure that certificates are not issued without proper authentication.**

**23** You wish to use Network Autodiscovery because it sounds easier. How are the networks learned and how do you ensure that only specific networks are included?

**Autodiscovery relies on the RIP protocol. Autodiscovery will advertise all of the networks learned through RIP. When using Autodiscovery, you must limit what networks are advertised to the Concentrator. Therefore, if you wish to limit the networks seen, you must limit the RIP advertisements that are broadcast by the routers connected to the interior interface of the Concentrator. There are no provisions for limiting the networks learned within the Concentrator configuration. You must also ensure that RIP is enabled on the interface within the Configuration | Interfaces screen.**

**24** What are the differences between a root certificate, a subordinate certificate, and an identity certificate?

**A certificate signed by itself is called a *self-signing* or *root certificate*. When one certificate issues another, the issued certificate is referred to as a *subordinate certificate*. A subordinate certificate can never issue another certificate. An identity certificate is used to authenticate a specific host on a network, while root and subordinate certificates may be used on a group of hosts within a network.**

**25** What are the maximum numbers of certificates that may be used on concentrators?

**The maximum number varies by model. On the 3005 a total of 6 root or subordinate certificates may be used, with a maximum of two identity certificates. On other concentrator models a total of 20 root or subordinate certificates and 20 identity certificates may be used. On all models, only a single SSL can be used.**

# INDEX

## Numerics

3DES (Triple Data Encryption Standard), 48

## A

Access Rights screen (VPN 3000 Series Concentrator), administration, 316–322

Action options, applying to filter rules, 273

adding filter rules to VPN Client, 272

addressing assignment method, configuring on VPN 3000 Series Concentrator, 147

admin password, configuring on VPN 3000 Series Concentrator, 150

Administer Sessions screen (VPN 3000 Series Concentrator), administration, 310

administering VPN 3000 Series Concentrators, 307

  Access Rights screen, 316–322

  Administer Session screen, 310

  Certificate Manager screen, 323

  File Management screen, 322

  menu options, 308–310

  Monitoring Refresh screen, 315

  Ping screen, 315

  Software Update screen, 310–312

  System Reboot screen, 313–315

Administration screen, VPN 3000 Series Concentrator management interface, 97–98

AH (Authentication Header), 40

  fields, 41

Always On option. *See* Stateful Firewall feature

answers to problem scenarios, 478–486

applying filter rules

  Action option, 273

  Destination address option, 274

  Destination port option, 274–276

  Direction option, 273

  ICMP Packet Type option, 276

  Name option, 273

  Protocol option, 273

  Source address option, 274

  TCP connection option, 273–274

  TCP/UDP source option, 274

assessing knowledge of required topics, 11

authentication

  IKE key types, 49

  interactive hardware client authentication, 375–376

  with preshared keys

    group preshared keys, 133

    unique preshared keys, 132–133

    wildcard preshared keys, 133

Authentication Data field

  AH, 41

  ESP, 43

authentication process for identify certificates, 225

Automatic Client Update feature, 283–284

auto-update

  monitoring events, 426–428

  VPN 3002 Hardware Client configuration, 423–426

AYT (Are You There), 268

  applying to firewall policy, 280

## B

backup servers

  VPN 3002 configuration, 412–413

branch office VPN routers, 28

browser-based manager, performing Quick Configuration for Cisco VPN 3000 Concentrator, 141, 144

  address assignment method, 147

  admin password, 150

  interface settings, 144–146

  internal authentication, 148

  IPSec tunnel group, 149

# D

# E

# F

# K-L

# M

# V

# W-Z

# Cisco Security Certification

### CCSP™ Cisco Secure PIX® Firewall Advanced Exam Certification Guide (CCSP Self-Study)
Christian Degu, Greg Bastien
1-58720-067-8 • **Available Now**

The CSPFA exam is one of the five component exams to the CCSP certification. *CCSP Cisco Secure PIX Firewall Advanced Exam Certification Guide* provides CSPFA exam candidates with a comprehensive preparation tool for testing success. With pre- and post-chapter tests, a CD-ROM-based testing engine with more than 200 questions, and comprehensive training on all exam topics, this title brings the proven exam preparation tools from the popular Cisco Press Exam Certification Guide series to the CSPFA candidate. It also serves as a learning guide for networkers interested in learning more about working with the PIX Firewall line of products.

### CCIE® Practical Studies: Security (CCIE Self-Study)
Andrew Mason, Dmitry Bokotey
1-58705-110-9 • **Available June 2003**

The Cisco Certified Internetworking Expert (CCIE) Certification from Cisco Systems is the most prestigious certification in the networking industry. In 2001, Cisco introduced the CCIE in Security. This exam, a combination of a written qualification exam with a one-day intensive lab exam is a highly sought after affirmation of a networkers security skills. A key to success in the intensive lab exam is hands-on understanding of how the security principles and concepts are executed in a real network. *CCIE Practical Studies: Security* provides a series of lab scenarios that help a CCIE candidate or advanced-level networker gain that expertise. The labs show how, with or without a lab of actual equipment, different concepts are applied. Chapters include background and technology overviews, directions on how to set up a practice lab, case study-based scenarios that show the step-by-step implementation of these concepts, and comprehensive labs that mimic those in the one-day lab exam. *CCIE Practical Studies: Security* serves as an invaluable guide in gaining networking security experience and in CCIE testing success.

### CCIE Security Exam Certification Guide (CCIE Self-Study)
Henry Benjamin
1-58720-065-1 • **Available Now**

*CCIE Security Exam Certification Guide* is a valuable self-study aid in preparing for the Security Qualification Exam. The book covers security and application protocols, security technologies, general and Cisco-specific security applications, as well as related general networking and operating system issues.

# CCIE Professional Development

**Network Security Principles and Practices
(CCIE Professional Development)**

Saadat Malik

1-58705-025-0 • **Available Now**

*Network Security Principles and Practices* is a comprehensive guide to network security threats and the policies and tools developed specifically to combat those threats. Starting with a general discussion of network security concepts and design philosophy, the book shows readers how they can build secure network architectures from the ground up. Taking a practical, applied approach to building security into networks, the book focuses on showing readers how to implement and verify security features and products in a variety of environments. Security aspects of routing protocols are discussed and various options for choosing and using them analyzed. The book goes into a detailed discussion of the security threats posed by increasingly prevalent LAN to LAN Virtual Private Networks and remote access VPN installations and how to minimize large vulnerabilities caused by these non-traditional network portals. Firewalls, including the PIX and IOS® firewalls, and underlying protocols are presented in depth. Intrusion detection is fully examined. The book shows the reader how to control dial-in access by setting up access servers with AAA, PPP, TACACS+, and Radius. Finally, protections at the service provider are discussed by showing the reader how to provision security at the service provider level.

## Cisco BGP-4 Command and Configuration Handbook
## (CCIE Professional Development)

William R. Parkhurst

1-58705-017-X • **Available Now**

*Cisco BGP-4 Command and Configuration Handbook* is an exhaustive practical reference to the commands contained within BGP-4. For each command/subcommand, author Bill Parkhurst explains the intended use or function and how to properly configure it. Then, he presents scenarios to demonstrate every facet of the command and its use, along with appropriate show and debug commands. Through the discussion of functionality and the scenario-based configuration examples, Cisco BGP-4 Command and Configuration Handbook helps you gain a thorough understanding of the practical side of BGP-4.

## Routing TCP/IP, Volume II
## (CCIE Professional Development)

Jeff Doyle, Jennifer DeHaven Carroll

1-57870-089-2 • **Available Now**

This book presents a detailed examination of exterior routing protocols (EGP and BGP) and advanced IP routing issues, such as multicast routing, quality of service routing, IPv6, and router management. Students learn IP design and management techniques for implementing routing protocols efficiently. Network planning, design, implementation, operation, and optimization are stressed in each chapter.

# Cisco CCNP BSCI Certification

## CCNP® BSCI Exam Certification Guide (CCNP Self-Study), Second Edition
Clare Gough
1-58720-078-3 • **Available Now**

*CCNP BSCI Exam Certification Guide*, Second Edition, is a comprehensive exam self-study tool for the CCNP/CCDP/CCIP BSCI exam, which evaluates a networkers ability to build scalable, routed Cisco internetworks. This book, updated with more than 100 pages of IS-IS protocol coverage, addresses all the major topics on the most recent BSCI #640-901 exam. This guide enables readers to master the concepts and technologies upon which they will be tested, including extending IP addresses, routing principles, scalable routing protocols, managing traffic and access, and optimizing scalable internetworks. CCNP candidates will seek out *CCNP BSCI Exam Certification Guide* as timely and expert late-stage exam preparation tool and useful post-exam reference.

## CCNP Self-Study: Building Scalable Cisco Internetworks (BSCI)
Catherine Paquet, Diane Teare
1-58705-084-6 • **Available Now**

*CCNP Self-Study: Building Scalable Cisco Internetworks* (BSCI) is a Cisco authorized, self-paced learning tool for CCNP, CCDP, and CCIP preparation. The book teaches readers how to design, configure, maintain, and scale routed networks that are growing in size and complexity. The book focuses on using Cisco routers connected in LANs and WANs typically found at medium-to-large network sites. Upon completing this book, readers will be able to select and implement the appropriate Cisco IOS® Software services required to build a scalable, routed network.

# Cisco CCNP Certification

## CCNP Preparation Library (CCNP Self-Study), Third Edition
Various Authors
1-58705-131-1 • **Available Now**

*CCNP Preparation Library*, Third Edition, is a Cisco authorized library of self-paced learning tools for the four component exams of the CCNP certification. These books teach readers the skills in professional level routing, switching, remote access and support as recommended for their respective exams, including for the new Building Scalable Cisco Internetworks (BSCI) exam.

Based on the four component exams of the CCNP certification, this four-book library contains *CCNP Self-Study: Building Scalable Cisco Internetworks* (BSCI), *Building Cisco Multilayer Switched Networks*, *Building Cisco Remote Access Networks*, and *Cisco Internetwork Troubleshooting*. These books serve as valuable study guides and supplements to the instuctor-led courses for certification candidates. They are also valuable to any intermediate level networker who wants to master the implementation of Cisco networking devices in medium to large networks.

## Cisco CCNP Certification Library (CCNP Self-Study), Second Edition
Various Authors
1-58720-080-5 • **Available Now**

Cisco Certified Network Professional (CCNP) is the intermediate-level Cisco certification for network support. This is the next step for networking professionals who wish to validate their skills beyond the Cisco Certified Network Associate (CCNA®) level or who want to have a path to the expert level certification of CCIE. CCNP tests a candidates skill in installing, configuring, operating, and troubleshooting complex routed LANs, routed WANs, switched LANs, and dial access services. Where CCNA requires candidates to pass a single exam, CCNP requires candidates to pass four written exams, including 640-901 BSCI, 640-604 Switching, 640-605 Remote Access, and 640-606 Support.

The official exam self-study guides for each of these exams are now available in this value priced bundle. These books, *CCNP BSCI Exam Certification Guide*, *CCNP Switching Exam Certification Guide*, *CCNP Remote Access Exam Certification Guide*, and *CCNP Support Exam Certification Guide*, present the certification candidate with comprehensive review and practice of all the key topics that appear on each of the CCNP exams.

Learning is serious buisiness. **Invest wisely.**

# Cisco CCNP Certification

## Internetworking Technologies Handbook, Third Edition

Cisco Systems, Inc.

1-58705-001-3 • **Available Now**

*Internetworking Technologies Handbook*, Third Edition, is an essential reference for every network professional. *Internetworking Technologies Handbook* has been one of Cisco Press' best-selling and most popular books since the first edition was published in 1997. Network engineers, administrators, technicians, and support personnel use this book to understand and implement many different internetworking and Cisco technologies. Beyond the on-the-job use, *Internetworking Technologies Handbook* is also a core training component for CCNA and CCDA® certifications. It is a comprehensive reference that enables networking professionals to understand and implement contemporary internetworking technologies. You will master terms, concepts, technologies, and devices used in today's networking industry, and will learn how to incorporate internetworking technologies into a LAN/WAN environment.

This Third Edition features new chapters on cable technologies, wireless technologies, and voice/data integration. After reading this book, networking professionals will possess a greater understanding of local and wide-area networking and the hardware, protocols, and services involved. *Internetworking Technologies Handbook* offers system optimization techniques that will strengthen results, increase productivity, and improve efficiency--helping you make more intelligent, cost-effective decisions for your network environment.